Palgrave Macmillan Studies in Banking and Financial Institutions

Series Editor: **Professor Philip Molyneux**

The Palgrave Macmillan Studies in Banking and Financial Institutions are international in orientation and include studies of banking within particular countries or regions, and studies of particular themes such as Corporate Banking, Risk Management, Mergers and Acquisitions, etc. The books' focus is on research and practice, and they include up-to-date and innovative studies on contemporary topics in banking that will have global impact and influence.

Titles include:

Mario Anolli, Elena Beccalli and Tommaso Giordani (*editors*)
RETAIL CREDIT RISK MANAGEMENT

Seth Apati
THE NIGERIAN BANKING SECTOR REFORMS
Power and Politics

Caner Bakir
BANK BEHAVIOUR AND RESILIENCE
The Effect of Structures, Institutions and Agents

Alessandro Carretta and Gianluca Mattarocci (*editors*)
ASSET PRICING, REAL ESTATE AND PUBLIC FINANCE OVER THE CRISIS

Dimitris N. Chorafas
BASEL III, THE DEVIL AND GLOBAL BANKING

Dimitris N. Chorafas
HOUSEHOLD FINANCE
Adrift in a Sea of Red Ink

Dimitris N. Chorafas
SOVEREIGN DEBT CRISIS
The New Normal and the Newly Poor

Stefano Cosma and Elisabetta Gualandri (*editors*)
THE ITALIAN BANKING SYSTEM
Impact of the Crisis and Future Perspectives

Joseph Falzon (*editor*)
BANK PERFORMANCE, RISK AND SECURITIZATION

Joseph Falzon (*editor*)
BANK STABILITY, SOVEREIGN DEBT AND DERIVATIVES

Juan Fernández de Guevara Radoselovics and José Pastor Monsálvez (*editors*)
CRISIS, RISK AND STABILITY IN FINANCIAL MARKETS

Juan Fernández de Guevara Radoselovics and José Pastor Monsálvez (*editors*)
MODERN BANK BEHAVIOUR

Franco Fiordelisi and Ornella Ricci (*editors*)
BANCASSURANCE IN EUROPE
Past, Present and Future

Josanco Floreani and Maurizio Polato
THE ECONOMICS OF THE GLOBAL STOCK EXCHANGE INDUSTRY

Jill M. Hendrickson
FINANCIAL CRISIS
The United States in the Early Twenty-First Century

Otto Hieronymi and Constantine Stephanou (*editors*)
INTERNATIONAL DEBT
Economic, Financial, Monetary, Political and Regulatory Aspects

Paola Leone and Gianfranco A. Vento (*editors*)
CREDIT GUARANTEE INSTITUTIONS AND SME FINANCE

Philip Molyneux (*editor*)
BANK PERFORMANCE, RISK AND FIRM FINANCING

Philip Molyneux (*editor*)
BANK STRATEGY, GOVERNANCE AND RATINGS

Victor Murinde (*editor*)
BANK REGULATORY REFORMS IN AFRICA

Bernardo Nicoletti
CLOUD COMPUTING IN FINANCIAL SERVICES

Özlem Olgu
EUROPEAN BANKING
Enlargement, Structural Changes and Recent Developments

Fotios Pasiouras
GREEK BANKING
From the Pre-Euro Reforms to the Financial Crisis and Beyond

Daniela Pîrvu
CORPORATE INCOME TAX HARMONIZATION IN THE EUROPEAN UNION

Ramkishen S. Rajan
EMERGING ASIA
Essays on Crises, Capital Flows, FDI and Exchange Rate

Allesandro Roselli
FINANCIAL STRUCTURES AND REGULATION: A COMPARISON OF CRISES IN THE UK, USA AND ITALY

Yasushi Suzuki
JAPAN'S FINANCIAL SLUMP
Collapse of the Monitoring System under Institutional and Transition Failures

Gabriel Tortella and José Luis García Ruiz
SPANISH MONEY AND BANKING
A History

The full list of titles available is on the website:
www.palgrave.com/finance/sbfi.asp

Palgrave Macmillan Studies in Banking and Financial Institutions
Series Standing Order ISBN 978–1–4039–4872–4

You can receive future titles in this series as they are published by placing a standing order. Please contact your bookseller or, in case of difficulty, write to us at the address below with your name and address, the title of the series and the ISBN quoted above.

Customer Services Department, Macmillan Distribution Ltd, Houndmills, Basingstoke, Hampshire RG21 6XS, England

---

Bank Stability, Sovereign Debt and Derivatives

Edited by

Joseph Falzon
Faculty of Economics, Management and Accountancy, University of Malta, Malta

palgrave
macmillan

First published 2013 by
PALGRAVE MACMILLAN

Palgrave Macmillan in the UK is an imprint of Macmillan Publishers Limited, registered in England, company number 785998, of Houndmills, Basingstoke, Hampshire RG21 6XS.

Palgrave Macmillan in the US is a division of St Martin's Press LLC, 175 Fifth Avenue, New York, NY 10010.

Palgrave Macmillan is the global academic imprint of the above companies and has companies and representatives throughout the world.

Palgrave® and Macmillan® are registered trademarks in the United States, the United Kingdom, Europe and other countries

ISBN: 978–1–137–33214–1

This book is printed on paper suitable for recycling and made from fully managed and sustained forest sources. Logging, pulping and manufacturing processes are expected to conform to the environmental regulations of the country of origin.

A catalogue record for this book is available from the British Library.

A catalog record for this book is available from the Library of Congress.

Contents

List of Figures

List of Tables

Notes on Contributors

Göran Bergendahl is Professor Emeritus, Gothenburg University, Department of Business Administration, School of Business, Economics and Law, Sweden. His research focuses on the development and use of quantitative methods such as linear and dynamic programming, asset liability and management, and production functions, for decision making in production, transport, pricing, investment and international finance. A main area of his research has been on banks and other financial institutions.

Frank Bezzina is Deputy Dean of the Faculty of Economics, Management and Accountancy, at the University of Malta. He teaches applied business statistics, decision modeling, risk analysis, and quantitative research methods on the faculty's degrees and MBA programs. His research interests focus on data collection and data analysis methodologies applied to business and management research. In 2012, he was awarded the Emerald Literati Network Highly Commended Paper Award for Excellence.

Giorgio Carlo Brugnoni is a doctoral student in Banking and Finance at La Sapienza University of Rome. He recently spent a period of study and research at Bangor Business School, Wales, UK. His main research interests include bank strategy, intermediation models, profitability, financial reporting and performance analysis, credit, liquidity management, financial crisis, regulation and supervision.

Giusy Chesini is an associate professor in Banking and Finance at the Faculty of Economics of the University of Verona, Italy, where she teaches corporate finance and the economics of financial markets and financial intermediaries. She is a researcher in the Polo Scientifico e Didattico di Studi sull'Impresa, an academic centre focused on the analysis of Italian enterprises. She is also a member of several academic associations. Her research interests include stock exchanges, and the evolution of financial systems, banking and risk management. She has participated in conferences on these subjects, to which she has contributed numerous papers.

Laura Chiaramonte is a lecturer in Banking at the Catholic University of Milan, Italy. She holds a PhD in Business Administration from the University of Verona. Her research interests include hedge fund strategy, the evolution of financial systems, the drivers and effects of bank acquisitions, domestic and cross-border banking consolidation in Europe, the causes and consequences of the subprime crisis, the role of credit default swaps in the recent financial crisis and the new liquidity rules for banks (Basel III).

Concetta Colasimone holds a PhD in Banking and Finance from La Sapienza University of Rome. Her main research interests include bank capitalization, credit risk analysis, funding, and profitability.

Joseph Falzon holds a PhD degree in Economics from Northwestern University, USA. He is currently the Head of the Department of Banking and Finance, and the Dean of the Faculty of Economics, Management and Accountancy at the University of Malta. He is the author of several foreign publications and of numerous papers on the Maltese economy. He has served as a consultant to several leading public and private organizations and financial institutions in Malta. His research interests include hedge fund strategies, portfolio management, and economic development. He currently also serves on the Executive Committee of the European Association of University Lecturers in Banking and Finance.

Josanco Floreani is a lecturer in Banking and Finance at the University of Udine, Italy. He is a member of a number of academic associations, including the Italian Association of University Teachers in Banking and Finance (ADEIMF) and the European Association of University Teachers in Banking and Finance (The Wolpertinger Club).

Elisa Giaretta is a PhD student in Business Administration and Management at the Faculty of Economics of the University of Verona, Italy. She is a researcher at the Polo Scientifico e Didattico di Studi sull'Impresa, an academic centre focusing on the analysis of Italian enterprises. She is also a member of the Italian Association of University Teachers in Banking and Finance (ADEIMF). Her research topics include asset management companies, private equity and venture capital. She has participated in Italian and international conferences on these subjects.

Simon Grima is a lecturer in the Department of Banking and Finance, Faculty of Economics, Management and Accountancy, at the University of Malta. He teaches corporate finance, banking, the principles of finance, GRC (governance, risk management and compliance), and financial derivatives. He has considerable experience in treasury, risk management and audit management in both governmental and financial institutions.

Krzysztof Kil is Assistant Professor of Banking and Finance at the Cracow University of Economics, Faculty of Finance, Poland. His research concentrates on the issues of bank stability and bank efficiency in Central and Eastern Europe.

Paola Leone is Full Professor of Banking and Finance at La Sapienza University of Rome. She is Coordinator of the Banking and Finance and International Finance and Risk Management programs. She is the author of several books, and has contributed numerous articles on banking and financial topics.

Her main research interests include banking, capital markets, risk management and mutual guarantee institutions. She has acted as consultant and trainer for various financial intermediaries, public and private entities and consulting firms.

Ted Lindblom is Professor of Business Administration at the University of Gothenburg, Sweden. His current research interests mainly concern corporate finance and banking. In the corporate finance area he particularly focuses on corporate governance, capital budgeting and financial structure decisions. In the banking area, his emphasis is on banking strategies, pricing, profitability and risk management under different market condition and regulatory frameworks. He has authored and co-authored several articles and books regarding these issues.

Ewa Miklaszewska is a professor in Banking and Finance at the Cracow University of Economics (CUE), Poland, where she chairs the Banking Division, and an associate professor of Economics at the Jagiellonian University in Cracow, Department of Management and Public Communication. She has held visiting positions at both foreign universities and Polish financial regulatory institutions. Her research interests focus on bank regulation and bank strategies.

Pierluigi Morelli works at the Research Department of the Italian Bank Association (ABI), where he is responsible for the econometric model of the Italian economy and the Italian banking system. He graduated in Statistics and Economics at La Sapienza University of Rome in 1988. From 1988 to 2009 he worked at the Centro Europa Ricerche (CER). As Research Director of the CER Monetary and Banking sector, he was in charge of the econometric models of the Italian economy, the banking sector, and the pension expenditure. He has published numerous articles on monetary economics, banking, social security and environment.

Marco Oriani is Full Professor of Banking at the Catholic University of Milan, Italy, where he is coordinator for the BA in Economics and Executive Masters in SME Management. He is a board member of several Italian financial intermediaries. He is the author of more than 90 publications, and his main areas of research include private banking, financial innovations and bank internationalization.

Ida C. Panetta is Associate Professor at La Sapienza University of Rome, where she teaches modules on International Financial Institutions and capital markets. She is a member of the academic board of the PhD in Banking and Finance. Her main research interests include liquidity risk management, banking regulation and supervision, corporate governance, and the security exchange industry. She has acted as a consultant and trainer to a number of banks and mutual credit guarantee institutions.

Giovanni B. Pittaluga is Full Professor of Economics at Genoa University, Italy, prior to which he was Associate Professor of Monetary Economics at Università Cattolica del Sacro Cuore, Milan, Italy (1991–1994) and Economist at the Research Department of the Bank of Italy (1983–1988). He was responsible for the budget of Regione Liguria in the periods 2000–2002 and 2005–2010. He is the author of books and articles in international journals in the area of monetary economics. His research interests include central banking, banking, inflation, international political economy and economic history.

Maurizio Polato is Full Professor in Banking and Finance at the University of Udine, Italy. He is a member of a number of academic associations, including the Italian Association of University Teachers in Banking and Finance (ADEIMF) and the European Association of University Teachers in Banking and Finance (The Wolpertinger Club).

Federica Poli is Associate Professor of Banking at the Catholic University of Milan, Italy, where she is Director of the MA in International Trade Management program. She holds a PhD in Business Administration from the University of Venice. Her main research areas include bank internationalization, bank organizational models, financial distribution channels and financial innovations. She is the author of several publications, including book chapters and manuals on banking and financial intermediation.

Pasqualina Porretta is a senior lecturer in Banking and Finance at La Sapienza University of Rome, where she teaches Risk Management in Bank and Insurance and Derivatives. She is a board member of the PhD in Banking and Finance program. Her main research interests include risk measurement and management (credit, market, liquidity and counterparty risk), capital regulatory frameworks, financial derivatives and credit guarantee institutions. She has acted as a consultant to a number of financial intermediaries, microfinance institutions, public entities and consulting firms.

Gert Sandahl is a senior lecturer in the Department of Business Administration of the School of Business, Economics and Commercial Law, University of Gothenburg, Sweden. His main research interests concern behavioral aspects of capital budgeting, capital structure decisions, corporate governance, innovation and incentives.

Elena Seghezza is a lecturer at Genoa University, Italy. She previously worked as an economist at the Department of Economic Affairs of the Italian Government and at the Organisation for Economic Cooperation and Development (OECD). She has a PhD in International Economics from the Graduate Institute of International Studies, Geneva. She has published several articles on political economy, interest groups, inflation and international trade.

Stefan Sjögren is an associate professor in the Department of Business Administration, School of Business, Economics and Law, University of Göteborg, Sweden. His research interests include capital budgeting, international finance, valuation, deregulation, efficiency measurement, venture capital and the valuation of ideas.

Franco Tutino is Full Professor of Banking at La Sapienza University of Rome, where he teaches Banking Management and Banking Strategies, Financial Reports and Performance Analysis. He has recently published books on banking liquidity management and the effects of Basel III on banking management. He has also recently written, with Roberto Nicastro, General Manager of UniCredit Group, an article on banking strategies and profitability. His main research interests include bank strategy, financial reporting and performance analysis, financial crisis and regulation, supervision, financial and liquidity management, profitability and intermediation models.

Leo A. van Eerden is Assistant Professor at VU University, Amsterdam, the Netherlands. His teaching and research are in the areas of financial crisis, the regulation of financial institutions and financial system design. He is co-founder of The Power of Risk, an independent risk-assessment network, and he has published a variety of books and articles on bank regulation and systemic risk management. As independent professional, he is involved with a number of pension fund management assessment committees.

Introduction

Bank Stability, Sovereign Debt and Derivatives comprises a selection of chapters originally presented as papers at the European Association of University Lecturers of Banking and Finance Conference (otherwise known as the Wolpertinger Conference) held at the University of Malta, Valletta, Malta, in August 2012 (see also the companion volume *Bank Performance, Risk and Securitization*).

The editor would like to thank all the referees who acted as reviewers to all the chapters published in this volume – the double-blind peer review process significantly improved their quality – and to the contributors, who meticulously incorporated their comments and suggestions.

The 2012 Conference was successful in attracting high-quality papers and creating a varied and interesting social program. As organizer, I would like to thank the following for their financial and logistical support: Malta Financial Services Authority, Central Bank of Malta, Bank of Valletta, APS Bank, Fimbank, Middlesea Insurance, Middlesea Valletta Life, Office of the President and the Ministry of Gozo.

Chapter 1 by Laura Chiaramonte, Federica Poli and Marco Oriani, examines the relationship between bank business models and financial stability, using evidence from the financial crisis in OECD countries. Based on a sample of cooperative, savings and commercial banks from OECD countries over the period 2001–2010, this chapter examines the contribution of cooperative banks to the stability of other banks operating in the same financial system, with particular attention to those of a larger size. To account for changing impacts of sample mutual banks in varying macroeconomic and financial conditions, the analysis encompasses two time periods: pre-crisis (2001–2006) and crisis (2007–2010). The results of the empirical analysis indicate that cooperative banks become a significant determinant of the financial stability only during the crisis period and show a positive relationship. Moreover, the authors' results indicate that only during a financial crisis does a greater presence of cooperative banks exert a positive and increasing influence on the stability of large banks in the same banking system. Hence, it seems that banking systems characterized by a high presence of cooperative banks will be able to face future periods of financial distress in a better way.

In **Chapter 2** Ewa Miklaszewska and Krzysztof Kil explore cooperative banking in Poland during the post-crisis record of stability and efficiency. Globalization and the growing complexity of banking firms, plus post-crisis bank restructuring based on massive public assistance to the largest banks, pose between them the question of whether in the global post-crisis environment there is still a role for locally based cooperative banks, with their traditional intermediation model. Facing lower competitive pressures from the environment/shareholders, and with a traditional business model with long-term objectives, cooperative banks should in principle behave more prudently and take fewer risks. The aim of this chapter is to determine whether Polish cooperative banks have a post-crisis performance record superior to that of universal banks, due to their safer business model. Using the bank stability index and Z-score indicator, the chapter concludes that the Polish cooperative banking sector is safe and profitable, but slightly inefficient, and needs pressure exerting on it in order to expand. The 'niche bank status quo' seems to fulfill the needs of both universal banks, which do not intend to operate in rural areas, and cooperative banks, which feel comfortable with their traditional functions. Thus, the policy conclusion of the paper is that although the current performance of the Polish cooperative sector is sound, regulatory support for this sector will be necessary in the long run, either through strengthening the position of associating banks, or by creating incentives for the largest cooperative banks to demutualise.

Chapter 3, by Franco Tutino, Concetta Colasimone and Giorgio Carlo Brugnoni, focuses on credit development, quality deterioration and the intermediation model, posing the question of whether bank size matters, using evidence from Italy during the financial crisis started in 2007. The chapter, based on financial statement data from about 500 Italian banks in the period between 2006 and 2010, analyses the development of loans to customers in Italy by bank size. The research focuses on its evolution over time, on the composition of loan portfolios by product breakdown, on the quality of credit exposures and on the main income effects. The aim is to assess the lending policies adopted by Italian banks during the recent financial crisis, by linking the resulting differences to bank size and to the characteristics of the intermediation model adopted. The analysis shows that to the heterogeneity emerged in the loans to customers development, in the deterioration of its quality and in the main income effects correspond significant differences in the business model in terms of orientation to the funding-lending credit intermediation activity with customers.

In **Chapter 4**, Pierluigi Morelli, Giovanni B. Pittaluga and Elena Seghezza focus on credit supply and the rise in sovereign debt risk in the eurozone. The aim of this chapter is to try to establish whether, and if so to what extent, a rise in sovereign debt risk can cause a credit crunch. By conducting an empirical analysis of the eurozone countries for the period between the first quarter of 2010 and the last quarter of 2011, the authors first estimate the potential losses for banks on different kinds of financial assets by using credit default swap prices. A subsequent econometric analysis of panel data allows us to show them potential losses on government securities have a negative impact on credit supply, and that this impact is significantly greater than that on other domestic and foreign assets. This evidence can be attributed to the role of government securities in banks' liquidity management. In the recent euro crisis, especially since the end of 2011, the ECB has properly adopted measures aimed at relieving the lack of liquidity suffered by the banks of countries hit by a deterioration in their public debt worthiness.

Chapter 5, by Paola Leone, Ida C. Panetta and Pasqualina Porretta, explores credit guarantee institutions, performance and risk analysis utilizing an experimental scoring methodology. In a financial system, in which SMEs have no substantial alternatives to bank lending, credit guarantee institutions (CGIs) can significantly contribute to facilitating the credit access of such firms by reducing the information asymmetries between the lenders and the borrowers, and in some cases by reducing the cost of funding. Financial crises and the new capital requirements are leading to increased interest in both practitioners and regulators for these financial institutions, which have traditionally acted as intermediaries between banks and enterprises. These changes in market and regulatory conditions have made it necessary to assess whether the new generation of CGIs is really able to support access to credit, and if so whether they can be considered a valid instrument for avoiding small lending problems. That is why, over the last 20 years, the literature has paid more attention to measuring their financial additionality or incrementality; the practitioners have paid more attention to measuring their creditworthiness, risk and performance profile. The validity and the strength of the support provided by CGIs to those who have difficulty in accessing credit, in fact, in the current competitive environment, are closely related to the solvency and solidity of CGIs. Nevertheless, these last two factors qualify and determine the ability of CGIs to survive in the current economic situation. It has therefore become crucial for a variety of the CGI's interlocutors, who interface with them in different roles (policymakers, intermediary banks, industry associations), to understand their risk and performance profile, and to attempt to measure the credit, even if in a rudimentary way. In this perspective, this chapter aims to define a quantitative scoring framework methodology that can express the risk and performance of a sample of Italian CGIs (Confidi) on an experimental position map. The construction of the ranking/position map on the basis of the CGI score is derived from a set of indices expressive of the balance of management and more representative of the production process of CGIs and their risk profile and performance. The present work is a first experimental exercise in the field of credit guarantee institutions ranking/scoring. Hence, it is subject to improvements and the possible future developments highlighted in the concluding remarks.

In **Chapter 6**, Ted Lindblom and Gert Sandahl explore the role of trade credit and the cost of capital. In this chapter, the authors show that working capital in the form of trade credit may constitute a significant share of firms' debt capacity. Despite its short-term debt characteristics, such capital seems to be a long-term element of the financial structure of the firm. This has implications for the determination of the cost of capital. The authors analyze the cost of different types of working capital in the context of firms' investment appraisal, arguing that cash committed to trade credit extended by suppliers should generally be omitted from free cash flow. The required rate of return should then be based on the *total* weighted average cost of capital, including the implicit (market-based) interest cost of trade credit. They argue, further, that the opportunity cost of trade credit should be expected to be higher than the average interest cost of interest-bearing debts, albeit lower than the *partial* weighted average cost of capital based on long-term (interest-bearing) debt and equity capital. Hence, in a (near-) optimal capital structure, the *total* weighted average cost of capital would be lower than the *partial* weighted average cost of capital.

In **Chapter 7**, Frank Bezzina, Simon Grima and Joseph Falzon explore the reasons that lead to the success of firms in achieving their objectives for using derivatives. This empirical study examines whether the five factors of 'proper derivative use' (risk management controls, expertise, perception, benefits and misuse) proposed by Bezzina and Grima (2012) account for the level of success of firms in achieving their objectives for using derivatives. The survey responses of 496 financial and non-financial firms that use derivatives revealed that the firms that were classified as being successful in achieving their objectives for using derivatives reported: (i) greater use of risk management controls; (ii) more expertise in dealing with derivatives, particularly in complex situations; and (iii) greater awareness of an array of benefits that derivatives offer to firms in managing and shifting risks. No significant differences were found in 'perception' and 'misuse' since, irrespective of the success of firms in achieving objectives for using derivatives, the firms agreed (on average) that derivatives are valuable financial instruments and that the financial losses incurred by firms when using derivatives result from the misuse of the said financial tools.

The findings of this study lend weight to the claim that derivatives can be useful tools in pursuing an investment strategy, provided there is full understanding of these instruments and responsible management of the risks (cf. Rutledge & Bertram, 1995). The study goes on to provide some interesting avenues for further research.

Chapter 8, by Göran Bergendahl and Stefan Sjögren, examines the management of foreign exchange exposures. This chapter focuses on how different firms handle the risks of economic losses caused by changes in currency exchange rates. It aims at investigating the principles and procedures used in the foreign exchange management of multinational corporations (MNCs). The study has a qualitative, longitudinal approach, based on personal interviews on three occasions; 1985, 1996, and 2008. The authors find that over these years the management of foreign exchange exposure has become a more centralized activity. This centralization is driven by the introduction of new administrative systems and new legislation (IFRS), by earlier 'hocks' from speculative behavior, and a higher focus on shareholder value. Swedish firms use their choice of currency as a competitive advantage, offering suppliers and customers the opportunity to invoice in their home currency. The introduction of the euro has not affected the exposure management operations to any great extent; the respondents view themselves as being risk-averse, and their most common argument for hedging is that they do it better than their shareholders. The product characteristics (standardized or customized) affect the hedging procedures; forwards, netting and swaps are used as hedging techniques, but new, advanced hedging derivatives are not in common use. Still, many firms do not distinguish between economic and transaction exposure. Finally, translation exposure is rarely hedged. Many treasurers state that they have taken up a position not to speculate; on the other hand they may well hedge expected exposures, despite the fact that such actions may well increase the currency risks. So even if they support the arguments pro hedging, a new controversy has emerged in terms of whether to hedge or not to hedge economic exposures. That issue has not yet led to a satisfactory solution.

In **Chapter 9**, Leo A. van Eerden focuses on risk governance and management control in Dutch pension funds. This chapter shows that risk management is a crucial task for pension fund boards and management. Two elements are, however, missing or undervalued in present risk management systems. First of all, traditional risk management is strongly model and data-biased, neglecting the 'human' factor, encompassing the governance of managerial processes. Secondly, traditional risk management has a strong bias towards 'market-fundamentalism', and the point is that a coherent vision on macroeconomic developments is absent. The strong plea of this chapter is to combine micro and macro prudential issues, and to integrate quantitative and qualitative elements in risk management. Risk cannot be eliminated completely, and future financial developments cannot be completely foreseen; nevertheless risk management is a fundamental task of the board, and even if it is outsourced remains the board's responsibility. In this chapter it is proposed to develop a frame of risk beliefs in order to cope with the human factor in risk management and to improve the risk management processes in pension funds. Risk management must focus primarily on conduct and secondly on systems; it is a process approach of (risk) conduct, incentives and motivation. Risk management needs to link the quantitative and qualitative aspects.

In **Chapter 10**, Maurizio Polato and Josanco Floreani develop a new risk-adjusted performance approach for measuring the value of securities exchanges. What exchanges are actually worth is not a simple question to answer, especially in the light of the consolidation process involving major exchanges. Prominent research argues that exchanges pursue consolidation strategies in order to exploit economies of scale and scope; by building large liquidity pools and engaging in trade-related activities, exchanges try to reduce volatility in revenues and manage uncertainty. The authors argue that this is, however, only part of the picture. since the risks that exchanges are exposed to are not comprehensively take into account. The aim of this chapter is to bridge the gap in knowledge about value drivers, developing a conceptual framework which captures the main variables impacting on the value of exchanges. The authors identify the main risks, ether endogenous and exogenous, which may adversely affect cost and revenue functions. This allows the authors to develop a risk-adjusted performance approach to tackle the problem of value creation in the securities industry.

Finally in **Chapter 11**, Giusy Chesini and Elisa Giaretta examine whether or not private equity investment has a positive impact on firms' profitability and on the growth of the target company. Interest in the private equity (PE) business has been recently revitalized due to the financial crisis, which requires, among other things, an improvement in the competitiveness and productivity of companies. The evidence from empirical research seems to suggest that private equity investments deliver strong returns to their investors by improving the operating performance of the target companies, but the results are not homogeneous. In this chapter, the authors aim to verify whether or not a portfolio of companies located within the same area in Italy improve their profitability on average after PE investment. In particular, the authors aim to discover if PE-backed companies increase their profit margins and cash flows more than their industry competitors do. The analysis utilizes a Probit model in order to test the statistical significance of some variables designed to measure the impact of private equity on target companies.

1

On the Relationship between Bank Business Models and Financial Stability: Evidence from the Financial Crisis in OECD Countries

Laura Chiaramonte, Federica Poli and Marco Oriani

1 Introduction

The cooperative credit sector represents an essential sector of the banking structure of many financial systems, especially in Europe where, in Austria, Finland, France, Germany, Italy and the Netherlands, the cooperative banks have a high market share (see Figure 1.1). In advanced economies and emerging markets outside Europe, cooperative banks generally have a lower share, but there are some countries where they play a non-negligible role, as in Japan and Canada, where in 2010 the share of the cooperatives was 15.72 per cent and 3.49 per cent, respectively.

During the recent worldwide financial turmoil, some authors (see Ayadi et al., 2010; Boonstra, 2010; Groeneveld, 2011; Mottura, 2011) and the European Association of Co-operative Banks, (EACB, 2010) argue that cooperative banks have fared relatively well, due essentially to a business model which pursues a healthy attitude to risk (with limited exposure to toxic assets), a longer-term perspective, a much stronger stakeholder focus and substantial capital buffers. These characteristics should reduce instability in more mutualized banking systems. However, the contribution of cooperative banks to the stability of the financial system in which they operate is still a controversial matter. Groeneveld and Sjauw (2009), Llewellyn (2009), Ayadi et al. (2010), EACB (2010), Stefancic (2010), Groeneveld (2011), and Stefancic and Kathitziotis (2011) show that the presence of cooperative banks enhances financial stability in certain countries. Hesse and Cihák (2007) find that a higher cooperative bank market share improves the stability of the average bank in the same banking system; however, they also argue that if cooperative banks are widespread, their presence may weaken commercial banks, particularly those that are already weak. Contrary to these findings, Barth et al. (1999), Brunner et al. (2004), Goodhart (2004) and Fonteyne (2007) maintain that cooperative banks tend to increase the fragility of their respective financial system for different reasons: firstly because their inefficiency may ultimately undermine their soundness, and secondly because cooperative banks are more vulnerable to shocks in credit quality and interest rates.

To date, no empirical studies have investigated the contribution of cooperative banks to bank stability, taking into account the recent financial crisis.

The mixed empirical results of the impact of cooperative banks on financial stability warrant further investigation, especially after the onset of the financial crisis. Based on a sample of cooperative, savings and commercial banks from OECD countries over the period 2001–2010, this chapter examines the contribution of cooperative banks to the stability of other banks, with particular attention to those of a larger size. Bank soundness is proxied by a very popular accounting measure: the Z-score (Boyd and Runkle, 1993).

To account for changing contributions made by sample mutual banks in varying macroeconomic and financial conditions, the analysis is carried

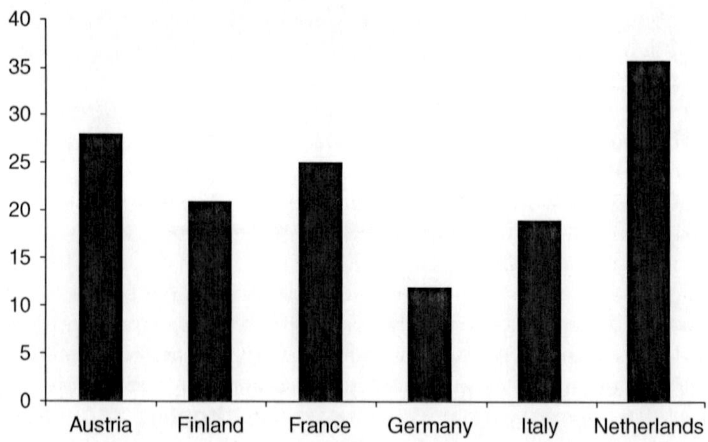

Figure 1.1 OECD countries with the highest cooperative banks' market share in 2010

Notes: The share of cooperative banks is calculated as the ratio of the sum of the total assets of all cooperative banks in the country to total assets of all banks – cooperative, savings and commercial banks – in the same country. Values on cooperative banks' total asset are collected from the European Association of Cooperative Banks (EACB); while values on all banks' total asset are collected from the Organisation for Economic Co-operation and Development (OECD). Data in the figure are in percentages.

Sources: EACB and OECD, authors' calculations.

out both in the pre-crisis period (2001–2006) and in the crisis period (2007–2010).

The empirical study is conducted using a random effect panel regression and focuses on bank-specific variables, on a set of dummy variables which account for specialized business models adopted by banks and on country-specific factors concerning macroeconomic and bank-industry specific factors. In addition to the traditional variables used by the related studies as country-specific factors, we also considered a banking systemic stability indicator: the aggregate Z-score (Beck et al., 2011).

The results of the empirical analysis indicate that cooperative banks become a significant determinant of the financial stability only during a period of crisis. Moreover, our results indicate that only during financial crisis does a greater presence of cooperative banks exert a positive and increasing influence on the stability of large banks in the same banking system. Hence, it seems that banking systems characterized by a strong presence of cooperative banks will be able to face future periods of financial distress in a better way.

Section 2 of this study reviews the relevant literature. Section 3 describes data sample and the variables used in our analysis. Section 4 presents the empirical methodology and summarizes the main results, while Section 5 shows the robustness tests. Finally, Section 6 concludes the chapter.

2 Literature review

The empirical publications examining the role played by cooperative banks within the banking stability puzzle is still limited, mostly because of their marginal importance in many developed countries, in comparison with that of commercial banks. Research, despite its scarcity, has thrown up mixed results in the last two decades.

Some empirical evidence points to cooperative banks generally having fewer incentives to take on risks, due to the lack of profit-maximization targets and the absence of many of the factors that lead rational managers in joint-stock banks to adopt short-term horizons (see Rajan, 1994; Hansmann, 1996; Chaddad and Cook, 2004). Hesse and Cihák (2007) use a well-known indicator of individual bank risk, the Z-score, and thus provide evidence that cooperative and savings banks are more stable than commercial banks, adding that the much lower volatility of the cooperative banks' returns more than offsets their relatively poorer profitability. Garcia-Marco and Robles-Fernandez (2008), Beck et al. (2009), Groeneveld and de Vries (2009), Beck et al. (2010), EACB (2010) and Liu et al. (2010) have since maintained that both cooperative and savings banks appear safer than their commercial counterparts. Iannotta, Nocera and Sironi (2007) evaluate the impact of alternative ownership models in 15 European countries, and find that mutual banks are of higher quality and have a lower asset risk than both private and public sector banks.

Moving from studies comparing the soundness of different business models with others focused on the appraisal of mutual banks' contribution to financial stability, there is evidence indicating that a greater presence of cooperative banks increases the stability of the average bank in the same banking system (Hesse and Cihák, 2007). Groeneveld and Sjauw (2009), Llewellyn (2009), Ayadi et al. (2010), EACB (2010), Stefancic (2010), Groeneveld (2011), and Stefancic and Kathitziotis (2011), although starting out from different datasets, time periods and countries, all argue that cooperative banks actually promote the stability of national banking systems by contributing to the diversity of business models and ownership structures adopted by bank intermediaries. They suggest that this makes the system more stable as a whole.

Despite the above-mentioned positive contributions attributable to cooperative banks, one line of research suggests that cooperative banking may increase the fragility of financial systems for several reasons. Firstly, explicit and implicit advantages granted to public or semi-public banks such as cooperative banks may exert downward pressures on the interest margins in traditional banking, thus pushing private sector banks to engage in more risky activities (see Barth et al., 1999; Goodhart, 2004). In addition, Hesse and Cihák (2007) argue that a large presence of cooperative banks apparently weakens commercial banks, in particular those commercial banks that are already weak. Secondly, other authors suggest that cooperative banks may have more difficulty adjusting to adverse circumstances and changing risks (see Brunner et al., 2004). Finally, cooperative banks are regarded as more vulnerable to sudden changes in credit quality and interest rates, as they are more focused on traditional credit intermediation than are other institutions, and therefore have higher exposure to credit and interest rate risk (see Fonteyne, 2007).

Here we study the role played by cooperative banks, using a sample of cooperative, savings and commercial banks from OECD countries over the period 2001–2010. To account for the varying roles taken by mutualized entities over time, specifically after the onset of the financial crisis, we have split our analysis into two sub-periods, the first covering the pre-crisis period, 2001–2006, and the second covering the period of crisis, 2007–2010.

3 Data sample and descriptive statistics

3.1 Data description

The study focuses on sample banks belonging to OECD countries operating according to three different business models: commercial, cooperative and savings banks.[1] Our sample covers the following countries: Australia, Austria, Belgium, Canada, the Czech Republic, Denmark, Finland, France, Germany, Greece, Hungary, Ireland, Italy, Japan, South Korea, Luxembourg, the Netherlands, New Zealand, Poland, Portugal, Spain, Slovenia, Sweden, Switzerland, the United Kingdom and the United States. Eight countries – Chile, Estonia, Iceland, Israel, Mexico, Norway, the Slovak Republic and Turkey – were excluded from the analysis because BankScope Database does not provide data on cooperative banks in these OECD countries.

We used only unconsolidated bank statements (BankScope Database consolidation codes U1 and U2), since most of the data concerning the sampled banks is unconsolidated. Hence, domestic and foreign subsidiaries are included as separate entities.[2]

Table 1.1 Sample distribution by business model (2001–2010)

Country/Specialization	Cooperative banks	Savings banks	Commercial banks
Australia	12	–	40
Austria	121	102	107
Belgium	10	16	58
Canada	22	4	63
Czech Republic	2	–	30
Denmark	8	59	59
Finland	2	2	19
France	127	46	230
Germany	1,483	584	270
Greece	1	1	22
Hungary	1	1	42
Ireland	2	1	31
Italy	594	63	183
Japan	650	1	175
Luxembourg	2	2	139
New Zealand	5		13
Netherlands	1	2	54
Poland	1	1	63
Portugal	2	5	40
Slovenia	2	1	20
South Korea	2	6	22
Spain	83	62	88
Sweden	1	81	38
Switzerland	10	247	221
United Kingdom	66	3	199
USA	19	1032	9068
Total	3,229	2,322	11,294

Notes: This table shows the sample distribution by business model in the OECD countries, over the period 2001–2010. The number of sample banks reported in the table refers only to those intermediaries considered in the random effect panel regressions.

Source: BankScope Database, authors' calculations.

Table 1.2 Descriptive statistics of cooperative banks' market share in sample OECD countries

Country/Sub-period	Pre-crisis period	Crisis period
Australia	4.44	0.75
Austria	29.17	24.65
Belgium	1.37	0.89
Canada	1.83	2.64
Czech Republic	3.87	6.06
Denmark	0.07	0.15
Finland	8.76	27.91
France	28.98	35.74
Germany	14.22	14.23
Greece	4.91	0.62
Hungary	1.71	1.91
Ireland	5.96	1.89
Italy	18.22	19.71
Japan	22.21	21.25
Luxembourg	0.49	0.04
New Zealand	0.15	1.01
Netherlands	48.13	29.07
Poland	4.24	3.32
Portugal	1.64	0.46
Slovenia	3.22	3.87
South Korea	4.55	2.90
Spain	9.32	6.23
Sweden	0.003	0.005
Switzerland	2.83	2.64
United Kingdom	4.79	4.79
USA	0.81	0.93

Notes: The table shows the cooperative banks' market share in each OECD country in the pre-crisis period (2001–2006) and in the crisis period (2007–2010). Data in the table are in percentages.

Source: BankScope Database, authors' calculations.

The final sample consists of 16,845 OECD banks, out of which 11,294 are commercial, 3,229 are cooperative and 2,322 are savings banks. See Table 1.1 for sample distribution by business model in each country; the data collected is end-of-year observations, from 2001 to 2010.

For each banking system in the sample, we calculated the market share of cooperative banks in terms of total assets in both sub-periods (see Table 1.2). The six countries with values above 10 per cent are the Netherlands, France, Finland, Austria, Japan, Italy and Germany. The remaining OECD countries exhibit lower market shares for cooperative banks.

Table 1.3 Breakdown of the natural Z-score logarithm by business model in each sub-period

	ln_Z		Equity to assets (%)		Roaa (%)		Standard deviation of Roaa	
Specialization	**Pre-crisis period**	**Crisis period**	**Pre-crisis period**	**Crisis period**	**Pre-crisis period**	**Crisis period**	**(% points)**	**Crisis period**
Cooperative	4.250	4.262	6.168	7.574	0.257	0.285	0.218	0.208
Savings	4.446	4.242	10.100	10.012	0.660	0.244	0.292	0.391
Commercial	4.140	3.700	11.510	11.601	1.216	0.747	0.380	0.549

Notes: This table displays the decomposition of the natural logarithm of the Z-score (ln_Z) by business model for OECD sample banks in the pre-crisis period (2001–2006) and in the crisis period (2007–2010). Roaa is Return on Average Assets. Reported descriptive statistics are calculated only for banks considered in the random effect panel regressions.

Source: BankScope Database, authors' calculations.

3.2 Measuring bank stability

This chapter uses as a dependent variable a widespread accounting measure of bank stability: the Z-score (see Boyd and Runkle, 1993; Maechler et al., 2005; Beck and Laeven, 2006; Laeven and Levine, 2006; Hesse and Cihák, 2007; among others).

This measure is calculated as:

$$\text{Z-score} = (\text{Roaa} + \text{Eta})/\sigma Roaa \tag{1.1}$$

Roaa is the bank's return on average assets, *ETA* represents the equity to total assets ratio, and *σRoaa* is the standard deviation of return on average assets. In order to capture the changing pattern of the bank's return volatility, we use a three-year rolling time window to calculate *σRoaa.*

The Z-score reflects the number of standard deviations by which returns would have to fall from the mean in order to wipe out bank equity. Higher Z-score values stand for lower probability of insolvency risk and greater bank stability.

Since the Z-score is highly skewed, we use the natural Z-score logarithm, ln_Z (see Ivičić et al., 2008; Laeven and Levine, 2009; Liu et al., 2010).

Data on *Roaa* and *ETA* are collected from BankScope Database on an annual basis, due to the limited availability of quarterly data for the majority of banks in our sample.

Table 1.3 summarizes the descriptive statistics of the breakdown of the natural Z-score logarithm by bank business model in the pre-crisis and crisis periods.

The cooperative banks' natural logarithm of the Z-score is higher than that of the savings banks only during the crisis years. In both sub-periods, the cooperative banks' ln_Z is higher than that of commercial banks. Moreover, cooperative banks are the only ones that showed a tendency to increase their stability from the pre-crisis period to the period of crisis (from 4.250 to 4.262). In contrast, the savings and commercial banks' average ln_Z value dropped from the first sub-period to the second; the savings banks' ln_Z dropped from 4.446 to 4.242, while that of commercial banks dropped from 4.140 to 3.700. This result can be largely explained by the low volatility of returns (proxied by the standard deviation of *Roaa*) of cooperative banks compared with that of commercial and savings banks (see Table 1.3). However, during the two sub-periods, the whole non-cooperative banking sector shows higher equity to total asset ratios and profitability (*Roaa*).

Table 1.4 provides international comparisons both of the ln_Z by institutional model and of the aggregate ln_Z (LN_Z) for all the sample banks, in each sub-period.

Although in the table we have shown the ln_Z data for both periods, the analysis has focused only on the crisis period, since it is more interesting to see

Table 1.4 International comparisons of the natural Z-score logarithm and its aggregate

	ln_Z				LN_Z			
	Cooperative banks		Savings banks		Commercial banks		Whole sample	
Country	**Pre-crisis period**	**Crisis period**	**Pre-crisis period**	**Crisis period**	**Pre-crisis period**	**Crisis period**	**Pre-crisis period**	**Crisis period**
Australia	4.513	3.662	–	–	3.294	3.437	3.047	3.634
Austria	3.896	3.906	4.250	3.709	3.741	3.223	3.962	3.612
Belgium	4.575	2.972	2.794	3.219	3.254	2.926	3.541	3.039
Canada	4.320	3.806	4.051	4.148	3.740	3.767	3.702	3.770
Czech Republic	–	4.092	–	–	3.154	3.675	3.289	3.623
Denmark	3.917	3.334	3.862	2.861	3.694	2.953	3.824	3.049
Finland	–	3.320	–	4.073	2.858	3.431	2.858	3.608
France	5.167	4.976	4.477	4.198	3.650	3.468	4.431	4.214
Germany	4.710	4.783	4.928	5.159	3.972	3.785	4.536	4.575
Greece	5.558	4.274	–	–	–	2.616	4.035	2.972
Hungary	4.133	3.266	2.857	–	3.528	2.998	3.366	3.020
Ireland	–	1.124	–	–	4.089	2.804	3.939	2.708
Italy	3.826	3.799	4.294	3.654	3.678	3.562	3.932	3.671
Japan	3.423	3.567	4.635	4.444	3.391	3.447	3.359	3.513
Luxembourg	5.057	3.959	–	–	3.537	3.213	3.534	3.214
New Zealand	3.761	4.222	–	–	3.549	2.665	3.752	3.072
Netherlands	3.578	3.988	3.910	2.180	3.829	3.430	3.772	3.199
Poland	–	3.215	–	3.656	3.030	3.323	2.980	3.316
Portugal	3.736	4.929	3.622	3.292	3.677	3.384	3.678	3.868
Slovenia	–	3.500	–	–	3.255	3.440	3.357	3.426
South Korea	1.774	0.307	1.593	–	2.597	3.420	2.114	2.534
Spain	4.884	4.246	–	3.680	3.463	3.761	4.173	3.895
Sweden	3.856	–	3.743	3.120	3.724	3.918	3.880	3.349
Switzerland	5.716	5.343	5.242	5.158	4.363	4.226	4.751	4.775
United Kingdom	4.979	4.185	–	3.160	3.777	3.218	4.378	3.521
USA	4.125	3.818	4.220	3.783	4.185	3.725	4.151	3.693

Notes: The table contains the international comparison both of the natural logarithm of the Z-score (ln_Z) by business model and of the aggregate natural Z-score logarithm (LN_Z), in the pre-crisis period (2001–2006) and in the crisis period (2007–2010). LN_Z is the country-wide natural Z-score logarithm across all banks for any given year and country (see Beck et al., 2011). Reported descriptive statistics are only calculated for banks considered in the random effect panel regressions.

Source: BankScope Database, authors' calculations.

how the different bank business models behaved in terms of stability during a period of financial stress in the countries considered. Table 1.4 shows that during the crisis period, in several OECD countries cooperative banks are the most stable in terms of ln_Z, followed by savings and commercial banks. This outcome holds for Australia, Austria, the Czech Republic, Denmark, France, Greece, Hungary, Italy, New Zealand, Spain, Portugal, Slovenia, Switzerland, the United Kingdom and the USA. Also in Luxembourg and the Netherlands, cooperative banks are the most stable during the crisis period, followed by commercial banks. In Belgium, Canada, Germany and Japan, savings banks look more stable in times of crisis, followed by cooperatives and then by commercial banks; in Finland and Poland as well, savings banks are the most stable in the second sub-period – better than commercial and cooperative banks. Finally, in Ireland, South Korea and Sweden, commercial banks turned out to be the most stable in times of crisis.

With reference to the aggregated Z-score, LN_Z, Table 1.4 identifies 11 countries where our proxy for banking systemic stability augmented from the pre-crisis to the crisis period, namely: Australia, Canada, the Czech Republic, Finland, Germany, Japan, Poland, Portugal, Slovenia, South Korea and Switzerland, while 15 countries registered a drop in LN_Z. However, in just some of these countries the proxy for systemic risk showed a significant drop: Denmark (from 3.766 to 2.908), Greece (from 4.035 to 2.972), Ireland (from 3.939 to 2.708), Spain (from 4.173 to 3.895) United Kingdom (from 4.378 to 3.521) and United States (from 4.151 to 3.693).

3.3 Explanatory variables

In our empirical analysis we explain bank stability as a function of bank-specific variables, a set of dummy variables which account for bank institutional models adopted by banks and country-specific factors (see Table 1.5).[3]

Bank-specific items of data are extracted annually from the BankScope Database, including proxies for bank size (natural logarithm of a bank's total assets in millions of euros: SIZE), liquidity risk (the ratio of net loans to deposits and short-term funding: LIQ), lending behavior (the ratio of net loans to total assets: CRED), efficiency (the cost-to-income ratio: CIR) and diversification (the ratio of non-interest income to net operating revenue: ID).

Moreover, in our analysis we considered two dummy variables to allow for varying intercepts for different institutional models. In particular, we included cooperative bank dummy (CBD) and savings bank dummy (SBD). The former takes the value 1 if the bank is a cooperative bank; the latter takes the value 1 for a savings bank. If commercial banks are relatively weaker (less stable) than cooperative or savings banks, the first (second) dummy variable would have a positive sign in the panel regressions explaining ln_Z.

For country-specific factors. we used the annual percentage change of GDP (GDPC). This variable is obtained from the World Economic Outlook

Table 1.5 Explanatory variables description and predicted sign

	Variable	Measure	Notation	Expected sign
Bank-specific	Size	ln (total assets)	SIZE	POSITIVE/ NEGATIVE
	Liquidity risk	Net loans to deposits and short-term funding	LIQ	NEGATIVE
	Bank lending behavior	Net loans to total assets	CRE	NEGATIVE
	Efficiency	Cost–income ratio	CIR	POSITIVE/ NEGATIVE
	Income diversification	Non-interest income to net operating revenue	ID	POSITIVE/ NEGATIVE
Dummies	Cooperative bank dummy	Equals 1 for cooperative banks; 0 otherwise	CBD	POSITIVE
	Savings bank dummy	Equals 1 for savings banks; 0 otherwise	SBD	POSITIVE
	Gross domestic product	Annual percent change in GDP	GDPC	POSITIVE/ NEGATIVE
Country-specific	Bank market concentration	Normalized Herfindahl–Hirschman index	n_HHI	POSITIVE/ NEGATIVE
	Cooperative banks' share	Cooperative banks' market share in a country per year	CMS	POSITIVE/ NEGATIVE
	Banking systemic stability	The country-wide natural Z-score logarithm across all banks for any given year and country	LN_Z	POSITIVE

Notes: n_HHI, CMS and LN_Z are calculated using data available from BankScope database. GDPC is available from World Economic Outlook Database (International Monetary Fund, IMF).

Source: Bank-specific and dummy variables are available from BankScope database.

Database (International Monetary Fund, IMF). In addition, we considered two bank industry-specific variables: the normalized Herfindahl–Hirschman index (n_HHI) and the share of cooperative banks (CMS). The normalized HHI index is calculated as:

$$n\_HHI = \frac{HHI - (1/N)}{1 - (1/N)} \tag{1.2}$$

where *HHI* is the sum of squared market shares (in term of total assets) of all banks in the country and *N* is the number of banks in the market. The items of data used to calculate this variable were extracted with annual frequency from BankScope Database.

Finally, for country-specific variables we considered a banking systemic stability indicator, the aggregate natural Z-score logarithm (LN_Z), which is the country-wide natural Z-score logarithm across all banks for any given year and country (see Beck et al., 2011). This variable is a proxy of country-specific systemic risk and it helps to capture any impact on the resilience of any single bank.

The explanatory variables and their hypothesized relationship with the dependent variable (ln_Z) are summarized in Table 1.5. The sign linking SIZE to ln_Z is uncertain; the relationship can be interpreted positively when the growth of bank size may give rise to the realization of efficiency gains and superior diversification ability which would result in higher banking systemic stability –but on the other hand, the relationship may be negative according to the Too Big To Fail (TBTF) incentive attributable to large banks to take on more risks. thus undermining their own stability and eventually that of the financial system in which they operate.

With reference to the relationship between LIQ and the banking systemic stability, we expected a negative sign, since a higher exposure to liquidity shortfalls would threaten banking stability. A negative sign was also expected between CRE and ln_Z, given that credit is risky area of banking business.

The sign linking CIR to ln_Z is doubtful. The relationship between our cost-efficiency proxy and bank stability is expected to be negative, assuming that generally speaking inefficiency provides an incentive to banks to take on riskier activities in order to improve their profitability (for evidence of the 'bad management' and 'moral hazard' hypotheses, see Berger and De Young, 1997; Kwan and Eisenbeis, 1997; Williams, 2004; and Fiordelisi et al., 2010). Additionally, since cooperative banks act as non-profit maximizing intermediaries which are willing to trade off their profits in order to be able to deliver financial services at below-market price to their customers, their competitive behavior may drive down the profitability and efficiency of other non-mutual banks, tempting the latter to raise their risk exposure to compensate for lost returns under moral hazard considerations. Contrary to the above findings, Altunbas et al. (2007), investigating the relationship between capital, loan provisions and cost efficiency for a large sample of commercial, saving and cooperative European banks over the period 1992–2000, do not find a positive relationship between inefficiency and risk taking by banks; inefficient European banks appear to hold more capital and take on less risk. Such a result may derive from a more relaxed attitude by regulators/regulations towards more cost-efficient banks (allowing the latter to trade off capital and risk taking) than to inefficient banks. Broadly speaking, cost-constrained banks may be inhibited from increasing their risks, possibly being also more reserve-constrained than efficient banks. Therefore, a positive relationship between CIR and ln_Z is also possible.

The sign linking ID to our bank stability measure is uncertain. The relationship can be interpreted both positively, when diversification can lead to a reduction in risk and therefore greater bank stability, and negatively, when it occurs in business or geographical areas poorly known by managers; in such a case, increasing diversification leads to a reduction of bank stability.

The direction of the relationship between GDPG and our proxy of bank soundness is uncertain. Intuitively, GDP growth is likely to have a positive impact on our dependent variable: with higher demand, indivisible production factors are better utilized, lowering average costs and improving managerial efficiency (Conrad et al., 2009) and this may help banks to reduce risks. However, there is some evidence suggesting that lending mistakes are more likely during boom periods than in recession (Jiménez and Saurina, 2006). There are two possible reasons for this. Firstly, when the economy is growing rapidly, banks become over-optimistic about borrowers' ability to repay, and this leads to more liberal credit policies with lower credit standards. This lending behavior tends to ultimately result in a higher level of impaired loans and borrower defaults. Secondly, in boom periods, the excessive competition that can prevail during an economic upturn may erode margins and encourage managers to seek higher-return (and therefore higher-risk) business. On the basis of the studies cited above, therefore, we expect a dual relationship: positive or negative.

The sign linking norm_HHI to banking stability is uncertain. According to the 'competition-fragility' view, monopoly rents gained by banks in less competitive markets discourage excessive risk-taking conduct, and enhance banks' ability to cope with demand/supply shocks (Allen and Gale, 2000, 2004; Carletti, 2008). According to this view, competitive markets limit the ability of banks to gain informational advantages from their relationship with borrowers, reducing their incentives to properly screen borrowers, thus increasing the risk of fragility (Beck et al., 2012). On this basis, a positive sign of the coefficient of the explanatory variable is expected.

In contrast to the above hypothesis, the competition stability view (Boyd and De Nicolò, 2005) maintains that more competitive banking systems result in more, rather than less, stability. If competition reduces the cost of financing, bank borrowers would be better able to repay their loan obligations, thus reducing the risk of bank instability caused by the occurrence of credit risk. However, in more concentrated markets, incumbent banks exert their market power by setting high interest rates on lending, thus providing incentives to borrowers to finance only high-risk projects – and this ultimately undermines the ability of debtors to repay loans, and consequently the stability of the bank itself. Additionally, less competitive markets represent breeding grounds where overlarge, complex and highly interconnected big banks have better access to subsidies from national safety nets and pursue excessive risk taking consistent with moral hazard behaviors. If competition enhances stability, then we may expect a negative sign of the norm_HHI coefficient.

With reference to CMS, on the basis of related studies, we hypothesized a dual relationship between the cooperatives' market share and bank stability. Barth et al. (1999) and Goodhart (2004) maintain that the presence of any non-profit-maximizing banking entities may make financial systems more fragile. Hence, an increase of cooperative share would result in a decrease of financial stability. On the other hand, Rajan (1994), Hansmann (1996) and Chaddad and Cook (2004) find that mutual banks tend to adopt less risky strategies than demutualised ones. In this case, an increase in the share of cooperative banks would encourage financial stability.

Finally, we expected a positive sign between ln_Z and LN_Z. Hence, an increase of the systemic stability (LN_Z) would correspond to an increase in the resilience of any single bank (ln_Z).

Table 1.6 reports descriptive statistics of the explanatory variables of bank stability, disaggregated by each of the periods considered.

The values of our explanatory variables did not change significantly from the pre-crisis period to the crisis period. The only exception was the average value of CIR, ID, GDPG, n_HHI and LN_Z.

With regard to bank-specific characteristics, the average values of SIZE, LIQ and CRE remained substantially unchanged for almost all sample banks. Table 1.6 indicates that SIZE grew moderately, from 5.10 in the pre-crisis period to 5.34 in the crisis period. Therefore, on average, the total assets of sample banks showed a slight tendency to increase. The average LIQ value of sample banks increased from 76.84 per cent to 82.63 per cent. The mean CRE value augmented from 61.15 per cent in the first period to 62.58 per cent during the crisis. Also, the average value of CIR and ID showed a significant variation. In particular, operational efficiency worsened during the crisis years, due probably much more to the deterioration of the bank operating income than the concomitant increase in operating costs. The average value of CIR grew from 66.84 per cent in the pre-crisis period to 73.14 per cent in the crisis period. ID decreased from 19.22 per cent to 16.54 per cent, given that in the crisis years the banks were less able to exploit diversified sources of income.

Table 1.6 Summary statistics on explanatory variables for sample banks

	Pre-crisis period		Crisis period	
Variable	**Mean (Std. Dev.)**	**Min.–Max.**	**Mean (Std. Dev.)**	**Min.–Max.**
Bank-specific variables				
SIZE	5.10 (1.710)	–0.168–13.953	5.34 (1.799)	–0.386–14.581
LIQ	0.760 (0.987)	0.00016–31.435	0.826 (0.781)	0.00008–35.822
CRE	0.611 (0.185)	0.00014–0.999	0.625 (0.186)	0.000024–0.999
CIR	0.668 (0.204)	–0.634–9.415	0.731 (0.307)	–5.935–13.53
ID	0.192 (0.684)	–116.090–91.473	0.165 (5.308)	–864–287.5
Country-specific variables				
GDPG	0.024 (0.009)	–0.009–0.071	0.001 (0.028)	–0.082–0.068
n_HHI	0.038 (0.061)	0.016–0.996	0.054 (0.055)	0.027–0.406
CMS	0.045 (0.079)	0.000–0.690	0.053 (0.081)	0.000–0.379
LN_Z	4.164 (0.310)	1.785–6.124	3.839 (0.495)	1.755–4.936

Notes: Reported descriptive statistics are calculated only for banks considered in the random effect panel regressions.

Source: BankScope Database, authors' calculations.

Table 1.7 Correlations for the pre-crisis and crisis period

	ln_Z	
Variable	**Pre-crisis period**	**Crisis period**
SIZE	0.0275*	–0.0178*
LIQ	0.0062	–0.0381*
CRE	0.0373	–0.0505*
CIR	–0.2105*	–0.2257*
ID	–0.0236*	0.0094*
GDPC	–0.0204*	0.1162*
n_HHI	0.0331*	0.1389*
CMS	–0.0197*	0.1068*
LN_Z	0.2479*	0.3187*

Notes: Only correlations for banks considered in the random effect panel regressions were reported. The variables with * are statistically significant at 5% level.

With reference to the macroeconomic factor, the average value of GDPG exhibited a considerable decline from the pre-crisis period (+2.47 per cent) to the crisis period (+0.15 per cent) due to the hoarding effect of a contraction in the main determinants of demand.

Looking at the banking industry-specific variables, n_HHI displayed an important tendency to grow, from 0.038 in the pre-crisis period to 0.054 in the crisis period. The rise in banking system concentration during the period 2007–2010 was principally due to M&A[4] operations aimed to avoid bailouts. However, the average level of concentration of sample banks remained low. We observe a similar pattern for the average value of CMS, which showed a tendency to increase from the first sub-period (3.86 per cent) to the second (4.86 per cent).

Finally, from the pre-crisis to the crisis period there was a worsening of the banking systemic stability. In particular, an LN_Z decrease, from 4.164 in the first sub-period to 3.839 in the second sub-period.

Finally, correlation coefficients were calculated between the explanatory variables and ln_Z (see Table 1.7). The correlation results enabled us to check whether the hypothesized relationships between dependent variable and each explanatory variable were correct (see Table 1.5). Table 1.7 shows that all the signs hypothesized in Table 1.5 are respected.

4 Empirical methodology and main results

To empirically check whether cooperative banks play a key role in shoring up the average bank stability, we used random effect panel data regressions. As already stated, in our empirical analysis we explain bank stability as a function of bank-specific variables (*BankSpec*), country-specific factors (*CountrySpec*) and a set of dummy variables which account for specialized business models adopted by banks (*CBD* and *SBD*) (see Equation 1.3). All explanatory variables are lagged with a one-year period, with the sole exception of CBD and SBD.

$$\ln\_Z_{it} = \alpha + \ln\_Z_{i,t-1} + \beta_1(BankSpec)_{i,t-1} + \beta_2(CountrySpec)_{j,t-1} + \beta_3 CBD_{i,t} + \beta_4 SBD_{i,t} +_{i,t} \quad (1.3)$$

In this setup, the indices *i*, *j*, and *t* stand respectively for bank, country, and time. *ln_Z*it is the risk measure of bank *i* at time *t*, with *i* = 1...N; *t* = 1...T. *ln_Z*i,t_1 is the one-period lagged risk measure. Like Ivičić et al. (2008) and Liu et al. (2010), we included lagged ln_Z in our specification in order to capture capital reserves built in the previous period. εit is the error.

All panel regressions were performed for both periods. Such sub-samples were created in order to detect possible changes in the contribution of cooperative banks to the resilience of financial systems. Table 1.8 summarizes the results of the random effect panel regressions.[5] In particular, the second and third columns refer to the entire sample of banks, while the fourth and fifth columns report the results for the least and most stable sample banks (belonging to the first and fourth quartile respectively). Finally, in order to test the impact of cooperative banks' market share on banks able to give rise to systemic risk, we also tested the model only on large banks, that is, with total assets greater than US$10 billion (see the sixth and seventh columns in Table 1.8). The role of cooperative banks varies considerably over time, as economic and financial conditions differ. The coefficients of cooperative banks' market shares become significant only during the crisis period, and exhibit a positive sign. The no-key role of cooperative banks' market shares during the pre-crisis period may be due to the fact that in boom business cycles, on the whole, most OECD banking systems tend to be stable (see also Table 1.3). Conversely, in an adverse macroeconomic scenario a significant percentage of cooperative banks' market share raises the stability of the financial system in which they operate, thanks to their specific institutional characteristics and healthy risk attitude.

The stabilizing power of cooperative banks is confirmed by the findings for the most stable sample banks (see the sixth and seventh columns in Table 1.8). Indeed, CMS is positively related with ln_Z only in this subsample and not in that of less stable banks. Hence, most stable banks seem to benefit from a high market share of the cooperative banks.

Moreover, considering the outcomes for large banks (see the last two columns of Table 1.8), it emerges that only during the crisis period does a greater presence of cooperative banks exert a positive and increasing influence on the stability of large banks in the same banking system. A possible explanation for this result is that the potential phenomena of banking instability might be smoother and spread more slowly in more mutualized banking systems, since interconnections between mutual banks and large commercial banks are certainly less strong than those existing between large commercial banks (due to the latters' extensive involvement in derivatives, wholesale funding and repurchase agreements).

Regardless of the sample observed (whole sample or sub-samples), we also obtained the following results. The banking systemic stability indicator (LN_Z) has, as expected, a positive sign in all statistically significant cases. Thus improvements in systemic stability result in corresponding improvements in the resilience of any single bank.

Table 1.8 shows that, as expected, in the pre-crisis period the liquidity risk variable (LIQ) did not play any part in bank stability in each sample investigated. LIQ becomes significant only during the crisis period, where indeed severe liquidity shortages experienced by banks triggered bailouts and new regulatory measures (see Basel Committee on Banking Supervision, 2010).[6]

The bank lending behavior variable (CRED) is also significant only during the crisis years. This variable has the negative sign expected, confirming that

Table 1.8 Random effect panel regressions

Variables	Whole sample		Least stable banks (1)		Most stable banks (2)		Large banks (3)	
	Pre-crisis period	Crisis period	Pre-crisis period	Crisis period	Pre-crisis period	Crisis period	Pre-crisis period	Crisis period
ln_Z (-1)	0.637***	0.657***	0.225***	0.212***	0.140***	0.166***	0.606***	0.576***
	(0.003)	(0.004)	(0.007)	(0.007)	(0.006)	(0.007)	(0.021)	(0.026)
SIZE (-1)	–0.008***	–0.040***	–0.0007	–0.027***	0.002	–0.003	–0.055*	–0.048*
	(0.002)	(0.002)	(0.004)	(0.004)	(0.003)	(0.004)	(0.028)	(0.023)
LIQ (-1)	–0.019	–0.031*	–0.014	–0.029*	–0.001	0.012	–0.013	–0.044*
	(0.010)	(0.014)	(0.014)	(0.012)	(0.013)	(0.026)	(0.006)	(0.023)
CRE (-1)	–0.004	–0.275***	0.091	–0.218***	–0.032	–0.150**	0.124	0.058
	(0.023)	(0.030)	(0.036)	(0.040)	(0.033)	(0.048)	(0.125)	(0.141)
CIR (-1)	–0.347***	–0.225***	–0.214***	–0.160***	–0.026	0.054	–0.363*	–0.045
	(0.023)	(0.020)	(0.028)	(0.021)	(0.042)	(0.047)	(0.148)	(0.083)
ID (-1)	–0.027	8.599	–0.006	0.0003	–0.046	0.002	–0.036	0.0007***
	(0.016)	(0.000)	(0.003)	(0.000)	(0.051)	(0.006)	(0.103)	(0.000)
GDPC (-1)	1.169**	-3.134***	4.086***	-2.764***	-1.693**	-0.742**	7.717**	-2.669**
	(0.370)	(0.182)	(0.615)	(0.321)	(0.492)	(0.219)	(2.388)	(0.883)
n_HHI (-1)	–0.117	–0.780***	–0.159	0.325	–0.346***	–0.191*	–0.102	0.545
	(0.067)	(0.085)	(0.137)	(0.169)	(0.094)	(0.097)	(0.220)	(0.475)
CMS (-1)	–0.045	0.341***	–0.707***	–0.156	0.380***	0.392**	0.435	1.181***
	(0.072)	(0.084)	(0.141)	(0.140)	(0.095)	(0.122)	(0.232)	(0.220)
LN_Z (-1)	0.304***	0.277***	0.181***	0.143***	0.158***	0.154***	0.220***	–0.053
	(0.015)	(0.012)	(0.023)	(0.022)	(0.020)	(0.016)	(0.056)	(0.055)
CBD	0.075***	0.124***	–0.145***	0.097**	0.080***	0.067**	0.272**	0.250***
	(0.017)	(0.017)	(0.032)	(0.030)	(0.021)	(0.024)	(0.093)	(0.069)
SBD	0.068***	0.153***	–0.036	0.054	0.000	0.027	–0.043	0.081
	(0.010)	(0.015)	(0.023)	(0.029)	(0.015)	(0.019)	(0.074)	(0.067)
Number of observations	56,858	45,195	10,946	13,932	15,561	9,920	1,545	1,677
R-squared	0.4957	0.5031	0.3056	0.1768	0.1137	0.1691	0.4949	0.4279

Notes: The dependent variable is the natural logarithm of the Z-score (ln_Z) which measures bank stability. The explanatory variables are bank-specific characteristics referring to bank size (SIZE), liquidity risk (LIQ), bank lending behavior (CRE), efficiency (CIR) and income diversity (ID). Country-specific factors referring to annual GDP growth rate (GDPG), to bank market concentration (n_HHI), to share of cooperative banks (CMS) and to banking systemic stability (LN_Z). CBS and SBD are cooperative bank dummy and savings bank dummy, respectively.

(1) Bottom quartile of banks used as the sample; (2) top quartile of banks used as the sample; (3) large sample banks are those banks with total assets greater than US$10 billion.
'Pre-crisis period' denotes the period from 2001 to 2006. 'Crisis period' denotes the period from 2007 to 2010.Standard errors of estimated coefficients are reported in parentheses. *** denotes coefficient statistically different from zero (1% level, two-tail test), ** 5% level, * 10% level.

credit activity is one of the riskiest areas of a bank, capable of weakening bank stability due to a strong deterioration in credit quality.

We found a negative relationship between the proxy of operational efficiency (CIR) and bank stability (see Table 1.8).

Our results also signal that the one-period lagged risk measure (ln_$Z_{i,t-1}$) and bank size variable (SIZE) are significant, having, as expected, a positive and negative relationship respectively with ln_Z. As ln_$Z_{i,t-1}$ renders bank'scapital buffers built in the past, the above evidence corroborates its significant positive relationship with present ln_Z. Regarding SIZE, its increase has a negative effect on bank stability, consistently with opportunistic behaviors arising from the Too Big To Fail (TBTF) status.

The normalized HHI index (n_HHI) displays a negative sign when it is significant. As a result, banking concentration seems to undermine financial stability, possibly because of the occurrence of moral hazard phenomena and excessive risk-taking by large banks.

When the annual GDP growth rate (GDPG) results a significant variable, it shows both of the hypothesized signs, confirming the uncertain relationship with bank stability.

Finally, the proxy for income diversification (ID) is never significant, with the sole exception of the sub-sample of large banks. In this case, ID is significant only in the crisis period, and exhibits a positive sign, thus providing evidence of the beneficial effects of diversification on large banks' stability.

5 Robustness tests

To check for any changing impact of cooperative banks on bank stability according to different levels of their market shares, we ran further random effect panel regressions, using two alternative thresholds of cooperative banks' market share: 5 and 15 per cent. Table 1.9 summarizes the results of the robustness tests. All the panel regressions were performed for the period preceding the crisis and for the following one. The first two panels of regressions relate to sample banks active in OECD countries where cooperative banks' market share is greater than or equal to 5 per cent and less than 5 per cent, while the other two panels of regressions concern banks active in OECD countries whose cooperative banks' market share is greater than or equal to 15 per cent and less than 15 per cent.

The results in Table 1.9 confirm what emerged from Table 1.8; OECD countries with a strong presence of cooperative banks (greater than or equal to the threshold of 5 or 15 per cent) exploit the positive effects exerted by mutual banks on average bank stability, mostly in times of crisis. Thus, Tables 1.8 and 1.9 together suggest that cooperative banks exert a stabilizing effect mainly in the period of crisis and on the growing cooperative banks' market shares.

Moreover, Table 1.9 shows that in OECD countries with very high market shares of cooperative banks (in our cases greater than 15 per cent), but only in the crisis period, the relationship between the aggregate banking stability proxy, LN_Z, and the single bank average stability turns out to be negative instead of positive, as resulted in all cases in which it is significant both in Table 1.8 and in Table 1.9. The latter (counterintuitive) findings suggest that in more mutualized banking systems, any decrease in systemic stability seems to stir banks into taking steps to improve their own future stability.

Table 1.9 Random effect panel regressions (robustness test)

	CMS > = 0.05		CMS < 0.05		CMS > = 0.15		CMS<0.15	
Variables	**Pre-crisis period**	**Crisis period**	**Pre-crisis period**	**Crisis period**	**Pre-crisis period**	**Crisis period**	**Pre-crisis period**	**Crisis period**
ln_Z (–1)	0.656***	0.629***	0.623***	0.669***	0.621***	0.640***	0.633***	0.659***
	(0.007)	(0.008)	(0.004)	(0.005)	(0.012)	(0.012)	(0.003)	(0.004)
SIZE (–1)	0.028***	-0.013*	0.002	–0.047***	0.055***	-0.010	0.002	–0.049***
	(0.006)	(0.005)	(0.002)	(0.003)	(0.009)	(0.007)	(0.002)	(0.003)
LIQ (–1)	–0.008	–0.035	–0.013	–0.016	0.016	0.037	–0.021	–0.028
	(0.017)	(0.025)	(0.010)	(0.018)	(0.025)	(0.027)	(0.011)	(0.017)
CRE (–1)	–0.013	–0.164*	0.006	–0.397***	-0.043	–0.268**	0.018	–0.304***
	(0.055)	(0.066)	(0.025)	(0.035)	(0.089)	(0.085)	(0.025)	(0.032)
CIR (–1)	–0.304***	-0.076*	–0.371***	–0.250***	-0.266***	-0.301***	-0.357***	-0.240***
	(0.056)	(0.040)	(0.027)	(0.022)	(0.065)	(0.084)	(0.025)	(0.021)
ID (–1)	–0.037*	0.0002	–0.027	–0.0004	–0.058**	0.0040**	-0.026	–0.0006
	(0.017)	(0.000)	(0.017)	(0.001)	(0.020)	(0.000)	(0.016)	(0.001)
GDPC (–1)	0.902	–1.404***	1.358**	–4.917***	11.975***	1.045	0.661	–2.166***
	(1.147)	(0.245)	(0.421)	(0.386)	(1.798)	(0.637)	(0.385)	(0.224)
n_HHI (–1)	0.298	–4.332***	-0.273**	–0.745**	0.267	–1.788**	-0.064	–0.831***
	(0.249)	(0.518)	(0.086)	(0.101)	(0.343)	(0.524)	(0.071)	(0.088)
CMS (–1)	0.030	0.296*	4.831***	-1.515	–0.130	3.362***	0.739***	1.937***
	(0.150)	(0.163)	(1.066)	(1.121)	(0.311)	(0.290)	(0.164)	(0.227)
LN_Z (–1)	0.301***	0.251***	0.234***	0.327***	0.380***	–0.455***	0.205***	0.166***
	(0.024)	(0.023)	(0.025)	(0.027)	(0.050)	(0.057)	(0.022)	(0.018)
CBD	0.193***	0.250***	0.137*	0.200**	0.209***	0.242***	0.027	0.110***
	(0.026)	(0.028)	(0.065)	(0.061)	(0.037)	(0.035)	(0.023)	(0.025)
SBD	0.281***	0.350***	0.017	0.096***	0.194***	0.138**	0.056***	0.136***
	(0.027)	(0.032)	(0.011)	(0.018)	(0.045)	(0.048)	(0.011)	(0.017)
Number of observations	11,164	11,426	45,694	33,769	4,803	5,408	52,055	39,787
R–squared	0.5651	0.5347	0.4658	0.4779	0.5485	0.4543	0.4774	0.5137

Notes: CMS: cooperative banks' market share.

Austria, Finland, France, Italy, the Netherlands and Japan are the only OECD countries with CMS values greater than both thresholds (0.05 and 0.15) in the two sub-periods considered.

Germany and Spain have CMS values greater than 0.05 but lower than 0.15 in the pre-crisis and crisis period. Ireland displays CMS values greater than 0.05 only in the pre-crisis period, while the Czech Republic shows CMS values greater than 0.05 only in the crisis period.

The other OECD countries considered (Belgium, Canada, Denmark, Greece, Hungary, Luxembourg, New Zealand, Poland, Portugal, Slovenia, South Korea, Sweden, Switzerland, the United Kingdom and the USA) show CMS values below 0.05 in both sub-periods.

'Pre-crisis period' denotes the period from 2001 to 2006. 'Crisis period' denotes the period from 2007 to 2010.

Standard errors of estimated coefficients are reported in parentheses. *** denotes coefficient statistically different from zero (1% level, two-tail test), ** 5% level, * 10% level.

In order to further test the robustness of our findings, we regressed the annual changes in our measure of bank stability on the same explanatory variables used. The results confirm those already discussed (see Table 1.8 above) as far the contribution of cooperative banks to bank stability is concerned.

6 Conclusions

Based on a sample of cooperative, savings and commercial banks from OECD countries over the period 2001–2010, this chapter investigates the role of cooperative banks in supporting bank stability (proxied by the Z-score). We used random effect panel regressions, and employed bank-specific and country-specific factors as explanatory variables, as well as a set of dummies to account for any difference in the resilience of the business model. In order to evaluate the relationship between the share of cooperative banks and the proxy of bank risk under varying financial conditions, we performed our analysis on two distinct periods, prior to the emergence of the financial crisis (2001–2006) and during the crisis period (2007–2010).

The results of the empirical analysis show that the cooperative banks' market share becomes significant only during the crisis period showing a positive sign. Hence, after the emergence of the recent financial crisis, OECD banking systems characterized by a high presence of cooperative banks seem to be better placed to weather any future periods of financial stress.

Moreover, our results indicate that only during financial crisis does a greater presence of cooperative banks exert a positive and increasing influence on the stability of large banks in the same banking system. A possible explanation for these results is that potential phenomena of banking instability might be smoother and spread more slowly in more mutualized banking systems, since interconnections between mutual banks and large commercial banks are certainly less strong than those existing between large commercial banks.

These results are of particular interest to both academics and policymakers, as they will contribute to the current debate on the regulation and design of banking sectors with better resilience to systemic crisis.

Notes

1. BankScope Database defines 'Commercial Banks' as those banks mainly active in a combination of Retail Banking (Individuals, SMEs), Wholesale Banking (large corporate) and Private Banking (not belonging to groups of saving banks, cooperative banks); Commercial banks are joint-stock companies, owned by the public and/or the private sectors. 'Cooperative banks' are defined as those banks that have a cooperative ownership structure and are mainly active in Retail Banking (Individuals, SMEs). According to Cuevas and Fischer (2006), cooperative banks are one out of the diverse member-owned financial intermediaries, such as credit unions, savings and

credit cooperatives. Their institutional governance, legal and regulatory status and scale and service portfolios vary widely across regions and between developed and developing countries. Among their common key futures there are: the provision of their services often solely to members and the principle of one-man/one-vote, as far as concern governance mechanisms are concerned. 'Savings Banks' are defined as those banks mainly active in Retail Banking (Individuals, SMEs). Savings banks may be profit or non-profit oriented. Their ownership structure often comes close to the shared ownership model, where control is shared between multiple interest groups: local regional governments, employees and different types of private investors.

2. BankScope Database provides the specialization of sample banks (commercial, cooperative, and savings) in each current year. It is possible, for instance, that some banks within the commercial bank subset may have been cooperative or savings banks in earlier periods. Given the large number of banks in the sample, it was not possible to individually check potential changes in specialization over time, as well as making allowances for any merger and acquisition (M&A) that may have occurred. However, like Hesse and Cihák (2007), we do not think that these limitations severely bias our results.
3. We employed the Variance Inflation Factor (VIF) test, but we did not find multicollinearity problems between the explanatory variables used in our analysis.
4. M&A – merger and acquisitions.
5. Due to multicollinearity problems, it was not possible to include country dummies in the model.
6. In December 2010, the Basel Committee announced the introduction of two new liquidity standards for banks: the Liquidity Coverage Ratio (LCR), rule of short term and the Net Stable Funding Ratio (NSFR), longer-term structural rule. See Basel Committee on Banking Supervision (BCBS, 2010).

References

Allen, F. and D. Gale (2000) 'Financial contagion', *Journal of Political Economy*, 108, 1–33.

Allen, F. and D. Gale (2004) 'Competition and systemic stability', *Journal of Money, Credit and Banking*, 36, 453–80.

Altunbas, Y., S. Carbo, E.P.M. Gardener and P. Molyneux (2007) 'Examining the relationships between capital, risk and efficiency in European banking', *European Financial Management*, 13, 49–70.

Ayadi, R., D. Llewellyn, R.H. Schmidt, E. Arbak and W.P. de Groen (2010) 'Investigating diversity in the banking sector in Europe: key developments, performance and role of cooperative banks', Brussels: Centre for European Policy Studies Banking and Finance, no. 28.

Barth, J.R., G.J. Caprio and R. Levine (1999) 'Banking systems around the globe: do regulation and ownership affect performance and stability?' World Bank Policy Research Working Paper, no. 2325.

Basel Committee on Banking Supervision (BCBS) (2010) *Basel 3: A Global Regulatory Framework for Liquidity Risk Measurement, Standards and Monitoring,* Basel, December.

Beck, T., O. De Jonghe and G. Schepens (2011) 'Bank competition and stability: cross-country heterogeneity', European Banking Center Discussion Paper, Tilburg University, no. 019.

Beck, T., O. De Jonghe and G. Schepens (2012) 'Bank competition and stability: cross-country heterogeneity', *Journal of Financial Intermediation*, available online 4 August 2012.

Beck, T., D. Coyle, M. Dewatripoint, X. Freixas and P. Seabright (2010) 'Bailing out the banks: reconciling stability and competition', London: Centre for Economic Policy Research.

Beck, T., H. Hesse, T. Kick and N. von Westernhagen (2009) 'Bank ownership and stability: evidence from Germany', Bundesbank Working Paper Series.

Berger, A.N. and R. De Young (1997) 'Problem loans and cost efficiency in commercial banking', *Journal of Banking and Finance*, 21, 849–70.

Boonstra, W.W (2010) 'Banking in times of crisis: the case of Rabobank', in M. Balling, J.M. Berk and M.O. Strauss-Kahn (eds), *The Quest for Stability: The View of Financial Institutions*. Vienna: SUERF.

Boyd, J. and D.E. Runkle (1993) 'Size and performance of banking firms', *Journal of Monetary Economics*, 31, 47–67.

Boyd, John H. and G. De Nicolò (2005) 'The theory of bank risk taking and competition revisited', *Journal of Finance*, 60, 1329–43.

Brunner, A., J. Decressin, D. Hardy and B. Kudela (2004) 'Germany's three-pillar banking system-cross-country perspective in Europe', IMF Occasional Paper, no. 233 (Washington: International Monetary Fund).

Carletti, E. (2008) 'Competition and regulation in banking', in A. Boot and A. Thakor (eds), *Handbook of Financial Intermediation and Banking*. Amsterdam: Elsevier.

Chaddad, F. and M. Cook (2004) 'Economics of organization structure changes: a US perspective on demutualization', *Annals of Public and Cooperative Economics*, 75, 575–94.

Conrad, A., D. Neuberger and L.T. Gamarra (2009) 'The impact of regional and demographic factors on the efficiency of German savings banks', University of Rostock Working Paper, no. 111.

Cuevas, C.E. and K.P. Fischer (2006) 'Cooperative financial institutions. issues in governance, regulation, and supervision', World Bank Working Paper, no. 82.

European Association of Cooperative Banks (EACB) (2010) 'European co-operative banks in the financial and economic turmoil', Research Paper Financial Services Research, no. 12.

Fiordelisi, F., D. Marques Ibanez and P. Molyneux (2010) 'Efficiency and risk in European banking', European Central bank Working paper Series, no. 1211, June.

Fonteyne, W. (2007) 'Cooperative banks in Europe', Policy Issues, IMF Working Paper (Washington: International Monetary Fund).

Garcia-Marco, T. and M. Roblez-Fernandez (2008) 'Risk-taking behavior and ownership in the banking industry: the Spanish evidence', *Journal of Economics and Business*, 60, 332–54.

Goodhart, C. (2004) 'Some new directions for financial stability', The Per Jacobsson Lecture (Basel: Bank for International Settlements).

Groeneveld, H. (2011) 'The value of European cooperative banks for the future financial system', Working Paper.

Groeneveld, H. and B. de Vries (2009) 'European co-operative banks: first lessons of the subprime crisis', *The International Journal of Co-operative Management*, 4, 8–21.

Groeneveld, J.M. and A. Sjauw-Koen-Fa (2009) 'Cooperative banks in the new financial system', Report prepared by Rabobank for the IMF/World Bank meeting in Istanbul, Turkey, October.

Hansmann, H. (1996) *The Ownership of Enterprise*. Cambridge, MA: The Belknap Press of Harvard University Press.
Hesse, H. and M. Cihak (2007) 'Cooperative banks and financial stability', International Monetary Fund (IMF) Working Paper.
Iannotta, G., G. Nocera and A. Sironi (2007) 'Ownership structure, risk and performance in the European banking industry', *Journal of Banking and Finance*, 32, 2127–49.
Ivičić, L., D. Kunovac and I. Ljubaj (2008) 'Measuring bank insolvency risk in CEE countries', Croatian National Bank Working Paper.
Jiménez, G. and J. Saurina (2006) 'Credit cycles, credit risk, and prudential regulation', *International Journal of Central Banking*, 2, 65–98.
Kwan, S. and R. Eisenbeis (1997) 'Bank risk, capitalization and operating efficiency', *Journal of Banking and Finance*, 21, 849–70.
Liu, H., P. Molyneux and J. Wilson (2010) 'Competition and stability in European banking: a regional analysis', paper presented at the Wolpertinger Conference, September 9–10, Bangor (UK).
Llewellyn, D.T. (2009) 'British building societies and the financial crisis: the continuation of the mutual business model', paper published in the Dutch translation in Mooij and Boonstra.
Mottura, P. (2011) 'Banche cooperative e crisi finanziaria. Forme istituzionali da valorizzare con modelli di governance appropriate', *Bancaria*, 12, 2–25.
Rajan, R.G. (1994) 'Why bank credit policies fluctuate: a theory and some evidence', *The Quarterly Journal of Economics*, 2, 399–441.
Stefancic, M. (2010) 'Cooperative credit network: advantages and challenges in Italian cooperative credit banks', Euricse Working Papers, no. 16.
Stefancic, M. and N. Kathitziotis (2011) 'An evaluation of Italian banks in the period of financial distress', *International Business & Economics Research Journal*, 10, 103–14.
Williams, J. (2004) 'Determining management behavior in European banking', *Journal of Banking and Finance*, 28, 2427–60.

2
Cooperative Banking in Poland: A Post-Crisis Record of Stability and Efficiency

Ewa Miklaszewska and Krzysztof Kil

> After all, there is an element in the readjustment of our financial system more important than currency, more important than gold, and that is the confidence of the people.
>
> Franklin D. Roosevelt, National Radio Address, 12 March 1933

1 Introduction

The deregulation of financial markets over the two decades surrounding the turn of the 20th/21st century has dramatically influenced the scale and complexity of banking firms, and created strong incentives towards universalism and globalization. In the pre-crisis period, universal bank strategies were largely directed towards expansion, while business models were centered on operational efficiency accruing from new sources of profits and high leverage. The preferred bank business model before the crisis was that of universal (conglomerate) banking, where bank expansion was based on non-interest income and non-depository funding. The global financial crisis of 2008 highlighted the riskiness of that model, and demonstrated that in many cases benefits from diversification from traditional banking have been overstated. Moreover, the crisis forced banks and regulators to redefine their priorities; in the area of bank management, priority has shifted from profit maximization towards balance sheet soundness. The most frequent restructuring pattern for global banks has been partial or total nationalization, as a result of which large global banks have contributed to inflated budget deficits and escalating public debts in major countries. The global financial crisis, which reached its peak with the demise of the investment bank model in September 2008 (pinpointed by the collapse of Lehman Brothers) has called into question the future of specialised banking. With countless cases of nationalization or forced takeovers of failing banks, questions have been raised as to the size and scope of banking activities, to what extent national and local competition is important for bank efficiency and stability, and whether there is still a place for the locally-based cooperative banks.

Post-crisis bank restructuring has concentrated on large banks, and the cooperative (mutual) sector has been of marginal importance to the regulators. Cooperative banking – retail banking carried out by locally-based small institutions such as credit unions, mutual savings banks, building societies or cooperatives – has long played an important role in their local environments, thereby enhancing bank reputation and trust. However, their one-person, one-vote legal basis has created an important barrier to growth and development. There is an extensive body of literature on the efficiency and restructuring of cooperative banks in Poland, and indeed globally. However, this chapter aims to analyze whether the global financial crisis of 2008 has changed the completive position of cooperative banks, placing a particular emphasis on the competitive advantages of the soundness of their business model, proximity to customers, and long-term strategic objectives. Hence, this chapter analyses the relative position and future prospects of commercial (universal) banks versus cooperative banks, using the Polish example, and seeks to answer the following questions: whether cooperative banks have a future in a global, complex world; whether cooperative banks, although socially important, will face further marginalization in the coming years; and whether the 2008 crisis can act as a stimulus to their expansion

The chapter is structured as follows: Section 2 analyses the evolution of commercial and cooperative bank business models, Sections 3 and 4 look at the position and strategies of cooperative banks in the Polish banking market, Section 5 discusses the lessons from past crises, while Sections 6 and 7 analyze commercial and cooperative bank soundness in Poland. Section 8 presents the future challenges for the cooperative banks and Section 9 concludes the chapter.

2 Rethinking the bank business model: the post-crisis perspective

The decades of deregulation and globalization of financial markets have resulted in the increasing scale and complexity of banks, and the expansion of conglomerate banking, with new sources of income and new areas of risk. On the one hand, banks have better access to funds, diversification of assets, and better management. On the other hand, their expansion has introduced new areas of risk stemming from geographical expansion, operational problems and non-depository incomes. Additionally, new areas of profit generate new sources of risk, such as the problem with liquidity in global firms. If traditional banks were structured according to the dimensions of their organizations, with a similar risk profile, then globally active financial institutions would select new models of strategic orientations, exploiting their global scale.

The global financial crisis has shown that the benefits from universalism and global scale have been in many cases overstated (Demirgüç-Kunt and Huizinga, 2009). It has also highlighted worries about the stability of large banking institutions (Duffie, 2011). Large global firms in many cases survived only thanks to direct or indirect government support (The World Economic Forum, 2010). This may suggest that locally-oriented cooperative banks are better equipped to cope with the crisis and post-crisis macroeconomic environment. However, bank efficiency can be measured not only by organizational and financial efficiency, but also by looking at product and technology innovativeness, and in this respect global universal banks are clearly ahead.

There is wide consensus as to the main reasons for the 2008 collapse of the banking systems in major countries: pre-crisis overconfidence in growth and prosperity (asset bubble) and consequent price uncertainty, the liberal policies of central banks (low interest rates, focus on consumer price inflation, and failure to consider asset price inflation), easy credit, shareholder pressure for returns, regulatory arbitrage from hedge funds, and the growing scale and complexity of banks. There were also more fundamental reasons, such as the wrong incentives being used in mortgage-based loans and the failure of risk management systems in securitization processes (Allen et al., 2009). At bank level, the fundamental problem was that of risky bank business models based on high leverage.

The bank business model – the way a bank operates and creates value for its shareholders and stakeholders – depends on certain external factors, such as types of activity and their scope and scale, but to some degree it also reflects the preferences of owners and managers. The 2008 crisis affected global financial stability and underlined the need to rethink some of the approaches adopted by the financial community in assessing bank performance. Recent development in banking markets, particularly in Spain – the need for massive aid to large banks, which have traditionally been leaders in efficiency – have shown that in order to have valid and sound performance indicators, it is necessary to monitor and evaluate the risks taken. In some cases, indicators such as RoA or RoE may be less of a performance measurement than the indicators of the relationship between banks and markets (ECB, 2010b). Hence, another lesson from the 2008 crisis is that the most important elements in the assessment of bank performance are risk level, corporate governance and business models leading to efficiency in the long run.

For universal banks, an additional question is how to prevent moral hazard behavior. Conducting commercial and investment banking activities within a single institution is a variant of the 'too big to fail' (TBTF) problem, as commercial and investment banks have different risk profiles. The investment bank trades actively in the capital markets, where bubbles and crashes are endemic. Combining both types of institutions extended the protection which is given to commercial banks to investment banking, thereby artificially reducing the cost of capital (McKinsey, 2009). This encouraged the growth of larger and more complex institutions, and transferred their restructuring costs to the public.

Although the global universal bank model is based on inherent problems with size and complexity, its Polish variation can be characterized by

Table 2.1 Bank business models: globally and in Poland

	Global universal banks	Polish universal banks	Polish cooperative banks
Operating risk (leverage, ST financing)	High (L/D>100%)	Low (L/D around 100%)	Low (L/D<100%)
Systemic risk	Large systemic size of top banks (absolute and relative to GDP)	Competitive market structure, the largest five banks' assets <50% of GDP	Small market share (6% of total banking assets)
Organizational structure	Complex, conglomerate model	Simple: concentration in consumer market	Simple: concentration in local firm financing
Profitability/risk	High	High profitability, moderate risk	High profitability, low risk
Innovations	High	Moderate	Low

Source: Own presentation.

a relatively simple organizational structure and strong capitalization (particularly with Tier 1 capital), low leverage, and concentration on the profitable consumer market (Table 2.1). For Polish banks, the economic crisis of 2008 was an imported factor, resulting in a slowing down of growth and increasing regulatory costs, from both new national and European legislation. One future threat is that new European regulations might penalize the cross-border banking model, which has been the basis of economic and financial growth in Poland and other Central and East European Countries (CEE: Banking Outlook, 2010 and 2011).

3 Polish banking market structure and the position of cooperative banks

The banking sector in Poland at the end of 2011 comprised the central bank (NBP), 47 commercial banks, 19 credit institution branches, and 574 cooperative banks. The cooperative sector follows a two-level model and currently there are: two cooperative associations, one headed by Bank Polskiej Spółdzielczości SA (BPS SA) with 366 banks, and the other by Spółdzielcza Grupa Bankowa (SGB-Bank) with 207 banks; and one cooperative bank, Krakowski Bank Spółdzielczy, which operates independently (ZBP, 2012). Globally, cooperative banks have different regulations and structure. In Poland, among a number of locally active credit institutions, until recently only cooperative banks had a banking licence. However, cooperative banks will face more intense competition, as in October 2012 a new regulation incorporated into the banking sector another mutual organization, the SKOK, which till that point had enjoyed unregulated status.

Cooperative banks in Poland constitute a small but important part of the banking industry. They are mutually owned, follow the cooperative principle of one-person, one-vote, and are regulated under both banking and cooperative legislation. Their market shares for loans and deposits are 6 per cent and 8 per cent respectively. For comparison, in the EU cooperative banking sector, the market share of domestic deposits and loans stands at around 20 per cent each (EACB, 2011). On the other hand, they operate locally in areas where they have their headquarters, and mainly serve households, small and medium-size businesses, farmers, and local authorities, particularly in small towns and villages. The stated mission of the cooperative banks is to support their customers, as well as members of local communities, as opposed to the profit-maximizing objectives of commercial banks (Table 2.2). This, however, constitutes also their main weakness: problem with corporate governance and access to capital (Fonteyne, 2007).

Since 1989, cooperative banks have undergone comprehensive restructuring processes in order to adapt to market economy rules, and to adjust to

Table 2.2 Comparison of commercial and cooperative banks: main features

	Cooperative banks	Commercial banks
Main legal background	Act concerning the Operations of Cooperative Banks, their Affiliation and Affiliating Banks of 7 December 2000; Banking Law of 1997	Banking Law of 1997 and Commercial Code of 2000
Minimum capital requirements/capital adequacy	€1 million, Basel ratios	€5 million, Basel ratios
Scale/size/organizational structure	Local/small/simple	National/large/complex
Mission	To support their members and the local community	To maximize profitability for owners
Owners	Cooperative members (Polish)	Shareholders (global)
Owner control	Weak (one-owner, one-vote)	Strong (one-share, one-vote)
Main customers	SME, rural and small town population, local governments	Urban population, big enterprises, SME, public institutions
Range of banking products and services	Limited	Full
Supervision/deposit insurance	KNF, BFG	KNF, BFG

Source: Based on Groeneveld and Sjauw-Koen-Fa (2009); Siudek (2010); McKinsey (2012) and Szelągowska (2012).

Table 2.3 Bank liquidation (1995–2011)

	1995	1996	1997	1998	1999	2000	2001	2002–2011
Commercial banks	2	1	–	–	1	1	–	–
Cooperative banks	48	30	6	4	–	–	1	–

Source: BFG Annual Report (2011, p. 23).

EU requirements. This restructuring was painful, the situation of the cooperative sector in the mid-1990s being particularly difficult. As a consequence, many cooperative banks went bankrupt (Table 2.3) and their number has plummeted, from 1510 in 1995 to just 574 today. In 1994, the Polish Parliament passed an Act on the Restructuring of Cooperative Banks and of the Bank of Food Economy, which established a legal framework for a three-tier structure of the cooperative banking sector with one bank (BGŻ SA) at the top, nine regional banks in the middle, and the cooperative banks at the bottom, with a compulsory affiliation. As this legislation did not succeed in stabilizing the sector, a new so-called Millennium Law was introduced in 2000, with new capital rules and a two-tier structure, and eleven affiliated banks. They later consolidated themselves into three, and then, in 2012, two, banks: BPS and SGB-Bank.

On the whole, cooperative banks have benefited from the consolidation process; while the number of cooperative banks was declining, bank branches and staff were expanding, and the cooperative sector managed to adjust to EU regulatory requirements. The sector still plays a prominent role in serving and financing agriculture, rural development and SME financing. Today cooperative banks serve over 10 million customers, through a countrywide network of 4600 branches. The main areas of cooperative bank activities are small and medium towns, as well as villages. Since Poland's accession to the European Union, cooperative banks have become an important channel through which money from the Common Budget is transferred to farmers and local authorities nationally (Siudek, 2010).

Poland's cooperative banks have a limited scale and scope of operations. At the end of 2011, loans constituted 55 per cent of their assets (40 per cent for households and micro–enterprises, and 15 per cent for the firms, mostly SMEs), followed by interbank loans (30 per cent). They financed their assets in 77 per cent by deposits, mostly from households. In the countryside, cooperative banks faced important competition from credit unions (SKOKs), which that year possessed deposits equal to 27 per cent of those in cooperative banks (ZBP, 2012). Although SKOKs represent only 1.4 per cent of total banking sector assets, they have grown at a remarkable rate since their implementation in 1992. SKOKs operate for people on low incomes, especially those who do not have accounts with other banks. In 2010, there were 61 SKOKs, with 1800 branches serving over 2 million customers (15 per cent of Polish households). Their assets in June 2010 were over US$4 billion (World Bank, 2010). SKOKs were regulated by the Credit Union Act of 1995, which provided for self-regulatory solution. The new Credit Union Act of 2009, implemented in October 2012, shifted SKOK supervision to Polish Financial Supervision Authority (KNF), and the protection of depositors to the Bank Guarantee Fund (BFG), as in the case of regulated banking institutions, commercial and cooperative. This was a move in the right direction, as many surveys have indicated that customers cannot differentiate between self-regulated SKOKs and fully regulated cooperative and commercial banks (KNF, 2012b).

Overall, the Polish banking sector in the post-crisis period has been characterized by good performance, as well as by solid and sound fundamentals, as indicated by Table 2.4, which represents the profitability of the largest Polish banks and that of their foreign owners. Polish subsidiaries, on average, have generated higher profits than their mother companies in the post-crisis period. As frequently indicated in the literature, the main reasons for their good performance have been: good macroeconomic environment, traditional business model and competitive market structure dominated by foreign-owned banks (fully capitalized subsidiaries) with capital coming in from many countries. At the same time, Polish banks are facing new global challenges and risks, mostly connected with the high participation of foreign capital in banking assets. In terms of the ownership structure of Polish banking sector assets at the end of 2011, commercial banks were controlled by capital

Table 2.4 Profitability of foreign owners and Polish subsidiaries (2011)

1. Majority owner of Polish Bank	**2. Polish subsidiary**	**ROA (1)**	**ROA (2)**
KBC (Bel.)	Kredyt Bank SA	0.00	0.74
BNP Paribas (Fr.)	BNP Paribas Bank Polska	0.31	0.10
Crédit Agricole (Fr.)	Credit Agricole Bank Pol.	–0.09	1.01
Santander (Sp.)	Bank Zachodni WBK SA	0.43	1.95
Santander (Sp.)	Santander Cons. Bank SA	0.43	2.40
Commerzbank (Ger.)	BRE Bank SA	0.10	1.13
Deutsche Bank (Ger.)	Deutsche Bank Polska SA	0.18	1.81
Deutsche Bank (Ger.)	Deutsche Bank Polska PBC	0.18	0.68
BCP (Por.)	Bank Millennium SA	–0.84	0.83
Nordea (Sweden)	Nordea Bank Polska SA	0.37	0.84
UniCredit (It.)	Bank Polska Kasa Opieki	–0.98	1.98
Citi (US)	Bank Handlowy w Warsz.	0.59	1.73
GE Company (US)	Bank BPH SA	–	0.56
ING (Hol.)	ING Bank Śląski SA	–0.29	1.29
Rabobank (Hol.)	Bank Gosp. Żywnościowej	0.35	0.38
Raiffeisen (Aus.)	Raiffeisen Bank Polska SA	0.74	1.08

Source: Data based on KNF (Polish FSA), 2012a.

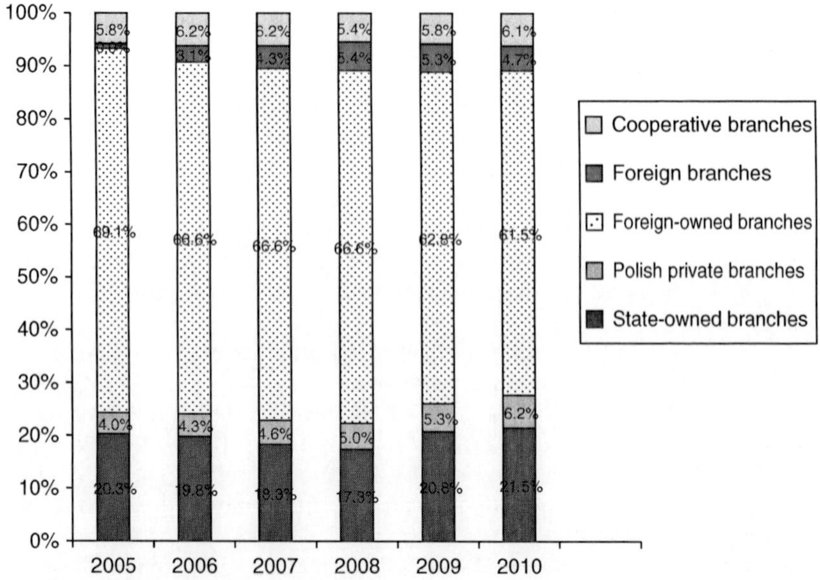

Figure 2.1 Polish banking market: structure of assets (2005–2010)
Source: Own calculations based on KNF (2011).

coming from Poland (35 per cent), Italy (12.5 per cent), Germany (10.5 per cent), the Netherlands (8.5 per cent), the US (6.2 per cent), Spain (5.7 per cent), France (5.1 per cent), Portugal (3.9 per cent), and other countries (12.6 per cent) (MF, 2012). Although foreign capital dominated in the largest banks, the average foreign institution share in banking assets is lower in Poland than in other CEE countries. The Polish Treasury is a majority owner in four large banks, PKO BP, BGK, BOŚ SA, and also Bank Pocztowy SA (in total over 20 per cent of assets), while Polish private capital constitutes over 6 per cent of total assets. Cooperative banks, also owned almost solely by Polish capital, constitute another 6 per cent of total assets (Figure 2.1).

Market concentration in Poland is low, with the two largest banks possessing 26 per cent of the total market share, and the five largest 45 per cent. Profitability and efficiency indicators for both universal and cooperative banks are good (Table 2.5). Bank capitalization is also sound: at the end of 2011, the capital adequacy ratio for Polish banks amounted to 13.13 per cent Tier 1 ratio at the level of 11.74 per cent (Figure 2.6).

In terms of asset size, the Polish banking sector has been dominated by subsidiaries of global universal banks, although numerically the cooperative sector dominates (Table 2.6). Cooperative banks represent 90 per cent of the total number of banks, 25 per cent of bank branches and 20 per cent of employment, but possess only 6 per cent of banking sector assets. They are

Table 2.5 Bank performance (%)

	ROA			ROE			C/I		
	2009	2010	2011	2009	2010	2011	2009	2010	2011
Total sector	0.81	1.03	1.28	8.37	10.21	12.78	54	52	51
Universal banks	0.83	1.10	1.32	8.22	10.19	12.98	53	51	50
Cooperative banks	1.18	1.12	1.24	10.54	10.46	11.88	72	69	67

Note: For description of performance indicators see Bikker and Bos (2008).

Source: Own calculations based on data from KNF 2011a, 2011b.

Table 2.6 Number of commercial and cooperative banks in Poland

	2006	2007	2008	2009	2010	2011
a. Banking sector total:						
no. of banks	647	645	649	643	646	640
no. of branches	11 927	12 847	13 655	13 910	14 170	–
b. Universal banks:						
no. of banks	63	64	70	67	70	66
no. of branches	8 712	9 414	10 114	10 134	10 306	–
c. Cooperative banks:						
no. of banks	584	581	579	576	576	
no. of branches	3 215	3 433	3 541	3 776	3 864	574

Source: Own calculations based on data from Polish FSA (KNF 2011a, 2011b).

small, locally-based institutions: most have assets below €20 million, and only 66 are relatively large, with assets above €50 million (BFG, 2010b).

Cooperative banks provide traditional services, such as savings and loans, to non-members as well as to members. Their market perspectives are good. According to a Pentor opinion survey among banks (Pentor, 2012a), retail banking will still be the engine for profitability and growth in Poland, particularly in the household sector, followed by the SME sector financing, while more sophisticated services, such as bank assurance, mortgage-based products or investment banking, are perceived by the surveyed bankers as being of marginal importance in the near future (Figure 2.2).

However, some households have a rather negative perception of their future financial position, and among the factors which most negatively influence their perception are: age (particularly for people above 50), low education (primary and vocational training) and/or low income (Pentor, 2012b). The Pentor Research also showed that 76 per cent of bank customers trust banks, but they also trust other institutions that accept deposits, particularly the credit union (SKOKs). However, although one third of Polish households do not have a bank account (34 per cent of people over 18), it will be difficult to include them in the financial sector, as in these households the dominant

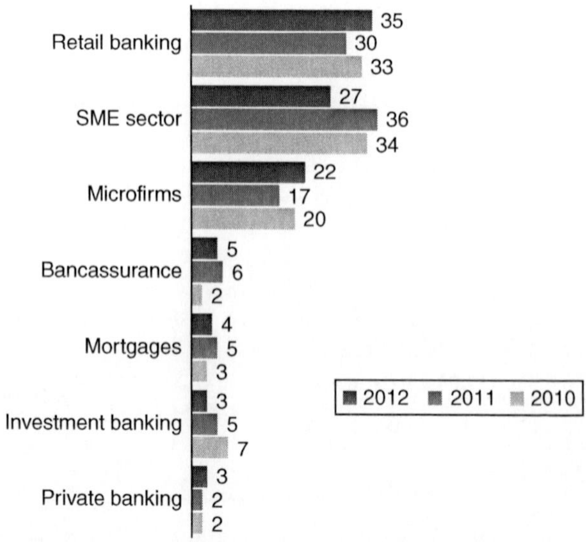

Figure 2.2 Poland: banking segments with the highest growth potential

Source: Pentor (2012a).

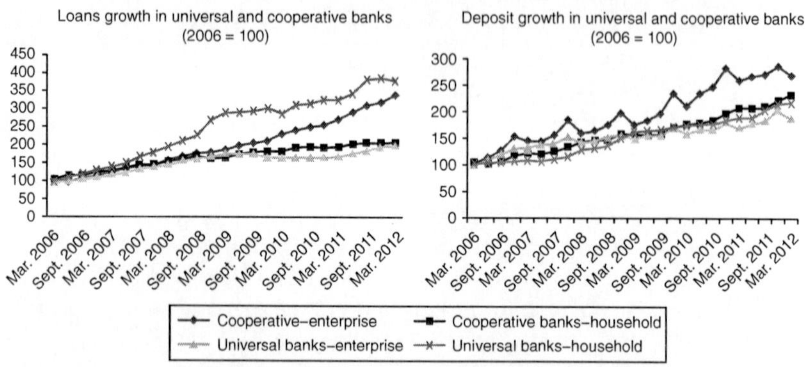

Figure 2.3 Dynamics of loans and deposits growth in commercial and cooperative banks (2006 =100%)

Source: Own calculations based on data from Polish FSA (KNF 2011a, 2011b).

way of thinking is to consider indebtedness (bank loans) as a negative factor, indicating a lack of control over their lives. These people are indifferent to banking; they are mostly older people, or people living in the countryside, and they exhibit a very negative attitude towards banking services and products (self-exclusion).

There is relative discrimination against retail clients in the countryside, as cooperative banks tend to concentrate on local enterprises and not on combating exclusion (Figure 2.3). As a consequence, retail clients in the Polish countryside have reduced access to banking products.

4 Cooperative bank model: safe, but of limited impact

Despite years of globalization and the consolidation of business entities, local cooperatives of various types today represent 3–5 per cent of the world's GDP (McKinsey, 2012). According to the European Association of Cooperative Banks (EACB, 2011), this segment has over 180 million European customers, 50 million members, 65,000 banks, €4 trillion in assets, and around 20 per cent of Europe's deposits and loans market share. It includes such important groups as Credit Agricole, Crédit Mutuel and Banque Populaire in France, Rabobank in the Netherlands, DZ Bank in Germany, Banco Popolare, UBI Banca and Banca Popolare di Milano in Italy, Migros and Coop Bank in Switzerland, and the Raiffeisen system in several countries in Central and Eastern Europe (Table 2.7).

Table 2.7 Largest cooperative associations in EU (full members of EACB, 31 December 2010)

EACB largest member organizations	Assets (EUR mil.)	ROE %	C/I %	TC ratio %	No of banks	Banking outlets	Mkt share dep. (%)	Mkt share credits (%)
France								
Crédit Agricole	1 730 846	n.a	61	11.7	39	11 500	n.a	n.a
Crédit Mutuel	591 309	11	61	4.6	18	5 875	14.2	17.0
BPCE	349 000	5	78	11.1	20	2 938	6.7	7.6
Germany	1 020 313	13	63	13.7	1 138	13 474	19.4	16.9
Italy								
AN BP	481 472	5	58	11.2	100	9 514	26.9	24.7
FEDERCASSE	179 960	2	74	15.2	415	4 375	7.3	7.2
Netherlands	652 536	8	64	5.2	141	911	40.0	29.0
Austria								
Raiffeisenbank								
Genossenschaf-	255 220	10	66	11.4	551	1 738	29.3	25.5
tsverband	65 167	5	62	17.0	80	1 042	7.2	7.3
Spain	119 455	4	53	n.a.	80	5 079	6.6	5.3
Finland	83 969	6	59	12.8	213	554	32.5	33.0
United Kingdom	51 764	4	72	4.6	n.a.	342	5.0	1.5
Portugal	13 213	3.6	67	13.4	86	691	4.5	3.10
CEE:								
Poland	17 625	12	69	13.6	576	4 395	8.9	5.7
Hungary	5 075	8	69	20.8	112	1 520	8.6	2.8
Bulgaria	1 168	8	73	13.5	30	266	4.1	2.3
Slovenia	911	0.5	77	13.4	n.a.	88	2.7	1.6

Source: Own presentation based on financial data from EACB *Annual Report* 2011.

Local cooperative banking includes retail banking carried out by credit unions, mutual savings banks, building societies and cooperatives (Rabobank, 2009). Cooperative banks are traditionally strong in retail banking, which is characterized by stable returns and comparatively good access to savings and deposits, with limited income from wholesale banking (EACB, 2011). The cooperative model has performed well in the post-2008 crisis period in many countries, although there are many challenges ahead (Oliver Wyman Report, 2012).

Polish cooperative banks benefit from a stable deposit base, low reliance on wholesale funding and low complexity of asset structure. This sector survived the 2008 crisis without major problems (see Table 2.8), although the implementation of post-crisis regulations will impose new costs concerning the quality of capital, higher capital requirements, the introduction of leverage ratio and new liquidity standards (McKinsey, 2011). According to cooperative bank forecasts, with a stricter definition of Tier 1 capital, around 30 cooperative banks may have a short-term problem with adequate capital. A bigger problem will be the introduction of the liquidity ratio (implementation of CRD IV liquidity requirements), particularly for the association banks. In a two-level cooperative banking model, the associating banks take liquid instruments from the subordinated cooperative banks, and not from the market. If association banks start to take deposits directly from the market, this will be in direct competition with the subordinated banks, thereby risking problems with their owners. Currently, there is an attempt to reach a compromise by implementing the so-called IPS system (Individual Protection Scheme) with a joint liquid fund for all associating members, which, however, will require further integration of cooperative banks.

Polish cooperative banks did not participate in the pre-crisis boom, as did the universal banks, and this resulted in their marginalization (Figure 2.4). However, their stable performance meant they did not have problems with

Table 2.8 Cooperative sector in Poland: basic statistics

	1995	1997	1999	2001	2003	2005	2007	2009	2011
No. of banks	1510	1295	781	642	600	588	581	576	574
No. of branches	n.a.	2550	2619	2878	3151	3598	4014	4374	4600*
Employment (000)	n.a.	14.6	14.4	16.0	18.0	28.6	30.1	31.7	32.8
Capital adequacy (%)	8.4	11.1	12.8	13.9	14.2	14.7	14.0	13.4	13.4
Assets (PLN bn.)	n.a.	11.3	15.4	21.5	25.7	36.4	48.9	61.7	78.4
Loans (PLN bn.)	n.a.	5.5	8.1	11.3	14.8	18.0	27.9	36.2	44.3
Deposits (PLN bn.)	n.a.	7.6	11.1	16.1	19.1	25.0	32.2	45.7	60.0
RoE	n.a.	14.3	30.8	18.0	19.4	12.2	17.3	10.5	11.9
C/I	n.a.	71.5	74.2	69.4	75.1	72.2	70.0	73.0	68.7

Note: *Estimation.

Source: Own calculations, based on NBP Summary Evaluation of the Financial Situation of Polish Banks (various years).

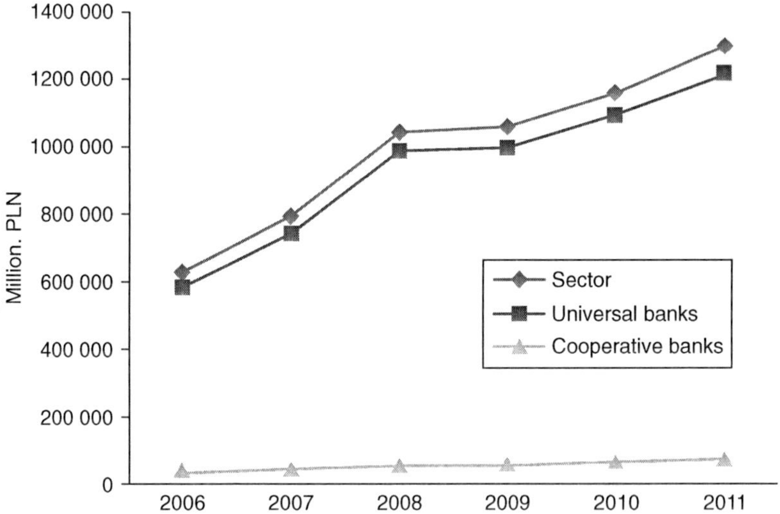

Figure 2.4 Dynamics of asset growth in the Polish banking sector
Source: Own calculations based on data from Polish Financial Supervision Authority.

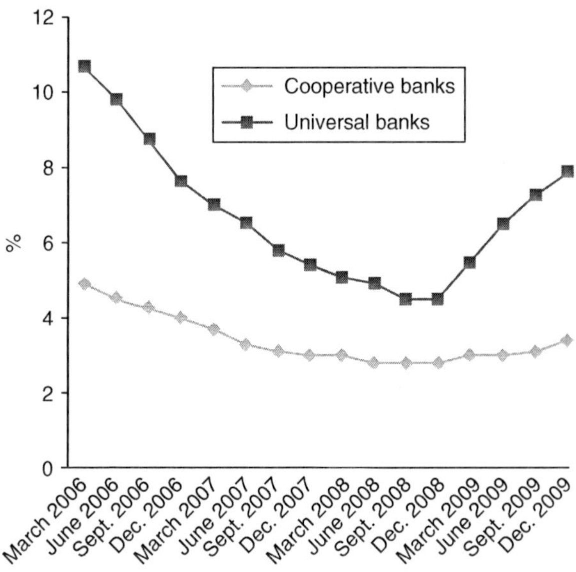

Figure 2.5a Non-performing loans
Source: Own calculations based on data from Polish Financial Supervision Authority.

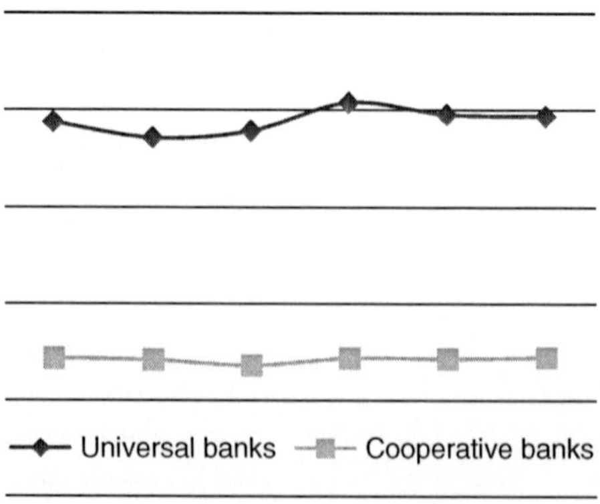

Figure 2.5b Off-balance sheet transactions to total assets

Source: Own calculations based on data from Polish Financial Supervision Authority.

the growth of non-performing loans, off-balance sheet transactions and capital adequacy, as was the case for universal banks (Figure 2.5).

5 Cooperative and mutual banks: lessons from past crises

Cooperative banks, because of their rigidities and weak capital base, may increase the fragility of financial systems, for while those banks generally have low incentives for risky behavior, their focus on traditional lending to local members and small enterprises tends to imply relatively large and correlated exposures to credit risk.

Globally, regionally based saving banks went through a number of crises and required numerous rescue measures. There were also different regulatory responses to local bank problems. One of the earliest crises was that of Savings and Loan Associations (S&Ls) in the US in the 1980s. This crisis was initially related to the interest rate rigidity of S&Ls imposed by Regulation Q in 1960, which created a gap between the cost of short-term liabilities and long-term fixed rate mortgage repayments. After the deregulation of the 1980s (Depository Institutions Deregulation and Monetary Control Act, 1980) and a period of interest rate instability after the 1979 oil crisis, many of the associations became insolvent. But deregulation did allow S&Ls to offer a wider array of products: they were allowed to make commercial and consumer loans, loans for real estate developers, and direct investments in real estate. As a result, in the 1980s and early 1990s, S&Ls suffered large losses and declined significantly in numbers (from approximately 4000 in 1980 to less than 2000 by the mid-1990s). In 1989, newly elected President George W. Bush announced a rescue program for the S&Ls industry, and later that year 318 thrifts were resolved with total assets of US$135 billion, and in 1990, 213 with total assets of US$130 billion. Only in 1993–1995 did the industry begin to stabilize. The overall rescue program for the sector was estimated at US$153 billion, of which US$124 billion was paid by the US taxpayer and US$29 billion by the thrifts themselves (World Savings Banks Institute, 2006). The regulatory response to the S&L crisis was tardy and inefficient, partially due to the fact that the associations had strong political backing in their local communities. Consequently, it took the whole of the 1980s to solve the problem and most of the thrifts were dismantled.

The 2012 crisis of the Spanish regional banks (*cajas*) may also raise certain questions as to the impact of local banks on overall stability. Spanish saving banks, many controlled by local politicians, were the principal participants in the real estate boom in the pre-2008 crisis period. Loans to the real estate sector increased from 4 per cent of total lending by credit institutions to the domestic private sector in the early 1990s, to 18 per cent in 2009, and in 2011 troubled assets totaled €176 billion, which amounted to 52 per cent of loans to real estate developers and 18 per cent of Spanish GDP (IMF, 2012). The Spanish government undertook a number of restructuring actions; among others, the creation of the Fondo de Restructuracion Ordenada Bancaria (FROB) in 2009, whose goal was to help restructure and consolidate the Spanish banking industry. The FROB complemented the tasks of the Bank Guarantee Fund (FGD: *Fondo de Garantia de Depositos*), which focused more on bank resolutions and deposit protection, while the FROB, together with the Bank of Spain, has been responsible for active involvement in the restructuring of Spanish banking, including the savings bank sector.

In response to the savings bank crisis, a new banking conglomerate, Bankia, was created in December 2010, the product of the merger of seven mutually owned Spanish regional *cajas*, in an attempt to create a common defense against bad real estate loans. At the time of its creation, Caja Madrid, owned by the government of the Community of Madrid, held a controlling interest of 52 per cent, followed by Bancaja (38 per cent) and La Caja de Canarias, Caja de Ávila, Caixa Laietana, Caja Segovia and Cana Rioja. In 2011 Bankia offered shares to the public in an IPO (Bankia, 2011) and in 2012 Bankia was the fourth largest Spanish bank, with 12 million customers. In May 2011 it was partially nationalized by the government of Spain as a rescue measure: FROB took 45 per cent in Banka shares, for €4.5 billion. However, this did not solve the problem; in May 2012 the new president of Bankia announced expected losses exceeding €4 billion and requested a bailout of €19 billion.

Both the US thrifts crisis of the 1980s and the more recent problems of the Spanish *cajas* demonstrate the potential fragility of locally-based mutual banks. However, a major part of the blame in both crisis situations can be attributed to strong political links and inefficient regulations. The Spanish solution of mega-merging problematic banks has not so far solved any problems, and has only succeeded in shifting it from regional to national level, making potential resolution much more costly and complex. Hence the lessons from past crises of locally-based mutual banks is that strong political links and inefficient regulations may create problems which require public resolution.

6 Cooperative bank soundness in Poland: BFG risk index

While the mission of the commercial banks is to maximize shareholder value, in the case of cooperative banks profits are only supposed to be a means of achieving a broader range of objectives. Facing less competitive pressures from the environment and from their shareholders, and with more long-term objectives, cooperative banks should opt for a traditional business model, behave more prudently and take fewer risks. In principle, this should lead to more prudent risk-taking and lower variability of returns. Many studies have confirmed the remarkable stability of local banks (Ianotta, Nocera and Sironi, 2007; Cihak and Hesse, 2007; Beck et al., 2009), particularly in the post-crisis period (Rabobank, 2011). They point to the fact that cooperative banks tend to be more stable than commercial banks, because of lower volatility of returns, which offsets their lower profitability and capitalization. Therefore, the aim of the empirical part of this chapter is to compare the safety and stability of commercial and cooperative banks in Poland, using two main indicators: the Bank Guarantee Fund (BFG) risk index and the Z-score indicator, interpreted frequently as a distance-from-bankruptcy index.

The Polish Bank Deposit Guarantee Fund (BFG) has developed its own bank assessment system, on the basis of which an index of risk in the commercial and cooperative banking sector has been produced. The construction of the risk index went through three phases (Sowińska, 2006):

- in the first version (1996–1997) the synthetic index was based on 11 indicators, and the evaluation was based on a positive interpretation (whether bank standing is better than the referential score),
- in the second version (1999–2001) the synthetic index was based on 48 indicators, but the evaluation was based on a negative interpretation (whether bank standing is worse than the referential score),
- in the third version (2001–2006) the synthetic index was based on 13 basic balance sheet indicators, supplemented by non-balance sheet factors important for bank stability. The evaluation was also based on a negative interpretation: the aim was to identify banks for which the financial situation was deteriorating and as a result posing a risk to banking sector stability,
- since 2010, the index construction has been in the process of being modified to new reporting standards, and new bank risk data is not yet available (BFG Safe Bank, 2010a, p. 33).

In BFG methodology, the assessment of an individual bank's financial position is based on four principal analytical areas: efficiency, quality of assets,

Table 2.9 BFG bank assessment methodology

Principal risk areas	No. of indicators in each area	Worst score for commercial banks	Worst score for cooperative banks
1. Efficiency	4	–35 points	–35 points
2. Asset quality	3	–22.5 points	–27.5 points
3. Off-balance sheet positions	2 for commercial banks 1 for cooperative banks	-7.5 points	
4. Solvency	4	–35 points	–37.5 points
Total		–100 points	–100 points

Source: Sowińska (2006), pp. 53–54.

quality of off-balance-sheet position and solvency (Table 2.9). Individual banks are given ratings, and the risk index is computed for the whole sector, and for the commercial and cooperative bank sub-sectors.

This risk index is an aggregated, standardized assessment of: solvency, efficiency, quality of assets and off-balance sheet commitments – weighted by the share of each bank's deposits in the banking sector. The measure is calculated separately for commercial and for cooperative banks. It is presented on a scale from 0 (no threat to bank stability) to 100 (the highest level of potential threat). Changes in index values reflect changes in bank risk assessment. Figure 2.6 presents the level of risk indices for commercial and cooperative banks.

The BFG risk index demonstrates the stable position of the Polish banking sector till mid-2008. The stability of both commercial and cooperative banks was a result of a high credit expansion, which in turn resulted in the increased efficiency of banks. A significant drop in the index took place, however, at the turn of 2008/2009, particularly for commercial banks. While cooperative banks exhibited a good and stable standing throughout the crisis period, demonstrating a remarkable resilience to the crisis, the risk index for commercial banks rapidly deteriorated in the crisis period of 2008–2009, changing from a good to a satisfactory rating. Commercial banks were most affected by their increasing portfolio of non-performing loans, which negatively influenced bank capitalization (Figure 2.7) and the consequent growth of required reserves and a decrease in ROA. Only the cost–income ratio remained stable for commercial banks. However, even these banks were at a safe distance from poor standing (below -30 points), supporting the assertion that overall the Polish banking sector came safely through the crisis period.

7 Cooperative bank soundness in Poland: Z-score index

Banking risk can be defined as adverse impacts on profitability from several sources of uncertainty (Bessis, 2002). Its most important aspect is solvency risk, that is of being unable to absorb losses generated by all types of risks with the capital available. A measurement tool capable of approximating this kind of risk is found in the Z-score, an index of bank sensitivity to risk (default) which is frequently used in the literature as a method for measuring bank stability. The Z-score soundness index estimates the likelihood that a company will run out of capital on the basis of its capitalization and profitability, and the volatility of its returns. It is often referred to as 'distance to bankruptcy', as the index measures the number of standard deviations the ROA must decrease by before a bank's equity is depleted.

Thus the Z-score tells us what the distance from default is, measured by the standard deviation of profits expressed by ROA (Lown, Osler, Stragan and Sufi; 2000). So, the higher on average the ROA and CAR (capital/assets) are in a given period, and the more stable the returns, the higher the Z-score. The higher the score, the safer the bank. It points up the riskiness of volatility of returns, and is based on the notion that the source of default is losses not covered by adequate capital.

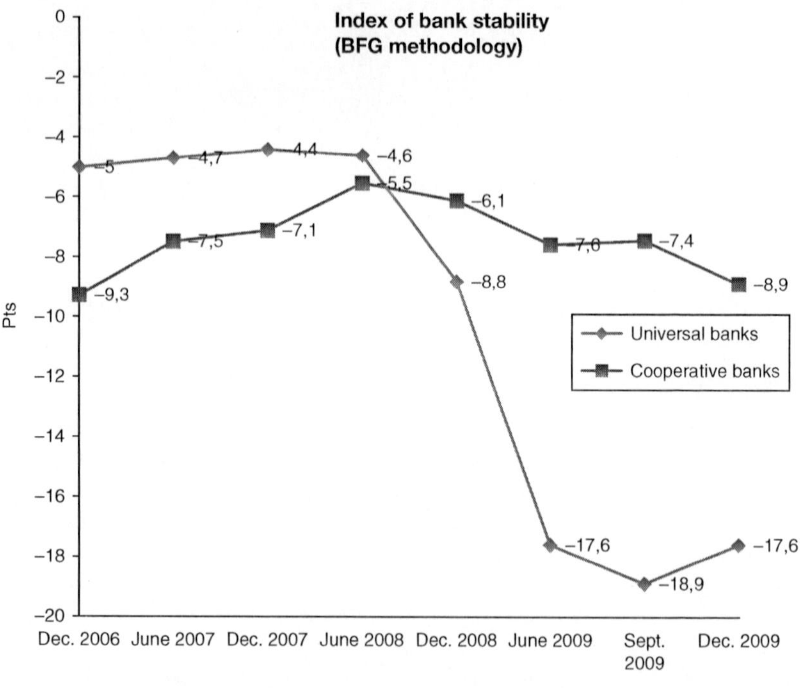

Figure 2.6 Bank Guarantee Fund (BFG) risk index of commercial and cooperative banks

Source: Own presentation based on data presented in the BFG Annual Reports for 2007 (p. 21), 2008 (p. 34), 2009 (p. 31) and 2010a (p. 33).

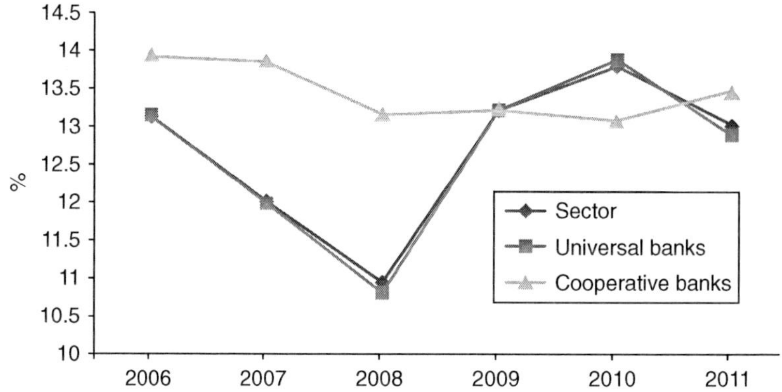

Figure 2.7 Capital adequacy of Polish universal and cooperative banks (2006–2011)
Source: Own calculations based on the data from the KNF (Polish FSA).

$$Z-score=\frac{\dfrac{\sum_{t=1}^{n}\dfrac{2\pi_t}{A_t+A_{t-1}}}{n}+\dfrac{\sum_{t=1}^{n}\dfrac{E_t+E_{t-1}}{A_t+A_{t-1}}}{n}}{\sigma_{ROA}}=\frac{ROA+CAR}{\sigma_{ROA}}$$

where:
A_t = assets in a period t;
π_t = net profit in t;
$2\pi_t/(A_t + A_{t-1})$ denotes the average value of ROA in t;
σ_{ROA} = standard deviation of ROA;
E_t = bank equity in t;
$(E_t + E_{t-1}) / (A_t + A_{t-1})$ denotes CAR in t;
n = number of researched periods (years).

The index is based on the following assumptions (Hannan and Hanweck, 1988):

- bankruptcy occurs when losses exceed bank equity,
- ROA is calculated as net profit divided by average assets in a period,
- CAR reflects equity divided by average assets,
- profits have a normal distribution,
- ROA is a random variable with finite mean and variance.

Thus the least safe banks are those which have relatively little equity to prevent the absorption of losses, and they are characterized by unstable profits. Table 2.10 presents Z-score calculations for commercial and cooperative banks operating in Poland, in quarterly moving, rolling windows. In calculating the Z-score, a moving average was used to illustrate the dynamics of change better in the index; that is, how quickly, as a result of deteriorating financial performance, the banking sector moved towards bankruptcy.

Table 2.10 and Figure 2.8 show that the 2008 crisis resulted in a strong lowering of the Z-score index for the entire banking sector. For commercial banks, a rapid deterioration in the index resulted primarily from their pre-crisis high profitability. A drastic decline in ROA caused a rapid increase in the variability of the standard deviation. As a result, between 2009 and mid-2010 the ability to absorb losses in the commercial banking sector decreased to a level close to 20. Only from the end of 2010 can a reversal trend be observed, particularly for cooperative banks. However, for commercial banks there was a second lowering of the score, in 2011. Changes in the value of the Z-score index for the cooperative banking sector were, however, less dramatic. This sector started with a lower value, but at the beginning of 2009 the value of the Z-score for cooperative banks had risen to such a degree that it was for the first time higher than that of the commercial banks. In the first quarter of 2010, the minimum value of the cooperative Z-score index was 47. Then

Table 2.10 Z-score for Polish commercial and cooperative bank (April 2006–June 2011)

Quarter/ year	Total banking sector			Commercial banks			Cooperative banks		
	ROA	CAR	Z-score	ROA	CAR	Z-score	ROA	CAR	Z-score
II/06	1.72%	7.90%	X	1.79%	7.88%	X	1.35%	9.77%	X
II/ 06	1.74%	7.73%	X	1.76%	7.68%	X	1.38%	9.53%	X
IV/06	1.67%	7.57%	X	1.80%	7.57%	X	1.37%	9.14%	X
I/ 07	1.73%	7.64%	X	1.75%	7.61%	X	1.41%	9.28%	X
II/07	1.77%	7.53%	X	1.79%	7.54%	X	1.40%	9.24%	X
III/07	1.80%	7.49%	213.55	1.82%	7.50%	386.96	1.47%	9.27%	247.11
IV/07	1.85%	7.50%	161.90	1.88%	7.55%	226.85	1.50%	9.36%	188.83
I/08	1.83%	7.58%	149.21	1.85%	7.63%	206.28	1.59%	9.44%	128.23
II/ 08	1.89%	7.58%	124.98	1.90%	7.60%	178.62	1.68%	9.52%	91.24
III/08	1.88%	7.59%	159.47	1.90%	7.70%	167.92	1.74%	9.51%	77.21
IV/ 08	1.53%	7.55%	76.24	1.52%	7.72%	70.65	1.70%	9.62%	85.24
I/09	1.23%	7.50%	37.58	1.21%	7.67%	35.56	1.56%	9.80%	107.07
II/09	0.95%	7.62%	24.45	0.93%	7.83%	23.51	1.38%	9.98%	88.12
III/ 09	0.77%	7.83%	19.39	0.74%	7.96%	18.86	1.24%	10.18%	61.58
IV/09	0.78%	8.09%	18.33	0.76%	8.12%	17.94	1.18%	10.24%	49.11
I/10	0.82%	8.38%	20.49	0.79%	8.45%	20.15	1.18%	10.24%	47.00
II/10	0.86%	8.55%	31.09	0.84%	8.60%	30.93	1.20%	10.22%	54.78
III/10	0.90%	8.61%	56.82	0.89%	8.67%	56.72	1.15%	10.23%	76.71
IV/10	1.02%	8.66%	98.70	1.02%	8.72%	93.76	1.12%	10.22%	134.90
I/ 11	1.11%	8.66%	72.61	1.12%	8.66%	67.67	1.11%	10.16%	255.39
II/11	1.18%	8.66%	62.72	1.18%	8.61%	58.65	1.12%	10.13%	347.99

Source: Own calculations based on data from KNF (Polish FSA).

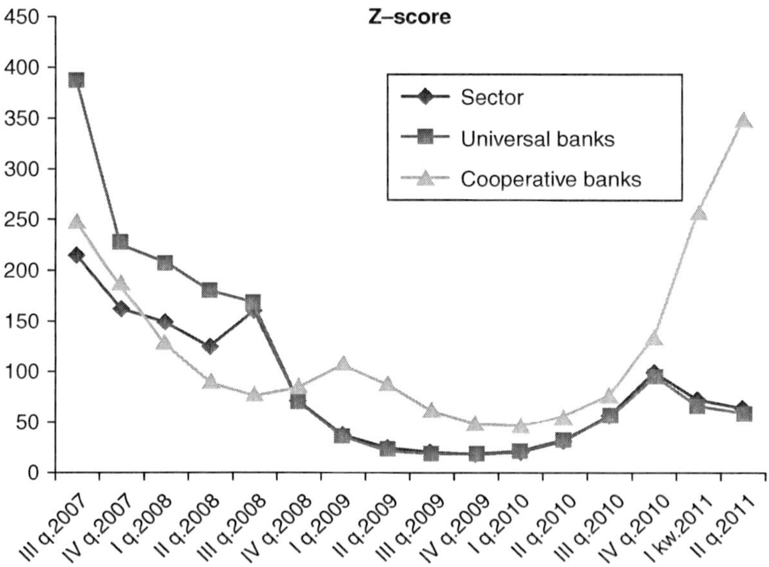

Figure 2.8 Z-score index for commercial and cooperative banks
Source: Own calculations.

in 2011, the increase in the index level was also much higher for cooperative banks, demonstrating their stable position throughout the crisis. This was largely due to the stable nature of their relationships with customers.

8 Future challenges for the cooperative sector

The Polish cooperative banking sector is safe and profitable, although slightly inefficient, with a relatively high C/I ratio. However, having considerable growth potential, this sector needs pressure exerting on it in order to expand. The niche bank status quo seems to satisfy both the universal banks, which do not intend to operate in rural areas, and the cooperative banks, which feel comfortable in their traditional markets and functions. In the universal banking sector, there is strong competition in the retail market, while cooperative banks have in many cases local monopolies. By concentrating on local enterprise financing, they face only limited competitive pressures. However, this strategy, although successful in the short term, is posing a number of long-term threats. First, there are possibilities that universal banks will start to show an interest in servicing the countryside, particularly its rich segments, and will thus provide direct competition to cooperative banks, not to mention the credit unions – SKOKs. Second, the cooperative sector is expanding its shifts away from household towards enterprise financing (Tables 2.11 and 2.12), which entails more risk than the traditional intermediation, focused on the households.

In addition, the cooperative sector may have more profound problems than the universal banks with implementing some post-crisis regulation, such as the implementation of liquidity requirements in CRD IV, which will be particularly difficult. While local cooperative banks have an excess of liquidity, they deposit a large part of their liquid assets in associating banks and consequently, 30 per cent of their net interest income comes from interbank activities. However, interbank deposits are not accepted in the new liquidity requirements. So the Polish regulatory authorities (KNF, 2012c) have suggested implementing an Institutional Protection Scheme (IPS) for joint liquidity. This innovative structure within the banking system is intended to ensure the solvency and liquidity of a group of affiliated institutions (BIS, 2010): firstly, it entails all participants relinquishing the capacity to determine and implement business strategies and internal risk control to the central body of the IPS; the second pillar of this structure comprises the mutual liquidity and solvency pacts between the participating cooperative banks; and its third pillar is a commitment to the stability of the agreements. Thus the IPS results in much tighter cooperation within a group of affiliating banks than in the past. However, there is considerable resistance among some cooperative banks to giving up their independence. So another solution is to split the sector, making IPS obligatory for small cooperative banks, and the rest, with capital of over €5 million, to function independently (Table 2.13). But this solution would result in a considerable weakening of the remaining cooperative associations.

So far, it has not been the intention of the regulatory authorities to interfere directly with the cooperative banking structure, as it was done in the 1994 and 2000 Cooperative Laws. However, this may be advisable, considering their foregone growth potential and the new challenges ahead. Regulatory intervention should be aimed either at strengthening the position of 'mother banks' for cooperative groups in an IPS mechanism, or at

Table 2.11 Loans and deposit structure for Polish commercial and cooperative banks, 3 Q 2012 (in %)

a. Loans structure	**Commercial banks**	**Cooperative banks**
Households	59.87	63.90
SME	17.57	25.83
Large firms	12.47	0.61
Local self-governments	4.55	8.61
Central government	5.06	0.25
Others	0.48	0.80
b. Deposits structure	**Commercial banks**	**Cooperative banks**
Households	63.85	79.83
Firms	25.53	7.54
Local self-governments	2.53	9.46
Others	8.09	3.17

Source: Based on BPS (2012), pp. 19–20.

Table 2.12 Changes in loan structure of commercial and cooperative banks (2008–2011)

	Commercial banks			Cooperative banks		
	2008, 2Q	2010, 2Q	2011, 2Q	2008, 2Q	2010, 2Q	2011, 2Q
Households	55.7	62.0	61.8	74.7	70.5	67.1
Firms	40.2	31.3	30.0	19.8	22.1	24.1
Local and central governments	3.8	6.2	7.8	4.9	6.7	8.0
Others	0.3	0.5	0.4	0.6	0.7	0.8

Table 2.13 The asset size of cooperative banks

Own capital	<5 mil. Euro	>5 mil. Euro
No. of cooperative banks	473	90
Asset size (PLN bn.)	43.1	38.4
% of total assets	53%	47%

Source: KNF (2012c).

encouraging the strongest cooperative banks to demutualize, in emulation of the Bank Conversion Act of 1986 in the UK.

Building Societies were once very popular local mutual banks in Britain. Borrowers and depositors were society members, setting policy and appointing directors on a one-member, one-vote basis. Their main purpose was to provide mortgages for members, but they often provided other retail banking services, such as current accounts, credit cards and personal loans. Regulation allowed societies to access wholesale bond and money markets, in order to fund mortgages. The Building Societies Conversion Act of 1986 resulted in a bottom-up restructuring of the sector; it permitted societies to demutualize if more than 75 per cent of members voted in favour of doing so, and members' rights were exchanged for shares; in response to the incentives provided by the act, a number of the larger societies made a decision to do this. After demutualization, some of them were acquired or merged, and others became independent companies quoted on the London Stock Exchange. The process began with the demutualization of the Abbey National in 1989. Then, from 1995 to 1999, the eight largest societies, with two thirds of building society assets, demutualized. This wave of demutualizations halted in 2000, when the remaining societies modified their rules of membership to ensure that anyone joining a society for the first time would, for the first few years, be unable to make any profit out of demutualization. Today, this sector is a fraction of its historical size: there are only about 50 institutions remaining, but they actively compete with commercial banks for consumer banking services, especially mortgage lending and deposits.

9 Conclusions

The main purpose of this chapter has been to compare the performance of commercial and cooperative banks in Poland from a post-crisis perspective, paying particular attention to the issue of their stability and soundness. Both the BFG bank risk index and Z-score indicator clearly demonstrate the stable position of cooperative banks in Poland in the period analyzed. The global financial crisis of 2007–2009 has highlighted the fact that the safety of banks is largely determined by a healthy balance sheet. In the post-crisis period, cooperative banks, with their traditional business model, have come out with the highest Z-score (low risk of default) and satisfactory profitability. However, their secure position has been achieved at the expense of 'niche bank status' and marginal market share (6 per cent of total assets), and the threat of further marginalization in the coming years, due to new competitive threats from the mutually owned credit unions (Spółdzielcze Kasy Oszczednościowo-Kredytowe, SKOKs) which have recently been granted a regulated institution status. This, together with new regulatory challenges, connected with the implementation of Basel III rules (particularly the new liquidity requirements in CRD IV and a new definition of core capital components) will require the creation of a new cooperative model in Poland.

In doing this, learning from the experiences of other countries, such as the UK Demutualisation Act of 1986, will be educational. Thus the policy recommendation of this chapter is that although the current performance of the Polish cooperative sector is stable and sound, regulatory support for this sector is advisable in the long run, either through strengthening the position of associating banks, or by creating incentives for the largest cooperative banks towards demutualization.

References

Allen, F., A. Babus and E. Carletti (2009) 'Financial crises: theory and evidence', *Annual Review of Financial Economics*, 1, 97–116.

Bankia (2011). *Boletin del Accionista*, www.bankia.com (date accessed 5 December 2013).

Beck, T., H. Hesse, T. Kock and N. von Westernhagen (2009) *Bank Ownership and Stability: Evidence from Germany,* http://www.fdic.gov/bank/analytical/cfr/2009/june/CFR_SS_2009 _beck.pdf.

Bessis, J. (2002) *Risk Management in Banking* (Chichester: Wiley).

BFG: Bankowy Fundusz Gwarancyjny, *Annual Reports* for 2007, 2008, 2009, 2010 and 2011.

BFG (2010a) 'Report of BFG Activity', *Safe Bank,* no. 2(41).

BFG (2010b) Pruski, J. 'Sytuacja finansowa sektora banków spółdzielczych w Polsce', www.bfg.pl/sites/default/files/dokumenty/forum-liderow-bs.pdf (date accessed 5 December 2013).

BFG (2011) Pruski, J., 'Cooperative Banks Leaders' Forum', http://www.bfg.pl/sites/default/files/dokumenty/forum_liderow_bs_prezentacja_bfg.pps (date accessed 5 December 2013).

Bikker, J. and J. Bos (2008) *Bank Performance: A Theoretical and Empirical Framework for the Analysis of Profitability, Competition and Efficiency* (London: Routledge).

BIS (2010) Aríztegui, J., *Savings Bank Restructuring and Institutional Protection Schemes*, available at http://www.bis.org/review/r101222e.pdf (date accessed 5 December 2013).

BPS (2012) Bank wspólnych sił, no. 6.

CEE (2010) 'Strategic Analysis', http://www.unicredit-tiriac.ro/data/files/CEE_BankingOutlook-2010.pdf.

CEE (2011) 'Banking in CEE: The New Growth Model', *Banking Outlook*, January, UniCredit.

Cihak, M. and H. Hesse (2007) 'Cooperative banks and financial stability', *IMF Working Paper*, no. 2, Washington D.C.

Demirgüç-Kunt, A. and H. Huizinga (2009) 'Bank activity and funding strategies: the impact on risk and return', CEPR Discussion Paper, no. 7170.

Duffie, D. (2011) *How Big Banks Fail* (Princeton: Princeton University Press).

EACB (2011) *The Annual Report*, www.eurocoopbanks.coop.

ECB (2010a) *EU Banking Structures*, Frankfurt, October.

ECB (2010b) 'Beyond ROE – How to Measure Bank Performance', appendix to the *Report on EU Banking Structures*, Frankfurt, September.

Fonteyne, W. (2007) 'Cooperative banks in Europe – policy issues', IMF Working Paper, no. 159, Washington D.C.

Groeneveld, H. and A. Sjauw-Koen-Fa (2009) 'Cooperative banks in the new financial system', *Economic Research Department of the Rabobank Group*, Utrecht.

Hannan, H. and G.A. Hanweck (1988) 'Bank insolvency risk and the market for large certificates of deposit', *Journal of Money, Credit and Banking*, 20, 203–211.

Ianotta, G., G. Nocera and A. Sironi (2007) 'Ownership structure, risk and performance in the European banking industry', *Journal of Banking and Finance*, 31, 2127–2149.

IMF (2012) Financial Sector Assessment Program Update, Spain, May.

KNF (2011a) *Raport o sytuacji banków w 2007–2010*, Warszawa. Available at: http://www.knf.gov.pl/opracowania/sektor_bankowy/dane_o_rynku/Dane_miesieczne.html

KNF (2011b) Informacja o sytuacji banków w I półroczu 2011, Warszawa.

KNF (2012a) Kwasniak, W., *Współczesne wyzwania ekonomiczne banków w swietle prognozowanego spowolnienia gospodarczego*, http://www.knf.gov.pl/images/wyzwania_ekonomiczne _bankow_tcm75-29765.pdf (date accessed 4 October 2012).

KNF (2012b) Zaufanie do wybranych instytucji sektora finansowego, March 2012, http://www.knf.gov.pl/Images/material_prasowy_Pentor_dla_KNF_tcm75-29870.pdf.

KNF (2012c) Kwasniak, W., Pozadane_kierunkI_zmian_modelu funkcjonowania_bankowoscI_spoldzielczej_17_09_2012_tcm75-31843.

Lown, C., Osler, C., Stragan, P. and Sufi, A. (2000) 'The changing landscape of the financial services industry: what lies ahead?' *FRB NY Economic Policy Review*, October.

McKinsey (2011) The State of Global Banking: In Search of a Sustainable Model.

McKinsey (2012) McKinsey on Cooperatives.

McKinsey Quarterly (2009) Learning from Financial Regulation's Mistakes, June.

MF (2012) Polish Ministry of Finance: Kondycja oraz perspektywy rozwoju polskiego sektora bankowego w 2012 roku na tle Europy, available at: www.mf.gov.pl.

NBP (2011) Raport o stabilności systemu finansowego, Warszawa.

NBP (various years) Summary Evaluation of the Financial Situation of Polish Banks. Warsaw.

Oliver Wyman Report (2012) Mc Carroll, V. and S. Habberfield, *The Outlook for Co-operative Banking in Europe*, www.oliverwyman.com.

Pentor (2012a) *Barometr nastrojów ekonomicznych,* www.pentor.pl/publikacje_barometr_ nastrojow.xml.

Pentor (2012b) *Monitor Bankowy*, January, www.pentor.pl/publikacje_monitor_bankowy.xml

Rabobank (2009) The European Banking Sector and the Co-operative Banks, January. Available at www.rabobank.com/content/images/OverviewEurCo-opbankingsector_% 20200901_tcm43–80349.pdf

Rabobank (2011) Special Report: Cooperative Banks in the Spotlights, no. 12.

Siudek, T. (2010) 'Polish cooperative banking sector in the face of systemic transformation and European integration in agriculture', *Agricultural Economics*, 3, 116–134, www.agriculturejournals.cz/publicFiles/18335.pdf

Sowińska, I. (2006) 'Metodyka Bankowego Funduszu Gwarancyjnego w zakresie oceny zagrożeń sytuacji finansowej banków', *Bezpieczny Bank*, 2(31).

Szelągowska, A. (2012). *Współczesna bankowość spółdzielcza* (Warszawa: CeDeWu). The World Bank (2010), Credit Unions in Poland: Diagnostic and Proposals on Regulation *and Supervision,* Report No. 59432, December, pp. 1–93.

World Economic Forum Report (2010) The Future of the Global Financial System: Navigating the Challenges Ahead.

World Savings Banks Institute and European Savings Banks Group(2006) *A Comparative Analysis of the US and EU Retail Banking Markets*, September.

ZBP (2012) Polish Bank Association, *Banki 2011* (Warszaw: ZBP).

3

Credit Development, Quality Deterioration and Intermediation Model: Does Bank Size Matter?

Evidence from Italy between 2006 and 2010

Franco Tutino, Concetta Colasimone and Giorgio Carlo Brugnoni

1 Introduction

In Italy, the effects of the global financial crisis started in 2007 caused both a significant downturn in the trend in loans to customers and a serious deterioration in the quality of credit exposures. Although widespread, this phenomenon took on different characteristics according to bank size; during the worst phase of the crisis, loans provided by larger banks grew significantly less than did those provided by smaller banks. In contrast, the deterioration in credit exposures mainly affected small and minor banks.

This chapter analyses the lending activity of Italian banks by size during the period between 2006 and 2010, focusing on its evolution over time, on the composition of loan portfolios by product breakdown, on the quality of credit exposures and on the main income effects. The aim is to find elements that outline the lending policies adopted by banks during the financial crisis, also linking the heterogeneity shown in the evolution of loans to customers to the bank size and to the fundamental characteristics of the intermediation model adopted. We specifically investigate the way in which the differences identified in terms of greater or lesser orientation towards the funding–lending credit intermediation with customers could explain the heterogeneity shown in the development of loans to customers and in its quality during the financial crisis started in 2007. The underlying hypothesis is that to different funding and investment policies, to different assets and liabilities composition strategies correspond divergent banking management conditionings and, consequently, dissimilar financial and capital constraints to the credit supply.

This chapter is structured as follows. Section 2 provides a brief review of the main studies carried out on credit development in Italy during the financial crisis started in 2007, and highlights the contribution of the research to the literature. Section 3 illustrates the dataset used in the analysis, the characteristics of the sample of banks investigated and the methodology adopted. Section 4 analyses the trend in loans to customers during the financial crisis by bank size. Section 5 shows the main evidence about the composition of loan portfolio by product breakdown. Section 6 analyses the lending activity from a qualitative point of view. Section 7 examines the main effects on income in terms of interest income and impairment losses on loans to customers. Section 8 links the heterogeneity shown in the credit development by bank size to the main differences in terms of intermediation model adopted. Section 9 concludes the chapter, summarizing the main findings and giving some closing remarks.

2 Literature review and contribution of the research

The effects of the financial crisis on the credit supply of Italian banks has aroused the interest of numerous scholars, who have investigated relevant dimensions and determinant factors.

Some studies (Panetta and Signoretti, 2010; Del Giovane, Ginette and Nobili, 2011) focus on the role played by supply and demand factors in affecting the trend in loans to customers in Italy between 2007 and 2009.

Panetta and Signoretti (2010) use data on loans at an aggregate level provided by the Bank of Italy, the Italian results of the *Bank Lending Survey*[1] and the findings of some surveys on credit supply and demand factors conducted on Italian firms. Del Giovane, Ginette and Nobili (2011) combine qualitative information from the Italian results of the *Bank Lending Survey* with quantitative information on loans provided by the Italian banks participating in the survey. These analyses show the significance of both supply and demand factors in influencing the trend in loans to customers, revealing a tighter restriction on the supply side between the end of 2008 and the beginning of 2009.

Other studies (Albertazzi and Marchetti, 2010; De Mitri, Gobbi and Sette, 2010; Di Battista, Nieri and Patarnello, 2010; Di Battista and Nieri, 2011; Gambacorta and Mistrulli, 2011; Bonaccorsi di Patti and Sette, 2012) provide a more in-depth analysis of the significance of certain specific features of banks, in terms of financial structure, capital constraints, business models and intensity of the customer relationship in affecting the credit supply policies adopted by Italian banks during the financial crisis started in 2007.

Albertazzi and Marchetti (2010) analyze data on loans to firms in the period between September 2008 and March 2009, showing that banks with low levels of initial capitalization largely restricted the supply of loans to their customers, especially the riskier firms. This phenomenon is more significant in larger banks than smaller ones. The authors link the reasons for this size heterogeneity to the lower constraints imposed by the Basel II risk-sensitive capital requirements, to a significant informational advantage and to more flexible credit allocation processes in smaller banks compared to the larger ones.

De Mitri, Gobbi and Sette (2010), analyzing data from a sample of more than 30,000 Italian firms, show that during the financial crisis started in 2007 the more stable and strong the customer relationship was, the less relevant the restriction in the credit supply was.

Di Battista, Nieri and Patarnello (2010) use balance sheet data from a sample of 31 Italian banking groups that represent around 80% of the system, analyzing the trend in loans to customers between December 2006 and June 2009, focusing in particular on the periods from June 2007 to June 2008, and from June 2008 to June 2009. The authors adopt two analytical approaches. To assess the main differences by size of intermediary, they divide the sample into three classes (large, medium and small) based on the total assets and – secondarily – on the number of branches. To identify the operating conditions that could have influenced the heterogeneity detected in the credit supply – liquidity and funding constraints, capital constraints, the quality of the credit exposures, the business model adopted, and size – the authors divide the sample into three types of bank (more dynamic, averagely dynamic, less dynamic) using the rate of credit growth between June 2008 and June 2009. The analysis by size shows that the larger groups slowed down their loans to customers more consistently than did medium and small groups, and that in the case of smaller groups a higher dynamism in the mortgage supply emerged. However, as highlighted by the authors themselves, the size factor can be relevant only for larger groups, and that would only partially explain the different trends in the credit supply between intermediaries. The analysis of operating conditions shows that the most dynamic groups are characterized by: less stringent capital constraints; a financial structure mainly focused on funding from customers rather than from the interbank market; a business model mostly oriented to credit intermediation; a poorer quality of credit exposures in the portfolio; and a smaller size on average.

Di Battista and Nieri (2011) analyze balance sheet data from a sample of 44 intermediaries (including 31 banking groups and 13 independent banks) representative of approximately 85% of the banking system, and they investigate the determinant factors of the differences shown in the credit supply policies adopted by Italian banks between 2006 and 2009. The authors, in particular, conduct their analysis by comparing the observed trends with reference to two distinct classes of banks: that of the most dynamic intermediaries, which in the period analyzed registered a higher growth of loans to customers than average; and that of the less dynamic intermediaries, which, in contrast, registered growth rates below average. The objectives of the analysis, carried out by adopting a descriptive approach, are to verify:

if the starting operating conditions and peculiarities in terms of business model in the period before the second phase of the financial crisis (from December 2006 to June 2008) affected the credit development in the immediate aftermath; and if in the most acute phase of the crisis (from July 2008 and December 2009) significant differences could be traced in the lending policies in terms of product breakdown and pricing between the two classes of banks. The assumption underlying their methodological choice is that the heterogeneity observed in the behavior of Italian banks should be detectable in the diversity of challenges faced by the funding side, in different financial constraints and in the characteristics of the business model adopted, apart from an exclusive reference to the size factor. The study, in particular, demonstrates that banks found to be more dynamic in providing loans to customers during the financial crisis started in 2007 were those characterized by: less stringent capital constraints; a financial structure more oriented towards funding from customers; and a business model mostly oriented to credit intermediation. Moreover, the analysis indicates less restrictive pricing policies adopted by more dynamic banks, a smaller size of the latter on average and a greater focus on the supply of mortgages.

Gambacorta and Mistrulli (2011) use data on the cost of loans to firms between the second quarter of 2008 and the first quarter of 2010, showing that banks' specific characteristics, in terms of size, liquidity, capitalization and intensity of customer relationship, affected the level of interest rates charged by banks. The study highlights that smaller banks – characterized by a business model more oriented to lending, liquid, well capitalized and characterized by a stronger customer relationship – increased the spread on loans to customers less than did other intermediaries.

Bonaccorsi di Patti and Sette (2012), referring to loans to firms between 2007 and 2008, show that supply conditions worsened most for the banks that were most exposed to the interbank market and for those that made the most use of securitization, while the initial capital position of banks did not significantly affect the credit supply. According to Bonaccorsi di Patti and Sette (2012), in contrast to the arguments of Albertazzi and Marchetti (2010), the initial level of capital influenced lending indirectly, with higher capital reducing the elasticity of lending to the shocks on the funding side. In spite of the initial capital level, the credit supply had been significantly affected by the deterioration of the bank capital.

The main aspects investigated by the studies examined are highlighted in Table 3.1. With regard to the size factor, it is explicitly taken into account in some of them. However, they are not mainly concerned with the size as a factor that is able to explain the trend in loans to customers.

In particular, Di Battista, Nieri and Patarnello (2010) study the trend in loans to customers, also focusing on the intermediary size. The consolidated analytical approach adopted, however, does not enable to achieve results highlighting significant differences in terms of size. As underlined by the

Table 3.1 Literature review – synthesis of the main aspects investigated

	Demand factors	Supply factors					
			Banks' specific factors				
			Capitalization	Funding	Business model	Customer relationship intensity	Size
Panetta and Signoretti (2010)	X	X					
Del Giovane, Ginette and Nobili (2011)	X	X					
Albertazzi and Marchetti (2010)			X			X	X
De Mitri, Gobbi and Sette (2010)						X	
Di Battista, Nieri and Patarnello (2010)			X	X	X		X
Di Battista and Nieri (2011)			X	X	X		X
Gambacorta and Mistrulli (2011)			X			X	X
Bonaccorsi di Patti and Sette (2012)			X	X			

Source: Own elaboration.

authors themselves, the size factor would be significant only for larger banking groups, and it would only partially explain the difference in credit supply performance between intermediaries. Gambacorta and Mistrulli (2011) conduct an analysis by bank size, referring exclusively to the pricing policies adopted by banks, but without considering the relevant differences in terms of the trend in loans to customers. Albertazzi and Marchetti (2010) focus their analysis of the differences by bank size on the relationship between credit development and capitalization. Di Battista and Nieri (2011), although not deliberately conducting an analysis by bank size, show some significant heterogeneities in the development of loans to customers.

The research conducted in our work aims to offer a contribution to the analysis of the trend in loans to customers during the financial crisis started in 2007, by linking the heterogeneity by bank size to the impacts and the constraints based on the different business models and lending policies adopted by banks. The work, furthermore, analyses in depth loans to customers by bank size, also considering, in addition to the mere trend aspects, the composition of loan portfolio by product breakdown, the quality of credit exposures, and the main effects that lending to customers has on income; these are aspects that in our opinion have not yet been fully studied together and that are particularly relevant for the impacts that follow for the banking management as a whole, including the orientation to the credit supply. The research, after all, differs from the other contributions analyzed for other profiles as well: the size, the type of composition and the representativeness of the sample; the extension of the period analyzed; and the methodology of analysis adopted. For further information, in particular on the methodological differences, please refer to Section 3 below.

The choice of adopting a reading key focused on difference by bank size aims to integrate the main results achieved so far in the literature, first by adding elements of differentiation compared to the more recent contributions, and also to check if the size factor could be significant in explaining the heterogeneity by bank size shown in the evolution of loans to customers during the financial crisis. The accepted hypothesis is that conducting the analysis by bank size enables the specificities of the business models adopted by intermediaries to be taken into account, thus emphasizing the impacts that they bring in terms of lending to customers. Such impacts may also result from the different credit supply policies adopted by banks, which are the consequence of the heterogeneities shown in the intermediation model and of the opportunities and constraints which may ensue.

Looking at the reality of Italian banking, the analysis of the credit development by bank size seems to taken on a significant relevance. First of all, the Italian financial system is notoriously bank-based; therefore, distortions in the credit supply may have a sizeable impact on the economy (Gambacorta and Mistrulli, 2012). Second, the Italian banking system is characterized by an evident size heterogeneity, as a high number of small and minor local banks coexist with a significantly lower number of larger and multi-national banks. Third, the crisis had a different impact on banks according to their different size, the top five banking groups suffering relatively more from the drying of wholesale funding markets than did the smaller intermediaries (De Mitri, Gobbi and Sette, 2010).

3 Data, sample and methodology

The analysis has been conducted on the basis of data from individual financial statements from around 500 Italian banks extracted from ABI Bilanci FAST. [2]

The use of data from individual, instead of consolidated, banking financial statements does not ensure that the consolidated business policies and strategies which actually affect the lending policies adopted by banks that belong to banking groups will be taken into account. At the same time, however, the

Table 3.2 Sample representativeness by number of banks and volume of total assets (number of banks, volumes in euro millions, percentage values)

	Sample	Italian banking system	Sample representativeness (1)
	2006		
Number of banks	495	793	62.42%
Total assets, volume	1,932,130	2,793,245	69.17%
	2007		
Number of banks	493	806	61.17%
Total assets, volume	2,092,660	3,331,830	62.81%
	2008		
Number of banks	493	800	61.63%
Total assets, volume	2,309,501	3,634,564	63.54%
	2009		
Number of banks	493	789	62.48%
Total assets, volume	2,341,692	3,690,692	63.45%
	2010 (2)		
Number of banks	487	761	63.99%
Total assets, volume	2,136,282	3,750,113	56.97%

Notes: (1) Ratio, respectively, between the number of banks included in the sample and the total number of banks in the banking system, and between the volume of total assets of the banks from the sample and the volume of total assets of the banks of the banking system.

(2) The reduction of the sample representativeness in term of volume of total assets registered in 2010 is due to: the contraction registered in the volume of total assets of two major banks (Banca Nazionale del Lavoro SpA and Intesa Sanpaolo SpA) and three large banks (Dexia Crediop SpA, Banca Popolare di Verona S. Geminiano e S. Prospero SpA and Banca Popolare di Bergamo SpA) included in the sample; and to the effects of the merger by incorporation in the holding UniCredit SpA of the subsidiaries UniCredit Banca SpA, UniCredit Banca Di Roma SpA, UniCredit Corporate Banking SpA, Banco di Sicilia SpA, UniCredit Family Financing Bank SpA and UniCredit Private Banking SpA. For further details refer to the considerations about the total assets development reported in Section 4 (Table 3.10).

Source: Own elaboration; data on the sample of banks are collected from *ABI Bilanci Fast*; data on the Italian banking system are collected from Bank of Italy (2006, 2007, 2008, 2009, 2010), appendix, glossary, banks.

use of individual financial statements enables the study to be extended to a sample of intermediaries which is more representative of the Italian banking system composition by bank size. It is therefore possible to conduct an analysis by bank size which turns out to be more significant than ever before.

The sample of banks analyzed represents almost 60 per cent of the banking system in terms of the number of intermediaries and volume of total assets (Table 3.2) and has been designed around the same institutions throughout

Table 3.3 Classification of banks by size

	Average intermediated funds (1)
Major banks	More than €60 billion.
Large banks	Between €26 and €60 billion.
Medium banks	Between €9 and €26 billion.
Small banks	Between €1.3 and €9 billion.
Minor banks	Less than €1.3 billion.

Notes: (1) Weighted average of the intermediated funds from the last five quarters before the valuation date, assigning weight 1 to the final quarters and weight 2 to the middle quarters. The lower weighting assigned to the final quarters of the year enables us to mitigate the influence of distortions related to the typical seasonality of the data in December (Bank of Italy, 2010, appendix, methodological notes, table a17.7, p. 218); 'volume of intermediated funds' means volume of total assets.

Source: Bank of Italy (2010), appendix, methodological notes, table a17.7, p. 218.

Table 3.4 Sample composition by bank size and comparison with the banking system (number of banks, percentage on the total)

	Sample		Italian banking system		Sample		Italian banking system		Sample		Italian banking system	
	2006				2007				2008			
Major banks	9	1.82%	10	1.26%	7	1.42%	8	0.99%	7	1.42%	8	1.00%
Large banks	7	1.41%	13	1.64%	7	1.42%	12	1.49%	7	1.42%	12	1.50%
Medium banks	21	4.24%	39	4.92%	21	4.26%	39	4.84%	21	4.26%	36	4.50%
Small banks	85	17.17%	152	19.17%	85	17.24%	152	18.86%	85	17.24%	151	18.88%
Minor banks	373	75.35%	579	73.01%	373	75.66%	595	73.82%	373	75.66%	593	74.13%
	2009				2010							
Major banks	7	1.42%	8	1.01%	4	0.82%	5	0.66%				
Large banks	7	1.42%	12	1.52%	6	1.23%	11	1.45%				
Medium banks	21	4.26%	35	4.44%	21	4.31%	34	4.47%				
Small banks	85	17.24%	148	18.76%	84	17.25%	142	18.66%				
Minor banks	373	75.66%	586	74.27%	372	76.39%	569	74.77%				

Source: Own elaboration; data on the entire sample of banks collected from *ABI Bilanci Fast*; data on the Italian banking system collected from Bank of Italy (2006, 2007, 2008, 2009, 2010), appendix, glossary, banks.

the five years analyzed. In this way, the sample results homogeneous over time and, therefore, more significant for the purposes of the research. The sample has been divided into five size classes of banks – major, large, medium, small, minor – according to the classification designed by the Bank of Italy[3] following the criteria reported in Table 3.3, taking particular care to ensure that the incidence of the different classes of banks in terms of the number of intermediaries included in the sample will be as consistent as possible with respect to the system (Table 3.4). The variation in the number of banks in 2007 and 2010 are exclusively related to the mergers that involved some of the selected intermediaries of major, large, small and minor size. This led to an inevitable formal change in the composition sample size, but did not affect its homogeneity or its temporal significance in any way.[4]

Table 3.5 Reading path of bank financial statements – loans to customers

Information source		Financial statements items	Profiles of analysis
Balance sheet	Assets	▪ Loans to customers ▪ Total assets	Overall trend
Notes to the financial statements	Part B Balance sheet	▪ Current accounts loans ▪ Mortgages ▪ Consumer financing loans (1)	Product breakdown
	Part C Income statement	▪ Interest income on loans to customers ▪ Impairment losses on loans to customers	Income effects
	Part E Information on risks and relative hedging policies	▪ Loans to customers – non-performing loans (2) ▪ Loans to customers – bad debts ▪ Loans to customers – sub-standard loans ▪ Loans to customers – restructured exposures ▪ Loans to customers – past due exposures	Quality of credit exposures

Notes: (1) Credit card loans, personal loans and loans repaid by automatic deductions from wages.
(2) Non-performing loans = bad debts + sub-standard loans + restructured exposures + past due exposures.

Source: Own elaboration on the basis of the items from the financial statements and from the notes to the financial statements of banks (Bank of Italy, 2005).

The methodology adopted distinguishes this research from most of the other contributions on the subject, which are mainly focused on the use of econometrical models (Albertazzi and Marchetti, 2010; De Mitri, Gobbi and Sette, 2010; Del Giovane, Ginette and Nobili, 2011; Gambacorta and Mistrulli, 2011; Bonaccorsi di Patti and Sette, 2012).

In order to analyze in depth the trend of loans to customers in the years of the financial crisis, thus tracing the main differences by bank size and interpreting the possible underlying credit policies, the adoption of a descriptive business–economic analytical approach is useful. Even though econometrical models provide relevant information about the statistical significance of the determinant factors of a specific investigated phenomenon, they do not entirely enable us – in our view – to grasp and completely take into account the numerous individual specificities that can affect the empirical evidence. Only an accurate descriptive business–economic analysis could provide the detailed information necessary for a more complete interpretation.

This work analyses the evolution of loans to customers between 2006 and 2010 according to the reading path of bank financial statements proposed in Tutino (2009).[5]

In particular, attention is focused on items from the balance sheet and from the notes to the financial statements which permit the extraction of useful information in order to analyze the development of loans to customers from the point of view of: its evolution over time; the composition of loan portfolio by product breakdown; the quality of the credit exposures; and the main income effects (Table 3.5).

The analysis of the composition of the loan to customers portfolio by product breakdown (Section 5) focuses on current account loans, mortgages and consumer financing loans: banking products which, as a whole, represent more than 50 per cent of the total amount of loans to customers (Table 3.12). These three banking products being typical, an analysis of their evolution and their relative relevance in the loan to customers portfolio may allow significant considerations on some essential aspects of the lending policies adopted by banks in the period analyzed to emerge.

The analysis of the quality of credit exposures (Section 6) has been conducted by focusing not only on the non-performing loans – the first significant indicator of a deterioration in a credit portfolio – themselves, but also on the evolution and impact of their different components. In particular, by order of those decreasing in risk and increasing in solvency, the bad debts (indicators of the *current risk*, as they are exposures whose symptoms of insolvency have manifested and been confirmed over time) the sub-standard loans, the restructured exposures and the past due exposures – which are, instead, indicative of the *potential risk* at different degrees of intensity.[6]

The trend of the different financial statement items under investigation has been analyzed, both generally and by size of bank, either annually, or for the entire period under analysis. The purpose has been to point out short-term and long-term trends at the turn of the financial crisis started in 2007.

Special attention has been paid to 2009 – an iconic year, since it witnessed the main impacts of the financial crisis on the granting of loans to customers – and to 2010 – significant for the first main effects of the recovery strategies adopted by banks.

Furthermore, the analysis has been conducted using the balance sheet indicators shown in Table 3.6, useful for studying in greater depth the lending to customers activity by bank size in terms of composition of loan portfolio by product breakdown, quality of credit exposures and income effects.

Trend in loans to customers has been then analyzed, linking the heterogeneity shown by bank size back to the differences detectable in terms of the intermediation model (Section 8).

As pointed out by Tutino and Nicastro (2011), the main features of the business model of banks, despite their wealth and complexity, can be attributed to the following aspects of synthesis: *funding and investment markets; the composition of assets and liabilities*; *products and services*; *organizational structure*, including the quality of corporate governance; *management equilibriums* – profitability, liquidity, capitalization, risk – and relations of interdependence between them.

In this chapter, according to the approach adopted and to the data analyzed, we consider only the aspects related to the credit intermediation structure: funding and investment markets; composition of assets and liabilities. Thus it is possible to track the main features of the business model adopted by banks in terms of the credit intermediation structure, especially with reference to activities with customers. The indicators used are reported in Table 3.7.

The underlying idea is that by analyzing the assets and liabilities structure of the balance sheet, different specificities of the intermediation models can emerge according to size; specific characteristics of the business models, which the strategic management decisions and the lending policies adopted by banks lead back to.

Other significant and specific factors that can affect banks' lending policies to customers can be found in other aspects which characterize the bank business models, as outlined above. On some of these – in particular on the maintenance conditions of satisfactory management equilibriums – are based the researches cited in the literature review and their significant results (Section 2).

Table 3.6 Loans to customers – indicators of analysis

Indicators		Formulas		Interpretation
Assets composition		$CI^{assets}_{loans\ to\ customer\ j\ t} = \frac{Loans\ to\ customer_{j\ t}}{Total\ assets_{\ j\ t}}$	[3.1]	Indicator of the incidence of loans to customers on total assets.
Loan portfolio composition by product breakdown		$CI^{producr\ breakdown}_{i\ j\ t} = \frac{Type\ of\ product_{i\ j\ t}}{Loans\ to\ customers_{\ j\ t}}$	[3.2]	Indicator of the composition of the loan to customers portfolio by product breakdown.
Quality of credit exposures	Stock indicators	$I^{STOCK}_{d\ j\ t} = \frac{NPL_{d\ j\ t}}{Loans\ to\ Customers_{j\ t}}$	[3.3]	Indicators of the incidence of the non-performing loans on the total volume of loans to customers.
	Flow indicators	$I^{FLOW}_{d\ j\ t} = \frac{(NPL_{d\ j\ t} - NPL_{d\ j\ t\text{-}1})}{Performing\ loans\ to\ customers_{\ j\ t\text{-}1}}$	[3.4]	Indicators of the intensity of the deterioration over time of the credit exposures. Capturing changes in the different types of non-performing loans compared to the volume of performing loans enables us to measure the deterioration of the credit exposures in a more significant way than by using the simple percentage variation calculated on the volume of non-performing loans.

			[3.5]	As detailed information by bank size is not available, this indicator enables us to estimate the interest rates effectively charged by banks on loans to customers. Therefore, it enables us to obtain useful indicative information about the pricing policies adopted by banks. A similar approach has been adopted in Di Battista, Nieri and Patarnello (2010) and in Di Battista and Nieri (2011). However, as neither the cost of funding from customers nor the impairment losses on loans to customers is taken into account, it is not appropriate to analyze the profitability of the lending to customers activity as a whole.
Income effects	Gross interest return on loans to customers	$GIR_{\text{loans to customers } j\,t} = \frac{II_{\text{loans to customers } j\,t}}{\frac{\text{Loans to Customers}_{j\,t} - \text{Loans to customers}_{j\,t-1}}{2}}$		
	Net interest return on loans to customers	$NIR_{\text{loans to customers } j\,t} = \frac{II_{\text{loans to customers } j\,t}}{\frac{\text{Loans to Customers}_{j\,t} - \text{Loans to customers}_{j\,t-1}}{2}}$	[3.6]	Although the net interest return on the loans to customers indicator takes into account the cost of loan quality deterioration, it also assumes that credit quality deterioration and the consequent impairment losses do not occur in the year of the loan provided.

Notes: NPL = non-performing loans; II = interest income; IL = impairment losses; i = current account loans, mortgages, consumer financing loans; d = non-performing loans, bad debts, sub-standard loans, restructured exposures, past due exposures; j = major banks, large banks, medium banks, small banks, minor banks, total.

Source: Own elaboration on the basis of the items from the financial statements and from the notes to the financial statements of banks (Bank of Italy, 2005).

Table 3.7 Credit intermediation model – balance sheet and income statement indicators

Indicators	Formulas		Interpretation
Intermediation structure	$CI^{assets}_{a\,j\,t} = \frac{\text{Asset item}_{a\,j\,t}}{\text{Total assets}_{\,j\,t}}$	[3.7]	Intermediation structure from the assets side.
	$CI^{\text{liabilities and equity}}_{l\,j\,t} = \frac{\text{Liability item}_{l\,j\,t}}{\text{Total assete}_{\,j\,t}}$	[3.8]	Intermediation structure from the liabilities side.

Notes: a = financial assets, loans to banks, loans to customers; l = deposits from banks, deposits from customers, debt securities in issue, financial liabilities, equity; j = major banks, large banks, medium banks, small banks, minor banks, total.

Source: Own elaboration on the basis of the items from the financial statements and from the notes to the financial statements of banks (Bank of Italy, 2005).

4 Development in loans to customers by bank size

During the financial crisis started in 2007, lending to customers by the banks included in the sample analyzed showed a significant slowdown, beginning to grow more rapidly again only in 2010.

The data in Table 3.8 shows that the slowdown in lending to customers started in 2008, then increased sharply in 2009, when the effects of the financial crisis had manifested significantly. But then in 2010 loans to customers began to grow only slowly again, registering a growth rate almost similar to that in the findings for 2008.

The trend in loans to customers between 2006 and 2010 varied widely, according to bank size. In 2008, while loans provided by large banks slowed down significantly, credit provided by medium, small and minor banks registered less of a slowdown.[7] The heterogeneity shown in the trend in loans to customers by bank size became more profound by 2009. While customer loans provided by medium, large and major banks contracted, those provided by small and minor banks continued growing rapidly, although at a slower rate than in the previous year. In 2010, on the other hand, the major banks seem to have registered a far more rapid growth in customer loans than did the smaller intermediaries, partially recovering from the slowdown registered in the previous two years. In reality, even in a context of generalized growth – confirmed by the increase of 8.13 per cent registered by the loans to customers with regard to the entire sample of banks examined – it should be noted that there have been changes in the composition of the size groups.[8]

Table 3.8 Loans to customers by bank size (percentage rates of change)

	2007–2006	2008–2007	2009–2008	2010–2009	2010–2006
Major banks	7.50	9.83	–1.66	13.62	31.92
(Without MPS) (1)	5.92	–1.42	–5.02	17.88	16.91
(Without UC) (2)	5.14	22.66	–3.46	1.55	26.44
Large banks	8.49	2.23	–0.50	0.37	10.77
Medium banks	9.80	5.76	–1.14	3.96	19.35
Small banks	12.01	8.39	5.23	3.73	32.52
Minor banks	13.01	12.31	6.51	7.62	45.49
Total	9.18	8.08	0.32	8.13	28.01
(Without MPS) (1)	8.59	3.32	–0.80	9.10	21.43
(Without UC) (2)	8.71	11.97	0.00	2.98	25.34

Notes: (1) MPS = Banca Monte dei Paschi di Siena SpA; (2) UC = UniCredit SpA.

Source: Own elaboration on data from *ABI Bilanci Fast*.

Overall, the percentage rates of change registered during the entire period of time under analysis show that the best performing banks in terms of lending to customers during the financial crisis started in 2007 have been the minor banks, followed closely by the small ones.

This evidence, symbolic of the important role that smaller intermediaries played in supporting the financing of the real economy in the most difficult years of the financial crisis, leads us also to think about the qualitative problems – both current and prospective – that could arise from the credit expansion strategies that have already been put into place. For further information, please refer to the analysis of the quality of the credit exposures conducted in Section 6.

Furthermore, the fact that heterogeneity has shown up in the trend of loans to customers – albeit in a less evident way – in 2007 as well, leads us to extend the analysis and the related considerations away from an exclusive reference to the financial crisis started in 2007, focusing instead on the specificities that typically characterize banks of different size in terms of intermediation structure and on the related constraints that arise in terms of changes in the trend of credit to customers (Section 8).

The slowdown in the volume of loans to customers in 2008 and 2009 inevitably caused a slight reduction of their incidence on the total assets of banks in respect to the sample as a whole (Table 3.9). While the relevance of loans to customers provided by minor banks had been almost stable, the large banks registered a gradual increase; medium and small banks saw a slowdown in 2008, followed by a recovery in 2009; and major banks experienced a gradual reduction. In 2010, this ratio increased significantly, deviating by about 10 percentage points compared to 2008 and 2009 and the two previous years. This evidence might at first glance seem indicative of a revision of

Table 3.9 Loans to customers by bank size – assets composition indicators (percentage values)

	2006	2007	2008	2009	2010
Major banks	47.17	46.36	44.84	42.63	56.63
Large banks	56.70	63.91	65.66	67.64	73.85
Medium banks	68.78	68.36	67.76	71.16	73.88
Small banks	64.17	64.59	63.88	65.59	68.96
Minor banks	69.94	71.80	71.84	71.74	74.36
Total	55.36	55.80	54.65	54.07	64.09

Source: Own elaboration on data from *ABI Bilanci Fast*.

Table 3.10 Total assets by bank size (percentage rate of change)

	2007–2006	2008–2007	2009–2008	2010–2009	2010–2006
Major banks	9.37	13.56	3.43	–14.46	9.88
Large banks	–3.75	–0.50	–3.41	–8.07	–14.95
Medium banks	10.48	6.70	–5.86	0.13	11.11
Small banks	11.29	9.60	2.47	–1.33	23.32
Minor banks	10.09	12.24	6.65	3.84	36.85
Total	8.31	10.36	1.39	–8.77	10.57

Source: Own elaboration on data from *ABI Bilanci Fast*.

the lending policies and business strategies adopted by banks, towards an intermediation model more oriented on lending to customers. However, the impact on the composition ratios that also stems from the general reduction in the total assets should be taken into account (Table 3.10).[9]

5 Empirical evidence by product breakdown

The analysis of the trend of current account loans, mortgages and consumer financing loans enables us to highlight some fundamental characteristics of the lending strategies adopted by banks in terms of composition of loan portfolio by product breakdown and to think about the main changes occurring in the period analyzed.

The trend in loans to customers by product breakdown and the relative portfolio composition certainly reflect both the lending policies adopted by banks and the evolution of the demand by households and firms. As the analysis of the role played by demand factors in influencing the trend in loans to customers during the financial crisis is not one of the objectives of this research, in this chapter we focus only on the supply side aspects, to investigate the main characteristics of the lending policies underlying the composition of the loan to customers portfolio by product breakdown.

The data reported in Table 3.11 shows a significantly heterogeneous dynamic by product breakdown. In 2008 mortgages registered a relevant slowdown, while current account loans increased. In 2009 and 2010 mortgages grew rapidly, while current account loans contracted. Consumer financing loans, strongly contracted in 2008 and in 2009, grew more rapidly in 2010.

Overall, between 2006 and 2010 current account loans increased by 9.03 per cent; mortgages registered a growth of 41.17 per cent; and consumer financing loans a growth of 40.73 per cent. This phenomenon could reflect the adoption by banks of credit policies more prudently oriented to reduce the generally most risky and unpredictable components of the loans portfolio (typically the current account loans) by moving their own investment to more guaranteed types of loans (typically the mortgages). The rapid growth registered by mortgages and consumer financing loans (the types of product mainly, and typically, targeted at households) could also be indicative of increasing attention being paid by banks to household financing, and their preference for it. Similar considerations are expressed in Di Battista, Nieri e Patarnello (2010) and in Di Battista e Nieri (2011).

The development of current account loans, mortgages and consumer financing loans underwent different trajectories according to bank size. In the case of small and minor banks, current account loans registered a slight slowdown in 2008, contracting in 2009 and 2010. The loans provided by medium and major banks, which had grown in 2008 and contracted in 2009, began to grow again in 2010, although at a slower rate. However, in the case of larger banks, current account loans contracted progressively.

Overall, considering the entire period analyzed, while current account loans provided by major banks increased by 8.85 per cent and those provided by large banks contracted by 23.71 per cent, current account loans provided by small and minor banks registered an increase between 18 and 20 per cent.

Regarding mortgages: the slowdown registered in 2008 was more severe the more the bank size increased; the recovery registered in 2009, although widespread, was highly relevant in the case of minor banks; in 2010, while large, medium, small and minor banks registered a slowdown, major banks increased their volume further. According to Bank of Italy (2010, p. 205) major banks would have significantly increased mortgages to households with the twin aims of limiting asset riskiness and increasing availability of eligible assets as collateral in funding operations.

As for consumer financing loans, the decrease registered in 2008 and 2009 is mainly due to major and large banks, joined by small banks in 2008 and minor banks in 2009. Similarly, the growth registered in 2010 is mainly due to major banks, followed by minor and small banks. The relevant growth

Table 3.11 Loans to customers – product breakdown by bank size (percentage rates of change)

	2007–2006	2008–2007	2009–2008	2010–2009	2010–2006
	Current account loans				
Major banks	3.36	23.72	-16.78	2.29	8.85
Large banks	-5.12	-11.66	-2.62	-6.53	-23.71
Medium banks	7.39	9.30	-1.30	2.10	18.28
Small banks	12.05	11.08	-0.56	-2.62	20.52
Minor banks	13.09	11.70	-5.25	-1.20	18.25
Total	5.62	12.25	-7.83	-0.23	9.03
	Mortgages				
Major banks	2.94	-5.25	13.12	27.95	41.17
Large banks	9.33	-8.78	11.86	1.15	12.83
Medium banks	12.37	6.34	13.92	7.23	45.97
Small banks	12.91	8.04	11.30	6.58	44.71
Minor banks	14.15	13.76	15.83	8.93	63.84
Total	8.26	0.78	13.09	14.41	41.17
	Consumer financing loans				
Major banks	-6.76	-20.06	-16.42	178.39	73.43
Large banks	4.84	-32.41	-9.83	1.01	-35.46
Medium banks	41.82	-0.77	-0.28	-3.23	35.81
Small banks	6.60	-15.16	20.99	15.41	26.28
Minor banks	0.32	24.72	-4.94	30.25	54.91
Total	16.81	-8.41	-0.15	31.74	40.73

Source: Own elaboration on data from *ABI Bilanci Fast*.

registered by consumer financing loans provided by major banks was due to the incorporation in the holding UniCredit SpA of the subsidiary UniCredit Family Financing Bank SpA, a medium-sized intermediary – not included in the selected sample of banks – specializing in providing consumer financing loans. Even if a clearly heterogeneous trend by bank size does not emerge, the data relating to major, large and medium intermediaries shows a progressive dynamic of contraction, especially from 2008 – excluding, that the increase registered in 2010 by major banks and the slight recovery of large banks that same year. Small and minor banks seem to register, on the contrary, a significantly more intense dynamic, despite the slowdowns registered in 2008 and 2009. Overall, purposely not taking into account the data relating to major banks, between 2006 and 2010 consumer financing loans grew more rapidly in minor banks, followed by medium and small. Large banks, in contrast, registered an overall contraction of 35.46 per cent, due to the continuous contraction registered over time. The data relating to medium banks, however, is strongly conditioned by the particularly rapid growth in 2007, followed by contractions until 2010.

Table 3.12 Loans to customers – product breakdown by bank size – composition indicators (percentage values)

	2006	2007	2008	2009	2010
	Current account loans				
Major banks	13.40	12.88	14.51	12.28	11.05
Large banks	20.86	18.25	15.77	15.43	14.37
Medium banks	15.37	15.04	15.54	15.52	15.24
Small banks	20.67	20.68	21.19	20.03	18.80
Minor banks	26.30	26.32	26.18	23.29	21.38
Total	16.78	16.23	16.86	15.49	14.29
	Mortgages				
Major banks	40.49	38.77	33.45	38.47	43.33
Large banks	45.76	46.11	41.15	46.25	46.61
Medium banks	42.16	43.15	43.38	49.99	51.56
Small banks	48.08	48.47	48.31	51.10	52.50
Minor banks	51.80	52.33	53.00	57.64	58.34
Total	43.47	43.10	40.19	45.31	47.94
	Consumer financing loans				
Major banks	1.47	1.28	0.93	0.79	1.93
Large banks	1.21	1.17	0.77	0.70	0.71
Medium banks	4.96	6.40	6.00	6.06	5.64
Small banks	3.41	3.25	2.54	2.92	3.25
Minor banks	1.55	1.38	1.53	1.37	1.65
Total	2.44	2.61	2.21	2.20	2.68

Source: Own elaboration on data from *ABI Bilanci Fast*.

The dynamic that emerged generated a significant recomposition of the loans to customers portfolio, focusing more on the mortgages than on current account loans (Table 3.12). While the incidence of current account loans reduced – although only slightly – the ratio between volume of mortgages and total amount of loans to customers increased, from 43.47 per cent in 2006 to 47.94 per cent in 2010. As the intermediary size increases, so the incidence of current account loans and mortgages on the volume of total loans to customers reduces progressively. Basically, the relevance of the most typical and traditional banking lending types of product decreases, producing a focus more on the lending activity on different types of product (such as *repos, factoring, leasing*).

This size heterogeneity could also be indicative of the adoption of different business diversification strategies. The incidence of consumer financing loans – products which represent a limited part of the loan to customers portfolio – reduced slightly in 2008 and 2009, increasing again in 2010.[10] This type of product has a relatively greater role in the case of medium and small banks, followed closely by minor and major banks. The rapid growth of the consumer financing loans registered by major banks in 2010 inevitably caused a relevant increase in the incidence of this product, despite not exceeding the data relating to medium and small banks.

6. The quality of loans to customers exposures

The transmission of the financial turmoil to the entire economy, the uncertain economic outlook and the consequent difficulties in production and employment faced by firms and households inevitably affected the risk profile of borrowers, adversely affecting the quality of banks' credit exposures. While in 2007 the non-performing loans grew by only 3.60 per cent, in 2008, 2009 and 2010 they increased by 25.58 per cent, 60.42 per cent and 21.26 per cent respectively. In just four years, the volume of non-performing loans had more than doubled, growing by 153.10 per cent between 2006 and 2010 (Table 3.13).

The deterioration of exposures of credit to customers, although widespread, took different connotations according to bank size.[11] Overall, during the period analyzed, small intermediaries registered a much more rapid increase in non-performing loans, followed closely by intermediaries of major and medium size.

By separately analyzing the evolution of bad debts, sub-standard loans, restructured exposures and past due exposures, there emerges a significantly heterogeneous trend, in regard both to the different types of non-performing loans, and to bank size.[12]

The deterioration of the credit quality and the heterogeneity shown by bank size becomes increasingly more evident by looking at the stock and flow indicators shown in Table 3.14.

Between 2006 and 2010 the overall incidence of non-performing loans on the volume of loans to customers increased by about 3 percentage points, rising from 3.01 per cent in 2006 to 5.96 per cent in 2010. The ratio in question has a substantially growing trend the smaller the bank size, underlining a more rapid deterioration in the credit exposures for smaller banks with respect to the larger ones. Smaller intermediaries – which during the financial crisis had proved better performers in terms of lending to customers (Section 4) – might, in order not to endanger their customer relationship and strong local roots, have adopted less conservative lending policies, thus exposing themselves to greater current and prospective credit risks instead.

The incidence of bad debts and sub-standard loans on the total of credit exposures grew significantly, between 2006 and 2010 increasing from 1.25 per cent to 1.98 per cent and from 1.12 per cent to 2.62 per cent respectively. In particular, as the bank size increases, the incidence of non-performing and sub-standard loans (which represent the two most significant types of non-performing loans) decreases, thus clearly confirming the most rapid deterioration being registered by the credit exposures of smaller banks.[13]

Table 3.13 Loans to customers by bank size – non-performing loans (percentage rate of change)

	2007–2006	2008–2007	2009–2008	2010–2009	2010–2006
	Non-performing loans				
Major banks	–2.92	5.38	88.45	32.91	156.23
Large banks	11.63	10.30	73.32	8.46	131.49
Medium banks	9.48	60.61	26.35	12.20	149.25
Small banks	7.35	33.38	73.51	12.62	179.78
Minor banks	7.73	40.59	25.81	19.76	128.21
Total	3.60	25.58	60.42	21.26	153.10
	Bad debts				
Major banks	6.64	–28.40	39.02	61.78	71.72
Large banks	0.37	–24.52	52.32	36.81	57.89
Medium banks	12.91	11.44	40.08	30.76	130.48
Small banks	11.85	24.27	47.63	34.62	176.24
Minor banks	9.85	33.64	45.54	34.17	186.67
Total	8.11	–8.90	42.46	44.34	102.50
	Sub-standard loans				
Major banks	–3.95	48.23	87.91	25.84	236.65
Large banks	30.91	48.22	67.71	–7.46	201.12
Medium banks	5.89	145.25	3.03	6.26	184.28
Small banks	13.49	43.06	76.52	11.64	219.97
Minor banks	7.33	27.66	29.30	22.71	117.41
Total	5.96	61.19	52.10	15.38	199.72
	Restructured exposures				
Major banks	–14.00	49.00	327.04	40.44	668.43
Large banks	51.72	–10.23	401.90	79.57	1127.59
Medium banks	13.64	–4.89	193.46	98.09	528.28
Small banks	–36.69	14.02	296.72	87.60	437.28
Minor banks	78.26	36.59	12.50	103.17	456.52
Total	–5.38	27.54	303.14	55.08	654.47
	Past due exposures				
Major banks	–28.20	38.72	100.56	–7.22	85.32
Large banks	–5.71	4.66	37.64	–63.75	–50.77
Medium banks	6.82	29.84	65.43	–32.75	54.29
Small banks	–3.14	31.49	90.26	–24.30	83.43
Minor banks	9.44	18.34	63.80	–15.18	79.93
Total	–9.45	29.04	80.59	–21.17	66.34

Source: Own elaboration on data from *ABI Bilanci Fast*.

Table 3.14 Loans to customers by bank size – non-performing loans – stock indicators and flow indicators (percentage values)

		Stock indicators					Flow indicators				
		2006	2007	2008	2009	2010	2007–2006	2008–2007	2009–2008	2010–2009	2010–2006
		Non-performing loans									
	Major banks	2.98	2.69	2.58	4.95	5.79	-0.09	0.15	2.34	1.71	4.80
	Large banks	2.35	2.42	2.61	4.55	4.92	0.28	0.26	1.97	0.40	3.17
	Medium banks	2.84	2.84	4.31	5.50	5.94	0.28	1.77	1.19	0.71	4.37
	Small banks	3.10	2.97	3.66	6.03	6.55	0.24	1.02	2.79	0.81	5.75
	Minor banks	4.53	4.32	5.41	6.39	7.11	0.37	1.83	1.48	1.35	6.09
	Total	3.01	2.86	3.32	5.31	5.96	0.11	0.75	2.08	1.19	4.76
		Bad debts									
Current risk	Major banks	1.42	1.41	0.92	1.30	1.85	0.10	-0.41	0.37	0.84	1.05
	Large banks	1.04	0.97	0.71	1.09	1.49	0.00	-0.24	0.38	0.42	0.62
	Medium banks	1.24	1.28	1.34	1.90	2.39	0.16	0.15	0.56	0.62	1.67
	Small banks	1.01	1.01	1.16	1.63	2.11	0.12	0.25	0.57	0.60	1.84
	Minor banks	1.10	1.07	1.27	1.74	2.16	0.11	0.38	0.61	0.63	2.15
	Total	1.25	1.24	1.05	1.48	1.98	0.10	-0.11	0.46	0.69	1.32

		Sub-standard loans									
POTENTIAL RISK	Major banks	0.94	0.84	1.13	2.16	2.39	-0.04	0.41	1.02	0.59	2.28
	Large banks	0.84	1.01	1.46	2.46	2.27	0.26	0.50	1.02	-0.19	1.72
	Medium banks	1.02	0.98	2.28	2.38	2.43	0.06	1.47	0.07	0.16	1.94
	Small banks	1.25	1.27	1.67	2.80	3.02	0.17	0.56	1.33	0.35	2.84
	Minor banks	2.63	2.50	2.84	3.45	3.94	0.20	0.72	0.88	0.84	3.24
	Total	1.12	1.08	1.62	2.45	2.62	0.07	0.68	0.87	0.40	2.30
Restructured exposures											
	Major banks	0.17	0.13	0.18	0.79	0.98	-0.02	0.07	0.61	0.34	1.16
	Large banks	0.09	0.13	0.11	0.56	1.00	0.05	-0.01	0.46	0.47	1.05
	Medium banks	0.09	0.10	0.09	0.26	0.49	0.01	0.00	0.17	0.27	0.51
	Small banks	0.10	0.06	0.06	0.23	0.42	-0.04	0.01	0.19	0.22	0.47
	Minor banks	0.03	0.04	0.05	0.06	0.11	0.02	0.02	0.01	0.06	0.14
	Total	0.12	0.11	0.13	0.51	0.73	-0.01	0.03	0.40	0.30	0.83
Past due exposures											
	Major banks	0.41	0.27	0.34	0.70	0.57	-0.12	0.11	0.36	-0.05	0.36
	Large banks	0.36	0.31	0.32	0.44	0.16	-0.02	0.01	0.12	-0.29	-0.18
	Medium banks	0.48	0.47	0.58	0.96	0.62	0.03	0.14	0.39	-0.33	0.27
	Small banks	0.72	0.62	0.76	1.37	1.00	-0.02	0.20	0.71	-0.35	0.62
	Minor banks	0.73	0.71	0.74	1.14	0.90	0.07	0.14	0.50	-0.19	0.61
	Total	0.49	0.41	0.48	0.87	0.63	-0.05	0.12	0.40	-0.19	0.33

Source: Own elaboration on data from *ABI Bilanci Fast*.

Flow indicators show that with reference to the entire period analyzed it was the non-performing loans that increased the most as the bank size decreased. In particular, in the case of bad debts, sub-standard loans and past due exposures the more the bank size increases, the more each trend decreases; this is unlike restructured exposures.

Overall, the analysis of the quality of the credit exposures conducted in this section shows that smaller banks, which adopted more expansive lending policies during the financial crisis – continuing to lend to customers at relatively vigorous rates in a context of generalized slowing (Section 4) – registered a more rapid growth in both the volume of non-performing loans and their relative incidence, with particular intensity in the case of bad debts and sub-standard loans – the two types of non-performing loans which undoubtedly incorporate the highest risk. Therefore, the lending policies adopted may be destabilizing in the long term. Consequently, it is possible that in the coming years these banks will be forced to reduce their lending to customers in order to deal with the excessive risks taken during the financial crisis.

In fact, all other factors being equal, the deterioration of credit exposures leads to an inevitable negative impact on the credit supply, since it reduces profits and erodes bank capital.[14] Moreover, for banks perceived as more risky, it may be difficult to raise unsecured debt or equity funds to finance their lending activities or to meet capital requirements, thereby making the provision of credit more difficult and costly.

7 The main effects on income: interest income and impairment losses on loans to customers

The slowdown in the trend in loans to customers and the deterioration of the credit exposures inevitably contributed to affect bank income results.[15] On the one hand, the slowdown in the loan development – and, more important, the generalized decrease in the interest rates – caused a relevant impact on income through a contraction of the interest income from the credit activity with customers. On the other hand, the deterioration of the credit quality negatively affected the income statement through the increasing impairment losses on the credit exposures in portfolio.

As highlighted by the data reported in Table 3.15, the reduction of the interest income on loans to customers was particularly rapid in 2009 and continued, although more slowly, in 2010. Overall, between 2006 and 2010, the interest income on the volume of loans to customers registered a contraction of 21.27 per cent.

The decrease in interest income affected all the size categories of banks in our sample, although more dramatically in the case of minor banks. In 2009, the interest income of minor banks reduced by 70.64 per cent, while the other intermediaries registered contractions of between 39 and 60 per cent. In 2010, while the interest income of large and medium banks began to grow

Table 3.15 Interest income and impairment losses by bank size (percentage rates of change)

	2007–2006	2008–2007	2009–2008	2010–2009	2010–2006
	Interest income on loans to customers				
Major banks	10.98	37.86	–39.63	–10.28	–17.13
Large banks	23.67	13.51	–48.54	14.59	–17.22
Medium banks	24.99	21.79	–55.58	16.63	–21.13
Small banks	30.03	17.23	–39.78	–9.75	–17.15
Minor banks	30.82	22.11	–70.64	–9.17	–57.40
Total	19.66	26.99	–46.37	–3.40	–21.27
	Impairment losses on loans to customers				
Major banks	0.74	40.39	83.32	4.64	171.28
Large banks	36.98	79.81	4.92	–25.86	91.61
Medium banks	18.36	95.88	12.59	–8.26	139.47
Small banks	15.95	70.50	46.25	–15.62	143.97
Minor banks	56.47	53.62	30.15	8.77	240.29
Total	12.75	62.21	45.88	–3.69	156.97
	Interest income – impairment losses on loans to customers				
Major banks	12.07	37.61	–51.68	–15.83	–37.28
Large banks	22.59	7.54	–56.58	29.30	–25.99
Medium banks	25.66	14.73	–66.66	30.29	–37.37
Small banks	31.37	12.74	–50.74	–7.53	–32.53
Minor banks	29.36	19.93	–79.58	–19.32	–74.43
Total	20.33	23.80	–57.34	–3.29	–38.54

Source: Own elaboration on data from *ABI Bilanci Fast*.

again, in the case of minor – and major – banks, the reduction in interest income continued. Overall, between 2006 and 2010 the interest income on loans to customers of minor banks reduced by 57.40 per cent, while the other intermediaries registered contractions of between 17 and 20 per cent.

The fact that smaller banks – those that in the period analyzed registered the strongest growth in the volume of loans to customers (Section 4) – have had the most rapid contraction in the volume of interest income leads us to think about a possible greater incidence of the interest rate effect: the hypothesis that seems to pertain is that the most dynamic banks, in providing loans to customers during the financial crisis, may have more rapidly adopted pricing policies as a competitive strategy to capture maximum market share in a context of a relevant slowdown of the lending activity of larger banks. In this regard, Gambacorta and Mistrulli (2011) show that between the second quarter of 2008 and the first quarter of 2010 smaller banks, and those characterized by a business model more oriented to the lending activity, increased

Table 3.16 Gross and net interest return on loans to customers (percentage values)

	2007	2008	2009	2010	2007	2008	2009	2010
	Gross interest return				**Net interest return**			
Major banks	4.89	6.20	3.61	3.06	4.46	5.65	2.63	2.09
Large banks	4.77	5.15	2.63	3.01	4.38	4.48	1.93	2.49
Medium banks	5.27	5.96	2.59	2.98	4.49	4.75	1.54	1.97
Small banks	5.58	5.94	3.35	2.89	4.73	4.83	2.23	1.92
Minor banks	6.04	6.55	1.76	1.49	5.45	5.74	1.06	0.81
Total	5.15	6.02	3.10	2.88	4.58	5.20	2.13	1.97

Source: Own elaboration on data from *ABI Bilanci Fast*.

the spread on loans to customers less than other intermediaries, maybe in the hope of preserving their customer relationships.

At the same time, however, it should be considered that smaller banks may have not been able to correctly incorporate in the price charged on the loans they provided the credit risk they had effectively taken.

Analyzing the data relating to the gross interest return on loans to customers (Table 3.16) an evident turnaround emerges between 2008 and 2009. Between 2007 and 2008, the value of this indicator increased by one percentage point, from 5.15 per cent to 6.02 per cent. But between 2008 and 2009 it reduced by around 3 percentage points, and in 2010 it decreased to 2.88 per cent. The most rapid reduction is attributable to minor banks: they registered a decrease of around 5 percentage points, down to less than one third of the value registered in 2008. Furthermore, while until 2008 the gross average return on loans to customers would decrease as the bank size increased – excluding the data relating to the major banks in 2008 (6.20 per cent) – in 2009 this relationship was inverted, confirming the considerations previously expressed about the greater incidence of the interest rate effect on the interest income on the trend in loans to customers of minor banks. Similar considerations are expressed in Di Battista, Nieri and Patarnello (2010) and in Di Battista and Nieri (2011).

To consider the income effects due to credit quality, we analyzed the trend registered by the impairment losses on loans to customers. Table 3.15 shows that the strong deterioration of the credit exposures inevitably caused relevant impacts in terms of the growth of this negative income component: between 2006 and 2009 the impairment losses on loans to customers increased overall by 156.97 per cent. In particular, after having grown very strongly in 2008 and 2009, they registered a turnaround, decreasing slightly in 2010. Minor banks registered impairment losses on loans to customers growth of as much as 240.29 per cent between 2006 and 2010, deviating significantly from the average value relating to the other intermediaries. As already highlighted in

Section 6, a relevant deterioration in the credit quality and the concomitant significant increase in the related impairment losses, negatively affecting the total profitability – moreover already influenced by the decrease in the volume of interest income – correspond to the greater dynamism of smaller banks in providing loans to customers during the financial crisis. In connection with that, it needs to be highlighted that the differences between banks in terms of impairment losses on loans to customers could, in addition to the effective credit deterioration, also be due to balance sheet policies aimed to preserve the (already weak) total profitability.

Netting the volume of interest income with the impairment losses on the volume of loans to customers (Table 3.15) and calculating the net interest return on loans to customers (Table 3.16), the total income effect due to the qualitative and quantitative credit development during the financial crisis emerges even more prominently. Consistently to the earlier findings, income effects affected minor banks the most, both in 2009 and in the period 2006–2010 as a whole.

8 Loans to customers, credit supply and the intermediation model: considerations of relevant factors

The credit supply policies adopted by banks during the financial crisis were undoubtedly influenced by the specificities of the intermediation models of reference and by the related underlying management strategies.

Different vulnerabilities regarding the exogenous conditionings, and also different financial and capital constraints on the credit supply, correspond to different funding and lending policies, as well as to differentiated strategies relating to the assets and liabilities composition.

Therefore, the roots of the heterogeneity shown in the development of credit to customers by bank size could be linked, first of all, to the differences in the specific characteristics of the intermediation model adopted by banks and to the different resulting vulnerabilities. Moreover, it could be due to the lending opportunities which arise from the economic and financial conditions of the customers and from the competition with other banks.[16]

The data on balance sheet composition reported in Table 3.17 shows that the intermediation model adopted by the banks included in the sample selected is characterized by the prevalence of funding–lending credit intermediation with customers, although with significant differences by bank size. The main, and basically traditional, way of practising banking in Italy is therefore confirmed.

Between 2006 and 2009, more than 54 per cent of assets are represented by loans to customers, and more than 34 per cent of liabilities consists of deposits from customers. In 2010, the incidence of loans and customer deposits increased respectively by up to 64 per cent of assets and 40 per

Table 3.17 Intermediation structure – assets and liabilities (1) (percentage values)

		Assets					Liabilities					
		2006	2007	2008	2009	2010	2006	2007	2008	2009	2010	
		Loans to customers/total assets					Deposits from customers/total assets					Funding
Customers	Major banks	47.17	46.36	44.84	42.63	56.63	32.39	30.20	27.55	26.95	35.79	
	Large banks	56.70	63.91	65.66	67.64	73.85	33.56	37.83	36.63	40.73	39.04	
	Medium banks	68.78	68.36	67.76	71.16	73.88	41.77	40.06	41.78	45.13	45.84	
	Small banks	64.17	64.59	63.88	65.59	68.96	50.44	48.99	48.01	50.57	48.67	
	Minor banks	69.94	71.80	71.84	71.74	74.36	51.70	49.62	47.81	48.85	48.58	
	Total	55.36	55.80	54.65	54.07	64.09	37.57	36.33	34.66	35.48	40.55	
		Loans to banks/Total assets					Deposits from banks/Total assets					
Interbank	Major banks	32.08	31.04	33.03	33.54	15.87	25.96	25.16	29.39	28.77	18.57	
	Large banks	19.10	18.65	22.18	20.16	12.57	21.89	24.16	17.19	16.19	20.49	
	Medium banks	16.78	19.16	19.29	15.29	10.61	24.67	25.67	21.43	17.78	21.83	
	Small banks	15.37	15.24	19.11	17.41	13.31	13.91	15.11	15.43	14.49	17.59	
	Minor banks	7.23	7.55	8.76	8.37	6.48	2.91	3.28	3.00	2.92	5.00	
	Total	24.41	24.24	26.46	25.83	13.65	22.31	22.44	23.48	22.40	18.11	
							Debt securities in issue/Total assets					
	Major banks						25.12	25.24	25.32	27.05	26.15	
	Large banks						28.83	23.34	29.89	28.14	24.98	
	Medium banks						17.41	17.92	19.48	19.06	14.72	
	Small banks						18.57	18.62	20.70	19.96	18.85	
	Minor banks						23.12	26.20	30.94	31.65	30.30	
	Total						23.34	23.01	24.56	25.31	23.44	

		Financial assets/Total assets					Financial liabilities/Total assets					
Financial assets	Major banks	8.43	6.29	6.01	7.24	10.12	3.81	4.09	3.63	3.40	4.42	Financial liabilities
	Large banks	14.46	10.30	5.22	4.53	7.02	3.29	3.99	5.74	4.67	4.81	
	Medium banks	7.53	5.71	5.75	6.77	8.30	3.74	4.07	5.67	5.85	5.17	
	Small banks	14.16	14.24	10.46	10.63	11.22	3.79	4.07	3.79	2.86	2.73	
	Minor banks	18.36	16.51	15.31	15.90	15.20	7.70	6.41	4.63	3.49	3.33	
	Total	10.34	8.31	7.07	7.96	10.09	3.97	4.21	4.23	3.81	4.25	
							Equity/Total assets					
	Major banks						9.06	11.12	9.89	10.14	11.27	
	Large banks						7.95	6.27	5.89	6.43	7.05	
	Medium banks						8.04	7.95	7.72	8.70	8.86	
	Small banks						8.88	8.84	8.24	8.44	8.53	
	Minor banks						11.54	11.44	10.87	10.77	10.39	
	Total						8.89	9.81	9.01	9.41	10.03	Equity

Notes: (1) This table has been specifically designed in order to highlight the composition of assets and liabilities by operating sectors: customers, interbank, financial assets; funding, financial liabilities, equity.

Source: Own elaboration on data from *ABI Bilanci Fast*.

cent of liabilities. However, as already highlighted, the effects which resulted from the general contraction of total assets should also be considered.[17]

Loans to banks and deposits from banks, which between 2006 and 2009 represented more than the 24 per cent of assets and 22 per cent of liabilities, significantly reduced their relevance in 2010, to around 13 per cent of assets and 18 per cent of liabilities. Moreover, the data shows a significant turnaround in the trend compared to that of previous years, when banks invested more in the interbank market than the amount they raised. The instability of the interbank market and the issues related to liquidity management caused the banks to reduce their exposure to other intermediaries, due to a general crisis of confidence.[18]

Looking at the differences by bank size, the data seems to identify fundamental specificities of the intermediation model: the smaller the bank is, the more closely oriented to the funding-lending credit intermediation with customers activity it results. Between 2006 and 2010, the smaller the bank is, the greater the proportion of assets and liabilities represented by loans to customers and deposits from customers is, while the larger the bank is, the greater the proportion represented by loans and deposit on the interbank market is.[19]

The difficulties met in terms of funding affected banks in varying intensities during the financial crisis, and this has surely played a significant role in influencing their credit supply. The liquidity crisis and the operational difficulties which had characterized the wholesale interbank market in the most acute years of the financial crisis undoubtedly affected the business of larger intermediaries, whose financing significantly depends on this funding channel.[20] On the other hand, smaller banks, which typically mainly draw on retail customers for their funds, have been able to support their lending activity thanks to a source of funds that has been less affected by the consequences of the international financial turmoil.[21]

A positive relationship seems to exist between the more or less traditional characteristics of the business model adopted and the dynamism in the lending to customers. Larger banks, generally characterized by business models less traditionally oriented to credit intermediation with customers, registered the greatest slowdown in lending to customers during the crisis (Section 4). Smaller banks, on the other hand, characterized by business models more traditionally focused on credit intermediation with customers, registered a slower slowdown. As the incidence of credit intermediation activity increases relative to the other operating areas (financial and securities intermediation, provision of services, interbank intermediation), so does the availability of credit in times of crisis and the interest of banks in providing such credit – with the likely intent of preserving its own core business – in the hope of maintaining its relationship with its customers unchanged. Similar considerations are outlined in Di Battista, Nieri and Patarnello (2010) and in Di Battista and Nieri (2011).

9 Conclusions

The analysis conducted in this chapter enables us to highlight the effects of the financial crisis started in 2007 on the lending activity of Italian banks by intermediary size, showing significant and sometimes relevant heterogeneities in terms of overall trend, composition of loan portfolio by product breakdown, quality of credit exposures and income effects.

The slowdown in the loans to customers registered during the financial crisis started in 2007, although widespread, turned out to be relatively more rapid in the case of major banks, whereas small and minor banks were significantly more dynamic in providing loans. Although widespread, the deterioration in the credit quality affected the smaller banks the most, showing how the policies of credit expansion adopted during the financial crisis could actually be disadvantageous in terms of quality. The contraction in the volume of interest income and the reduction in the interest return on loans to customers interested smaller banks the most. Similarly, the generalized increase in the loan to customers impairment losses turned out to be greatly significant in the case of minor banks, confirming again that the greater dynamism in providing loans to customers during the financial crisis corresponded with a relevant deterioration of the quality of loans.

Overall, the research conducted has revealed significant heterogeneities by bank size relating to the different profiles of analysis investigated, and highlighting how the size factor represents a significant aspect in explaining the trend in loans to customers in the Italian banking system during the financial crisis. Size, however, cannot be considered as a determinant factor in itself; what is really important are the management and strategic policies that characterize banks, also depending on the size, and which determine and affect their specificity.

Banks of different sizes feature significant differences in terms of assets and liabilities structure. From these aspects derive – simultaneously – constraints and opportunities for the management and operational choices of banks. The reasons for the heterogeneity shown in the trend in loans to customers by bank size could – and must – be investigated; therefore, in the different specificities found in the intermediation model adopted by banks and in the different resulting vulnerabilities.

Looking at the differences in the credit development during the financial crisis by bank size helps us find the fundamental reasons for the different underlying lending policies adopted by banks – reasons which can be attributed to the constraints and conditions caused by the strategic business choices in terms of assets composition, funding composition, reliance on the interbank market, financial structure and liquidity management. The crisis showed that these aspects affect the extent of banks' exposure to exogenous turbulences and that they may represent, therefore, important constraints on the development of credit.

All in all, the results of this analysis provide useful information about the financial crisis started in 2007, as well as important elements on which to base the evaluation of business strategies and lending policies which could be adopted by banks in the future.

Notes

1. The *Bank Lending Survey* is conducted quarterly by the Bank of Italy on behalf of the Eurosystem on a sample of the eight major Italian banking groups, representing 60% of the whole system by volume of loans. It provides qualitative information on any changes to the criteria of lending to customers and to the credit demand conditions, and on the main factors which affect their evolution. For further information on the survey, refer to Berg et al. (2005) and European Central Bank (2003).
2. The database ABI Bilanci Fast, managed by the Italian Banking Association, includes data from the individual and consolidated financial statements of almost all banks and banking groups of the Italian banking system, except data related to branches of foreign banks and cooperative banks not belonging to Federcasse (Italian Federation of Cooperative Banks).
3. For further information, see Bank of Italy (2010), appendix, methodological notes, table a17.7, p. 218. For a detailed list of the banks included in the different size groups see Bank of Italy (2006, 2007, 2008, 2009, 2010), appendix, glossary, banks.
4. In detail: the reduction in the number of major banks in 2007 to seven was due to the merger between Unicredito Italiano SpA and Capitalia SpA and between Banca Intesa SpA and Sanpaolo IMI SpA; the reduction in the number of major banks in 2010 to four was due to the merger by incorporation in the holding UniCredit SpA of the subsidiaries UniCredit Banca SpA, UniCredit Banca di Roma SpA and UniCredit Corporate Banking SpA; the reduction in the number of large banks in 2010 to six was due to the merger by incorporation in the holding UniCredit SpA of the subsidiary Banco di Sicilia SpA; the reduction in the number of small banks in 2010 to 84 was due to the merger by incorporation in the holding UniCredit SpA of the subsidiary UniCredit Private Banking SpA; the reduction in the number of minor banks in 2010 to 372 was due to the merger between Banca Monteriggioni Credito Cooperativo Società Cooperativa and Banca di Credito Cooperativo del Chianti Fiorentino Società Cooperativa.
5. Chapter 8, 49–53.
6. Restructured loans are a consolidated risk in terms of agreement between the parties. For more in-depth information about the analytical approach adopted for the study of the quality of credit exposures, see Tutino, Bastianini and Parascandolo (2005), Chapter 12, 283–315.

7. With regard to the major banks, the growth rate registered in 2008 was higher by approximately 2 percentage points than that registered in 2007, and was strongly influenced by the growth of the volume in loans to customers provided by one of the main Italian banking intermediaries included in the size group of major banks. In particular, after the merger by incorporation of the subsidiaries Banca Agricola Mantovana SpA and Banca Antonveneta SpA in the holding Banca Monte dei Paschi di Siena SpA, the volume of loans to customers attributable to the latter increased by 93.31 per cent. Therefore, excluding Banca Monte dei Paschi di Siena SpA from the sample would result in a contraction of loans to customers provided by major banks as early as 2008. As Banca Agricola Mantovana SpA and Banca Antonveneta SpA are not included in the sample analyzed, data relating to the other size classes are not affected in any way by these merger operations.
8. In fact, while interpreting data on 2010, it is necessary to consider the effects in terms of increase of the loans to customers volume provided by major banks related to the merger by incorporation in the holding UniCredit SpA of the subsidiaries Banco di Sicilia SpA and UniCredit Family Financing Bank SpA. This merger operation involved also the subsidiaries UniCredit Banca SpA, UniCredit Banca di Roma SpA and UniCredit Corporate Banking SpA, but these banks were already included among the major banks. Their incorporation in the holding does not introduce, therefore, any distortion in the data related to the size group of reference. The operation, furthermore, involved the subsidiary UniCredit Private Banking SpA, whose incorporation, as it does not provide loans to customers, did not affect the volume of loans to customers. By excluding UniCredit SpA from the sample, indeed, a less rapid growth of loans to customers provided by major banks and an heterogeneity by size similar to the previous years would emerge. Moreover, as Banco di Sicilia SpA and UniCredit Private Banking SpA were included in the analyzed sample until 2009 –among large banks and small banks respectively –the data referring to these two size classes should also be interpreted taking this modification into account.
9. In fact, considering that in 2010 the volume of total assets declined significantly (Table 3.10), the relevant increase registered in the incidence of loans to customers on the total assets should also be linked, in addition to the increase of the volume of loans, to the reduction of other assets. Similarly, in 2010 the ratio between loans and total assets underwent a rapid increase in the case of major and large banks, which could have been influenced by the strong contraction registered by the volume of total assets relating to the two size classes (Table 3.10). In particular, the reduction of over 14 per cent by major banks is due to the contraction of the volume of total assets of Banca Nazionale del Lavoro SpA and of Intesa Sanpaolo SpA, as well as to the effects relating the merger by incorporation in the holding UniCredit SpA of the subsidiaries UniCredit Banca SpA, UniCredit Banca Di Roma SpA and UniCredit Corporate Banking SpA, which until 2009 had been included in the major bank class. The reduction of around 8 per cent registered by large banks is due to the contraction of the volume of total assets of Dexia Crediop SpA, Banca Popolare di Verona S. Geminiano e S. Prospero SpA and Banca Popolare di Bergamo SpA, as well as to the removal of Banco di Sicilia SpA from the large banks class after its incorporation into the holding UniCredit SpA.
10. The decreasing dynamic registered in 2008 and 2009 could be due to reduced interest by banks in financing households in a period characterized by employment difficulties.

11. In 2008 non-performing loans grew more intensively in medium, small and minor banks. In 2009 the credit deterioration continued at a more rapid rate in major, large and small banks, while continuing to have a significant impact in medium and minor banks. Although at lower rate than the previous year, in 2010 the deterioration in exposure of loans to customers mainly affected the major banks.
12. Bad debts, which had grown rapidly in 2009 and 2010, registered a more rapid increase the more the intermediaries size decreased, between 2006 and 2010. Large and major banks registered a growth rate of bad debts higher than the other categories of banks only in 2010. Sub-standard loans, that had increased in a relevant way in 2008 and 2009, registered an overall stronger trend in the case of major banks, closely followed by the small ones. Restructured exposures, which had grown rapidly in 2009, registered an overall increasing trend as bank size increased. Past due exposures, which had grown progressively until 2009, contracted in 2010. Overall they registered both a much less rapid growth than the other types of non-performing loans and a substantially homogeneous intensity between the different bank size groups, although lower in the case of large and medium banks.
13. The incidence of restructured exposures, grown from 0.12 per cent in 2006 to 0.73 per cent in 2010, results instead in an increase as the bank size increases. Larger banks, which can more easily maintain long-lasting relationships with large customers, may be relatively more active – compared to smaller banks – in relevant debt restructuring operations. However, the incidence of past due exposures, which increased until 2008, declined during 2010, with a greater impact in the case of smaller banks.
14. For more information, refer to Altunbas, Gambacorta and Marqués-Ibáñez (2010).
15. For further information about the evolution of the Italian banks' profitability between 2006 and 2010 and on the relating improvement prospective strategies refer to Tutino and Nicastro (2011).
16. The trend of loans to customers reflects both the evolution of the credit demand by households and firms and the supply policies adopted by banks during the financial crisis. The analysis of the role taken by the demand factors in influencing the trend of credit to customers during the financial crisis is not one of the objectives of this research. For further information about that, please refer to the studies conducted by Panetta and Signoretti (2010) and Del Giovane, Ginette and Nobili (2011), whose results have already been briefly summarized in the literature review (Section 2). In this chapter, we are looking at the relationship between the trend of loans to customers and the features of the supply policies adopted by banks.
17. See Table 4.3 and – relating to the credit to customers – the considerations presented in Section 4.
18. See La Ganga and Vento (2012).
19. As for the other items: the financial assets, whose relative importance in the balance sheet slightly fell between 2007 and 2009, represent a minority part of the assets, more relevant in the case of small and minor banks; debt securities in issue represent more than 23 per cent of liabilities and on average, registering a relative higher incidence in the case of minor, major and large banks; the relevance of financial liabilities, particularly limited in respect to the entire period analyzed, does not show evident differences by bank size; the equity, whose share on the

total assets gradually increased between 2006 and 2010, slightly slowing down in 2008 and 2009, represents a larger share of liabilities in major and minor banks.
20. Refer to Mieli (2010) and Bonaccorsi di Patti and Sette (2012).
21. 'Banks which during the financial crisis supported the development in loans to customers with a greater intensity are also those generally characterized by a net positive position on the interbank market, a higher incidence of deposits from retail customers on total assets and a higher growth rate of this component of the liabilities.' (Di Battista, Nieri and Patarnello, 2010). 'Banks with a consistent and robust credit intermediation basis and less dependent on wholesale funding have been less affected by the crisis.' (Mottura, 2011).

References

Albertazzi, U. and D. J . Marchetti (2010) 'Credit supply, flight to quality and evergreen: an analysis of bank-firm relationships after Lehman', *Bank of Italy Working Papers*, 756/April.

Altunbas, Y., L. Gambacorta and D. Marqués-Ibáñez (2010) 'Bank risk and monetary policy', *Journal of Financial Stability*, 6, 121–9.

Bank of Italy (2010) *Annual Report.*

Bank of Italy (2009) *Annual Report.*

Bank of Italy (2008) *Annual Report.*

Bank of Italy (2007) *Annual Report.*

Bank of Italy (2006) *Annual Report.*

Bank of Italy (2005) *Il bilancio bancario: schemi e regole di compilazione*, Circular 262 of 22 December 2005, 1° update of 18 November 2009.

Berg, J., A. Van Rixtel, A. Ferrando, G. De Bondt and S. Scopel (2005) 'The bank lending survey for the euro area', *European Central Bank Occasional Paper Series*, 23/February.

Bonaccorsi di Patti, E. and E. Sette (2012) 'Bank balance sheets and the transmission of financial shocks to borrowers: evidence from the 2007–2008 crisis', *Bank of Italy Working Papers*, 848/January.

Del Giovane, P., E. Ginette and A. Nobili (2011) 'Disentangling demand and supply in credit developments: a survey-based analysis for Italy', *Journal of Banking & Finance*, 35, 2719–32.

De Mitri, S., G. Giorgio and E. Sette (2010) 'Relationship lending in a financial turmoil', *Bank of Italy Working Papers*, 772/September.

Di Battista, M.L. and L. Neri (2011) 'Lending policies in Italian banks during the financial crisis', *Bancaria*, 3, 11–19.

Di Battista, M.L., L. Neri and A. Patarnello (2010) 'Gli effetti della crisi sull'offerta di credito da parte delle banche', *ASSBB Osservatorio Monetario*, 1, 42–56.

European Central Bank (2003) 'A bank lending survey for the euro area', *European Central Bank Monthly Bulletin*, April, 65–75.

Gambacorta, L. and P.E. Mistrulli (2011) 'Bank heterogeneity and interest rate setting: what lessons have we learned since Lehman Brothers?' *Bank of Italy Working Papers*, 829/October.

La Ganga, P. and G. Vento (2012) 'Il mercato interbancario', in F. Tutino (ed.) *La gestione della liquidità nella Banca* (Bologna: Il Mulino), pp. 321–364.

Mieli, S. (2010) 'To grant credit in the crisis era', *Bancaria*, 3, 11–17.

Mottura, P. (2011) 'Cooperative banking after the crisis: the necessity of a reform', *Bancaria*, 12, 2–25.

Panetta, F. and F.M. Signoretti (2010) 'Domanda e offerta di credito in Italia durante la crisi finanziaria', *Bank of Italy Occasional Papers*, April, 63.

Tutino, F. (2009) *Il bilancio delle banche. Introduzione alla lettura* (Roma: Bancaria Editrice).

Tutino, F., G. Bastianini and M. Parascandolo (2005) *La performance delle banche. Flussi informativi, analisi di gestione, valutazione* (Roma: Bancaria Editrice).

Tutino, F. and R. Nicastro (2011) 'Italian banks' profitability: improvement strategies, business models, constraints', *Bancaria*, 9, 1–18.

4

Credit Supply and the Rise in Sovereign Debt Risk in the Eurozone

Pierluigi Morelli, Giovanni B. Pittaluga and Elena Seghezza

1 Introduction

Since the financial crisis of 2007–2008, much has been written about the consequences of the fragility of the banking systems of several countries, as that fragility affects these countries' deficit and debt and the resulting crisis. The need to save the banking system from a severe insolvency crisis has prompted the governments of many countries to support their economies by implementing expansionary fiscal policies, with the state taking on the losses of banks in difficulty. In many cases this has resulted in a significant increase in public deficits and debts.

Representative of this are the cases of United States and United Kingdom, whose public debt rose from 69.6 to 102.9 per cent of GDP, and from 54.8 to 86.0 per cent respectively, between 2008 and 2011.

The euro crisis has highlighted a further connection between public debt default and the stability of the banking system. Since the spring of 2010, uncertainty about the sustainability of public debt in Portugal, Italy, Greece and Spain (the so-called PIGS countries) has generated doubts about banks' soundness.

Most of the existing theoretical literature on how sovereign default affects a country's economy pays no attention to the repercussions of public debt default on the stability of banks and their behavior. It assumes, in fact, that governments can shield the financial system from the effects of sovereign debt default either (a) through a selective default at the expense of foreign holders of government bonds or (b) through bailouts of banks hit by heavy losses resulting from the default. Several objections have been made to these contributions. Some scholars (Broner et al., 2010; Brutti, 2011) have observed that it is difficult to identify the foreign bondholders and, therefore, pursue a selective default. Others (Gennaioli et al., 2012) have pointed out that, in case of default, a country is unlikely to be able to save banks hit by heavy losses in government bonds. Two further observations can be added. Firstly, it is important to take into account not only the effects of actual sovereign debt default, but also the consequences of default expectations, that is, of a rise in sovereign credit risk. Secondly, government securities play a special part for banks in funding management. On the one hand, government bonds represent a form of liquidity for banks, both in the sense that the market for these securities is large and deep and because banks have tended to used them as collateral to secure financing on the interbank market or from the central bank. On the other hand, the rating on sovereign debt is a signal of the creditworthiness not only of the country itself, but also of its banks. Indeed, that rating measures the depth of guarantee that a state can provide to potential foreign lenders as to the degree of solvency of domestic banks.

Accordingly, the main objective of this chapter is to ascertain whether or not a rise in the risk on government securities affects a bank's propensity to grant loans, and, if so, whether this effect is greater than that due to a rise in other types of financial asset riskiness. In line with this objective, empirical tests were designed to verify whether, and to what extent, the Eurozone sovereign debt crisis has resulted in a credit crunch.

Section 2 is devoted to a survey of the literature on the effects of sovereign debt default on the banking system. In Section 3 we present a version of the Bernanke and Blinder (1988) model, where the rise in sovereign debt risk affects the conditions of banks' funding. As shown in Section 4, the conclusions of the model match the effects of the deterioration of some Eurozone countries' worthiness on the riskiness and balance sheets of these countries' banking firms. Section 5 gives an illustration of an empirical test aimed at ascertaining whether the recent rise in the risk of some Eurozone countries has caused a credit crunch. In the Conclusions, we suggest some policy implications.

2 Literature review

Until recently, cases of sovereign default were related solely to developing countries and emerging countries, that is, countries heavily indebted on foreign financial markets. Default costs were mainly attributed to two factors (Eaton and Gersovitz, 1981): repudiation costs and the explicit sanctions resulting from sovereign defaults. With regard to the latter point, it is assumed that the insolvent country, having suffered a loss of reputation, must pay a higher interest rate when seeking further credit from abroad, However, applying this penalty requires a high degree of coordination between potential creditors, and such coordination becomes less likely as more credit markets become competitive, that is, there is a higher number of potential creditors (Wright, 2005). This and other considerations have led several scholars to focus on the role of direct sanctions (Bulow and Rogoff, 1989 and De Paoli et al., 2006). Sanctions imposed on a defaulting country can take many forms, such as trade embargoes and exclusion from access to international markets (Sturzenegger and Zettelmeyer, 2005). Historical experience shows, however, that recourse to direct sanctions has been infrequent (Sturzenegger and Zettelmeyer, 2006); in the most recent empirical studies, there has been consistent evidence of costs to reputation being greater than the costs of sanctions (Tomz, 2007). At the end of the first decade of the 21st century, in view of the looming possibility of sovereign defaults in developed countries, an increasing number of scholars have focused on the effects of these defaults on the domestic economy. The empirical contributions have identified two regularities (Reinhart, 2010):

1. Sovereign defaults and banking crises tend to happen together;
2. Sovereign debt crises are costly in terms of credit and output.

In point (1), we refer to the results given by Reinhart (2009). It appears that after 1970, 70 of the 82 cases of banking crises found in the sample were accompanied by a sovereign default crisis.

Several explanations have been given for point (1). Livshits and Schoors (2011) showed that the governments of highly indebted countries may choose not to adopt prudential regulation, inducing banks to buy government bonds at lower prices than would otherwise occur. Bolton and Jeanne (2011) show that sovereign defaults aggravate the fragility of the banking system due to the processes of contagion that characterize highly integrated economies. In negatively influencing the stability of the banking system, sovereign defaults eventually affect both the credit market and output adversely, as well.

Theoretical contributions have shown that the costs of sovereign default in terms of lost output are greater in countries with more developed financial systems than those in other countries. This is probably mainly due to the disruptive effects of a sovereign default on banks (Gennaioli et al., 2012).

A growing number of empirical studies focus on the effects of sovereign default on the bank credit market and on output (point 2). On this aspect, Borensztein and Panizza (2009) conducted an econometric analysis on 149 countries for the period 1975–2000, adopting the methodology of Rajan and Zingales (1998) and its subsequent application by Dell'Arriccia et al. (2005); they identified 111 banking crises and 85 instances of sovereign debt default. On the basis of this data, they came to the conclusion that in the case of sovereign debt default the probability of a banking crisis increases by a factor of 5. Nevertheless, the results of this test do not support the hypothesis that sovereign defaults cause a credit crunch in the banking sector.

Furceri and Zdzienicka (2011) reached different results. By conducting an analysis on 154 countries for the period from 1970 to 2008, they found that sovereign default has pronounced negative effects on bank lending. Similar results have been obtained by Sandleris (2012) with reference to the cases of sovereign default between 1980 and 2000. Meanwhile, limiting their analysis to the credit granted by non-residents, Arteta and Hale (2008) find evidence that at times of sovereign debt crisis this form of financing to firms in emerging markets shrank significantly. This not only has a negative effect on the level of production, but also damages the GDP growth rates of these economies and makes it more likely that there will be subsequent debt crises.

The various empirical contributions on the links between sovereign default and the bank credit market, even those that confirm the hypothesis that defaults cause a credit crunch, consider as sovereign debt crises situations in which the state restructures its debt and does not repay its creditors entirely. In this way these contributions portray only the ex-post debt crisis and their effects, but fail to depict the effects of a pronounced and persistent rise in sovereign debt risk, such as that which characterized some of the Eurozone countries from spring 2010.

This chapter refers to the effects on credit supply of an increase in the probability of default instead of actual sovereign default. These effects can be evidenced by the model presented in the next section.

3 The model

In order to clarify how a rise in public debt risk can cause a credit crunch, we use a modified version of Bernanke and Blinder's model (1988). In particular, we add two hypotheses to the traditional Bernanke and Blinder model:

- There is a default risk with regard to government securities. This risk, indicated by σ, affects the structure of the financial portfolio of banks and of the private sector;
- The liabilities of banks consist of both deposits and refinancing by the central bank. Refinancing is a function of the market value of the securities given as collateral, $RIF = RIF(\sigma)$; the higher the default risk on government securities, the lower their market value and the amount of refinancing.

We start by considering the market for bank loans. The demand for loans depends on the rate of interest on loans:

$$L^d = L(r_L) \tag{4.1}$$

where L^{d} is the demand for loans, and r_{L} is the interest rate on loans. The supply of loans L^{S}can be determined as a residual, given the liabilities and assets of banks. The latter, apart from loans, take the form of long-term government securities, $\overline{B}_{t-1}^{LT}$; short-term government securities, B_t^{ST}; required reserves, *ROB*; and excess reserves, *RL*. We assume long-term government securities as exogenous because they were bought in previous periods; their value is considered at purchase price and is therefore given. On the liability side we have deposits, D_{t} and the refinancing by the central bank, RIF_{t}. Thus the balance sheet constraint of the bank can be expressed in this way:

$$\overline{B}^{LT}_{t-1} + B_t^{ST} + L_t^s + ROB_t + RL_t = D_t + RIF_t \tag{4.2}$$

The demand for Treasury bills by the bank depends positively on their interest rate, r_B, and negatively on the interest rate on loans, rL, and on the risk on sovereign debt. Required reserves are a share, τ, of deposits, while excess reserves depend negatively on the interest rate on short-term government securities and positively on the risk of sovereign debt, σ.[1] The demand for deposits, $D(r_B, \sigma, \overline{y})$, depends negatively on the interest rate on Treasury bills and public debt risk, and positively on income. The amount of central bank refinancing, RIF (σ), is a function of the value of bank collaterals, in particular of the value of government securities. The supply of credit is therefore:

$$L_t^s + (1-\tau)D_t + RIF(\sigma) - q(r_B, \sigma)D - B_t^{ST}(r_B, r_L) - \overline{B}^{LT}_{t-1} \tag{4.3}$$

The credit market is in equilibrium when supply and demand are equal. Analogously, the money market is in equilibrium when M^D $M^{\wedge S}$.

The demand for money base is given by $CIRC + ROB + RL$. We assume currency, CIRC, is proportional to the amount of deposits and that it is a positive function of the risk on sovereign debt, $CIRC = c(\sigma)D$, and that excess reserves are equal to $q(rB,\sigma)D$. The demand for money, therefore, is $M^d = c(\sigma)D + D$. The supply of money is equal to the refinancing of banks by the central bank multiplied by the money multiplier, that is, by $\dfrac{1+c(\sigma)}{c(\sigma)+\tau+q(r_B,\sigma)}$.

The money market is in equilibrium when the demand for and the supply of money are equal, that is, when deposits are equal to:

$$D = \frac{RIF(\sigma)}{[c(\sigma)+\tau+q(r_B,\sigma]} \tag{4.4}$$

Replacing the value of deposits established above in the supply of loans function, we get the equilibrium condition for the loans market:

$$L_t^d(r_L,) = (1 - \tau - q(r_B,\sigma)) \frac{RIF(\sigma)}{[c(\sigma) + \tau + q(r_{B,\sigma})]} + RIF(\sigma) - B_t^{ST}(r_B, r_L) \text{ - } \tag{4.5}$$

The effects on the credit market of a rise in the risk of sovereign debt are the following:

$$\frac{\partial r_L}{\partial \sigma} = \frac{\dfrac{RIF}{[c+\tau+q]^{q_\sigma}} + \dfrac{(1-\tau-q)}{[c+\tau+q]^2}[(c+\tau+q)RIF_\sigma - RIF(c_\sigma - q_\sigma)] + RIF_\sigma}{L^d_{r_L} + B^{ST}_{r_L}} > 0 \tag{4.6}$$

That is to say, an increase in government debt risk determines an increase in the interest rate on loans. This is due to the fact that when σ rises, the amounts of excess reserves and currency increase and the level of refinancing by the central bank decreases. Of course, the increase in the rate of interest on loans reduces the equilibrium level of loans:

$$\frac{\partial L^s}{\partial \sigma} = \frac{\partial L^d}{\partial r_L}\frac{\partial r_L}{\partial \sigma} < 0 \tag{4.7}$$

The central bank can counter the fall in the amount of loans supplied in several ways. Firstly, it can affect the money multiplier by reducing the rate of reserve requirement, thus increasing the money multiplier:

$$\frac{\partial r_L}{\delta \tau} = \frac{\frac{(1+c)}{(c+\tau+q)^2} RIF}{L^d_{r_L} + B^{ST}_{r_L}} > 0 \tag{4.8}$$

Secondly, it can change its refinancing rules. In particular, it can evaluate the securities given by banks as collateral, not at their market price but at the book price. This is equivalent to assuming that the refinancing does not depend on the risk of sovereign debt:

$$\frac{\partial r_L}{\partial \sigma} = \frac{-\frac{RIF}{[c+\tau+q]^{q_\sigma}} + \frac{(1-\tau-q)}{[c+\tau+q]^2}[-RIF(c_\sigma + q_\sigma)]}{L^d_{r_L} + B^{ST}_{r_L}} > 0 \tag{4.9}$$

Thirdly, if refinancing is less than its threshold, the central bank can expand its amount by injecting liquidity into the system.

This model has shown that an increase in sovereign debt risk affects the bank funding conditions, and has also shown what the central bank can do to counter any credit crunch that may arise. In the next section we compare the conclusions of the model, in particular the negative effect of the rise in sovereign debt risk on bank funding conditions, against the experience of some Eurozone countries. This comparison is important in order to establish whether or not the data is consistent with the topic of this chapter, which is that an increase in sovereign debt risk in Europe is one of the causes of the fall in the credit supply.

4 The rise in sovereign debt risk and the banking system

Since the spring of 2010, the spread between interest rates on government securities with the same maturity in different Eurozone countries and the

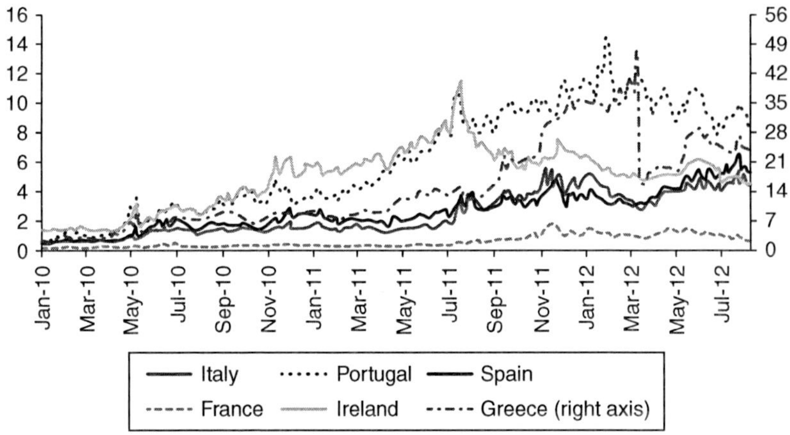

Figure 4.1 Interest rate spread *vis-à-vis* the Bund

Source: Authors' calculations based on Datastream statistics.

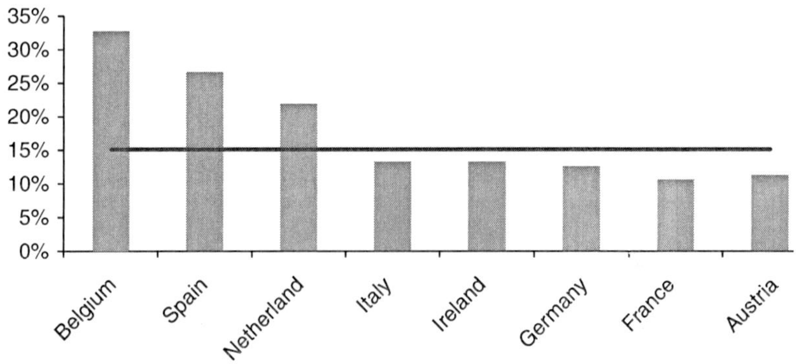

Figure 4.2 Share of government securities held by banks on outstanding government securities

Source: Authors' calculations based on data from ECB and National Central Banks.

interest rate on the German Bund has risen significantly. Figure 4.1 focuses on selected Eurozone countries that are considered more at risk.

In the Eurozone the share of public debt held by banks varies significantly. However, for almost all countries, it is higher than 10 per cent of the total public debt issued (Figure 4.2).

Figure 4.3 Difference between Euribor and OIS (three months)
Source: Authors' calculations based on data from Datastream.

Given the euro crisis current at the time of writing, early 2013, the question inevitably arises how this crisis might affect the funding costs of banks and ultimately the credit supply. To this end we use the model presented above to understand the channels through which a rise in sovereign debt risk can influence the costs of funding. Such channels, according to BIS (2011), Davies (2011) and Angeloni and Wolff (2012), are of four types:

3. The fall in the price of government bonds reflects negatively on the value of collateral that banks can use to secure wholesale funding. On the interbank market, this may induce potential lenders to exclude government bonds from the pool of eligible collateral or to apply high cuts to sovereign securities. This factor helps to explain why the volume of transactions in the EONIA market has significantly decreased since 2010, in particular since the latter part of 2011, and why the spread between the Euribor and the OIS simultaneously increased (Figure 4.3).

Refinancing at the central bank may also become more problematic. This was not the case with the refinancing at the ECB, which took into account the nominal value of government securities, taking on the risk of default.

1. The downgrading of the banks of many countries of the Eurozone has contributed to the deterioration of the conditions applied in the EONIA market and to the contraction in the quantities exchanged. This downgrading is largely a consequence of the downgrading of government bonds held in the portfolio of these banks.[2]

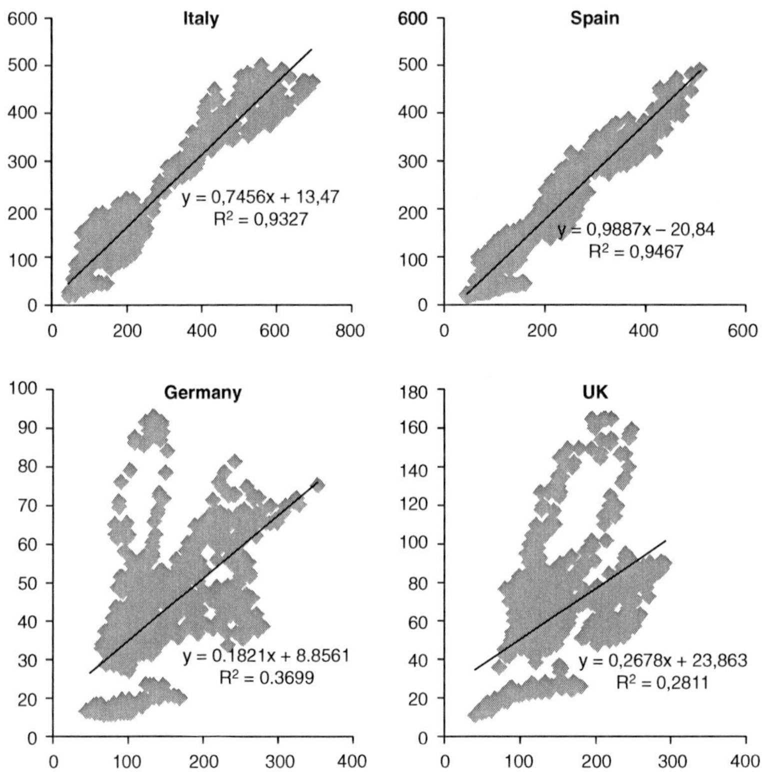

Figure 4.4 Correlation between sovereign and banking credit default swaps

Source: Authors' calculations based on Datastream.

2. All the countries characterized by an increase in spread have a strong correlation between the price of credit default swaps (CDS) on sovereign debt and that of domestic banks. This correlation, in the period between January 2008 and July 2012, was in fact higher than 90 per cent for Italy and Spain, while it was lower than 40 per cent for Germany and the United Kingdom (Figure 4.4). The deterioration in the creditworthiness of the sovereign debt reduces the confidence of savers in the ability of government to guarantee – either implicitly or explicitly – the stability of the banking system. This loss of confidence makes savers less willing to hold bank liabilities, primarily deposits. It is no coincidence that over 2010–2012 the Eurozone money multiplier decreased drastically (Figure 4.5).

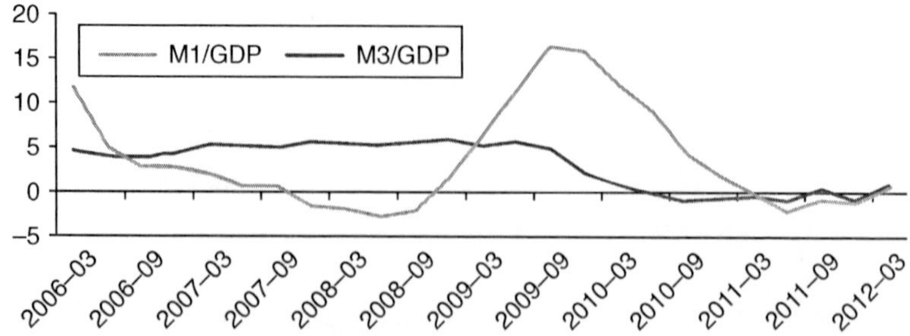

Figure 4.5 Eurozone money multiplier (annual growth rate)

Source: Authors' calculations based on ECB online statistics.

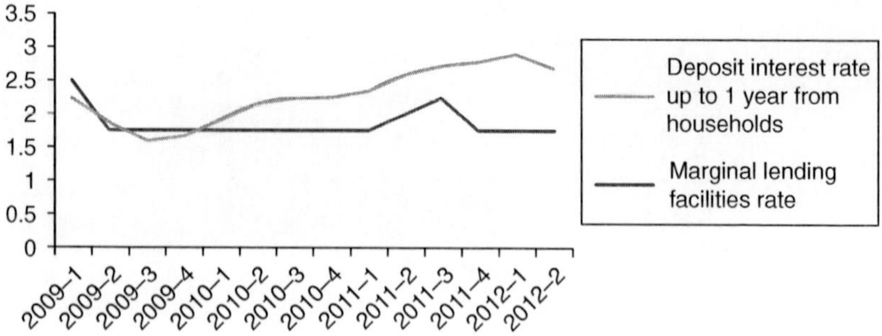

Figure 4.6 Interest rate on deposits

Source: Authors' calculations based on ECB online statistics.

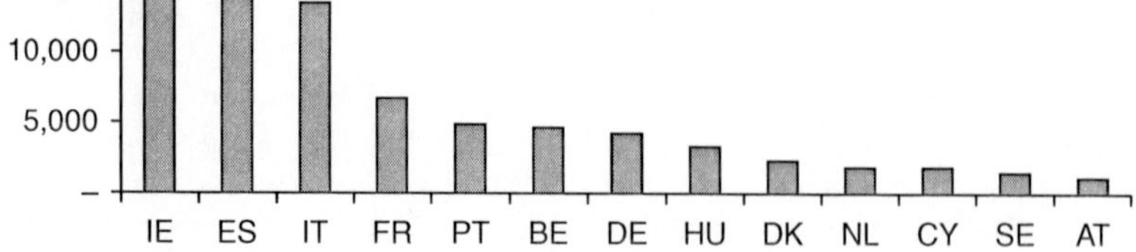

Figure 4.7 Capital account losses on government securities (in billions of euros)

Source: Authors' calculations based on EBA (2011).

The rise in sovereign debt risk was associated with an increase in the interest rate on deposits (Figure 4.6):

3. The rise in sovereign debt risk causes a fall in the price of government securities in bank portfolios, and consequently leads to capital account losses in financial bank portfolios and a fall in the price of bank shares. This makes the issuance of new shares more costly for them. Figure 4.7 shows that for some Eurozone countries, capital account losses on government securities have been particularly severe.

The propensity of banks to extend credit is affected not only by the link between the cost of funding and the conditions applied to loans, but also by the so-called balance sheet channel. Indeed, a fall in the price of a government's securities will inevitably reduce the value of the collateral that firms can offer to banks. Besides, if governments seek to counter the deterioration of the creditworthiness of sovereign debt by implementing restrictive fiscal policies and causing a contraction of aggregate demand, the cash flow of firms worsens. In short, the rise in sovereign debt risk tends to affect the risk of potential borrowers of banks, either directly or indirectly.

The factors outlined above lead us to expect that the decrease in the market price of government securities due to their higher risk affects the credit supply, and that this repercussion is more pronounced than that caused by the decrease in the market price of other assets. As we will see in the next section, this assessment has been tested econometrically.

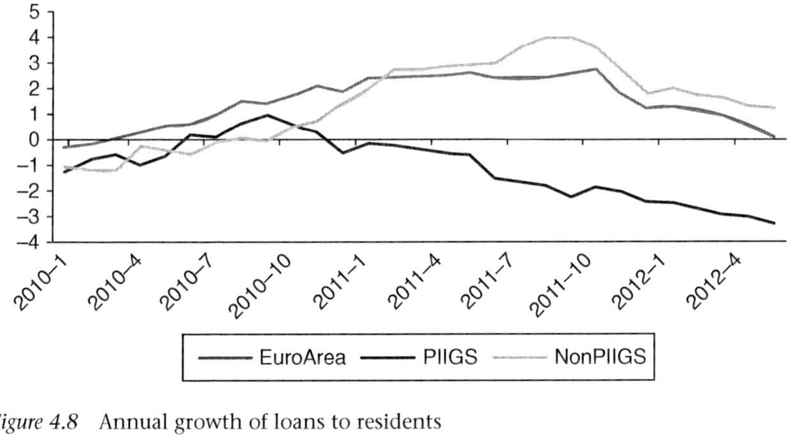

Figure 4.8 Annual growth of loans to residents

Source: Authors' calculations based on ECB online statistics.

5 The empirical estimates

The recent financial turmoil which has affected some Eurozone countries provides a good bench test to evaluate the effect of the change in the sovereign debt risk on the growth rate of credit.

Figure 4.8 shows the annual growth rate of loans to residents, broken down according to the Eurozone countries that have suffered the financial turbulence of the two years leading up to the time of writing.

It is to be noted that with the emergence of significant losses in the assets held in bank portfolios, the growth rate of loans in the countries worst hit by the crisis has been quite clearly declining, both in absolute terms and relative to other countries.[3]

Meanwhile, in the Eurozone, the differential between the interest rate applied to loans to non-financial corporations and that applied to the marginal lending facilities increased significantly in 2012.

5.1 Data and main methodological issues

To evaluate how the rise in the risk on financial assets, in particular on sovereign debt, has affected the propensity of Eurozone banks to grant credit, we estimated a panel data regression of the growth of loans in eight Eurozone countries on their banks' potential losses due to changes in the degree of risk of their financial portfolio.

The sample period is from the first quarter of 2010 to the last quarter of 2011 (the period when the Eurozone sovereign debt crisis developed) and

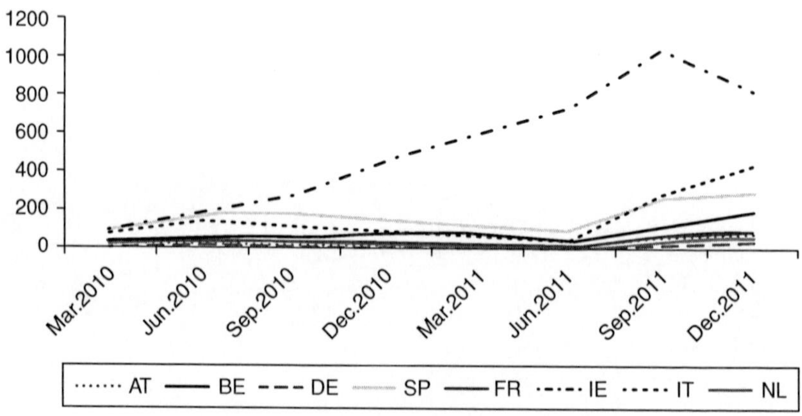

Figure 4.9 Price of banks' CDS contracts (one year)

Source: Authors' calculations based on Datastream.

relates to the banking systems of France, Germany, Italy, Spain, Holland, Ireland, Belgium and Austria. The sample selection is constrained by the availability of data regarding the BIS database on the foreign portfolio of European banks and data from National Central Banks (NCB).

The banks' potential losses were estimated by using the market price of CDS contracts as a proxy. As Figure 4.9 shows, around the end of the first decade of the 21st century, and primarily in the second half of 2011, the prices of banks' CDS contracts for some Eurozone countries, like Italy and Spain, significantly increased.

In order to ascertain the possible different effects of potential losses on different assets, we estimated separately the potential losses of government securities, of other domestic assets, and of foreign assets.

The source of these items of data is as follows: total assets data on outstanding amounts of these assets are taken from the ECB, while government bond amounts are given by NCBs. Then in order to estimate losses on non-resident assets we used the database of the Bank for International Settlements, which reports the breakdown of the portfolio of foreign assets according to country. The database takes into account the breakdown of the portfolio for each banking system in over 200 countries. As we have said, we have CDS prices for 69 countries, so it was necessary to allocate to some countries the value of the CDS of the most similar country in terms of geography and creditworthiness – but obviously, we do have the actual

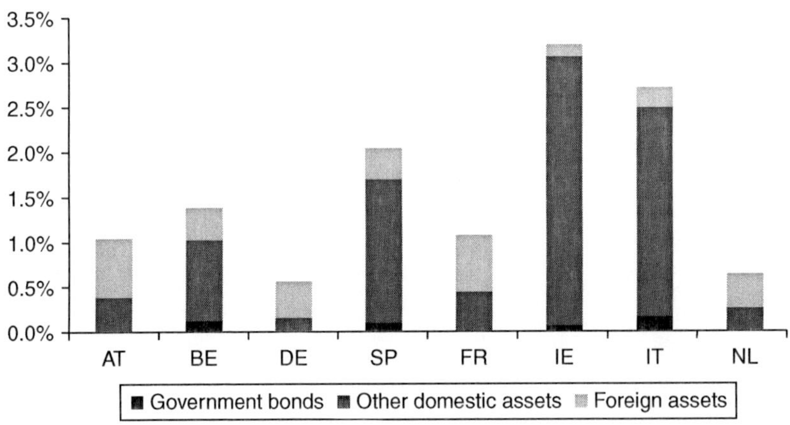

Figure 4.10 Composition of banks' potential losses (as percentage of total assets; values at December 2011)

Source: Authors' calculations based on BIS and Datastream data.

CDS prices for the most important countries in terms of shares of the foreign portfolio.

The losses were evaluated using one-year CDS prices for each kind of asset. Multiplying that price by the end-quarter amount of each type of asset, we obtained the potential losses relative to those components of the banks' financial portfolios. We were thus able to estimate the potential losses for the three groups of assets and for the eight banking systems of the sample.[4]

Figure 4.10 shows the share of the potential losses in the three types of assets on total assets for each of the eight countries considered. The figure clearly shows that the overall extent of potential losses in government securities is limited, except for Ireland, Italy, Spain and Belgium. The Italian banks' potential losses on government securities amounts to 0.16 per cent of total assets, followed by Belgium, with a 0.12 per cent share, while Irish banks have a yet lower value of losses on government securities (0.07%). These differences are determined not only by the market price of CDS but also by the weight of government bonds in banks' portfolios. In this respect the Belgian banks have the highest amount in total assets (8.6%), with Italian and Spanish banks presenting shares ranging from 5.2 to 5.5 per cent. After these three countries, the weight of government bonds in the total portfolio decreases significantly, reaching a maximum value of 2.4 per cent for Dutch banks, and a minimum of 1.3 per cent for Irish banks.

As for the potential losses in the other two types of assets, there is evidence that four countries (Belgium, Ireland, Italy and Spain) have higher potential losses on domestic assets (excluding government bonds), while the remaining four (Germany, France, Austria, and the Netherlands) have higher such losses on foreign assets.

Figures 4.11 gives the estimates of overall losses as a share of total assets for the eight banking systems.

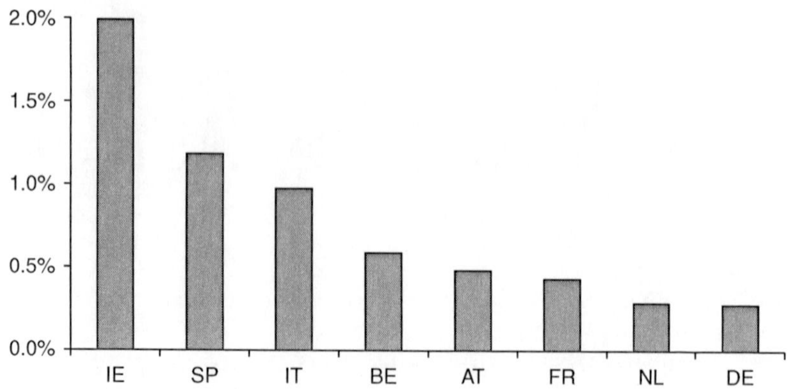

Figure 4.11 Potential losses share on total assets (average value 2010–2011)

Source: Authors' calculations based on BIS and Datastream data.

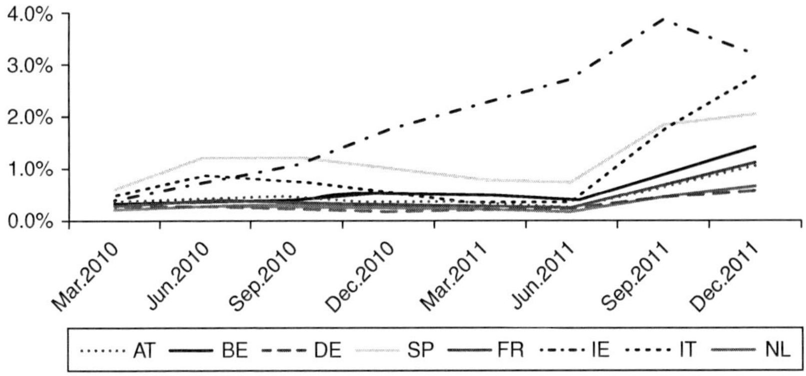

Figure 4.12 Share of potential losses on total assets (January 2010–April 2011)

Notes: AT, Austria; BE, Belgium; DE, Germany; SP, Spain; FR, France; IE, Ireland; IT, Italy; NL, Netherlands

Source: Authors' calculations based on BIS and Datastream data.

As shown in Figure 4.11, Irish banks suffered exceptional losses, while Spanish and Italian banks recorded losses of around 1 per cent of assets. The potential losses for the other countries of the Eurozone are significantly lower: Austrian and Belgian banks recorded losses of around 0.5 percentage points, and for the other countries the losses were even lower; in fact for German banks they were zero.[5]

More precise proof of the weight of potential losses against total assets can be obtained considering a time-series graph of such losses. Figure 4.12 shows the trend in the weight of losses against total assets for the eight banking systems for the period between March 2010 and December 2011.

This figure clearly shows that after June 2011 all banking systems faced a marked increase in potential losses. The countries afflicted by a deterioration of their creditworthiness show banks' total potential losses exceeding 2 per cent of total assets, while only two countries (the Netherlands and Germany) record potential losses for banks as less than 1 per cent of their total assets.

5.2 The results

Now that we are in possession of the data on potential losses across the various type of assets, we are in a position to estimate a panel regression on the eight countries considered for the period from the first quarter of 2010 to the last quarter of 2011, during which the annual growth of banks' credit to residents, GLOANS, regressed against the weight of potential losses on government securities (LossesGS), other domestic assets (LossesODA), and foreign assets (LossesFA).

Table 4.1 Descriptive statistics (percentage values)

	Losses on other domestic assets	Losses on foreign assets	Losses on government securities	Growth rate of banks' credit to residents	Growth rate of banks' credit to residents over GDP growth
Mean	0.57	0.18	0.03	0.13	–2.32
Median	0.25	0.14	0.01	0.85	–1.58
Maximum	3.68	0.66	0.16	9.00	6.65
Minimum	0.03	0.03	0.00	–12.60	–11.02

Source: Authors' calculations based on BIS, ECB, Eurostat and Datastream data.

In short, the equation to be used is as follows:

$$Gloans = c + \alpha LossesGS + \beta LossesODA + \gamma LossesFA + u \tag{4.10}$$

Table 4.1 reports some descriptive statistics of the variables used in the regressions.

In accordance with the theoretical model exposed in Section 3, we expect that all signs will be negative, that is, an increase in the potential losses on the assets held by banks in their portfolios will reduce the banks' supply of credit. However, we expect differences in the magnitude of the coefficients; in particular, we expect a higher coefficient on potential losses due to government securities because they, more than other securities, are used as collateral for refinancing.

To take into account any non-linearity in the relationship between potential losses and credit growth, we have divided the values of the various assets into two classes: high and low (Table 4.2).[6]

Table 4.2 gives the regression results for the period between the first quarter of 2010 and the fourth quarter of 2011:

1. the link between potential losses and credit growth is not only statistically significant for all three classes of assets considered, but is able to explain a high percentage – over 90 per cent – of the total variability of the phenomenon.
2. non-linear effects are significant only for domestic assets (securities and other assets), while there are no significant differences in the coefficients of potential losses on foreign assets in relation to the magnitude of the loss. Therefore, with only one reference to domestic assets, the responsiveness of credit growth to potential losses decreases with the increase in the size of the losses. [7]

Table 4.2 The relationship between credit growth and potential losses on bank assets

Dependent variable	**Percentage growth of loans**		**Ratio between the percentage growth of loans and that of GDP**	
Variable	**Coefficient**	**Std. error**	**Coefficient**	**Std. error**
Constant	0.07***	0.2	0.04**	0.02
Potential losses on other domestic assets (high losses)	−2.06***	0.66	−2.03**	0.85
Potential losses on other domestic assets (low losses)	−12.42***	3.30	−8.41**	3.42
Potential losses of foreign assets	−15.85**	6.43	−19.89***	6.00
Potential losses on government securities (high losses)	−59.53**	25.50	−62.47**	29.44
Potential losses on government securities (low losses)	−141.56***	40.01	−131.34***	44.29
R-squared	0.938			0.898

Notes: Sample: 2010Q1 2011Q4; cross-section and period fixed dummy variables; cross-sections and periods included: 8; number of observations: 64.

3. the elasticity of credit to potential losses on government securities is higher than that of potential losses on other kind of assets.

The higher impact on credit growth of potential losses on government securities compared to potential losses on the other assets is also apparent from Figure 4.13. Using the average of the eight countries at the end of 2011, the figure shows the share of the three kinds of losses out of total potential losses, and their effects on the growth rate of domestic credit.

As the figure shows, for the eight countries the potential losses on bonds represent an average of 3.8 per cent of total potential losses; however, their dampening effect represents 24 per cent of the total dampening effect.

Obviously, in the event of an increased risk on sovereign credit, a country may avert the risk of default by implementing corrective fiscal policies. Such policies inevitably affect domestic demand; and as a result the demand for credit tends to contract. In order to take this aspect into account, Table 4.2 also provides the estimates when the intensity of credit, measured as the

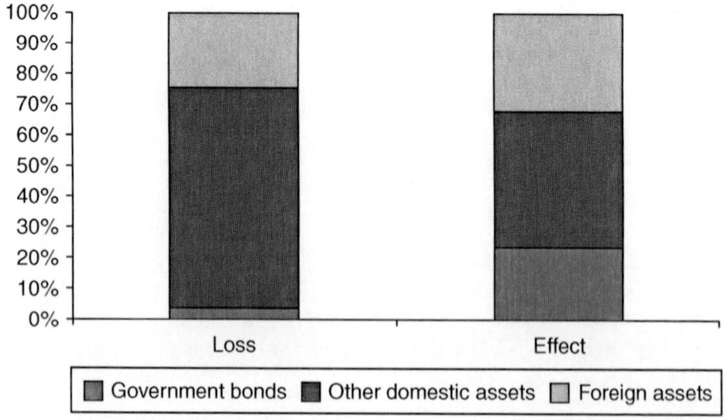

Figure 4.13 Losses on banks' assets and their effects on the growth rate of loans
Source: Authors' calculations based on BIS and Datastream data.

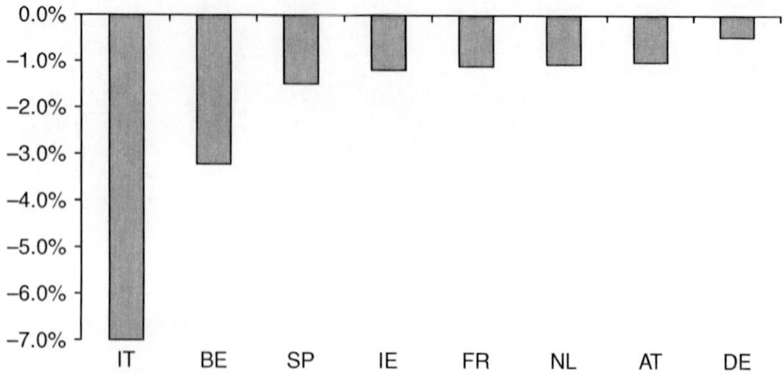

Figure 4.14 Effects of losses on government securities on loans' supply in the Eurozone (annual percentage; June 2011–December 2011)
Source: Authors' calculations.

ratio between credit growth to residents and GDP growth, is used as the dependent variable, rather than the growth of loans to residents. As Table 4.1 shows, the results show only marginal changes.

Based on the estimated coefficients of this regression, we can provide an estimate of the negative effect produced by the potential losses on government securities on the growth of credit to residents.

In Figure 4.14 we give the estimated reduction in the annual growth rate of loans between June and December 2011 due to changes in the creditworthiness of sovereign bonds. The Italian banks seem to be those most seriously affected by the Euro crisis of the second half of 2011, with a negative effect on the growth of loans, compared to the dynamics of mid-2011, equivalent to 7 percentage points, followed at some distance by the Belgian banks, and then, some way further behind, the banks of all the other countries.[8]

The ECB countered the credit crunch in three main ways. Firstly, it modified the Eurosystem collateral rules on refinancing. In particular, the Eurosystem suspended the application of the minimum credit rating threshold for the securities issued by countries that had adopted a fiscal consolidation approved by the European Commission and the IMF. Secondly, from January 2012 the reserve requirements were lowered from 2 to 1 per cent. Lastly, but most importantly, especially between the end of 2011 and the beginning of 2012, the ECB injected a huge amount of liquidity into the system. Between June 2010 and June 2012, the monetary base in the Eurozone increased by 34.8 per cent compared to an increase in M1 and M3, of 4.3 and 5.2 per cent respectively.

In 2011 and 2012, the dependence of Eurozone banks on ECB financing increased significantly. This increase was particularly high for the banks of the PIGS countries, for which the downgrading of the sovereign debt was more important.[9]

The compensatory action by the ECB has been partially successful; even though it could not prevent the credit crunch from happening it has alleviated it.

6 Conclusions

The Eurozone crisis manifested itself initially in the spring of 2010, with the eruption of the Greek public finance cataclysm. The crisis then expanded in the second half of 2011; the spread on ten-year government bonds of some Eurozone countries compared to the German Bund widened significantly, with a simultaneous downward revision in the creditworthiness of these countries by the ratings agencies and an increase in the prices of CDS on their sovereign debt.

In order to determine whether the current (as at 2013) debt crisis in the Eurozone has affected the propensity of banks to grant loans to the private sector, we conducted an econometric analysis by regressing the growth of credit to the private sector and the intensity of credit on potential losses on banks' assets. These kinds of losses were estimated on the basis of CDS prices and separately with respect to government securities, other domestic assets and foreign assets.

The results of the estimates, relative to eight countries of the Eurozone for the period from March 2010 to December 2011, suggest two main conclusions. First, the rise in sovereign debt risk negatively affects the propensity of banks to grant loans to the private sector. Secondly, changes in the propensity of banks to grant credit depends more on changes in the creditworthiness of sovereign debt than on those of other assets. The influence of potential losses on government securities on the propensity of banks to provide credit is eleven times higher than that of losses on other domestic assets, and nine times higher than that of losses on foreign assets.

These results are consistent with a modified version of the Bernanke and Blinder (1988) model illustrated in Section 3. Government securities, in fact, hold a crucial place in banks' liquidity management. On the one hand, these assets are in themselves a form of liquidity; on the other, government securities are used as collateral for raising funds on the interbank market and obtaining liquidity from the central bank.

The results of the econometric estimate enabled us to measure the impact of the worsening of the Eurozone crisis in the second half of 2011 on the growth of bank loans. On the basis of the coefficients of the estimates we assessed that in the second half of 2011 the decrease in bank loans due to the potential losses on government securities was almost zero for Germany and the Netherlands, but was significantly marked for other countries, and for Italy in particular.

Therefore, the measures adopted by the ECB to relieve the shortage of liquidity suffered by the banks of some Eurozone countries contributed to the alleviation of some forms of credit crunch in these countries.

Notes

1. The risk of sovereign debt also affects the demand for short-term government securities, but the effect is less, and so for the sake of simplicity we consider it null.
2. See among others Dailami (2012).
3. Of the five PIIGS countries (that is, PIGS plus Ireland), only Italy had a marginally positive growth rate, in May 2012. However, none of the non-PIIGS countries showed a fall in loans.
4. This type of estimate, almost always made using CDS prices, has recently been used by regulatory authorities, in particular the EBA, with the aim of determining the minimum capital amount needed by banks at the end of 2011.
5. For comparison, consider that at present the Italian banking sector has adjustments and provisions in the income statement totaling 0.5 percentage points of assets. But given the nature of these estimates, and especially their market origin, it is likely that they exaggerate the losses of the countries under attack, and probably underestimate the losses of the stronger countries.
6. In particular, for the potential losses on other domestic assets, the two classes are divided by the value of 0.3 per cent, and for bonds by the value of 0.04 per cent. These values are fixed for all countries considered.
7. This lower reactivity is consistent with normal bank management practices. They can tackle the problem more decisively when the volume of losses is lower, while they have to evaluate their actions more closely in situations of significant increase in the degree of riskiness of their overall assets. However, in the sample period,

it is probable that this difference in reactivity is due mainly to the set of unconventional measures implemented by the ECB and the Eurogroup to counter the systemic crisis of the Euro – for example, the two exceptional refinancing operations carried out by the ECB to reduce the liquidity crisis that was impeding the ability of the European banks to operate.

8. The low value for the Spanish and Irish banks is due both to the fact that the change in creditworthiness between June and December of 2011 was more limited than in Belgium and Italy (see Figure 4.2); in the Irish case it is due to the small size of the portfolio.
9. Access to refinancing with the ECB has been helped by modifications being made to the Eurosystem collateral rules; the Eurosystem suspended the application of the minimum credit rating threshold for securities issued by countries that had adopted a fiscal consolidation approved by the European Commission and the IMF.

References

Angeloni, C. and G. Wolff (2012) *Are Banks Affected by Their Holdings of Government Debt?* Bruegel Working Paper no. 2012/07.

Arteta, G. and G. Hale (2008) 'Sovereign debt crises and credit to the private sector', *Journal of International Economics*, 74, 53–69.

Bank for International Settlements (2011) 'The impact of sovereign credit risk on bank funding conditions', CGFS Papers, no. 43.

Bernanke, B. and A. Blinder (1988) 'Credit, money and aggregate demand', *American Economic Review*, 78, 435–9.

Bolton, P. and O. Jeanne (2011) 'Sovereign default risk and bank fragility in financially integrated economies', NBER working paper, no. 16899.

Borensztein, E. and V. Panizza (2009) 'The costs of sovereign default', IMF Staff Papers, no. 56, 683–741.

Broner, F., A. Martin and J. Ventura (2010) 'Sovereign risk and secondary market', *American Economic Review*, 100, no. 4, 1523–55.

Brutti, F. (2011) 'Sovereign defaults and liquidity crises', *Journal of International Economics*, 84, 65–72.

Bulow, J. and K. Rogoff (1989) 'Sovereign debt: is to forgive to forget?' *American Economic Review*, 79, 43–50.

Dailami, M. (2012) 'Looking beyond the Euro area sovereign debt crisis', The World Bank *Economic Premise*, 76, 1–9.

Davies, M. (2011) 'The rise of sovereign credit risk: implications for financial stability', *BIS Quarterly Review*, September, 59–70

De Paoli, B., G. Hoggarth and V. Saporta (2006) 'Costs of sovereign defaults', *Financial Stability Paper*, no. 1, Bank of England.

Dell'Arriccia, G., E. Detragiache and R. Rajan (2005) 'The real effect of banking crises', *Journal of Financial Intermediation*, 17, 89–112.

Eaton, J. and M. Gersovitz (1981) 'Debt with potential repudiation: theoretical and empirical analysis', *Review of Economic Studies*, 2, 289–309.

European Banking Authority (2011) *2011 EU-wide Stress Test. Aggregate Report.* London.

Furceri, D. and A. Zdzienicka (2011) 'How costly are debt crises?' IMF working paper, no. 11/280.

Gennaioli N., A. Martin and S. Rossi (2012) 'Sovereign default, domestic banks and financial institutions', Barcelona Graduate School of Economics, Working paper no. 622.

Livshits, I. and K. Schoors (2009) 'Sovereign default and banking', UWO working paper.

Rajan, R. and L. Zingales (1998) 'Financial dependence and growth', *American Economic Review*, 88, 559–86.

Reinhart, C. (2010) 'This time is different chartbook: country history's on debt, default, and financial crises', NBER working paper no. 15815.

Sandleris, G. (2012) 'The costs of sovereign defaults: theory and empirical evidence', Universidad Torcuato di Tella, mimeo.

Sturzenegger, F. and J. Zettelmeyer (2005) 'Haircuts: estimating investors losses in sovereign debt restructurings, 1998–2005', IMF working paper 05/137.

Sturzenegger, F. and J. Zettelmeyer (2006) *Debt Defaults and Lessons from a Decade of Crises*. Cambridge, MA: MIT Press.

Tomz, M. (2007) *Reputation and International Cooperation: Sovereign Debt across Three Countries*. Princeton, NJ: Princeton University Press.

Wright, M.L.J. (2005) 'Coordinating creditors', *American Economic Review*, Papers and Proceedings, 95, 388–392.

5

Credit Guarantee Institutions, Performance and Risk Analysis: An Experimental Scoring

Paola Leone, Ida C. Panetta and Pasqualina Porretta

1 Introduction

The credit guarantee consortia (known as Confidi) are a major phenomenon in Italy, since they play different roles in the relationship between banks and enterprises. They offer mutualistic guarantees aimed at alleviating financial constraints on their small or medium-sized (SMEs) shareholding or syndicated enterprises.

Confidi reduce asymmetric information, since they exploit members' confidential information; they conduct a form of social control, in order to prevent opportunistic and disloyal behavior; through trade associations they gain in-depth knowledge of the distinctive features of the fields they operate in; they collectively negotiate interest rates and other conditions with the banks concerning lending. They are therefore financial intermediaries, undertaking a fundamental role in codifying information regarding the territory and its enterprises, assessing SMEs and providing them with financial advice for more effective credit management.

Confidi select and monitor consortium member enterprises, especially the smaller enterprises that have greater problems in accessing credit, and seem to have found important support from the mutual guarantee schemes in the past few years.

In the current economic situation, the support provided by Confidi is often fundamental for enterprises, even though it seriously undermines the stability of the Confidi themselves. The said intermediaries – *partners* in a lending chain along which the functions of origination, funding, risk assumption and public fund transmission take place – may represent a weak link, especially during the current crisis, because they do not always comply with the profitability requirement, the new capital ratio and higher unexpected losses.

Public interventions in favor of Confidi, from which they have always benefited, might reduce the profitability requirement, since they ensure the credit access, that is the net benefits for members, if aimed at reducing the risk or connected with projects of strategic management reorganization of each guarantee intermediary especially intended for each of their fields (industry, crafts, tertiary) – a challenge that requires Confidi to reset a sustainable business model, under the economic and financial profile, while at the same time maintaining the mutualistic nature. The sustainability of the Confidi's business model, their reputation and their creditworthiness today, represent key elements to successfully competing in today's market, but are at the same time areas of analysis for a range of interlocutors, lenders and borrowers of guarantees who interface with them (policymakers, industry associations, bank intermediaries, etc.). All these entities need to understand and measure the areas of such analyses to develop tools, even rudimentary ones, for assessing the creditworthiness of the guarantee intermediaries able to measure in a standardized and objective way their solvency, solidity and credibility: the risk and performance profile. From this perspective, this chapter aims to define a quantitative scoring framework methodology able to express the risk and performance of a Confidi sample on an experimental position map. The construction of the ranking/position map on the basis of Confidi scores is derived from a set of indices showing the balance of management and more representative of the production process of Confidi and their risk profile and performance. After a brief literature review, this chapter explains the main theoretical and operational steps designed to achieve that result.

The methodological and operative steps that we have carried out to perform the research objective are:

a) analyze the annual reports and their principle of the Confidi sample
b) select different *information profiles* that contribute to the balance of management of the Confidi, and express their creditworthiness and sustainability and so their risk and performance profile
c) identify a set of key performance-risk indicators for each information profile,
d) undertake a univariate analysis of the indicators considered most significant for each information profile,
e) undertake an analysis of the latent structures and identification of multi-profile indicators derived from the single indices,
f) construct the experimental positioning map for the assignment of a rating/score for the Confidi analyzed through the use of multi-profile indicators.

This is a first experimental exercise in this field. The surveyed sample consists of both Supervised and Unsupervised Italian CGIs, in order to assess the different economic, financial and funding policy of each of these macro-categories of intermediaries, their ranking within the surveyed sample, and their capacity to survive in the near future. The analysis refers to the 2007–2010 period and evaluates the performance trend of the Confidi during the different phases of the current international financial crisis.

2 Credit Guarantee Scheme performance: evidence from the literature

Credit Guarantee Institutions (CGIs) have been part of the financial services landscape for SMEs since the end of World War II. The literature generally states that SMEs still suffer from limited access to bank financing around the world, even in the most developed countries, basically because of the existence of ex-ante and ex-post information asymmetries (Mankiw, 1986; Gittell & Kaen, 2003; Craig et al., 2008; Best Report – EU, 2006), the high administrative costs of small-scale lending and perceived high risk (Cowling and Mitchell, 2003; Davies, 2007; Berger & Udell, 2006), and the lack of collaterals (Pozzolo, 2004; Beck et al., 2008; Makhool et al., 2005).

Since these are the main reasons for SMEs experiencing difficulties in accessing credit all over the world, most academics agree that the CGIs could be the solution (Honohan, 2008); the role of a CGI is to act as a third-part intermediary risk sharer and facilitator between a bank and SME-borrowers. The overriding question posed in most recent literature is: have CGIs met their goals in solving SMEs' financing problems? And furthermore, have CGIs been effective and efficient in doing this?

During the 1990s CGIs were much criticized by academics for their high administration costs; for being subsidy-dependent; for increasing the danger of 'moral hazard' (cf. Navajas, 2001) and for contributing to a weakening of credit morality (cf. Vogel & Adams, 1997; Levitsky, 1997). The failure of many credit guarantee schemes in the 1980s and 1990s, mainly in developing countries, also led to controversy about their sustainability and efficiency. These failures, however, were mostly due to deficiencies in the wider institutional environment: the schemes were politicized, and neglected financial criteria or economic conditions affecting the borrower's ability to repay (Davies, 2007).

During the second half of the 1990s many CGIs were reformed, and (especially in EU countries) after the introduction of Basel II further reforms and restructuring processes of the sector took place. In fact, since the introduction of Basel II, the relevance of CGIs for banks has been related to the possibility of offering mitigation instruments. Since they can be qualified as guarantors according to Basel II prescriptions (becoming a supervised intermediary), their products allow banks to reduce regulatory capital for their loan portfolio.

These reforms and restructuring processes in the sector make it necessary to assess whether the new generation of CGIs has been able to solve previous deficiencies and can be considered a valid instrument for avoiding small lending problems. That is why, over the last 20 years, the literature has paid more attention to CGIs. For the above reasons, this renewed interest is due to the involvement of policymakers in supporting such schemes, and the related necessity of proving the marginal benefits of using taxpayer funds. Intervention by governments can take place at different levels (regional, national, etc.) and assumes different forms, as in Leone & Vento (2012):

- the provision of a legal and prudential framework, setting up rules regarding the management, the extent of their commitments, solvency requirements;
- support for the beneficiary SMEs, subsidizing the guarantee fee;
- financial support to guarantee schemes.[1]

The degree of government involvement and the amount of resources allocated varies between countries, but in any case, especially during actual economic downturn, this reinforces the necessity for a comprehensive evaluation of CGIs. To evaluate the performance of CGIs, the literature has explored the following profiles:

- *Financial Additionality or incrementality* (hereafter FA);
- *Economic Additionality* (hereafter EA);
- *Financial Sustainability* (hereafter FS).

FA concerns direct benefits to SMEs and banks as a result of intervention by the CGIs. For the SMEs, such benefits[2] mainly take the form of:

- Access to the bank credit market, or increasing the size of loans and/or the extension of loan maturities;
- More favorable conditions in terms of interest rates and/or the reduction of transaction costs;
- A reduction of the collateral required in order to obtain credit;
- A faster loan processing time.

Much empirical research (see Table 5.1) has attempted to determine whether the loans are actually additional, that is, whether they would or would not have been made without the intervention of the CGIs. These papers come to widely differing conclusions regarding outcomes, due to differences in the structure of the CGIs in the economies in which they operate, and in the research methodology used.[3] The results suggest that CGIs contribute to facilitating the access of SMEs to credit by increasing the amount of available credit.

EA refers to the improvement in the overall economy due to the increased access and availability of credit for SMEs. These gains generally take the form of increased employment levels or workers' salaries, increased profits for owners, and increased tax revenue for the government (Green, 2003). Although EA refers to the indirect benefits of the presence of CGIs, it is of crucial relevance because it helps policymakers assess whether or not to support their survival. However, although it is a primary objective of research, very few contributions have measured EA produced by guarantee schemes, due to the difficulty in modeling the multitude of variables involved by isolating the impact of guarantees from the rest of the economy (see Table 5.2),[4] and the lack of reliable microdata.

Table 5.1 Measurable dimension of financial additionality investigated in the literature (last 10 years)

Dimension of FA considered	Effect of CGI interventions	Literature Author (year) – Country
Access to credit	* Increase in commercial bank loans to clients who previously did not have access to credit	Benavente et al. (2006) – Chile; BIS (2010) – UK; Brash and Gallagher (2008) – US; Busetta, Presbitero (2008) – Italy; Cowling (2010) – UK; GAO (2007) – US; Larraín and Quiroz (2006) – Chile; Useugi et al. (2006) – Japan; Zecchini, Ventura (2009) – Italy.
	* Increase in loan size	Cowan et al. (2008) – Chile; Riding et al. (2007) – Canada.
Loan conditions	* Longer repayment period	GAO (2007) – US.
	* Lower interest rate	Anuchitworawong et al. (2006) – Thailand; Boocock, Sharif (2005) – Malaysia; Brash & Gallagher (2008) – US; Bennett et al. (2005) – Chile, Egypt, India, Poland; Busetta, Presbitero (2008) – Italy; Columba et al. (2009) – Italy; Zecchini, Ventura (2009) – Italy.
Relationship between banks and small firms	* Reduction in collateral demand by bank	Wilcox, Yasuda (2008) – Japan.
	* More rapid loan processing	Busetta, Presbitero (2008) – Italy.

Source: Based on Panetta (2012).

Finally, the financial sustainability (FS) of the CGIs is strictly related to the way in which they are organized and managed, and aims to achieving the objectives of the FA and EA without betraying the principles of sound management. This is a crucial point for policymakers, since the government needs to ensure that such schemes will increase overall welfare sufficiently to justify the cost of the subsidies. Evaluating the FS means assessing whether CGIs have the ability to properly allocate resources and generate appropriate levels of self-financing.

Performance studies have produced more limited evidence, and mainly focus on which funding model ensures the best performance. Academics

Table 5.2 Measurable dimensions of economic additionality investigated in the literature (last 10 years)

Dimension of EA considered	Effect of CGIs interventions	Literature
Improvements in commercial and economic activity	*Increase in investments of firms/sectors benefited	Lelarge et al. (2008) – France; Schmidt, van Elkan (2010) – Germany; Uesugi et al. (2006) – Japan.
	*Increase of sales in firms benefited	Benavente et al. (2006) – Chile.
	*Increase in performance ratio in firms benefited	Lelarge et al. (2008) – France; Oh et al. (Author (year) – Country Uesugi et al. (2006) – Japan.
	*Increase in the number of employees	Anuchitworawong et al. (2006) – Thailand; Bradshaw (2002) – US; Boocock, Sharif (2005) – Malaysia; Craig et al. (2007, 2008) US; Honcock et al. (2008) – US; Riding, Haines (2001) – Canada; Riding et al. (2007) – Canada.
Improvement in income and quality of life	*Increase in entrepreneurs' income	Hancock et al. (2008) – US.
	*Increase in employees' income	Hancock et al. (2008) – US.
Improvement in welfare	*Increase in tax income	Boocock, Sharif (2005) – Malaysia; Bradshaw (2002) – US; Riding et al. (2007) – Canada; Schmidt, van Elkan (2010) – Germany.

Source: Based on Panetta (2012).

indicate that the financial performances of CGIs are better in countries where CGIs are mainly operated by the private sector (Beck et al., 2008) and there is also a general consensus that governments may play a key coordinating role only in the initial stages of development. In the medium term, a government's role is more limited, taking the shape of counter-guarantor or lender of last resort. The CGIs that function best are those exhibiting the most sustainability and which operate at some distance from governments: as demonstrated by Beck et al. (2008), CGIs' default rates tend to be higher when governments are involved in credit risk assessment and recovery (Beck et al. 2008, p. 22). Many authors (see Green, 2003) also agree that mutual schemes[5] are preferable because they have the advantage of needing less government funds due to member contributions. Moreover, the members of mutual guarantee institutions are motivated to ensure that the programme administration is diligent in carrying out its duties, because any default will put the group's capital at risk and could result in worse borrowing conditions for companies in the future (Columba et al., 2008). Even when the mutual model is considered one of the best private ones for CGI, there is evidence of weak performance in some countries and the need for direct or indirect public support to comply with their mission.

The significant differences worldwide in the operational mechanisms make it rather difficult to carry out cross-country assessments of CGI sustainability or to define the best practices. This, together with differences in the CGI's annual reports, makes it extremely difficult to identify performance indicators useful for comparison. This is why the literature tends to focus on single countries or on qualitative studies. Although a number of publications deal with the operating procedures of CGIs (Green, 2003; Deelen & Molenaar, 2004; Best Report, 2006; Davies, 2007), very few studies have examined how to measure performance in any depth (GoNetwork, 2006; Deelen & Molenaar, 2004; Jonsson, 2009). Even with these limitations, some performance indicators are quite common in the analysis of CGIs' performances (see Table 5.3).

The FS of the scheme and the extent to which it requires a continuing cash subsidy from public funds is, in relation to the institution's default rate, the volume of activity in relation to the financial capacity (degree of leverage) of the guarantee institution, its cost–income ratio, and the extent to which losses can be partially or wholly covered by reserves or recovered from SME borrowers (recoverability of losses).[6]

One of the most widely used indicators is the degree of leverage measuring for the extent to which a CGI can expand its portfolio of guarantees with respect to the capital raised both from both public and private sectors; it measures the impact of the endowment of a CGI's own funds on the granting activity. The dimension and the composition of this indicator are influenced by the legal framework or supervisory rules, if applicable, and/or the internal policies of the single institution. No model has yet been developed to calculate the optimum leverage level.[7] However, experience has shown that long-established schemes, operating in industrialized countries, may achieve leverage of up to 26 times the fund's value (see Best Report, 2006). On the other hand, in developing and emerging economies with unstable macroeconomic environments, it is advisable to adopt a more conservative stance and restrain leverage to five or at most ten times the fund's value (Green, 2003, p. 50). According to Deelen & Molenaar (2004, p. 54), well-functioning guarantee funds attain leverage from 5:1 to 10:1.

Table 5.3 – Measurable dimension of financial sustainability investigated in the literature (last 10 years)

Dimension of FS considered	CGIs' performance indicators
Quantity and quality of guarantee portfolio	*Degree of leverage (also known as multiplier) *Default rate *Pay-out rate *Net loss rate *Recovery rate *Guarantee portfolio at risk
Profitability of the business	*Return on Guarantee and services *Return on investments
Efficiency	*Cost to income *Guarantee processing time

Source: Based on Panetta (2012).

In order to determine the most appropriate and negotiable level of leverage it is necessary to consider the default rate, which is another indicator used to evaluate CGI performance, although this does not allow us to determine the optimal level because:

i) a low default rate may imply limited activity and high-risk aversion (Green, 2003 p. 59), instead of being a signal of CGI's greater capacity of screening;
ii) a high default rate may imply inefficiencies in the scheme that incentivizes its use for poor credit propositions (Graham, 2004, p. 18).

In addition, high default rates (above 5 per cent default) over a long time span will lead to the depletion of the fund if it is not consistently supported through subsidies or sufficient income from investments (Jonsson, 2009).[8]

The FS of CGIs will depend on the capacity of the guarantor to cover its costs (mainly operational costs and defaults) either by charging fees to its clients, or through direct subsidies from donors, or from revenue from the guarantee fund's investments. The guarantee fund's returns are generated by the guarantee operations (guarantee fees) as well as by the return on its investments in the capital market.[9] Accordingly, appropriate pricing of the guarantee service is an important part of a guarantee scheme, both in terms of incentives for lenders and borrowers, as well as for the sustainability of the scheme (Beck et al., 2008, p. 19), since the fee is the income covering default risks[10] and limiting government intervention (Graham, 2004). The fee should be sufficient to deter unconstrained firms from applying to the programme, and low enough to allow constrained firms to take on debt.

Schemes that modulate their guarantee fees according to the borrowers' risk level may reduce their dependence from public funds.

The literature has generally paid less attention to CGI costs, both operational and in underwriting losses and provisioning (worth mentioning are the Italian studies conducted by Piatti, 2008; Baravelli and Leone, 2010; Aldrighetti & Erzegovesi, 2007; Erzegovesi, 2008; Quaglia et al., 2012).

This capacity to cover costs and evaluate the efficiency of CGIs are generally assessed by means of the cost–income ratio; differences in income statement forms between countries generate different margins used as denominators (fee revenues, investment revenues, intermediation margins, etc.) and the types of costs considered (operating, underwriting losses, provisioning expenses, etc.) as numerators of the ratio. In any case, academics demonstrate a generalized low profitability of the CGIs, making capital injection from both public and private shareholders necessary. Guarantee schemes everywhere are subsidized by the public system, by utilizing sums from general taxation or other specific sources, even in countries where the private model mainly prevails or where big players operate (KPMG, 2011) and also in the case of supervised guarantee institutions (that is, in Spain and France).

If, in order to survive, CGIs seem to require some kind of economic support from governments in a time when resources are scarce, politicians must carefully assess where to direct their efforts. This chapter therefore contributes to the debate by proposing a methodology for CGIs' performance analysis, using a sample of Italian CGIs. Our ultimate goal is to synthesize all the investigated profiles in order to assign a score that allows us suggest those CGIs worthy of public support.

3 Structure and content of the financial statements of the Confidi in the sample: a brief analysis

The integrated manner of reading the financial statements of Confidi taken into examination, preparatory to the construction of the methodological framework for the allocation of the score, has been developed starting from the analysis of the production process of the guarantee.

For the purposes of this analysis, it is useful to recall the ways in which a Confidi, particularly a Supervised Confidi, operates. Depending on the type of guarantee provided, this can be traced back to:

- *limited* guarantees, when granting ineligible monetary guarantees on the risk funds entered among the liabilities and invested in unavailable financial *assets* (segregated guarantees) or in the case of tranched cover, as a result of which the Confidi respond to the first loss on the portfolio share, subject to tranching covered by cash collateral;
- *unlimited* guarantees, when issuing guarantees as a result of which the Confidi also responds with its own assets. This is the case of subsidiary

guarantees in the event of losses superior to the risk provisions allocated in the budget, or of eligible guarantees for which, as determined by Bank of Italy circular 263/2006, the Confidi responds with excussion on first demand by the bank and with its own resources. The constraint of capital adequacy is provided only for Supervised Confidi, but no such obligation is incumbent upon Unsupervised Confidi.

The different forms of operation, for which defined different levels of responsibility and technical forms of guarantee are provided, have an impact on relations between the capital components, the role of risks and the makeup of costs and revenues. The analysis of these three elements and their relationships is useful both for the analysis of the financial statements of Confidi belonging to the selected sample, and for the definition of their information profiles against which to select the set of indicators to be treated statistically in order to determine the score.

About the links between *guarantees granted, net shareholders equity and total financial assets*, it may be observed how the possibility of expanding the guarantee activities with unlimited liability depends on the size of the equity, which operationally may increase through the subscription of members, self-financing and obtaining public and private contributions. Monetary resources collected through such a financing channel are available for discretionary investments without constraint. The limited guarantees are, conversely, fed by liability funds for specific purposes whose resources are invested in financial *assets* with availability constraint, since they are intended to cover specific losses and impairments.

The different operations and type of financial investments are reflected by the Supervised Confidi on the absorbed capital towards the requirements of prudential supervision and, hence, on the strategic investment decisions compatible with the pursuit of the conditions of solvency and profitability.

With regard to the relationship between *guarantees granted and connected risks*, it is clear how with the provision of loan guarantees by signature, the Confidi assume the credit risk whose quantification requires a distinction to be made, within the context of the guarantees issued, between the *in bonis* positions and those stranded and impaired. This distinction makes it possible to identify the extent of the write-downs to be made in the financial statements and to be accounted for in the provisions for adjustments and risk provisions. For financial statements prepared in accordance with IAS, adjustments to the value of collateral are only justified for operations with unlimited liability in the face of losses incurred by the bank, but for the purposes of a prudential risk management adjustments for limited liability would also be required. With respect to credit risk management, special importance is taken on by the techniques of risk transfer in its many forms, including the relevant ones of the counter-guarantees in the face of guarantees given to member companies. Where these tools are appropriate for supervisory purposes, they reduce the Confidi's risk both in terms of expected loss and of absorbed regulatory capital.

The third aspect of the analysis, that is *the relation between the portfolio of guarantees and performance*, allows the evaluation on the one hand of typical revenues, and on the other of the associated costs. With regard to revenue, the characteristic components are the fees, directly connected to the activity of provision of guarantees and income generated by the financial investments. In terms of costs, we refer to those relating to risks and structure. The difference between costs and revenues is the income for the year that, given the mutual constraints, should be of such amount as to sustain on the one hand the growth of the Confidi and, on the other, their solvency. This assumption must be interpreted in light of the different operating modes that require the pursuit of different equilibria. In particular, the return on capital is binding in the case where the Supervised Confidi, working with unlimited liability, should hold for regulatory purposes an amount of capital adequate to cover the risk taken on, a step not forbidden for other types of operations.

3.1 The Confidi sample: main feature

From the methodological point of view, we have analyzed the annual reports of a sample of 17 first-level Confidi,[11] members of a single second-level Confidi belonging to the tertiary sector.[12] First-level Confidi are characterized by the prevailing participation of SMEs which, within the bounds of the objectives regarding their reinforcement and coordination, have favored the establishment of second-level consortia or cooperatives in charge of reinsurance and counter-guarantees. Second-level Confidi offer provisions of guarantees on medium- and long-term loans, and also reinsure first-level Confidi.

In 2010 the surveyed Confidi accounted for approximately 94.4 per cent of the member institutions of the second-level Supervised Confidi. They had over 136,571 enterprises as members offering a total amount of €2,857 billion of guarantees; 50 per cent of the surveyed institutions have their registered office in the North of Italy, 28 per cent in the Centre and 22 per cent in the South.

From the annual reports assessment of the surveyed Confidi for the 2007–2010 period a first asymmetry emerged: Unsupervised Confidi continued to apply the national standards such as the Italian Legislative Decree 87/1992 in drawing up the balance sheets, while Supervised Confidi applied the IAS/IFRS standards (Bank of Italy, 14/02/2006). Starting from Confidi's production process, we define a logical scheme applicable to both Unsupervised and Supervised Confidi, and to define the relations between assets, liabilities and economic structure. The surveyed institutions comprise only two supervised financial intermediaries, while the other 15 belong to the Unsupervised Confidi type.

Table 5.4 Distribution of Confidi by number of employees (2007–2010)

	2010 Nr of Confidi		2009 Nr of Confidi 7		2008 Nr of Confidi 8		2007 Nr of Confidi 6	
No. of Employees	**No of Confidi**	**%**	**No of Confidi**	**%**	**No of Confidi**	**%**	**No of Confidi**	**%**
From 1 to 4	9	69.2	7	58.3	8	53.3	6	54.5
From 5 to 9	1	7.7	2	16.7	4	26.7	2	18.2
From 10 to 49	2	15.4	3	25.0	2	13.3	3	27.3
Over 50	1	7.7	–	–	1	6.7	–	–
Total no of Confidi	13	100	12	100	14	100	11	100
Total no employees	141		107		147		85	
Average	10.9		8.9		9.8		7.7	
Median	3.0		5.5		4.0		4.0	3.0

Source: Author's own calculations.

Table 5.5 Number of member enterprises (2007–2010)

	2010	2009	2008	2007
No of surveyed Confidi	16	12	14	14
Total value	136,571	123,632	127,594	110,427
Average value	8,536	10,303	9,114	7,888
Median	2,749	3,436	3,275	3,111
Standard deviation	15,073	16,695	16,150	13,732

Source: Author's own calculations.

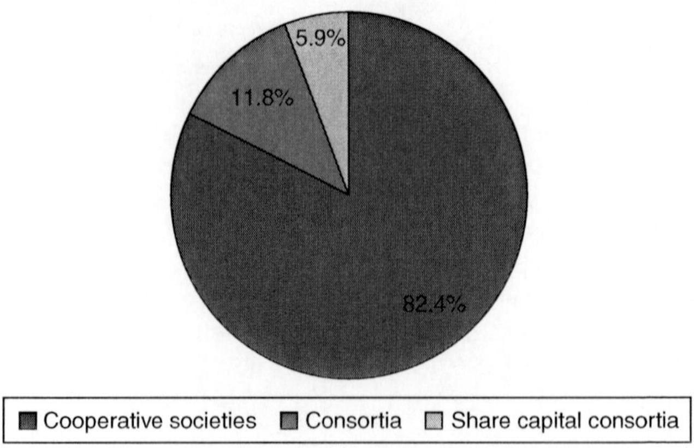

Figure 5.1 Distribution of the surveyed Confidi by legal status

Table 5.6 Distribution of surveyed Confidi by number of member enterprises

	Member enterprises									
	Up to 2000		From 2001 to 5,000		From 5001 to 15,000		Over 15,000		No. of surveyed Confidi	
Year	No.	%	No.	%	No.	%	No.	%	No.	%
2010	6	37.5	5	31.3	3	18.8	2	12.5	16	100
2009	4	33.3	3	25.0	3	25.0	2	16.7	12	100
2008	5	35.7	4	28.6	3	21.4	2	14.3	14	100
2007	5	35.7	4	28.6	3	21.4	2	14.3	14	100

Source: Author's own calculations.

As far as their *legal status* is concerned, most of the surveyed Confidi are cooperative societies, as shown in Figure 5.1, while the remaining 17.6 per cent comprises consortia and share capital consortia.

As for their size, in terms of *organizational complexity*, as shown in Table 5.4, most of the surveyed Confidi have a small number of employees. The surveyed guarantee institutions employed, in total, 141 employees in 2010, with an average value of 10.9. The median indicates, however, that in that four-year period, 50 per cent of Confidi employed less than six staff members. As shown in Table 4, over 59 per cent of Confidi employed less than six staff members[13] during the four-year period, with the sole exception of one large-sized company with 'over 50 employees'.

Analyzing the total number of member enterprises (Table 5.5) allows the dimensional structure of the surveyed Confidi to be assessed. In 2010, the surveyed mutual guarantee institutions had approximately 136,571 *member enterprises* (Table 5.5) with an average value of 8536 members in the same year, against a total of 110,427 registered in 2007. The median also shows that for 50 per cent of all Confidi their average number of members accounted for less than 4000 enterprises during a three-year period. Table 5.6 shows a significantly higher concentration of Confidi in the lower bands, accounting for a smaller number of members. Nonetheless the total amount of Confidi member enterprises grew by approximately 23.7 per cent; therefore the consortia should grow ever closer to the local area and its enterprises.

3.1.1 The guarantee portfolio

The amount of guarantees granted is one of the most significant values used to compare the size of the surveyed Confidi. As of 31 December 2010, the guarantees stock granted by the Confidi included in the sample accounted for €2858 billion (Table 5.7) with a 13.1 per cent increase over the four-year period. The high standard deviation recorded might be a consequence of the Confidi's distribution: most of them granted guarantees for small amounts, while only a limited number of them granted guarantees for significant amounts.

Figure 5.2 shows that the supervised institutions have granted over 85 per cent of the guarantee stock while Unsupervised Confidi, even if greater in number, managed the remaining 15 per cent. It is worth noticing that over the four-year period the market share controlled by the smaller size Confidi increased from 12 per cent in 2007 to 15 per cent in 2010, while the market share controlled by Supervised Confidi decreased as a consequence of

Table 5.7 Guarantee stock granted by surveyed Confidi (€000s)

	2010	2009	2008	2007
Total value	2,857,887	2,984,502	2,960,226	2,525,670
Average value	168,111	175,559	174,131	148,569
Median	30,805	27,492	22,822	19,286
Standard deviation	529,883	574,526	589,838	505,234
Variation coefficient	3.15	3.27	3.39	3.40
Herfindahl Index	6432	6,888	7,338	7,391

Source: Author's own calculations.

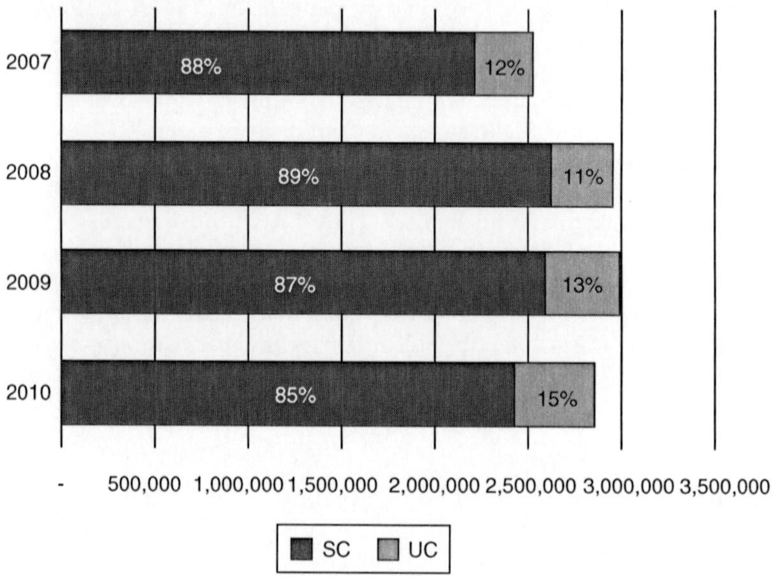

Figure 5.2 Breakdown of guarantees granted by surveyed Confidi by Type (€000s, %)
Note: SC: Supervised Confidi; UC: Unsupervised Confidi.

Table 5.8 Guarantees granted and collateralized loans: Unsupervised Confidi and Supervised Confidi

		Guarantees granted * (A)	Collateralized loans* (B)	Average coverage ratio (C) = A/B	Nr of surveyed Confidi
	Total	342,518	888,791	38.5%	9
2010	UC	76,721	198,723	38.6%	7
	SC	295,366	690,068	42.8%	2
	Total	589,894	1,185,414	49.8%	6
2009	UC	43,596	94,382	46.2%	5
	SC	546,298	1,091,032	50.1%	1
	Total	126,901	311,513	4.7%	10
2008	UC	86,244	189,401	45.5%	9
	SC	40,657	122,112	33.3%	1
	Total	113,205	272,774	41.5%	11
2007	UC	96,115	217,129	44.3%	10
	SC	17,090	55,645	30.7%	1

Notes: (*)€000s; UC: Unsupervised Confidi; SC: Supervised Confidi.

Source: Author's own calculations.

concurrent causes following reorganization, which itself followed the aggregation and transformation processes.

In order to verify the actual capability of Confidi to facilitate SMEs' access to credit, we analyzed which guarantees are affected by the issued loans. Table 5.8 shows the comparison between the annual guarantee stock granted and the loans granted to member enterprises. The average coverage ratio was equal to 39 per cent in 2010, while it was 42 per cent in 2007. The two types of Confidi did not share the same percentages: except for 2010, the average coverage ratio of the Supervised Confidi is always lower than that of Unsupervised Confidi.

It is worth drawing attention to the analysis of the guarantees received by the Confidi included in the sample, in order to identify the mitigation activity. To this end, the portfolios of the guarantees received by Unsupervised and Supervised Confidi respectively were compared. Table 5.9 shows how the risk transferred by Unsupervised Confidi grew over time, although the risk mitigation policy did not become a strategic tool for Supervised Confidi considering the almost insignificant amounts of the counter-guarantee operations over the four-year period compared to other types of hedging characterized by the granting of single and mutual guarantee deeds by members (in the 2007–2009 period).

Table 5.9 Evolution of counter-guarantee received by type of Confidi: aggregate value and main statistics (€000s)

	2010	2009	2008	2007
Total	112,814	900,737	774,304	540,878
Unsupervised Confidi	45,759	32,348	22,195	18,580
Supervised Confidi	67,055	868,389	752,110	522,298
Average value	9,401	90,074	96,788	67,610
Unsupervised Confidi	4,576	4,043	3,699	3,097
Supervised Confidi	33,527	434,195	376,055	261,149
Median	4,853	3,345	2,650	1,358
Unsupervised Confidi	4,182	2,805	1,901	1,358
Supervised Confidi	33,527	434,195	376,055	261,149
No. of surveyed Confidi*	12	10	8	8
Unsupervised Confidi*	10	8	6	6
Supervised Confidi*	2	2	2	2

Source: Author's own calculations.

3.2 Analysis of balance sheet

The balance sheets are analyzed considering the relations between the guarantee business and sources and uses of funds. To meet the purposes of the survey, we deemed it useful to break down the data of the Unsupervised and Supervised Confidi. At aggregate level Supervised Confidi represents 63 per cent of the aggregate invested capital.

3.2.1 Liabilities

Guarantee intermediaries generally use two main financing channels: shareholders' contributions and contributions received from public entities and, only partially, other sources such as guarantee deposits and subordinated loans. Through an in-depth analysis on the type of institutions, Supervised and Unsupervised, it is possible to highlight, on the liability side (Table 5.10):

- During the 2007–2009 period, the prevalence of *shareholders' equity* (SE) for both types of institutions and in particular for Supervised Confidi with values just below 70 per cent of the invested capital. In 2010, while for Unsupervised Confidi the incidence of the above-mentioned source did not change, it decreased significantly for Supervised Confidi due to a major downsizing of the *fund for guarantee*;

Table 5.10 Reclassified balance sheet (liabilities): Unsupervised Confidi and Supervised Confidi

		2010		2009		2008		2007		Var % 2007–2010
Confidi		**Value ***	%	**Value ***	%	**Value ***	%	**Value ***	%	
FL (A)	Supervised	3,434	1.4	440	0.2	990	0.4	1,814	0.8	89.3
	Unsupervised	7,563	5.2	6,270	4.8	4,473	3.9	2,319	2.2	226.1
GSL (B)	Supervised	133,824	54.2	57,127	22.6	41,310	17.7	46,263	21.3	189.3
	Unsupervised	42,414	29.1	38,577	29.8	32,321	28.1	31,702	29.7	33.8
OL (C)	Supervised	8,042	3.3	8,299	3.3	9,728	4.2	5,592	2.6	43.8
	Unsupervised	3,990	2.8	3,440	2.7	2,990	2.6	2,828	2.6	41.1
SE (D)	Supervised	101,678	41.2	186,737	73.9	181,545	77.7	163,001	75.2	–37.6
	Unsupervised	91,945	63	81,252	62.7	75,155	65.4	70,051	65.5	31.2
Tot (E)	Supervised	246,978	100	252,603	100	233,572	100	216,670	100	14.0
	Unsupervised	145,912	100	129,540	100	114,940	100	106,900	100	36.6

Notes: FL: Financial liabilities; GSL: Guarantee-specific liabilities; OL: Other liabilities; SE: Shareholders' equity. (*) €000s..

Source: Author's own calculations.

- *Guarantee-specific liabilities* (GSL), mainly consisting of provisions for risks and charge, had a significant incidence increasing by 189.3 per cent[14] for Supervised Confidi and by 33.8 per cent for Unsupervised Confidi over the four-year period.

Table 5.11 Shareholders' equity composition: Unsupervised Confidi and Supervised Confidi (000€s)

Voce	Confidi	2010	2009	2008	2007
+ Capital	Supervised	57,817	57,090	61,792	65,647
	Unsupervised	28,538	24,274	22,137	20,615
– Not disbursed capital	Supervised	–	–	–	32
	Unsupervised	192	230	234	225
+ Legal and statutory reserves	Supervised	31,882	30,927	36,192	7,943
	Unsupervised	13,702	16,172	15,001	13,769
+ Revaluation reserves	Supervised	2,951	–	–	–
	Unsupervised	321	–321	–321	–
+ Unavailable reserve funds	Supervised	11,367	92,140	81,541	60,830
	Unsupervised	49,128	39,991	36,838	34,216
+ Retained earning	Supervised	–	–	–	–62
	Unsupervised	149	141	229	216
+ Profit (loss) for the year	Supervised	- 2,340	6,580	2,020	28,676
	Unsupervised	299	583	807	900
+ Other	Supervised	–	–	–	–
	Unsupervised	–	–	–55	–560
Total	Supervised	101,678	186,737	181,545	163,001
	Unsupervised	91,945	81,252	75,155	70,051

Source: Author's own calculations.

Table 5.12 Regulatory capital for Supervised Confidi

	2010	2009
Total capital requirement	29,419,139	26,399,122
Capital requirement for credit	27,507,855	18,424,362
Capital requirement for operational risk	1,911,284	1,774,760
Regulatory capital	101,178,378	96,123,594

Source: Author's own calculations.

As far as the composition of the shareholders' equity is concerned, Table 5.11 shows an increase in share capital for Unsupervised Confidi, thanks to contributions from new members and reserves for retained earnings, while Supervised Confidi shows a decrease, due to aggregation processes. The Unavailable Reserve Funds, which represents the significant source of the capitalization for Confidi, is supplied mostly by the decrease for Supervised Confidi inasmuch as it is not attributable to equity, since it is not intended to cover the general risk.

As far as the risk-taking is concerned, and credit risk in particular, Supervised Confidi (Table 5.12) registered a limited absorption of capital with respect to the portfolio of granted guarantees, since technical segregated forms of guarantee prevail upon first-demand guarantees subject to their compliance with regulatory ratios. As a consequence, Supervised Confidi recorded a capital ratio far higher than the 6 per cent threshold provided for by supervisory regulations ,also taking into consideration the capital absorption for the other regulatory risks.[15]

The significant increase in the *Guarantee-specific liabilities* (GSL, Table 5.13) is due to:

i) the increase in provisions, especially as far as Supervised Confidi are concerned, proportional to the losses calculated using different parameters for the performing loan portfolio and the default portfolio;
ii) a new allocation of unavailable reserve fund (included in the shareholder equity) to provisions for risk and charge (included in the guarantee-specific liabilities) by Supervised Confidi.

The rather widespread use of deposits decreases within the guarantee-specific liabilities, both in terms of incidence upon the entire aggregate and in variations registered over the four-year period.

The incidence of public funds, regardless of their technical form, on the liabilities in the balance sheet (Table 5.14) was calculated in order to analyze the public support for Confidi's activities. The public support transversally affects several items of the liabilities: share capital, unavailable reserve funds, provisions for liabilities and charges, provisions for doubtful debts, provisions for general financial risks, and provisions for granted guarantees. As far as the Unsupervised Confidi are concerned, which did not provide detailed information on the public resources used for the items taken into consideration, the public support was calculated by adding segregated funds to *Unavailable reserve funds* of the liabilities, since according to the Explanatory Notes they were presumably funded mainly by public contributions. Supervised Confidi, however, provided significantly more detailed information on the public contributions they received. Table 5.14 concerning the analysis of the Unsupervised and Supervised Confidi shows two rather similar situations:

Table 5.13 Guarantee-specific liability: evolution and composition by type of Confidi (000€s)

Voce	Confidi	2010	2009	2008	2007
Segregated funds	Supervised	99,379	23,211	21,443	21,690
	Unsupervised	21,000	18,089	13,191	12,663
Bad debt provisions	Supervised	–	–	–	–
	Unsupervised	2,043	1,952	1,935	1,939
Provisions for guarantees	Supervised	14,855	14,503	1,276	3,809
	Unsupervised	4,372	3,433	2,616	2,039
Guarantee deposits	Supervised	19,591	19,413	18,591	20,764
	Unsupervised	14,999	15,102	14,579	15,060
Total	Supervised	133,824	57,127	41,310	46,263
	Unsupervised	42,414	38,577	32,321	31,702

Source: Author's own calculations.

Table 5.14 Incidence of public funds on the liabilities in the balance sheet by type of Confidi (%)

Type of Confidi	2010	2009	2008	2007
Supervised Confidi	44.9	45.7	44.1	38.1
Unsupervised Confidi	48.1	44.8	43.5	43.8
Total	46.	45.4	43.9	40.0

Source: Author's own calculations.

significant support by public funding for both type of Confidi, exceeding 40 per cent of the liabilities over the four-year period.

3.2.2 Assets

Table 5.15, concerning a first assessment of the reclassified balance sheets aggregated data, shows for both type of Confidi that the invested capital mainly consists of *Financial Assets* (FA, Table 5.15) and that investments in *Fixed Assets* (FXA, Table 5.15) tend to increase proportionally to aggregation processes evidently requiring an organizational structure and a greater amount of fixed assets.[16]

The figures below show the available and unavailable financial asset components in order to analyze how assets intended to hedge guarantees were used for that purpose. Both Unsupervised and Supervised Confidi registered an increase in unavailable financial assets, by 38.3 per cent and 28.9 per cent respectively, confirming the greater amount of segregate guarantees granted on unavailable monetary risk funds as well as the overdues already detected, for which Confidi intervenes in a subsidiary way.

Table 5.15 Reclassified balance sheet (assets): Unsupervised Confidi and Supervised Confidi

Type of Confidi		2010		2009		2008		2007		Var %
		Value*	**%**	**Value***	**%**	**Value***	**%**	**Value***	**%**	**2007–2010**
AFA (A)	Supervised	102,705	41.6	96,547	38.2	90,728	38.8	87,690	40.5	17.1
	Unsupervised	37,474	25.7	29,503	22.8	28,761	25	29,473	27.6	27.1
UFA (B)	Supervised	128,268	51.9	120,759	47.8	105,264	45.1	99,527	45.9	28.9
	Unsupervised	81,254	55.7	75,640	58.4	62,844	54.7	58,749	56	38.3
FA(C)	Supervised	230,973	93.5	217,306	86.1	195,992	83.9	187,216	86.4	23.4
	Unsupervised	118,727	81.4	105,142	81.2	91,605	79.7	88,222	82.5	34.6
RGP (D)	Supervised	466	0.2	28	0.01	759	0.3	830	0.4	–43.8
	Unsupervised	8,864	6.1	7,351	5.7	6,293	5.5	6,147	5.7	44.2
OA (E)	Supervised	8,298	3.4	19,026	7.5	21,559	9.2	20,473	9.5	–59.5
	Unsupervised	6,835	4.7	6,509	5.0	7,759	6.7	5,647	5.3	21
FXA (F)	Supervised	7,242	2.9	16,243	6.4	15,263	6.5	8,151	3.8	–11.2
	Unsupervised	11,485	7.8	10,537	8.1	9,284	8.1	6,884	6.4	66.8
Tot (E)	Supervised	246,978	100	252,603	100	233,572	100	216,670	100	14.0
	Unsupervised	145,912	100	129,540	100	114,940	100	106,900	100	36.5

Notes: AFA: available financial assets; UFA: unavailable financial assets; FA: total financial assets; RGP: receivable for guarantees paid; OA:other assets; FXA: Fixed assets. (*)€000s.

Source: Author's own calculations.

	Cash and cash balances		Receivable from banks		Receivable from financial institutions		Bonds		Shares and quote of funds	
	Supervised	Unsupervised	Supervised	Unsupervised	Supervised	Unsupervised	Supervised	Unsupervised	Supervised	Unsupervised
2010	22.6%	0.2%	23.6%	29.8%	0.0%	0.0%	0.0%	64.3%	53.8%	5.7%
2009	0.3%	0.3%	38.7%	39.1%	6.0%	0.0%	37.4%	52.5%	17.6%	8.1%
2008	0.1%	0.3%	36.2%	33.2%	7.1%	0.0%	31.4%	58.5%	25.2%	8.0%
2007	0.2%	0.3%	27.8%	31.3%	7.7%	0.0%	35.8%	61.7%	28.6%	6.7%

Figure 5.3 Breakdown of available financial assets

Source: Author's own calculations.

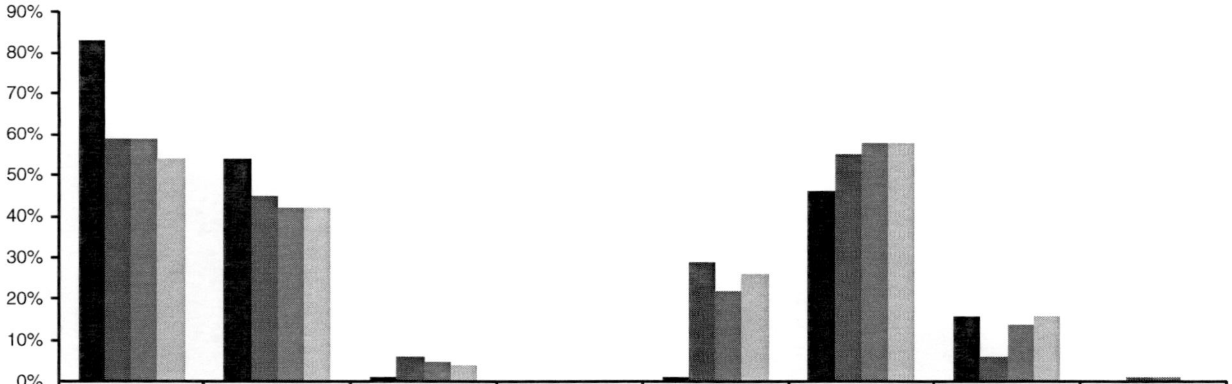

	Receivable from banks		Receivable from financial institutions		Bonds		Shares and que of funds	
	Supervised	Unsupervised	Supervised	Unsupervised	Supervised	Unsupervised	Supervised	Unsupervised
2010	83.0%	54.0%	1.0%	0.0%	1.0%	46.0%	16.0%	0.0%
2009	59.0%	45.0%	6.0%	00%	29.0%	55.0%	6.0%	1.0%
2008	59.0%	42.0%	5.0%	0.0%	22.0%	58.0%	14.0%	1.0%
2007	54.0%	42.0%	4.0%	0.0%	26.0%	58.0%	16.0%	0.0%

Figure 5.4 Breakdown of available financial assets

Source: Author's own calculations.

The percentage breakdown of the *Unavailable financial assets* (UFA, Figure 5.3) shows a widespread presence of zero-risk *assets* which grew notably in 2010, as well as a decrease in bond investments especially for Supervised Confidi. Similarly, Unsupervised Confidi demonstrate a higher decrease in *Available financial assets* (AFA, Figure 5.4) than do Supervised Confidi over the 2007–2009 period. As far as the *Available financial assets* are concerned, Supervised Confidi registered a significantly high value in terms of stock share, the riskiest component, exceeding 53 per cent of available assets in 2010, with a 120 per cent increase. This breakdown is the result of portfolio policies adopted to optimize the risk-return portfolio and increase the overall profitability in a scenario characterized by a significant decrease in the government bond quotation. In contrast, the available assets of Unsupervised Confidi are much more prudent, since they consist of a growing share of bonds, accounting for over 64 in 2010, with a 33 per cent increase over the four-year period.

Moreover, as Table 5.15 shows, Unsupervised Confidi registered a significant increase in the entry *Receivable for guarantee paid* (RGP, Table 5.15) over the four-year period, showing a worsening of the guarantee portfolio quality. Amounts owed to shareholders, implying the enforcement of the on-demand guarantee by the Confidi, recorded values above 5.5 per cent over the four-year period, with a peak in 2010 (6.1 per cent). The importance of this datum referred to the Unsupervised Confidi with respect to the overall aggregate value (91 per cent) of the relevant balance sheet item (RGP) is to be ascribed both to the accounting procedure of the portfolio risk and to the activities carried out by Supervised Confidi, more focused on subsidiary and segregated guarantees over the four-year period. This might

Table 5.16 Guarantees against impaired and non-performing loans (€000s)

	Confidi	2010	2009	2008	2007
Guarantee against non-performing loans	Unsupervised	7,368*	1,667**	6,902*****	6,789****
	Supervised	332,846**	309,269*	211,171*	154,939*
	Total	340,214	310,936	218,074	161,728
Guarantees against impaired loans	Unsupervised	na	na	622*	229*
	Supervised	178,108	na	na	na
	Total	178,108	na	622	229
Total guarantees against non-performing loans	106	7,368	1,667	7,524	7,018
	107	510,954	309,269	211,171	154,939
	Total	518,322	310,936	218,695	161,957

Notes: (*) Data related to 1 Confidi; (**) data related to 2 Confidi; (***) data related to 4 Confidi; (****) data related to 6 Confidi; (** ***) data related to 8 Confidi.

Source: Author's own calculations.

be a consequence of the higher devaluations for the credit risk rather than the reduction in the number of insolvencies between 2009 and 2010.

The specific nature of Confidi highlights the characteristic accounting profiles connected with the placement of the typical risk of these types of institutions. Guarantees are usually moved above the line only after the enforcement by the guaranteed intermediary. Therefore they are part of the overall credit risk assumed by the Confidi in their usual business. The typical risk below the line (guarantees against impaired and non-performing loans) must be also taken into consideration in order to carry out a proper risk analysis. Since only Supervised Confidi clearly and specifically defined this datum in their annual report, while Unsupervised Confidi hardly ever specified it in their Explanatory Notes, we can assume that the value of guarantee against substandard loans below the line, whenever present, is to be considered an optimistic underestimate (Table 5.16). Especially in the case of subsidiary guarantees, their entering among overdue loans is less immediate, since the enforcement usually follows the confirmation by the guaranteed intermediaries about losses. Confidi's underestimate of the substandard loans may affect profits due to higher capital devaluation and may also determine higher capital absorption, especially for Supervised Confidi.

3.3 Income statement analysis

The profitability analysis is carried out using the reclassified income statement with aggregate values, for Unsupervised and Supervised Confidi respectively.

Two different situations clearly emerge concerning the two Confidi macro-categories, at least in terms of cost–revenue relation and, in particular, efficiency. More specifically, Table 5.17 shows:

- the importance in operating income of the guarantee fees and financial asset return, for both Unsupervised and Unsupervised Confidi – which, however, show a decrease in the 2008–2010 period;
- a trend of growing costs (*Operating cost*, OC) with a notable increase, in the 2009–2010 period, for Unsupervised Confidi and in 2010 for Supervised Confidi, which resulted in the absorption of the income positive components expressed by the *Intermediation Margin* (IM), amounting to over 79 per cent for Unsupervised Confidi and 65.6 per cent (the highest value in 2010) for Supervised Confidi;
- a *Commission Margin* (CM) which is not adequate to cover the operating costs (OC), except in 2009 for Unsupervised Confidi, and
- the prominent role of the *Financial Operation Margin* (FOM) which improves the income situation; this circumstance is not found in Supervised Confidi, even if a notable drop of the financial contribution margin can be detected;

- a growth in the provisions (*Net provision for risk and charges*, PRC) which is more marked in 2010 for Supervised Confidi, due to a rise in the risk of the guarantee portfolio, specifically for 2010;
- the importance of public contributions, which played a significant role in hedging the risks actually incurred, especially by Unsupervised Confidi;
- the decrease of the *Net Operating Profits* (NOP), showing negative values in the four-year period, except in 2007 for Unsupervised Confidi, and only in 2010 for Supervised Confidi;
- the importance of the *Extraordinary Results* (ER), in particular for Unsupervised Confidi, in determining the differences of the two typical income parameters, that is, the operating income and the operating result.

In light of the gaps emerging from the dynamics of the income statement components, the analysis of the income aggregates was carried out for both type of intermediaries.

Unsupervised Confidi – Table 5.17 shows the growing trend of the *Commission Margins* (CM, Table 5.17) during the four-year period. Given that in practice the commissions are, at least in part, applied as a percentage of loans, this increase is to be ascribed to the growth in the guarantee granted. It can also be seen that revenues for additional services (consultancy, financial analysis, drawing up of business plans, etc.) do not have a significant impact (*Other net income*, ONI, Table 5.17).

The analysis of the financial margin (FOM, Table 5.17) reveals a positive and solid performance only in the 2007–2008 period. This phenomenon can be easily interpreted: most of the Confidi's profits come from debentures, current accounts, financial instruments and deposits. The conservative composition portfolio policy, characterized by investments in treasury bonds, limited the effects of the financial crisis, at least in 2007–2008, but not during the following years due to the sovereign risk of the Eurozone countries.

The growth of the guarantee portfolio draws attention to the innate risk of the Confidi activity and to the evaluation of the relevant dynamics. To that end, we should focus from an economic point of view on the costs resulting from the adjustments/provisions for the relating hedging (PRC, Table 5.17), that showed a growth trend (+ 124.4 per cent during the four-year period). Since no detailed information was provided in the Explanatory notes, it was not possible to split the losses from the provisions/adjustments. We can assume that the smaller Confidi, at least, adopted an inadequate provisions policy, thus incurring more frequent losses. On the other hand, the increase in the overdues registered by these institutions would justify stronger provisioning policies aimed at collecting more resources to cope with any future increase in disbursements.

Table 5.17 Reclassified income statement: Unsupervised Confidi and Supervised Confidi

Type of Confidi		2010		2009		2008		2007		
		Value*	**%**	**Value***	**%**	**Value***	**%**	**Var %**	**%**	**Value* 2007–2010**
CM (A)	Supervised	13,862	87.5	9,402	67.4	11,103	84.6	12,171	73.8	13.9
	Unsupervised	5,861	75.0	5,479	73.4	4,664	66.2	4,612	70.1	27.1
FOM (B)	Supervised	1,979	12.5	4,556	32.6	2,020	15.4	4,325	26.2	–54.2
	Unsupervised	1,957	25.0	1,989	26.6	2,385	33.8	1,968	29.9	–0.6
IM (C = A+B)	Supervised	15,841	100	13,958	100	13,124	100	16,496	100	–4.0
	Unsupervised	7,818	100.0	7,468	100	7,049	100	6,579	100	18.8
OC (D)	Supervised	10,400	65.6	6,026	43.2	8,054	61.4	9,576	58.1	8.6
	Unsupervised	6,184	79.1	5,346	71.6	5,067	71.9	4,701	71.5	31.5
OP	Supervised	5,441	34.4	7,932	56.8	5,070	38.6	6,920	41.9	–21.4
(E = C–D)	Unsupervised	1,634	21	2,122	28.4	1,982	28.1	1,878	28.5	–13.0
PRC (F)	Supervised	8,860	55.9	4,195	30.1	2,706	20.6	4,484	27.2	97.6
	Unsupervised	3,700	47.3	3,497	46.8	2,689	38.1	1,648	25.0	124.5
ONI (G)	Supervised	1,464	9.2	2,089	15	587	4.5	2,116	12.8	–30.8
	Unsupervised	932	11.9	92	1.2	–74	–1.0	–11	–0.2	111.9
NOP	Supervised	– 1,955	–2.3	5,826	41.7	2,951	22.5	4,553	27.6	–142.9
(H = E–F+G)	Unsupervised	–1,134	–14.5	–1,283	–17.2	–781	–11.1	220	3.3	–615.5
ER (I)	Supervised	–270	–1.7	824	5.9	–770	–5.9	24,264	147.1	–101.1
	Unsupervised	1,526	19.5	1,942	26	1,673	23.7	762	11.6	100.3
PBT	Supervised	– 2,225	–14	6,650	47.6	2,181	16.6	28,816	174.7	–107.7
(L = H+I)	Unsupervised	393	5.0	660	8.8	892	12.7	981	14.9	–59.9
T (M)	Supervised	115	0.7	70	0.5	161	1.2	140	0.85	–17.8
	Unsupervised	93	1.2	77	1.0	85	1.2	81	1.2	14.8
NP (N)	Supervised	– 2,340	–14.8	6,580	47.1	2,020	15.4	28,676	173.8	–108.2
	Unsupervised	300	3.8	583	7.8	807	11.4	900	13.7	–66.7

Notes: CM: Commission margin; FOM: Financial operation margin; IM: intermediation margin; OC: operating costs; OP: operating profits; PRC: net provisions for risks and charges; ONI: other net income; NOP: net operating profits; ER: extraordinary results; PBT: profit before taxes; T: taxes; NP: net profit. (*)€000s.

Source: Author's own calculations.

This adjustment of the previous years' inadequate policies makes the Unsupervised Confidi's income statement highly unstable. Such balance is heavily affected by a 31.5 per cent increase in operating costs, higher than that (+18.8 per cent) recorded by the *Intermediation Margin* (IM, Table 5.17). By introducing a breakeven *point* analysis aimed at determining the maximum value of sustainable costs, with no profitability, that also considers cost related to provisions for risk, Table 5.18 shows that in the four-year period the costs actually incurred are higher than the breakeven costs, thus reducing the capability of Confidi 106 to sustain the breakeven point. The role of public contributions is, therefore, fundamental in terms of an income statement rebalance, as can be inferred from the values recorded in the operating income.

Supervised Confidi – As for Unsupervised Confidi, the analysis of the aggregate data requires a closer examination of the commissions collected (Table 5.17) that as of 2010 are entered on an accrual basis only against the expenses relating to loan application and guarantee management. The same was done for commissions paid for the counter-guarantees received. The entering of the commissions in the medium- and long-term items by means of deferrals will allow the margin to be supported in case of a downturn in production, as occurred for a Supervised Confidi. The issue of deferrals is significantly reduced if operativity shifts to short-term exposures.

The performance of financial investments (FOM, Table 5.17), with reference to Supervised Confidi, was influenced by the kind of operativity of the larger Confidi, mainly characterized by segregated guarantees. This affected the policy of unavailable investments, characterized in large part by liquid assets. Nonetheless, the implementation in 2010 of a dynamic strategy of the financial portfolio through the sale of bond securities and the re-investment in shares did not affect the performance of the portfolio itself in a positive way.

In terms of costs, the considerable rise is to be ascribed to the transformation into supervised intermediaries, which required investments in

Table 5.18 Breakeven point analysis: Unsupervised Confidi

	2010		2009		2008		2007	
	Value*	%	**Value***	%	**Value***	%	**Value***	%
Total sustainable operating costs	4,118		3,971		4,360		4,931	
Operating cost	6,184	79.1	5,346	71.6	5,067	71.9	4,701	71.5

Note: (*)€000s.

Source: Author's own calculations.

Table 5.19 Breakeven point analysis – Supervised Confidi

	2010		2009		2008		2007	
	Value	**%**	**Value**	**%**	**Value**	**%**	**Value**	**%**
Total sustainable operating costs	6,981		9,763		10,418		12,012	
Operating cost	10,400	65.6	6,026	43.2	8,054	61.4	9,576	58.1

Note: (*) 000€.

Source: Author's own calculations.

the institution and, specifically, in human resources training (significant disbursements which represent inelastic fixed costs).

Another aspect which influenced the Confidi economic situation is the level of risk of the exposures undertaken against the guarantees granted, which resulted on the one hand in higher adjustments and provisions against *performing* and substandard exposures and, on the other, in higher losses covered by the use of funds.

The data on the commissions paid (Table 5.19) confirm, especially for larger Confidi, the inadequate recourse to counter-guarantees, especially at a point in time when *non-performing guarantees* are growing.

Finally, the relation between commission margin, operating costs and financial operation margin is worth mentioning. Specifically, the commission margins are high enough to cover operating costs. The contribution of the net interest income, even though improving the income situation, is not crucial to the covering of the costs of the Supervised Confidi. However, the breakeven analysis in Tables 5.18 and 5.19 show that the positive income sources cannot cover both operating charges and those resulting from provisions for risks and charges. With the correct assessment of the actual risk sustained by the management, problems of economic balance also emerge for larger Confidi. Before starting the subsequent analysis the point needs to be made that there have been many difficulties in the use of budgetary data, especially on account of the presence of accounting methods that are sometimes non-transparent and not sufficiently integrated with the information in the notes. The financial statement plays an important part as a starting point to guide the analysis and as an input information tool for the introduction of more complex accounting models. The shortcomings of this instrument, as has been verified in some Unsupervised Confidi financial statements, are not only that they do not facilitate the evaluations, but also that they can come back to bite those who are scoring the same Confidi. Despite these limitations, the analysis that follows proposes a technique, that, by coordinating the quotients derived from the financial statements in a suitable way, allows, the signs and symptoms of the management that are instrumental to applying quantitative scoring methods to be obtained in the most operative way possible.

4 Scoring/Ranking methodological framework

The analysis of the performance carried out so far is preparatory to the definition of a methodological framework to assign a quantitative score to sample Confidi, which represents a first experimental exercise in this field, as underlined in the introduction. This methodological framework was designed starting from an analysis of the core business features of the Confidi in question. As mentioned above, although they are *non-profit-oriented enterprises* devoted to the mutuality principle, Confidi must in any case pursue the financial and economic equilibria in both the short and long term. Starting out from this observation and from the main aspects of the Confidi production process already provided, we carried out the following activities aiming at defining a scoring/ranking methodological framework:

- Definition of the *information profiles* that make up the Confidi performance and risk profile, by identifying the relations between capital components and the other sources for hedging guarantee activity, risks and profitability resulting from the granting of the guarantees and the relevant provision of complementary and collateral services;
- Identification of a group of key performance-risk indicators for each *information profile*;
- Univariate analysis of the most significant indicators for each *information profile* through pseudo-inferential statistical techniques;
- Analysis of the latent structures that are more representative of the Confidi production process, in order to identify both performance and risk synthetic multi-profile indicators;
- Construction of a ranking experimental map to assign surveyed Confidi a rank/score using the multi-profile indicators.

4.1 Definition of information profiles, key performance-risk indicators and univariate analysis

Figure 5.5 shows the profiles that in our opinion determine Confidi management stability and define the guarantee management process. The content and the relevant economic, financial and capital impacts of the above-mentioned process can be referred to the following profiles:

- **Risk level of the guarantee portfolio** considered in terms of enforced, difficult and overdue guarantees. The indicators concerning this information

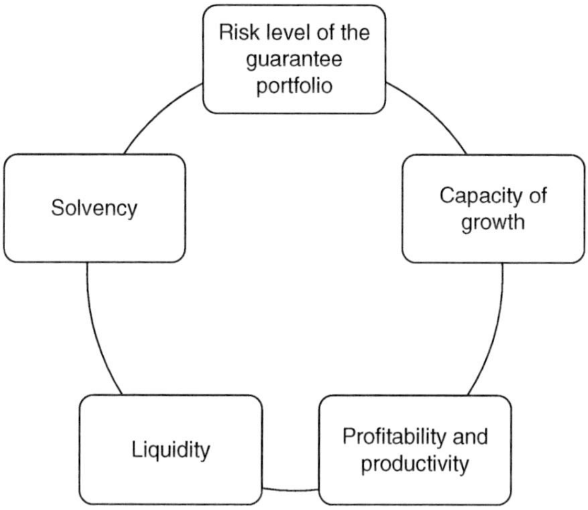

Figure 5.5 Information profiles

profile (Table 5.20) are aimed at measuring the potential and actual risk of the guarantee portfolio and its impairment rate;[17]

- **Solvency** in terms of adequacy of the hedging sources (capital and risk provisions) with respect to the risks and commitments assumed. The adequacy of the hedging sources depends on the size and breakdown of the provisions for doubtful debts, the provisions for guarantees granted, unavailable reserve fund and the segregated fund, as well as on the shareholders' equity and on the capital adequacy that define the Confidi's ability to absorb losses resulting from exposure due to on-demand guarantees. With respect to these facts we formulated the main indicators for this information profile;
- **Liquidity**, that is the intermediary's capability to face its commitments without affecting its ordinary business, in other words expected and unexpected cash flows over the short–medium and long term. From this perspective, we formulated tactical, operational (monetary equilibrium) and structural (financial equilibrium) liquidity indicators that draw inspiration from a measurement approach based on a temporal correlation between source and loan maturity, while at the same time considering the main features of Confidi operativity;
- **Profitability and productivity** analyzed through the decisive factors affecting cost and income levels and on the productivity of the guarantee process. From this perspective, we formulated indicators describing operational profitability, net profitability, profitability resulting from guarantee activity and collateral and complementary services supplied, and financial

margins obtained from the security portfolio management. As far as productivity is concerned, we formulated indicators providing information on the productivity per each staff member, on the average amount of each guarantee granted and the number of cases managed by each staff member;

- **Capacity of growth**, that is, the possibility for Confidi to expand the guarantee volume through the shareholders' equity and the liability segregated fund. From this perspective we formulated two leverages: one refers to the shareholders' equity assuming an active management of the portfolio characterized by the granting of on-first demand guarantees; the second refers to the shareholders' equity and the segregated fund, and is aimed at understanding the possible size of the guarantee portfolio growth, including segregated guarantees and guarantees drawn from segregated funds.

The profiles are tightly interconnected and strictly related to the guarantee production process. From our point of view, all of them define the Confidi's capacity to survive in the current market scenario. We identified 28 indices that in our opinion are able of representing each information profile.

Indicators which underwent statistical analysis were calculated using only the main aggregate data of the Income Statement and balance sheet of Unsupervised Confidi (that adopt the balance sheet scheme provided for the Italian legislative decree 1982) and of the Confidi, already changed into Supervised Confidi, but that in 2010 drew up their balance sheet according to the transition to IAS/IFRS standards (comparable to the previous balance sheet scheme). During the univariate analysis, we took into consideration 24 indicators using pseudo-inferential statistics techniques. As for the other four, we did not consider them, since the time-related accounting information required was insignificant or incomplete. The table below illustrated the indices selected for each information profile and how they are determined using the balance sheet data of the Confidi sample. Many of them derived from the traditional balance sheet ratio analysis adapted to the features of the guarantee process production.

For each indicator, which has passed the test of the abundance of available observations, an 'organ pipes' style histogram was constructed, featuring six uniform classes,[18] covering the entire range of variation, from the minimum to the maximum value. From a simple inspection of the organ pipe graph there can be inferred, even intuitively, one of the possible forms of distribution, namely: U-shape, inverted J (left half-U), J (right half-U), upside-down U (Normal). This solution, although statistically less robust than that based on the classical tests for normality, is preferred, because it is more efficient operationally. In the desire to achieve the most objective inference, as an alternative to the intuitive approach, we also carried out an interpolation of the empirical data with a second order polynomial (parabola), whose parameters were estimated by the least square method. Also, in cases of diagnostic

Table 5.20 Information profiles and relevant indicators

Information profiles	**Indices**	**How It Is Calculated**
Guarantee portfolio risk level	*Index 1: Actual risk index*	RGP/ Total outstanding guaranteed portfolio
	Index 2: Potential risk index	Non-performing guarantees/ Total outstanding guaranteed portfolio
	Index 4: Pay out rate	Enforcement/ Total outstanding guaranteed portfolio in the previous year
	Index 8: Risk provision ad equacy to difficult guarantees	Provisions for risk and charge /(RGP+ Non-performing guarantees)
Solvency	*Index 9: Risk Coverage ratio*	Shareholders' equity/(RGP+ Non-performing guarantees-provisions for risk and charge)
Capacity of	*Index 11: Leverage 1*	Total outstanding guaranteed portfolio /Shareholders' equity
growth	*Index 11b is : Leverage 2*	Total outstanding guaranteed portfolio /(Shareholders' equity +Segregated funds)
	Index 12: Structural liquidity ratio	Unavailable financial assets/ (Provisions for risk and charge+Reserves+Shareholders' equity)
	Index 13: Tactical Liquidity ratio	Available financial assets/ Enforcements
Liquidity	*Index 15: Operational Liquidity ratio*	Available financial assets / Total outstanding guaranteed portfolio
	Index 16: Liquidity mix composition	Unavailable financial assets /Total financial asset
	Index 17: ROE	Net profit/shareholders' equity
	Index 18: Operating profitability ratio	Operating profit/Total outstanding guaranteed portfolio
	Index 18 bis: Operating profitability ratio bis	Operating profit/Total outstanding guaranteed portfolio in the year
	Index 19: Credit risk cost ratio	Net provisions for risk and charge/Total outstanding guaranteed portfolio
Profitability	*Index 20: Other income ratio*	Other net income/Total outstanding guaranteed portfolio
	Index 21: Net Operating profitability	Net operating profit/ Total outstanding guaranteed

Continued

Table 5.20 Continued

Information profiles	Indices	How It Is Calculated
	Index 22: Commission Margin Profit ability	Commission margin/Total outstanding guaranteed portfolio
	Index 23: Financial management margin incidence	Financial management margin/ Commission margin
	Index 24: Return on financial asset	Interest income/Financial assets
	Index 25: Cost to Income ratio	Operating costs/Commission margin
	Index 26: Average size of guarantee granted	Guarantee granted/Number of practice
Productivity	*Index 27: Average number of practice per staff member*	Number of practice/Number of staff member
	Index 28: Average amount of guarantee per staff member	Guarantee granted/ Number of staff member

Note: The numeration is related to the 28 selected indices.

uncertainty, we analyzed the indicator against a previous period (if available), from past experience to assess whether it met the 'temporal stability' of the forms of distribution. For the subsequent transformation of the individual values of an indicator into ratings for each Confidi analyzed, it was necessary to predetermine the 'direction of the report', in order to identify which values of the distribution, sorted in ascending order, were to be considered more virtuous and which less so. Finally, to pass from the quantitative to the qualitative judgement, we set up a coherent system of rules and scores, which made it possible to assign a score to the first Confidi examined.

We elaborated this univariate statistical analysis for each of the 24 indices, as shown in Figure 5.6:

- the relevant value for each Confidi, whenever available, the Confidi *ranking*, sorted by growing indicator values and corresponding score from which the link between the two can be inferred;
- the creation of a bar chart illustrating the frequency distribution, with its relevant interpolation function (*best fit*), to objectively infer the distribution form, as shown in the following example concerning Index 9.

The univariate analysis of the selected indicators allowed us to infer the reflections on the performance of the frequency distributions observed each time in relation to the indices identified – and, therefore, to make a more

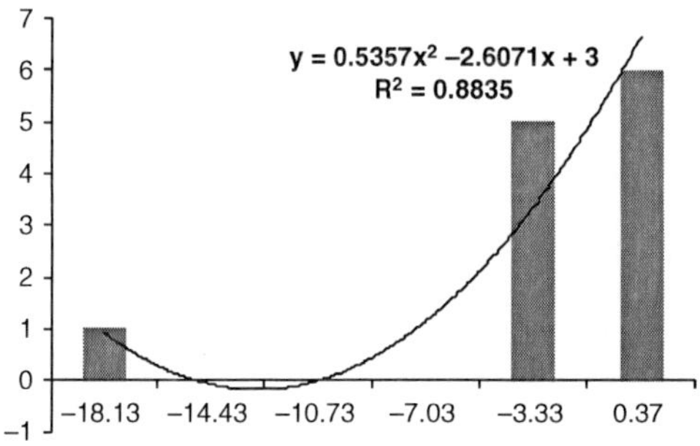

Confidi	Index value	Bar	Score
1	-0.53	6	2
2	na		na
3	na		na
4	-19.99	1	2
5	na		na
6	-1.97	5	4
7	-1.50	5	4
8	-0.21	6	2
9	-1.58	5	4
10	-1.62	5	4
11	2.22	6	2
12	-1.57	5	4
13	-0.64	6	2
14	-1.10	6	2
15	-1.20	6	2
16	na		na

Figure 5.6 Index 9: frequency distribution

accurate selection of the same for the purposes of constructing the main components of each information profile.

4.2 Analysis of the latent structures and identification of multi-profile indicators

We carried out a first exploratory analysis aimed at finding a simplified information structure suitable to represent the economic and financial equilibrium of the surveyed Confidi, in order to synthesize the information contained and distributed among the several indicators chosen for each information profile. From a methodological point of view, we applied a standard technique of statistical analysis: *principal component factor analysis*. This analysis is based on the observation that the quantity of information provided by each indicator is proportional to the variability of their appearance in the surveyed Confidi. It is aimed at significantly reducing the number of the indicators necessary to interpret the reference context, without losing any statistically relevant information. The *principal component analysis* is therefore focused on identifying the dimensions underlying the data structure, and the dimensions (latent factors or, as in this case, principal components) designed to sum up the interdependence of the intertwined relations between original variables, resulting from linear combinations of the initial indicators to obtain – by construction – the multi-profile feature we were aiming for.

This is achieved through a linear transformation of the variables projected onto a new Cartesian system: the new variable with a higher variance is projected onto the first axis, while the following variable, second in terms of variance, is projected onto the second axis and so on.

The complexity reduction is the result of the analysis of the main (in terms of variance) new variables.

Table 5.21 Multiple variability explained by each indicator

		Eigen values initial	
Component	Total	Variance %	Cumulative %
1	4.647	35.749	35.749
2	3.128	24.06	59.81
3	1.72	13.324	73.044
4	1.204	9.26	82.304
5	0.8	6.152	88.456
6	0.641	4.933	93.389
7	0.413	3.179	96.568
8	0.242	2.859	98.427
9	0.082	0.633	99.06
10	0.071	0.548	99.608
11	0.042	0.326	99.933
12	0.008	0.058	99.991
13	0.001	0.009	100

The algorithms used allow each component to progressively absorb a greater portion of the overall variability (and therefore of the information) with respect to the previous components. In other words, they are – in this case, by construction as well – 'independent' (uncorrelated). From a conceptual point of view this condition allows for an easier 'economic' interpretation of the analyzed scenarios, while from a more operative point of view it allows for the re-utilization of the new indicators for future aggregation and/or regression analyses without having to face the typical problems connected to the linear dependence of explanatory variables (multicollinearity).

The Latent Structure – Within the 24 indicators selected, we used the 13 balance sheet indexes providing information for all the 16 surveyed Confidi (the so-called 'active' indicators) in order to build the structures to be analyzed. Table 5.21 explains the multiple variability of each index.

The remaining 11 indices (so-called 'explanatory' indices) were instead used to better identify the meaning of the components (the underlying economic condition) progressively found, and therefore to finally select the most significant multi-profile indices. The first solutions obtained showed clearly that the performance aspects more directly connected to the portfolio quality were evenly distributed and, moreover, in a non-significant manner along the different axes of the latent structures identified by means of the standard procedure.

This – in general terms – implies that a further synthesis of the factorial axes towards a unique indicator (such as segmentation of the Confidi group)[19] is necessary.

Table 5.22 Mono-variability explained by the five components

Indices	Initial value	Final value
Ind11bis	1.000	0.967
Ind11	1.000	0.781
Ind12	1.000	0.3669
Ind17	1.000	0.897
Ind18	1.000	0.954
Ind19	1.000	0.945
Ind20	1.000	0.893
Ind21	1.000	0.794
Ind24	1.000	0.939
Ind15	1.000	0.959
Ind22	1.000	0.825
Ind23	1.000	0.915
Ind25	1.000	0.961

From this perspective, we used unsupervised segmentation techniques referring to the cluster analysis, aimed at dividing the initial group into subgroups (clusters) as similar as possible within the same group, and forming groups that differ from one another: the score assigned to each cluster will therefore represent their membership of one specific class.

More specifically we used a rotation technique of the identified latent structures (so-called Varimax) based on the criterion of maximizing the variability of each basic indicator on single components (Table 5.22).

Generally speaking, this implies a more even redistribution of the overall variability. Our specific aim was to identify an essential component featuring a low accounting relevance.[20]

Thus the 'sought' latent factor is found for, and it corresponds to the third principal component of the rotated structure (*careful management of the portfolio quality/profitability*). The explained overall variability portion is equal to approximately 17, which seems compatible with the reference information context. The first principal component of the 'rotated' solutions analyzed so far – the one that by construction absorbs the greater portion of the information provided by the 13 active indicators – does not, indeed, exceed 25 per cent of the total. This first principal component is the most representative in the production process of the Confidi surveyed in order to identify multi-profile synthetic indicators for risk and performance.

The factorial structure resulting from the statistical analyses is based upon five principal components that explain 88 per cent of overall variability. As already stated, the low concentration on each factor is in line with the reference context; it represents, on the one hand, the reduced number of Confidi involved, the framework characterized by objective unclearness and low presence in the initial database and, on the other hand, a significant independence – by construction – among the indicators of the different profiles. The five identified components are:

1. Growth factor of ordinary operations;
2. Financial management-oriented performance;
3. Portfolio quality/profitability-focused management;
4. Independent operational profitability factor;
5. Independent factor of profitability from collateral activities/services.

Scores are assigned to Confidi for each of the above-mentioned components by applying to each variable the coefficients included in Table 5.23.[21]

Portfolio quality/profitability-focused management – This third component of the proposed solution is the only factor in the analyzed structures that features clear significant correlations between the virtuous business management components and other components that provide information on profitability and guarantee portfolio quality undertaken more directly.

This is a real multi-profile indicator, since it sums up the various information areas defined during the methodology definition stage, and in particular risk level, solvency, liquidity and profitability. Productivity and potential size are not included in this first indicator, since they were absorbed by the first principal component (*Potential growth factor*).

The soundness of this latent structure is represented by the significant correlations in the 'right direction' among basic indicators with the multi-profile factor (as shown in Figure 5.7 below) that confirm from a logical and operational point of view that: *Portfolio quality/profitability-focused*

Table 5.23 Matrix of the component ranking coefficients

	Components				
	1	2	3	4	5
Indbis	0.367	0.116	–0.043	–0.021	0.177
Ind11	0.292	0.021	0.026	–0.113	0.151
Ind12	0.281	0.177	–0.094	–0.062	–0.033
Ind17	–0.104	0.112	0.477	–0.220	–0.302
Ind18	–0.055	0.050	0.216	0.352	0.170
Ind19	0.008	–0.096	–0.224	0.561	0.015
Ind20	0.124	0.153	0.015	0.051	0.842
Ind21	–0.015	0.010	0.401	–0.060	0.326
Ind24	–0.079	0.244	0.066	0.217	0.009
Ind15	–0.286	0.064	0.151	–0.109	–0.016
Ind22	–0.162	–0.424	–0.078	0.210	–0.091
Ind23	0.023	0.352	–0.040	0.060	0.197
Ind25	0.022	0.146	–0.251	–0.100	0.115

Note: Extraction Method: Principal Component Analysis; Rotation Method: Varimax with Kaiser normalization.

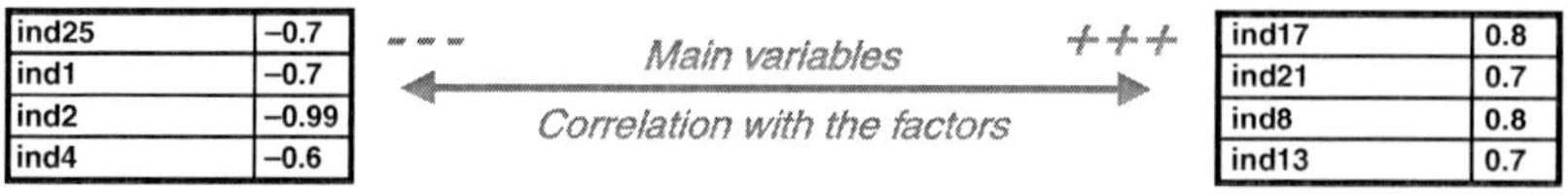

Figure 5.7 Indicators and sign of the correlations with multi-profile factor 3

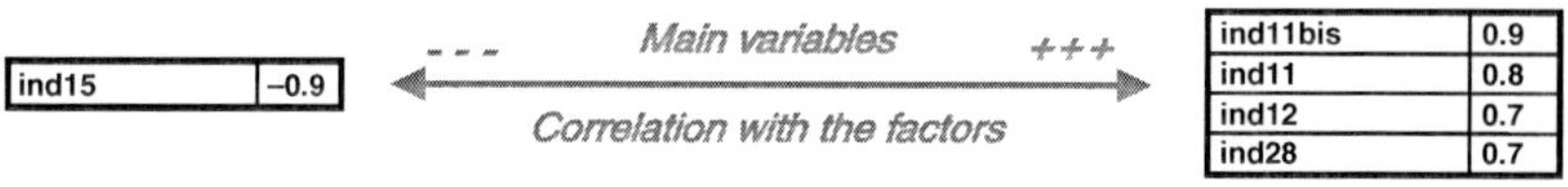

Figure 5.8 Indicators and sign of the correlations with multi-profile factor 1

management is positively correlated with the return on equity as well as with the ordinary operation contribution margin. In fact, the ratio between the operating result and the guarantee scale variable, the risk provision limit/consistency with respect to non-performing guarantees and with the ability of the guarantee intermediary to promptly face the immediate cash outflow requests (*Tactical liquidity ratio*). *Portfolio quality/profitability-focused management* is negatively correlated with the actual risk level, the potential risk and the guarantee portfolio enforcement rate, as well as with the efficiency level of the production process expressed by the *cost to income ratio* (see Figure 5.7).

Growth factor of ordinary operations – The other component of the rotated solution that we took into consideration was the *Growth factor of ordinary operations,* accounting for approximately 25 per cent of the overall variability. It is a rather low value. yet it proves the real independence of the balance sheet indexes chosen to represent the different profiles. This multi-profile indicator certainly represents a tendency or a potential growth of the specific guarantee business. The correlations between this profile and the size indicators (the two multipliers identified in the methodology stage), together with operational, structural liquidity ratio and productivity indicators, are significant and make good sense.

Business growth potentials are directly connected, from both the logical and operational points of view, to the funding sources, the long-term financial equilibrium (*Structural liquidity ratio*) and to the staff productivity. The *Growth factor of ordinary operations* instead shows a negative correlation with index 15 (Operational Liquidity gap ratio) which – in general terms – measures the ability of the Confidi to face guarantee commitments undertaken with all their financial assets, and certainly affects and defines potential growth and expansion in the guarantee business for the future (Figure 5.8).

4.3 The ranking map

The two principal components described might be used to provide a first – rather simple – key to the interpretation of Confidi ranking with reference to their information profiles and the relevant ratios analyzed. The result is a ranking map that is a strategic tool capable of suggesting corrective actions for the surveyed Confidi in terms of guarantee portfolio management and potential growth. However, we do not intend to categorically classify the good and the bad; that would be a mistake because we must also take into account some insufficiencies in the database used for the statistical analysis. This matrix is significant in yielding information, and is a flexible tool to accelerate structure assessment in order to acquire a more efficient guarantee management. The matrix (Figure 5.9) is divided into four quadrants, each representing a different combination of the quality-focused portfolio management, indicating along the abscissa axis the *portfolio guarantee management quality* and on the ordinate axis the *potential growth factor*. The central axes in the figure represent the mean value, by construction equal to zero.

The resulting ranking map is thus divided into four quadrants:

- Confidi with above-average scores for both variables (approximately 31 per cent of the total) are in the first quadrant (top right): the furthest distance from the central axes means falling within the range of the best guarantee portfolio management. These Confidi feature a careful guarantee portfolio

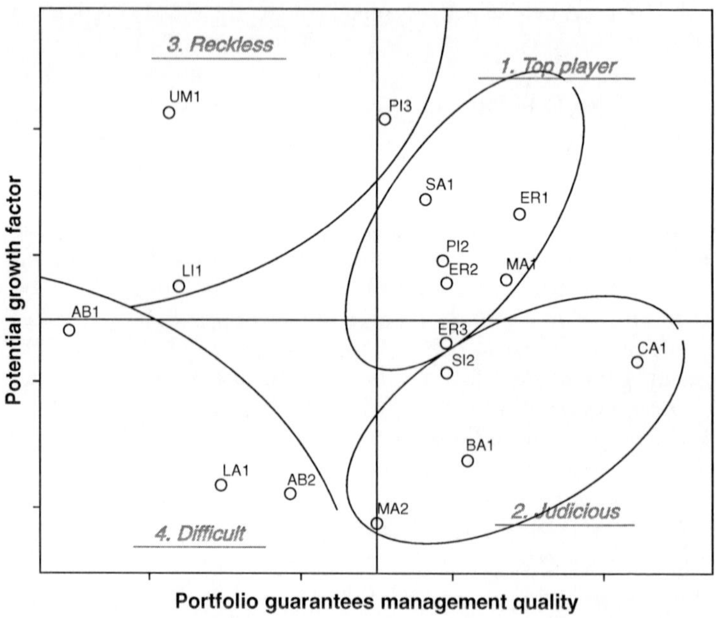

Figure 5.9 Mapping of the Confidi surveyed with respect to multi-profile components 1 and 3

management and relevant good profitability and solvency, along with good potential for growth/expansion of their business in the long term;
- Confidi that may be roughly defined as 'judicious' (approximately 25 per cent of the total) are in the second quadrant (bottom right); they feature below-average growth scores, yet with a significant virtuous performance index. These Confidi currently feature quality portfolio management and good net and operational profitability, and are figuratively solvent. On the other hand, they might in the long term suffer from liquidity problems and find it difficult to hedge the risk level of assumed commitments by using risk provisions and capital;
- 'Reckless' Confidi (19 per cent of the total) are in the third quadrant (top left). Their significant expansion factor does not fit with due care for the quality/sustainability of the commitments undertaken. These Confidi currently feature extremely low leverage, rather good productivity levels, satisfying structural balance levels – yet they suffer from a high current and potential risk level with a rather alarming pay-out ratio;
- Confidi with both scores below the mean sample values (the so-called 'difficult' Confidi, 25 per cent of the total) are in the fourth quadrant (bottom left), presenting the highest risk. They are undersized Confidi with impaired performance levels in terms of both profitability and risk level. These Confidi seem not to have any potential for future growth in terms of hedging sources available (capital and available risk provisions), and financial assets necessary to fund guarantee activity or productivity. Moreover they face a slight deterioration of the guarantee portfolio in terms of current and potential risk, and of guarantees already enforced by bank intermediaries.

This graphic representation is extremely easy to understand and provides useful indications about incentive and corrective actions for the surveyed Confidi from a strategic and operational point of view. Top players may benefit from actions aimed at consolidating their business, while judicious Confidi benefit from actions aimed at expanding hedging resources and the use of the same, plus productivity levels and by reconsidering the breakdown of the financial assets in the portfolio, in terms of quantity and quality. Reckless Confidi should be told to limit their business expansion and indiscriminate and anachronistic use of the multiplier; they should solve their problems connected to structural liquidity and staff productivity in order to streamline initiatives aimed at consolidating their business. As far as the difficult Confidi are concerned, rather than an undifferentiated initiative, a thorough monitoring of the economic, financial, capital and management situations of each will be necessary to better identify the corrective policies to be implemented in each of them, in terms of future growth potentials, current risk level, solvency, profitability and liquidity management of the guarantee business.

5 (Nearly) Final remarks

This research was intended as a first experimental exercise aimed at measuring and analyzing the *riskiness and performance* of a sample of Confidi with a ranking/scoring framework. The result of the methodology applied has been a ranking position map: a useful strategic tool able to suggest corrective actions for the surveyed Confidi in terms of guarantee portfolio management and potential growth.

The Confidi ranking within the reference context is the result of the information currently available according to the extent and modality selected by each Confidi to disclose them. In doing this, however, we do not pretend to have applied the results of our research, at least from a strictly statistical point of view, to the many different fields. We believe that in the future our work will be improved and developed. The first step will be to improve the database, by acquiring new information and by improving existing information with qualitative data. In the near future, in-depth assessments of the performance of guarantee intermediaries might be useful to:

a. thoroughly analyze the data currently missing,
b. develop a qualitative module aimed at assessing the processes, procedures and associated organizational issues of those surveyed,
c. establish a class of integrated *scoring* models for 'balance sheets & qualitative questionnaires',
d. analyze the ranking trends of each Confidi over time.

This would allow for a thorough monitoring of the performance and risk level of each Confidi, and for a subsequent complete assessment of their *financial stability*. This is a crucial issue also for policymakers, since those policymakers need to ensure that such schemes can properly allocate resources and generate appropriate levels of self-financing to justify the subsidy costs, and not merely produce a costly distortion.

Notes

1. In terms of equity, increasing the risk funds (provision accounts); providing counter guarantee of the CGIs' losses; providing subsidies for CGIs startup; reducing fiscal pressure (indirect taxation or income taxes) on CGIs.
2. Improvement of risk management through diversification opportunities and the possibility of transferring all or part of the risk assumed; acquisition of expertise in the evaluation of SMEs and startup of lending relationships leading to a progressive reduction in the use of collateral; reduction of costs related to collateral management.
3. Jonsson (2009), p. 62, describes two main approaches to the evaluation of additionality: (i) Studies compared a target group of firms which had benefited from guaranteed loans to a representative control group of firms which had relied on conventional bank loans (Zecchini & Ventura, 2009; ITPS, 2002; Uesugi et al.,

2006). (ii) Other studies relied on credit scoring (Riding et al., 2007, p. 52; GAO, 2007) in order to determine which firms of a group of firms that had all benefited from loan guarantees were truly 'additional', that is, they would not have benefited from a loan if the loan guarantee had not been in place.

4. For example, developing countries are more likely to detect higher growth rates of guaranteed enterprises, regardless of the quality of funded projects. In such cases, every type of financial support will produce positive results in terms of economic growth, but it is difficult to prove that the same results would not have been attained in the absence of CGIs.
5. Mutual guarantee schemes are, in general, independent, private mutual societies in enterprises; they are collective initiatives by independent businesses or their representative organisations. Member enterprises, through regular membership contributions, jointly guarantee credit advanced to one of their members.
6. The literature provides other indicators for measurement of FS, even though most studies mention, but do not measure, them.
7. Basel II and the EU directive proposal on Capital Adequacy represent the new guidelines. The Expert Group considered that a reasonable level for a mature Guarantee Scheme with a well diversified portfolio could reach atleast seven times the fund's value.
8. It is important to underline that there is much confusion about the calculation of default rates: (i) default from CGS's viewpoint is the claim made by the bank to the guarantor, but borrowers could be in difficulty before the bank decides to execute the grant, and furthermore banks differ in managing doubtful loans; (ii) confusion between provisioning a default and covering a default; (iii) difference in gross and net losses, depending on the intervention of a counter-guarantor and monies recovered on the debtor.
9. Because unused funds should not be invested in high-risk operations, these investments will have a relatively low return (Deelen and Molenaar, 2004, p. 53).
10. The premium has two important functions. First it provides an important source of income for the CGIs, which helps offset the cost of defaults. Secondly, imposing an additional cost on the borrower through the premium should ensure that only those businesses that cannot raise finance in the market under normal terms would choose to borrow under the CGIs.
11. The current Confidi system operates in Italy at different levels:The national coordination of Confidi bringing together national federations and implementing coordinated activities on common topics;National federations, responsible for coordinating, representing and assisting Confidi and which bring together Confidi referring to different trade associations;Second-level Confidi, responsible for coordinating, representing, assisting and offering some services to first-level Confidi's membership;First-level Confidi, to complete the outline of the Confidi system within the scope of the international coordination policy, mention should be made of the role played by the European Mutual Guarantee Association (A.E.C.M.), which brings together all European Mutual Guarantee institutions.
12. Tertiary sector of the economy – the service industries.
13. The lack of homogeneity in the number of surveyed Confidi providing information on their member staff in the explanatory notes affects the results over time.
14. With the aim of obtaining a higher transparency in the balance sheet data, the different allocation of item 141 by one Confidi affected the increase.
15. The Confidi's regulatory capital must always be equal or higher than the sum of the requirements against credit risks (counter-part risk included), operational risk, market risk (except for a trading portfolio below 5 per cent of the assets and not

exceeding €5 million) and exchange risk (except for a net open exchange position below 2 per cent of regulatory capital) according to a building block approach.

16. Supervised Confidi recorded a decrease in fixed investments, especially in equity investments, as a consequence of the application of the IAS/IFRS accounting standards.
17. From this perspective, the methods and the procedures by which banks communicate to each Confidi the risk level of guaranteed loans and enforce guarantees perform a crucial role.
18. The division into six classes is entirely subjective, considered by the authors to be fitting for the pseudo-inference of the forms of distribution of the different indicators selected.
19. The unsupervised segmentation techniques referring to the so-called 'cluster analysis', and aimed at dividing the initial group into subgroups (clusters) as similar as possible within the same group and different from one group to the other: the score assigned to each cluster will therefore represent their belonging to one specific class.
20. The Varimax method is based upon the orthogonal rotation of the reference system, that is, all structure axes are rotated in the same way. They are therefore uncorrelated, and the overall variability explained by the rotated structure is the same as that of the non-rotated structure. Maximizing the variance (Varimax) between factor weights implies that each component will increase the medium and large correlations – in terms of basic indicators – to the detriment of small correlations that might gain significance for another structure component, as in our specific case.
21. Factors are exact linear combinations of experimental variables. They are the result of the sum of the single experimental variables, or rather of their z values, multiplied by the relevant coefficients. The value and sign of these coefficients determine how, and how much, each factor is linked to the different experimental variables.

References

Aldrighetti, F. and L. Erzegovesi (2007) 'L'equilibrio gestionale dei Confidi vigilati: effetti sul pricing delle garanzie e sull'efficacia degli aiuti pubblici', 28 Marzo, http://smefin.net.

Anuchitworawong, C., T. Intarachote, P. Vichyanond (2006) 'The economic impact of small business credit guarantee', *TDRI Quarterly Review*, June, 17–21.

Baravelli, M. and P. Leone (ed.) (2010) *Il futuro dei Confidi in Italia*, Bancaria Editrice, Roma.

Beck, T., L.F. Klapper and J.C. Mendoza (2008) 'The typology of partial credit guarantee funds around the world', Policy research working paper 4771, World Bank.

Benavente, J.M., A. Galetovic and R. Sanhueza (2006) 'Fogape: an economic analysis', University of Chile Economics Department Working Paper 222.

Bennett, F., A. Doran and H. Billington (2005) 'Do credit guarantees lead to improved access to financial services? Recent evidence from Chile, Egypt, India, and Poland', Department for International Development, London, Financial Sector Team, Policy Division Working Paper.

Berger, A.N. and G.F. Udell (2006) 'A more complete conceptual framework for SME finance', *Journal of Banking and Finance*, no. 30 2945–66.

BEST Reports EC – European Commission (2006) 'Guarantees and mutual guarantees – BEST Reports, Guarantees and mutual guarantees', European Commission.

BIS – Department for Business, Innovation & Skills (2010) 'Small Firms Loan Guarantee (SFLG) Scheme Recipient and Comparison Group Survey Results', URN 10/511, January, OMB Research Ltd.

Boocock, G. and M.N.M. Shariff (2005) 'Measuring the effectiveness of credit guarantee schemes', *International Small Business Journal*, 23, 427–54.

Bradshaw, T. (2002) 'The contribution of small business loan guarantees to economic development', *Economic Development Quarterly*, 16(4), November, 360–9.

Brash, R. and M. Gallagher (2008) *A Performance Analysis of SBA's Loan and Investment Programs*. Washington DC: The Urban Institute.

Busetta, G. and A. Presbitero (2008) 'Confidi, piccole imprese e banche: un'analisi empirica', in Zazzaro A. (ed.), *I vincoli finanziari alle crescita delle imprese*, Carocci.

Columba, F., L. Gambacorta and P.E. Mistrulli (2008) 'Firms as monitors of other firms: mutual loan guarantee consortia and SME finance', Munich Personal RePEc Archive MPRA Paper No. 14032.

Columba, F., L. Gambacorta and P.E. Mistrulli (2009) 'Mutual guarantee institutions and small business finance', Temi di discussione, Banca d'Italia, n. 735, November.

Cowan, K., A. Drexler and A. Yanez (2008) 'The Effect of Partial Credit Guarantees on the Credit Market for Small Business: Chile', World Bank Conference on Partial Guarantee Schemes, March.

Cowling, M. (2010) 'The role of loan guarantee schemes in alleviating credit rationing in the UK', *Journal of Financial Stability Partial Credit Guarantees: Experiences & Lessons*, Focused Issue, 36–44.

Cowling, M. and P. Mitchell (2003) 'Is the small firms loan guarantee scheme hazardous for banks or helpful to small business?' *Small Business Economics*, 21(1), 63–71.

Craig, B.R., W.E. Jackson and J.B. Thomson (2007) 'On government intervention in the small-firm credit market and its effect on economic performance', Federal Reserve Bank of Cleveland Working Paper, no. 07–02.

Craig, B.R., W.E. Jackson and J.B. Thomson (2008) 'Credit market failure intervention: do government sponsored small business credit programs enrich poorer areas?' *Small Business Economy*, 30, 345–60.

Davies, I. (2007) 'People's Republic of China: development of small and medium-sized enterprise credit guarantee companies', Asian Development Bank.

Deelen, L. and K. Molenaar (2004) 'Guarantee Funds for Small Enterprises – A Manual for Guarantee Fund Managers', International Labour Organization (ILO).

Erzegovesi, L. (2008) 'Equilibrio gestionale dei Confidi "107"', DISA, Dipartimento di Informatica e Studi Aziendali, Università di Trento, Smefin tech reports, Trento.

GAO – United States Government Accountability Office, Small Business Administration (2007) 'Additional Measures Needed to Assess 7(a) Loan Program's Performance', http://www.gao.gov/new.items/d07769.pdf.

Gittell, R. and F.R. Kaen (2003) 'A framework for evaluating state-assisted financing programs (1)', *Public Finance and Management*, 3(3), 296–331.

GoNetwork (2006) 'Benchmark Analysis of the Credit Guarantee Organizations in the Central, Adriatic, Danubian and South-Eastern European Space' (CADSES).

Graham, T. (2004) 'Graham Review of the Small Firms Loan Guarantee Recommendations', HM Treasury.

Green, A. (2003) 'Credit guarantee schemes for small enterprises: an effective instrument to promote private sector-led growth?' SME Technical Working Paper Series, UNIDO.

Hancock, D., J. Peek and J.A. Wilcox (2008) 'The repercussions on small banks and small business of procyclical bank capital and countercyclical loan guarantees', AFA new Orleans Meetings Paper, available at SSRN.

Honohan, P. (2008) 'Partial credit guarantees: principles and practice', Conference on partial credit guarantees, Washington DC, 13–14 March, Trinity College Dublin.

ITPS (2002) 'Utvärdering av ALMI Företagspartner AB:s finansieringsverksamhet', Instituttet för tillväxtpolitiska studier.

Jonsson, M. (2009) 'Performance of Credit Guarantee Schemes (CGI)', Copenhagen Business School Working paper no. 24.
KPMG (2011) 'Credit Access Guarantees: A Public Asset between State and Market. International Survey on Guarantee Market Players', http://www.kpmg.com/it/it/issuesandinsights/events/pagine/creditguarantee.aspx.
Larraín, C. and J. Quiroz (2006) 'Estudio para el Fondo de Garantía de Pequeños Empresarios', Santiago: Banco Estado, Mimeographed.
Lelarge, C., D. Sraer and D. Thesmar (2008) 'Entrepreneurship and Credit Constraints, Evidence from a French Loan Guarantee Program', National Bureau of Economic Research (NBER).
Leone, P. (2010) 'Finanza d'impresa, soggetti pubblici e sistema delle garanzie: verso un nuovo assetto', in M. Baravelli and P. Leone (eds) Il futuro dei Confidi. Evoluzione dei modelli istituzionali, gestionali e organizzativi, Rome, Bancaria Editrice.
Leone, P. and G.A. Vento (2007) 'Basilea2 e business delle garanzie: quali opportunità per gli operatori istituzionali?', Atti del Convegno AIDEA06-Finanza e Industria in Italia, Il Mulino, Bologna.
Leone, P. and G.A. Vento (eds) (2012) *Credit Guarantee Institutions and SME Finance*. Palgrave Macmillan: London.
Levitsky, J. (1997) 'Best practice in credit guarantee schemes', *The Financier – Analyses of Capital and Money Market Transactions*, 4(1&2), February/May, 86–94.
Makhool, B., S. Boas and S. Bargouthi (2005) 'Financing Palestinian SME's', Palestinian Economic Research Institute (MAS), 6 September.
Mankiw, G.M. (1986) 'The allocation of credit and financial collapse', *The Quarterly Journal of Economics*, August, 455–70.
Navajas, A.R. (2001) 'Credit Guarantee Schemes: Conceptual Frame', Financial System Development Project, GTZ/FONDESIF, November.
Oh, I., J. Lee, A. Heshmati and G.G. Choi (2006) 'Evaluation of credit guarantee policy using propensity score matching', *Small Business Economics,* 33.
Panetta, I.C. (2012) 'An analysis of credit guarantee schemes: suggestions provided by literature', in P. Leone and G.A. Vento (eds), *Credit Guarantee Institutions and SME Finance*. Palgrave Macmillan: London.
Piatti, D. (2008) 'I Confidi. Gestione delle garanzie, redditività e pricing', Bancaria Editrice.
Pozzolo, A.F. (2004) 'The role of guarantees in bank lending', Economics & Statistics Discussion Paper no. 21/04, Dept. SEGeS, University of Molise, Italy.
Riding, A., J. Madill, J. and G. Haines (2007) 'Incrementality of SME loan guarantees', *Small Business Economics*, 29, 47–61.
Riding, A.L. and G. Haines Jr. (2001) 'Loan guarantees: costs of default and benefits to small firms', *Journal of Business Venturing*, 16(6), 595–612.
Schmidt, A.G. and M. van Elkan (2010) 'Macroeconomic benefits of German guarantee banks', Institute for Small and Medium-Sized Enterprises at the University of Trier (INMIT), Trier June 30.
Uesugi, I., K. Sakaiand G.M. Yamashiro (2006) 'Effectiveness of credit guarantees in the Japanese loan market', RIETI Discussion Paper Series 06-E-004, RIETI.
Vogel, R.C. and D.W. Adams (1997) 'Costs and benefits of loan guarantee programs', *The Financier,* 4(1&2), 22–29 February/May.
Zecchini, S. and M. Ventura (2009) 'The impact of public guarantees on credit to SMEs', *Small Business Economics*, 32, 191–206.

6
The Role of Trade Credit and the Cost of Capital

Ted Lindblom and Gert Sandahl

1 Introduction

Trade credit and other types of working capital, like inventory, may constitute significant components of a long-term investment in capacity expansion, particularly within businesses dependent on working capital, like wholesaling and retailing. Still the treatment of cash committed to these types of working capital is often lacking in consistency; the focus tends to be on net cash flow effects (see for example Allen, 1976; Kroll, 1985; Kaplan and Ruback, 1995; Mills, 1996). The standard approach is to regard the net of the initial working capital cash flow of a project as an investment that will be recovered at the termination of the project. Cash committed to inventory or trade credit in the form of receivables or payables, is thus implicitly assumed to be equally sensitive to changes in the economic environment. This may often, though, be considered as a major simplification or even an anomaly. Different types of working capital are exposed to different kinds of risk (cf. Cooley et al., 1975). Even in the deterministic case of certainty, it may be misleading to only consider net working capital if there is exposure to inflation (cf. Kim, 1979). As we will show in this chapter, a consistent treatment of cash committed to trade credit and inventory may be of vital importance not only for the investment appraisal decision, but also for an accurate determination of the overall cost of capital, and thus the optimal capital structure of the firm.

A firm's investments in long-term assets generally incur a large initial outflow of cash that must be financed. This is recognized as a fundamental reality in finance literature. Considerably less attention is, however, paid to the fact that many of these investments also affect cash committed to short-term assets and liabilities like inventory and trade credit; in reality, trade credit is a most common financial component in business-to-business transactions (Petersen and Rajan, 1997; Chee et al., 1999; Wilner, 2000; Huyghebaert, 2006). Such credit arises as a consequence of firms' deferral of the payment of goods or services sold instead of instant settlement of the transaction with a cash payment on the day of delivery/purchase. The resulting financial claim and debt is registered as a short-term asset and a short-term liability in the balance sheet statements of the supplier and the purchaser, respectively. In accounting and financial ratios, these claims and debts are often overlooked as capital employed or other, for net working capital, 'adjusted' measures are used.

In a survey of the capital structure of non-financial firms in the G7[1] countries, Rajan and Zingales (1995) report that trade credit in the form of short-term asset (accounts receivable) varied from 13 to as much as 29 per cent of total asset on average in 1991, whereas the corresponding share of short-term liability (accounts payable) varied between 11.5 and 17 per cent. Two decades later, we find similar levels of trade credit assets and liabilities in Swedish firms; Table 6.1 shows that the level of receivables varies between the studied industries, from 9 per cent of total assets in the industries with direct consumer contact (retail and hotels/restaurants) to 33 per cent in the construction industry. Also the payables vary between industries. The approximately 20 per cent payables in relation to total assets represent the top levels and these can be found in the construction, wholesale, and retail industries.

It is well worth noting that in the construction, wholesale, retail, and hotel/restaurant industries, the level of payables is well above the level of long-term debt in relation to total assets. Only in the energy sector, and perhaps in the mining industry, is the level of long-term debt clearly higher than the level of payables. It can also be noted that that the payables on

Table 6.1 Trade credit in Swedish firms in 2010

	R/A mean	P/A mean	LTD/A mean	P/LTD mean/ median	Number of firms
Mining	0.14	0.11	0.16	0.85/0.44	83
Manufacturing	0.23	0.14	0.15	9.49/0.66	5551
Energy, water & waste	0.11	0.07	0.30	2.65/0.10	351
Construction	0.33	0.19	0.10	11.94/0.97	6262
Wholesale	0.29	0.18	0.10	19.2/0.99	6892
Retail	0.09	0.22	0.12	12.8/1.23	4738
Hotels and restaurants	0.09	0.16	0.17	3.32/0.51	1506

Notes: R/A – Receivables/Assets; P/A – Payables/Assets; LTD/A – Long term debt/Assets; P/LTD – Payables/LTD.

Data source: *Retriever.*

average exceed the long-term debt (the variation between firms is high, as shown by the very different means and medians of payables to long-term debt). These observations indicate that payables represent important financial sources, even if this is denied in both theory and practice (Lindblom et al., 2011).

Table 6.1 shows not only that the use of trade credit varies between different industries. It also reveals that in some industries certain firms seem to rely relatively more heavily on trade credit as a source of finance than do other firms. In consumer-oriented industries, like retailing and hotels/restaurants, payables over total assets are greater than receivables over total assets. In the retail trade industry, financing of firms by trade credit seems to be almost as important as long-term financing. This conclusion about the importance of current debt as a long-run financial source is confirmed by some data concerning Danish and Swedish firms (see Table 6.2).

First of all, Table 6.2 shows increasing trade credit from suppliers; the average slope of the trade credit regression is positive (the number of observations per firm varies between 3 and 15). The annual increase is especially evident among Swedish firms working with consumer goods of the staple type, where the annual increase is 21 per cent of the average trade credit. Trade credit from suppliers is clearly not losing its importance; its role in the financial mix seems rather constant, as the trade credit ratio changes are fairly small, and are similar for the different measures. We can therefore conclude that trade credit in the form of payables represents approximately 10 to 20 per cent of the firm's total assets, and that its growth is closely related to the growth of the firms.

To some extent the use of trade credit is explained by the 'transaction motive' (Schwartz, 1974). The purchasing firm actually wishes to pay cash, but there will still be a delay in the financial settlement due to administrative costs of matching the time patterns of a payment transaction with the time patterns of a product (or service) delivery. The small trade credit (payables) to sales figures (see Table 6.2) seems to be in line with this notion. However, this motive is likely to have become less important, as both payment systems and internal cash management and logistics systems are far more sophisticated and efficient today than they were three to four decades ago. The 'financial motive' (also referred to by Schwartz) seems to remain, though, and even to grow in importance (Mian and Smith, 1994; Petersen and Rajan, 1997; Jain, 2001; Burkart and Ellingsen, 2004). According to Petersen and Rajan (1997) this is particularly true when ordinary credit from financial institutions is unavailable or when suppliers have better access to such credit than do the purchasing firms.

A supplier may act either as an intermediary between the financial institution and the (ultimate) borrower (Jain, 2001) or as a direct alternative to the

Table 6.2 The average proportion of trade credit in four industries in Sweden and Denmark

	Sweden								**Denmark**							
Consumer goods*	***Staples***				***Discretionary***				***Staples***				***Discretionary***			
Measure*	t/l	t/a	t/m	t/s	t/l	t/a	t/m	t/s	t/l	t/a	t/m	t/s	t/l	t/a	t/m	t/s
Number of firms	8	8	4	7	45	45	31	42	9	9	8	9	17	17	17	17
Average	0.21	0.12	0.15	0.40	0.22	0.16	0.18	0.08	0.22	0.09	0.11	0.09	0.19	0.10	0.17	0.08
Min	0.16	0.08	0.04	0.14	0.14	0.09	0.08	0.05	0.11	0.06	0.04	0.06	0.09	0.05	0.05	0.04
Max	0.32	0.27	0.32	0.94	0.31	0.39	0.33	0.14	0.36	0.13	0.24	0.14	0.35	0.18	0.37	0.19
Slope	–0.01	–0.05	–0.01	–0.07	–0.01	–0.01	–0.00	–0.00	0.02	0.00	–0.01	0.00	–0.00	0.00	0.00	0.00
Trade credit change – slope***	41174214 (7)				20381352 (45)				27691227 (9)				2825424 (17)			
Slope/average value of trade credit	0.21				0.15				0.08				0.11			
Capital goods*	***Trading companies***				***Miscellaneous***				***Trading companies***				***Miscellaneous***			
Measure*	t/l	t/a	t/m	t/s	t/l	t/a	t/m	t/s	t/l	t/a	t/m	t/s	t/l	t/a	t/m	t/s
Number of firms	6	6	6	6	37	37	31	37	8	8	8	8	15	15	15	15
Average	0.31	0.17	0.22	0.09	0.19	0.10	0.21	0.11	0.21	0.12	0.22	0.07	0.22	0.13	0.34	0.11
Min	0.25	0.14	0.11	0.07	0.13	0.07	0.08	0.06	0.15	0.09	0.09	0.05	0.16	0.09	0.15	0.07
Max	0.38	0.20	0.38	0.12	0.26	0.14	0.41	0.27	0.30	0.16	0.42	0.10	0.32	0.18	0.65	0.21
Slope	0.00	0.00	–0.02	0.00	0.00	0.00	–0.01	–0.01	0.00	0.00	–0.01	0.00	0.01	0.00	0.00	0.01
Trade credit change – slope***	9248412 (6)				132819584 (32)				15823477 (8)				14075245			
Slope/average value of trade credit	0.11				0.07				0.11				0.08			

Notes: (*) Industries according to GICS; (**) t = trade credit (payables), a = total assets, l = total liabilities, m = market capital and s = sales; (***) amounts in SEK and DKK, respectively.
Source: Ecowin.

bank (Biais and Gollier, 1997). This implies that 'upstream' suppliers, with good creditworthiness, use bank loans or other external/internal financial sources to extend trade credit to their customer firms downstream, and that these firms in turn use this credit to offer trade credit to their customers, and so on. This activity has attracted a lot of interest in the literature on trade credit, both theoretically and empirically. The main focus has then been on understanding and explaining why suppliers (or non-financial firms) engage in lending, and the rationale for this intermediary activity. Limited attention has been paid to the purchasing or borrowing firm's perspective. Certainly, it has been recognized that purchasing firms choose to use trade credit because they have poor, or practically no, access to ordinary bank credit (Nilsen, 2002;) but why a purchasing firm, with proper access to such credit, may still prefer trade credit seems to have been less explored.

As the Scandinavian examples in Table 6.2 (the maximum values of trade credit to total assets and trade credit to sales) indicate, the purchasing firms' use of trade credit, as a source of finance, is not uncommon even among well established firms (of the kind represented in the Ecowin database). This also matches the observation of Radjan and Zingales (1995). Thus, trade credit can in general, despite its character of a short-term debt, be seen as a long-term element of the financial structure of the firm. Firms may then lose market value if output prices fail to match the increasing costs represented in the working capital (Ashton et al., 2011; Goedhart et al., 2010). The cost of capital and of investments in working capital assets are affected by uncertain and long-run future price changes (Mishkin, 1992; Crowder and Hoffman, 1996; Horowitz, 2000).

With this background, we have chosen to analyze and demonstrate how cash flow related to working capital in the form of trade credit and inventory should be considered in the case of exposure to inflation and risk. We emphasize the importance of distinguishing between different types of working capital in the context of firms' investment appraisal. Particular interest will be paid to the cost and evaluation of trade credit extended by suppliers.

We begin the analysis with a recapitulation of what may be regarded as the standard case. There is exposure neither to risk nor to inflation. We then relax the condition of stable prices by allowing for inflation, and finally we show how to determine the cost of trade credit when the firm is exposed to different kinds of risk.

2 The standard approach

In most business firms, working capital (W) is initially needed for getting started and for smoothing payments or adapting them to the product and work flows. There are cash outflows for building up inventory (I) and delayed cash inflow when offering customers attractive terms of payment. Trade credit, represented by receivables (R), may be regarded as a fictitious outflow of cash that must be funded. However, the firm is also likely to receive trade credit from suppliers, represented by payables (P). This credit may be regarded as a fictitious cash inflow, reducing the need for financial funds. An investment in additional capacity will often change these cash flows. Under the assumption that business volume is constant over the economic life span of the investment the standard approach suggests the reverse cash flow will arise at the end of that time span when the investment is being terminated. This is shown in Figure 6.1.[2]

In accordance with the standard approach, the present value of committing cash to trade credit or inventory may be determined individually for each type of working capital, or in total in terms of net working capital. Given a hurdle rate (k) based on the opportunity cost of capital (OCC), the total cost in terms of net present value (NPV(W)) may be determined using Equation 6.1.

$$NPV(W) = P\,[1 - (1+k)^{-n}] - R\,[1 - (1+k)^{-n}] - I\,[1 - (1+k)^{-n}] \tag{6.1}$$

In a simple and uncomplicated world without any exposure to risk and inflation, or with only minor price changes, it is acceptable to apply the standard approach if prices do not include any implicit interest. Accordingly, a distinction between different types of working capital is unnecessary. The annual cost of net working capital (C(W)) then equals the hurdle rate times the initial cash flow, as demonstrated by Equation 6.2.

$$C(W) = W\frac{\left(1-(1+k)^{-n}\right)k}{1-(1+k)^{-n}} => C(W) = kW \tag{6.2}$$

When prices are less stable and inflation should be taken into account, a greater stringency is required in the treatment of working capital. The cost effect of having money tied up in receivables or freed up in payables cannot automatically be estimated and dealt with in the same manner as the cost of having cash locked up in raw materials, work in progress or other inventory.[3] Inventory investment (disinvestment) even varies as if used for 'project independent' purposes.[4] This observation underlines the need for a separate analysis of each type of working capital and even of the different types of inventory.[5] The inflation effect on trade credit, in terms of receivables and on inventory, in terms of finished goods or raw material inventories, will be further elaborated in the next section.

3 The cost of working capital under inflation

The cost of employing different types of working capital may vary substantially when cash flow is subject to inflation. However, it may also be

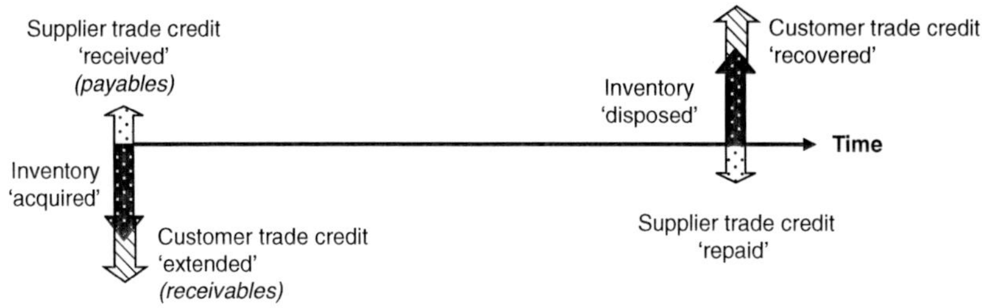

Figure 6.1 A general outline of working capital cash flow

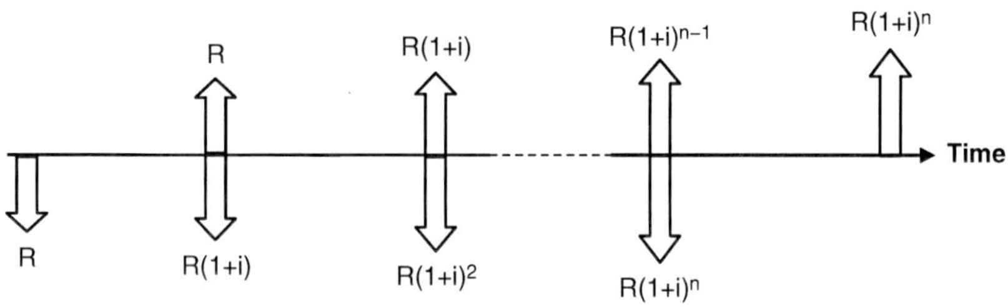

Figure 6.2 Cash tied up in receivables in nominal terms

important for firms in other industries to recognize existing cost differences between different types of working capital[6] when, for example, considering implementing just-in-time (JIT) production and replacing old, inefficient equipment with new, thereby also reducing the need for working capital in terms of inventory.

The short-term effects on working capital have to be recognized explicitly in order for nominal cash flow to be accurately described. Trade credit and inventory are frequently turned over during the economic life span of an investment project; this implies that additional cash is being tied up in such capital – at least in nominal terms. Allen (1976: 34) maintains that: 'These working capital supplements, or this working capital drain, can seriously reduce a project's rate of return.' This is, however, not completely true, as trade credit and inventory will be affected differently by inflation.[7]

3.1 Trade credit and inflation

Let us begin by examining how receivables and payables are affected by inflation. As neither form of trade credit is based on a contract explicitly stipulating a compensation for inflation, trade credit in the form of receivables will be drained, just as Allen suggests.[8]

Cash committed to trade credit differentiates from inventory in that over time the increasing amount of cash being tied up in receivables due to inflation is not balanced by a corresponding nominal value gain in the stock of receivables. This is illustrated in Figure 6.2.

The NPV of extending trade credit may be determined by using the nominal rate of return (k_{nom}) as in Equation 6.3.

$$NPV(R) = -R + R\left(\sum_{t=1}^{n}(1+i)^{t-1}(1+k_{nom})^{-t} - \sum_{t=1}^{n-1}(1+i)^{t}(1+k_{nom})^{-t}\right) \tag{6.3}$$

Equation 6.3 may be reformulated into Equation 6.4, which reveals the 'inflation-drain' component: $-\ R\cdot\Sigma\ i\ (1+i)^{t-1}\ (1+k_{nom})^{-t}$. It shows the PV of the periodical working capital drain.

$$NPV(R) = -R\left(1 + \sum_{t=1}^{n} i\,(1+i)^{t-1}(1+k_{nom})^{-t} - (1+i)^{n}(1+k_{nom})^{-n}\right) \tag{6.4}$$

If cash flow is deflated, that is divided by the inflation factor $(1+i)^t$, the periodical working capital drain may be computed in real terms. This is demonstrated in Equation 6.5, in which the NPV(R) is derived from real cash flow using the real required rate of return (k_{real}) determined by the relationship; $(1 + k_{nom}) = (1 + i)(1 + k_{real})$.

$$NPV(R) = -R\left(1 + \sum_{t=1}^{n}\frac{i}{1+i}(1+k_{real})^{-t} - (1+k_{real})^{-n}\right) \tag{6.5}$$

3.1.1 *Inventory and inflation*

Inventory is differentiated from trade credit in that the price of inventory items is likely to be constant in real terms. This means that the nominal value of inventory will follow the general price change due to inflation. As there is a time lag between the acquisition and the disposal of inventory, the business firm would then be gaining in nominal terms from holding items in inventory. More specifically, the nominal gain for a specific period would equal the product of the inventory value at the beginning of the period and the inflation rate (see Figure 6.3).

In principle, the firm will assimilate the nominal gain in the form of a reduction of its current cash outflow, and thus an increase of its net cash flow each period. In Equation 6.6, the magnitude of what may be referred to as 'inflation-gain' of holding an inventory periodically realized, is determined in terms of present value (PV(I)).

$$PV(I) = \sum_{t=1}^{n} I(i(1+i)^{t-1})(1+k_{nom})^{-t} \tag{6.6}$$

Clearly, a positive PV(I) of holding items in inventory is not an indicator of a positive NPV(I). There are still financial costs associated with inventory. The NPV is shown in Equation 6.7.

$$NPV(I) = -I + I\left(\sum_{t=1}^{n} \frac{i(1+i)^{t-1} + (1+i)^{t-1}}{(1+k_{nom})^{t}} - \sum_{t-1}^{n-1}(1+i)^{t}(1+k_{nom})^{-t}\right) \tag{6.7}$$

As the following relationship holds; $i\,(1+i)^{t-1} + (1+i)^{t-1} = (1+i)^{t}$, Equation 6.7 collapses into Equation 6.8.

$$NPV(I) = -I(1 - (1+i)^{n}(1+k_{nom})^{-n}) \tag{6.8}$$

In real terms, the computation of the cost of holding inventory in terms of NPV coincides with the standard approach when there is no exposure to inflation (see the second term in Equation 6.1). Hence, decision makers confronted with an investment in inventory need only consider the initial cash outflow and the terminal cash inflow, as shown in Equation 6.9.

$$NPV(I) = -I\,[1 - (1+k_{real})^{-n}] \tag{6.9}$$

In the absence of corporate taxes, we may thus conclude that cash committed to trade credit and inventory is affected differently by inflation. Whereas trade credit will be drained in nominal as well as in real terms, the value of inventory is not affected at all in real terms if prices are adjusted for inflation. The implication is that these two types of working capital

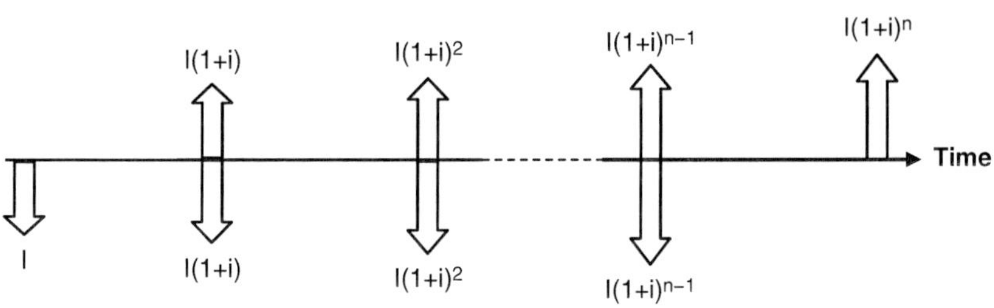

Figure 6.3 Cash tied up in inventory in nominal terms

should be treated differently whenever exposed to inflation. This distinction should also be made even when working capital is turned over more often. A more recurrent recovery and replacement of working capital will only mean a shortening of the discount period. In the extreme case of a very short turnover time, a continuous cash flow model is more appropriate for the analysis.

3.2 The cost of working capital after corporate tax

The presence of corporate tax (T) might be a complicating factor, even though changes in cash flow due to inflation are not directly subjected to tax payments. Taxes are paid according to the current regulatory framework (cf. Hamada, 1979). The tax to be paid for a specific year is determined by the obtained net income or accounting profit (revenue – cost) in nominal terms that year. This implies that working capital cash flow is unaffected by taxes;[9] it is true of trade credit in a system where profit and loss occurs when the product or service is delivered, not when it is paid. Again, though, inventory is different; provided that the so-called first-in-first-out (FIFO) principle is used for the valuation of goods sold, the nominal accounting profit earned can be regarded as the result of two events – an increase in the nominal value of inventory items due to inflation, and an increase in the nominal sales revenue as a result of the mark-up procedure. With the FIFO principle, the two components are taxed in each period; hence, the 'inflation gain' is taxed, like any other profit. This is considered in Equation 6.10, which shows the present value (PV(I,tax)) of the nominal gain after (proportional) tax of holding items in inventory.

$$PV(I,tax) = \sum_{t=1}^{n} I\left(i(1+i)^{t-1}(1-T)(1+k_{nom})^{-t}\right) \tag{6.10}$$

Equation 6.11 shows how to determine the after-tax cost of holding working capital as inventory in terms of NPV.

$$NPV(I,tax) = -I + I\left(\sum_{t=1}^{n}\frac{i(1+i)^{t-1}(1-T)+(1+i)^{t-1}}{(1+k_{nom})^{t}} - \sum_{t=1}^{n-1}\frac{(1+i)^{t}}{(1+k_{nom})^{t}}\right) \tag{6.11}$$

It is evident from Equation 6.12 (cf. note 4) that the financial cost of tax payments is more intelligible when cash flow is expressed in real terms:

$$NPV(I,tax) = -I\left(1+\sum_{t=1}^{n}\frac{i}{1+i}T(1+k_{real})^{-t} - (1+k_{real})^{-n}\right) \tag{6.12}$$

In Equation 6.12, the present value of the cost of an additional tax payment due to 'inflation gain' is expressed by the middle term. Thus, when the FIFO principle is applied there will be a periodic tax-related drain of working capital tied up in inventory in real terms as well.

The use of the alternative last-in-first-out (LIFO) principle would give another result. With the LIFO principle, the inflation gain would be untaxed as long as the inventory value remained constant (or increased). The levy would thus be postponed until the end of the project's economic life span, when the inventory is dissolved. Hence, in comparison to the FIFO principle, LIFO gives rise to a tax discount on inventory inflation gains. Equation 6.13 shows the cost of holding inventory working capital in terms of NPV when LIFO is used for the valuation of goods sold. (All cash flow is expressed in real terms.)

$$NPV(I, LIFO) = -I\left(1+\left(n\frac{i}{1+i}T-1\right)(1+k_{real})^{-n}\right) \tag{6.13}$$

4 The cost of working capital under exposure to risk

Firms are exposed to different kinds of risk that also affect cash flow related to working capital and the cost of such short-term capital. Working capital assets are exposed to a number of risks, mainly short-term ones related to sales volume and price as well as the settlement of payments. Estimates of these risks as well as other asset risks are likely to affect suppliers' risk assessments and their inclination to extend trade credit. It may seem natural to consider trade credit from suppliers as the major source of funds for working capital assets (cf. net working capital). Why this should be the case is not quite clear, though. In the remaining part of this chapter we are going to focus on the importance of distinguishing between asset and liability risks when determining the cost of working capital and whether cash committed to trade credit in form of payables should be considered as part of 'free' cash flow or included as a cost in the weighted average cost of capital (WACC).[10]

Inventory is exposed to the risk of becoming obsolescent, and thus to a decline in value.[11] The higher the risk of obsolescence, the higher the cost of holding items in inventory. Although this relationship is recognized in production and operations management literature (see for example Delft and Vial, 1996; Johnson and Anderson, 2000) in connection with the determination of the economic order quantity (EOQ), it is rarely taken into account explicitly in the literature on investment appraisal. The risk of obsolescence is implicit in the general rule that an investment project should be judged according to its marginal (beta) risk.

In principle, the problem of finding the opportunity cost for working capital assets is not much different from that of determining the relevant cost of capital for any other real investment. Where 'blueprint' investment opportunities are concerned, the financial cost in terms of the WACC is applicable.[12] In this case a firm beta according to CAPM and other market risk measures could be used in order to determine the costs of equity and debt. However, as different types of working capital are exposed to different kinds of risk, neither the opportunity cost of short-term assets nor the financial cost of short-term liabilities are likely to be correctly assessed if only the net working capital cash flow is considered. Hence, the accounting practice of joining a number of short-term assets and liabilities into a net working capital measure has no relevance in an investment appraisal context.

Receivables and payables are exposed to risks other than inventory, and some of these risks are type-specific. From the perspective of the individual firm, receivables are exposed to credit risk. But this is not the case for payables. Trade credit from suppliers does instead add to the financial risk of shareholders as the financial leverage or debt–equity ratio increases. From a risk perspective, there is thus a pronounced difference between having a net working capital of €2000 based on €10,000 in receivables and €8000 in payables, and having a net of €2000 when receivables and payables are €110,000 and €108,000, especially if the firms are of similar size. This lends further support to the conclusion that in investment appraisal, different types of working capital should be treated separately and not as a net amount.

4.1 The cost of trade credit

We argue that short-term assets are a part of the investment appraisal problem, whereas a short-term liability in the form of trade credit is, like other liabilities, assignable to the capital structure problem.[13] Such credit should thus be regarded as an element of the WACC.[14] This is, however, not recognized or adopted by mainstream literature in finance; instead there is a recurring recommendation that debt related to trade credit should be excluded from the WACC.

Copeland and Weston (1989: 530) argue that:

- payables and accruals may be thought of as 'free' capital
- the problem with including short-term liabilities is that the costs of non-interest-bearing short-term liabilities is already accounted for in the cash flows from operations.

Neither of these two arguments should be interpreted as though trade credit from suppliers is costless for the purchasing firm. In general, suppliers may be expected to compensate themselves for providing credit to their customers by including an interest fee within the price. This hidden price premium may be regarded as an implicit cost of payables. However, although such a premium may be included in prices, and thus cash flows from operations, it is seldom explicit in the cash flow analysis when evaluating an investment.

Providing an optimal capital structure, the inclusion of trade credit extended by suppliers as a part of the financial structure implies that it, like the rest of the WACC, is based on market values. Then the WACC is derived by Equation 6.14, where k_E is the required rate of return on equity (E), k_D the average interest rate on total interest-bearing debts (D), and k_P the implicit financial cost of a non-interest-bearing short-term liability as payables (P).[15]

$$WACC = (E\,k_E + D\,k_D + P\,k_P)\ /\ (E + D + P) \qquad (6.14)$$

As trade credit in the form of payables is explicitly a non-interest-bearing liability, its implicit financial cost may in principle be either equal to or greater than zero ($k_P \geq 0$). It seems unrealistic, though, that this cost should be zero or even close to zero; that would imply that suppliers, in general, disregard risk and interest on this form of lending to their customers, and as Wilner (2000) shows, customers are in certain cases prepared to pay interest on payables. So customers paying almost immediately provide the supplier with an unlooked-for interest-earning opportunity.

Another special case of an apparently costless short-term liability is likely to be more common in practice. In general, employees are not expected to ask for any interest on the salaries and wages due to them. This implies that working capital and other related short-term liabilities are sometimes to be regarded as imperfections or frictions in the payment system. As is evident from Equation 6.14, a prevailing occurrence of such an imperfection would result in a lowered weighted average cost of capital for the firm. The advantage in terms of a higher NPV may then be determined by adopting a required rate of return based on the relevant opportunity cost of both low cost and 'normal' cost liabilities.

In a perfect market, the opportunity cost of trade credit would equal the implicit interest charged by the supplier as a (hidden) price premium. That price premium would then be based on the relevant short-term market interest rate with a risk premium added. Such a risk premium varies with the business risk of the customer's operation; the greater the operational risk of the customer, the higher the risk premium, and thus the higher the implicit cost of trade credit extended by suppliers. This indicates that the implicit cost of such credit could even approach the opportunity cost of capital of the purchasing firm's operations.[16] In an unlevered firm (except for trade credit), however, the credit risk of the supplier is significantly reduced ,as equity absorbs losses in the operations of the purchasing firm. This means that in an otherwise equity-financed purchasing firm, it is almost risk-free for the supplier to extend trade credit. Therefore the implicit cost of trade credit (payables) may be close to the risk-free rate (k_{RF}), albeit never as high as the opportunity cost of capital of the purchasing firm, that is $k_{RF} < k_P < OCC$.

The adoption of interest-bearing debt of different kinds in the financial structure is likely to increase the implicit cost of trade credit extended by suppliers as the purchasing firm takes on more financial risk with the accumulation of debt. This is evident when the financial structure includes debt with collateral, as such senior debt has to be repaid before other claims in the case of financial distress. Hence, the implicit cost trade credit (payables) is likely to be higher than the average cost of interest-bearing debt, that is in a leveraged firm $k_D < k_P$.[17] Provided the firm is optimally financed, that is OCC = WACC, we get the relationship displayed in Equation 6.15.

$$k_D < k_P < WACC \qquad (6.15)$$

4.2 Trade credit as a part of free cash flow

Although it seems to be most logical to consider trade credit liabilities as part of the financial structure of the firm, it is possible to consider all cash flow causing this type of short-term liability as free cash flow, just as, for example, Copeland and Weston suggest. Cash flow from all kinds of debt may in fact be seen as free cash flow as long as double-counting is avoided. In the case of interest-bearing debt, this means that the adoption of a new loan is regarded as cash inflow, and instalment and interest payments as cash outflow, in a cash flow to equity approach. If the financial structure varies over the project life cycle, the cash flow to equity or the adjusted present value approach should be used. Double-counting is avoided by applying an over time adjusted rate of return based on the cost of equity (and the relevant market costs of debt not represented in free cash flow). In principle, the identical NPV should be obtained as when the required rate of return is based on the WACC, and debt is, thus, considered as a part of the financial structure and not as free cash flow.[18]

The inclusion of trade credit as a part of cash flow means that the implicit cost of such credit must not be included in the WACC; the appropriate weighted average cost of capital should instead be determined by a partial calculation based only on the required rate of return on equity and the average interest on total interest-bearing debts (cf. Copeland and Weston). The partially weighted average cost of capital ($WACC_p$) is given in Equation 6.16.

$$WACC_p = (E\,k_E + D\,k_D) / (E + D) \qquad (6.16)$$

It may be tempting to assume that $WACC_p$ equals the total WACC derived by Equation 6.14. As is easily verified, by inserting Equation 6.16 into Equation 6.14, this would mean that $k_P = WACC_p$.

$$WACC = ((E + D)\,WACC_p + P \cdot WACC_p) / (E + D + P) = WACC_p \qquad (6.17)$$

If the firm is optimally financed, that is WACC = OCC, Equation 6.17 is valid only in the risk-free case. The implicit cost of trade credit payables can never be as high as $WACC_p$ if there is exposure to risk.[19] As a part of the capital structure of the firm, trade credit will affect the financial risk-taking of shareholders and thereby also the required return on equity. Hence, $k_P < WACC_p$ (cf. Wilner, 2000). In accordance with Equation 6.16, the different costs of capital should be ordered as in Equation 6.18.

$$k_{RF} < k_D < k_P < WACC < WACC_p < k_E \tag{6.18}$$

A supplier offering trade credit to customers is most likely to face additional uncertainty. A number of events, from a simple, unplanned, payment delay to the bankruptcy of a customer, may incur additional costs. However, even though the risk of providing trade credit to customers is higher than the risk compensation implied in the short-term market interest rates, a risk premium equal to the margin between the customer's OCC and the appropriate market interest rate would be likely to give the supplier too high a risk compensation. It would not be sustainable. Purchasing firms should then be expected to have access to less costly debt alternatives. They would rather pay cash by utilizing an alternative financial source (like a bank credit line).

4.3 Trade credit and investment appraisal

'Free cash' related to trade credit extended by suppliers is likely to contribute positively to the NPV in an investment appraisal context. Otherwise it would not be of any interest to the firm to use this source of finance. In order to get the true contribution either a total WACC or a partial $WACC_p$ can be used.

When total WACC is used neither the 'fictitious' initial cash inflow for utilizing trade credit from suppliers nor the reverse conclusive or terminating cash outflow for settling the credit should be a part of the cash flow considered.[20] Furthermore, it means that all operational cash outflow that are related to the current payments of purchased items (equipment, goods or services) should be deflated with the implicit cost of payables (k_P), as this cost is already accounted for in the WACC.

When partial $WACC_p$ is used, the initial and conclusive cash flows related to trade credit are equal to the amounts on invoices. Payables generally display the amount due to be paid on the settlement of the credit; that is the actual credit includes the implicit interest charged by the supplier in the form of a hidden price premium. The crucial point is then to find the cost of capital associated with these price premiums. Evaluations of cash discounts are a method largely discarded as a means for finding the true cost;[21] pure play comparisons seem to be the only practical tool for this cost estimate.

4.4 Example

Let us demonstrate the difference between these two approaches by using the following example (cf. Allen, 1976). Assume a net investment in working capital of €40 million when the firm is purchasing goods for €11.8 million(on an after-tax basis) annually and utilizes a full year trade credit offered by the supplier. Let us further assume an annual cash flow (before purchasing) of €19 million after tax and that the WACC is equal to an expected rate of return of 18 per cent after tax. Provided that there is no exposure to risk, the partial weighted average cost of capital as well as the relevant opportunity cost of the trade credit (after tax) would be identical to the WACC, that is k_p = $WACC_p$ = WACC = 18 per cent. Hence, as shown in Figure 6.4, the actual trade credit is not €11.8 million but rather €10 million (€11.8 million /(1+.18).[22]

Figure 6.4 shows free cash flow when using $WACC_p$ as a hurdle rate. As the net investment in working capital is €40 million, the (gross) investment in working capital assets, that is inventory and trade credit in the form of receivables, is €50 million. Also shown is the net annual after-tax cash flow, which is €7.2 million. As the net present value of the net after-tax cash flow is zero, $WACC_p$ equals the internal rate of return (IRR).

The same result is obtained when applying the total WACC approach. As cash flow related to trade credit payables should then be excluded from free cash flow, the (gross) investment in working capital assets of €50 million is used. Moreover, the implicit interest charged by the supplier has to be 'cleaned' from the operational cash outflow for purchasing goods. Accordingly, the annual purchasing amount of €11.8 million should be deflated by k_p into €10 million. This results in an annual net after-tax cash flow of €9 million . As expected, this still gives IRR = 18 per cent and NPV = 0.

Let us now allow for exposure to risk, and assume that $WACC_p$ is still in accordance with the IRR and equal to 18 per cent.[23] Thus, NPV = 0 when including trade credit in free cash flow (cf. Figure 6.4). However, when using the total WACC approach, including trade credit as a part of the capital structure, net cash flows will be different from those in Figure 6.5. The relevant opportunity cost of trade credit extended by suppliers is now likely to be lower than 18 per cent. We assume k_p = 12 per cent (after tax) and

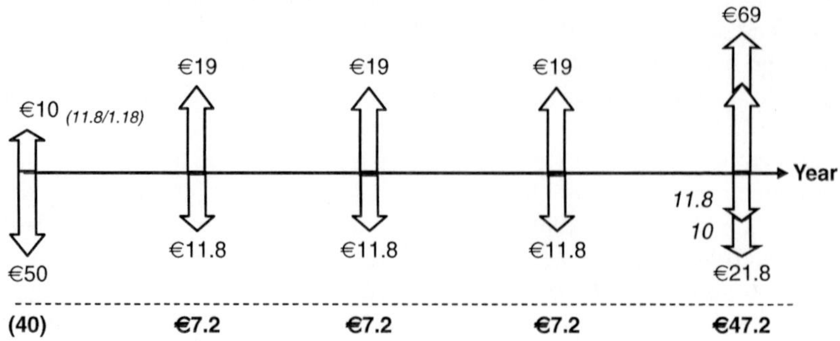

Figure 6.4 Trade credit as a part of free cash flow

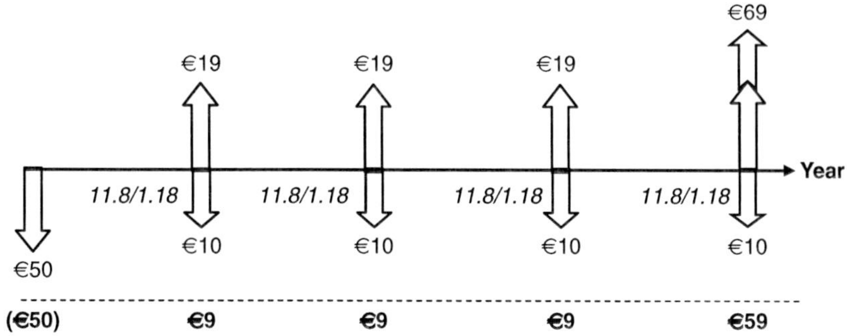

Figure 6.5 Trade credit as a part of the capital structure

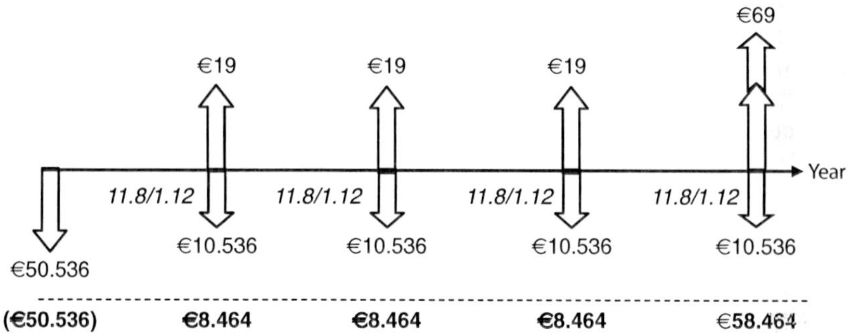

Figure 6.6 Trade credit as free cash flow, including an implicit interest of 12 per cent

that the implicit price premium charged by the supplier matches this cost. This means that the annual purchasing amount should be deflated by 1.12, which results in an annual net cash flow of after-tax equivalent cash outflow for the purchasing of goods that would be €8.464 million (€19 million – €10.536 million). Accordingly, as shown in Figure 6.6, the (gross) investment in working capital assets would be €50.536 million.

Equation 6.18 stipulates that the total WACC will be lower than $WACC_p$ in the case of exposure to risk, provided that the firm is optimally financed. Utilizing the fact that NPV = 0, we may derive WACC by calculating the IRR for the investment when cash committed to payables is not included as free cash flow. Under this approach, the IRR equals 16.75 per cent, which implies that WACC is 1.25 percentage units lower than $WACC_p$. However, this relationship only holds as long as the capital structure remains optimal.

The magnitude of the difference between the total and the partial weighted average cost of capital will vary for this investment in accordance with its profitability in terms of NPV; a positive NPV will increase the market value of the firm, which has implications for its capital structure. $WACC_p$ must therefore be adjusted downwards, in order to reflect the deviation from the optimal structure. In principle, the required adjustment will be different for each year, which of course makes it very difficult in practice to apply the partial weighted average cost of capital approach correctly. This is even more evident when the level of payables varies over the year (as when a strictly marginal principle is applied). In this respect the total WACC approach is superior, as we may assume that the firm continuously adjusts to the target (or optimal) capital structure. Hence, under the total WACC approach the hurdle rate may remain unchanged.

5 Concluding remarks

Despite its character of a non-interest-bearing short-term debt, trade credit is a significant element in the financial structure of the firm. In corporate finance literature, however, working capital seems to be treated more or less mechanically without any distinction made between cash flow assignable to the different types of short-term assets and liabilities. The focus on net working capital cash flow conceals important features of the different types of working capital. There is, furthermore, a lack of understanding of different types of working capital and that different types of working capital ought to be separated when cash flows are exposed to inflation or risk.

We have shown that netting working capital cash flows may be acceptable only in the simplest case, where prices are stable and certainty prevails. As soon as prices and business volumes are volatile, a greater stringency is required in the treatment of cash committed to trade credit and inventory. First, there is a dividing line between current assets and current liabilities with respect to risk. Second, trade credit and inventory should be treated differently when cash flows are exposed to inflation.

In the case of inflation cash tied up in trade credit (receivables) will be drained in real terms. The real value of inventory will however remain unaffected by inflation whenever there is a market for this type of asset. The nominal value of inventory may be expected to follow the general price changes due to inflation. We have labeled that as the 'inflation gain' of holding an inventory as opposed to the 'inflation drain' of extending trade credit. The implication is that cash committed to trade credit and inventory will show different patterns. We have demonstrated how these patterns should be considered in an investment appraisal context.

In the case of risk exposure we have emphasized that there are differences between trade credit and other types of working capital, in general, and between trade credit in the form of receivables and payables, in particular. As different types of working capital are exposed to different kinds of risk, it is essential to display the gross levels instead of net working capital. The financial risk will increase with the amount of debt committed to trade credit.

This has implications for the determination of the weighted average cost of capital. We argue that trade credit in the form of receivables and inventory should be regarded as parts of the investment appraisal problem, whereas trade credit in the form of payables should primarily be seen as a part of the capital structure and WACC. This is in contradiction to the general standpoint that payables are 'free' capital. Therefore, we have also demonstrated how to correctly include trade credit (payables) in free cash flow and use the partial weighted average cost of capital.

We have shown that the opportunity cost of trade credit should be expected to be higher than the average interest cost of interest-bearing debts, albeit lower than the partial weighted average cost of capital in the case of exposure to risk. Hence, in a (near) optimal capital structure, the total weighted average cost of capital would be lower than the partial weighted average cost of capital.

Acknowledgement

We wish to thank Vinnova for financial support.

Notes

1. At the time of writing, the G7 countries were the US, the UK, France, Germany, Italy, Canada and Japan.
2. In the analysis, we have assumed discrete cash flows even though they generally occur more or less frequently during the lifespan of an investment. In reality, continuous cash flows are extremely difficult for decision makers to estimate ex ante; such cash flows are hard to discern even ex post. Hence, in many cases it is rational to assume discrete cash flows instead of continuous ones. Following the standard simplification, when using discounted cash flow (DCF) methods, all cash flows within a certain period are assigned to the end of that period. If the period is as long as a whole year there may be a need for adjustments in the working capital cash flows (cf. Kim and Atkins, 1978).
3. This is seldom recognized in practice and academic literature. In a detailed (in many other aspects) model developed by Cooley et al. (1975), for instance, these different working-capital elements of the NPV calculation are not specified, so the true inflation effect on the cost of working capital cannot be determined by their model.
4. According to Carpenter et al. (1994) the inventory (dis)investment is used to absorb 'internal finance shocks'. They partly rely on Blinder and Maccini (1991) who found that the raw material inventory is much more volatile than either work-in-progress or finished goods. Just-in-time and other planning ideals of that kind, however, seem to reduce the inventories dependence on variations in the internal cash flow.
5. It should be noted, however, that the capital budgeting cash flow should rather be cleaned from the 'other purpose variations' in working capital than clouded with a number of utilization opportunities (except in a real options context) – cf. the difference between the asset and liability types of working capital; see also Aranoff (1992).

6. Cf. Miller and O'Leary (1997).
7. This effect in not recognized by Mills (1996) either, when he makes a similar kind of analysis – albeit in terms of NPV.
8. Released working capital through payables would of course mean an inflation gain to the company that is exactly the opposite outcome to tying up working capital in receivables. As there is no exposure to risk, we may allow for a netting of these types of working capital. The case of risk exposure will be dealt with in the next section.
9. We presume that there are no special tax rules for working capital.
10. In practice, the rates may be difficult to find, a fact recognized by Shinnar et al. (1989) when they solve their problem by using the average (economic in their case) cost of capital anyway.
11. Beside business risks, there are of course other risks, like the risk of fraud, robbery or accidents. Even though these risks are not considered explicitly in this chapter, we may note that they are all likely to increase the cost of working capital.
12. The WACC reflects the average expected return on assets. This holds even in the presence of taxes and default risks, if the firm displays an optimal capital structure. Accordingly, the WACC is an applicable alternative to OCC as a basis for determining a required rate of return that would fully compensate for the financial costs incurred by medium-risky or so-called 'blueprint' investments.
13. Some authors claim that the debt basis ought to be limited to long-term debt (or utilize such debt without further discussion in research, see for example Francis et al. (2000) – this must, however, be due to a misunderstanding of the role of short-term debt. Working capital is an important part of the firm's stock of capital (Fazzari and Petersen, 1993). Most important however, the short-term debt usually is a long-run component in the financial structure of the firm. As such, short-term debt then has to be considered in order to decide the firm's optimal financial structure.
14. Increasing debt is also expected to increase the financial risk of the investor (cf. Modigliani and Miller (1958) and all that followed). If the research by Bernard and Stober (1989) is to be trusted (they make a comparison with earlier, opposing, research results) significant coefficients larger than zero could not be found for inventory, receivables and payables in a regression model with market return as dependent variable. The conclusion is that we do not need to further complicate the discussion with a possible effect on the cost of other liabilities because of changes in the amount of payables.
15. There are also other kinds of short-term liabilities that are often excluded when determining WACC. Even though this analysis is limited to working capital in the form of payables only, a few clarifications may be made: Interest-bearing short-term liabilities are not different from other interest-bearing liabilities. The value of any debt is depending on the corresponding market interest rate and in that way with the risk embedded in the future cash flows considered.
16. We have not considered extreme risk or distress situations. It should be noted that the risk (for the lender) of payables, then, is lower than that of equity but higher than that of debt with collateral. It should also be noted that the risk of some other types of working capital debt is much lower because of high priority (this concerns, for example, corporate tax and salary debts).
17. We do not consider interest differences of debt with unequal time to maturity.
18. Because of sometimes rather complex project dependent changes in the financial structure of the company, the two approaches might give different results. If a

strict financial structure goal is to be upheld, a complete analysis of the financial cash flows would have to include the successive borrowings and repayments in order to preserve the optimal structure. If on the other hand the financial structure is allowed to change with other cash flows of a project, the weighted average cost of capital would have to be adjusted to the financial structure changes.

19. As an element in the long-run financial structure, payables would be exchanged for cheaper debt if k_P is higher than $WACC_p$.
20. Still, the purchase cost (less the implied interest rate) of the required resource should, of course, be regarded as a negative cash flow at the point of payment.
21. See Peterson and Rajan (1997) and Borde and McCarty (1998).
22. If this adjustment is not made the positive effects of trade credits on working capital are overestimated.
23. As there is exposure to risk we also assume that $WACC_p$ includes a risk premium.

References

Allen, B. (1976) 'evaluating capital expenditures under inflation: a primer', *Business Horizons*, December, 30–9.

Aranoff, G. (1992) 'Capital budgeting with technology choice and demand fluctuations in a simple manufacturing model: sample calculations and observations on output flexibility', *Managerial and Decision Economics*, 13, 409–20.

Ashton D., K. Peasnell and P. Wang (2011) 'Residual income valuation models and inflation', *European Accounting Review*, 20(3), 459–83.

Bernard, V.L. and T.L. Stober (1989) 'The nature and amount of information in the cash flows and accruals', *The Accounting Review*, 64(4), 624–52.

Biais, B. and C. Gollier (1997) 'Trade credit and credit rationing', *The Review of Financial Studies*, 10(4), 903–37.

Blinder, A. and L.J. Maccini (1991) 'The resurgence of inventory research: what have we learned?' *Journal of Economic Surveys*, 5(4), 291–28.

Borde, S.F. and D.E. McCarty (1998) 'Determining the cash discount in the firm's credit policy: an evaluation', *Journal of Financial and Strategic Decisions*, 11(2), 41–9.

Burkart, M. and T. Ellingsen (2004) 'In-kind finance: a theory of trade credit', *The American Economic Review*, 94(3), 569–90.

Carpenter, R.E., S.M. Fazzari and B.C. Petersen (1994) 'Inventory investment, internal-finance fluctuations and the business cycle', *Brookings Papers on Economic Activity*, 2, 75–138.

Chee K. Ng., J.K. Smith and R.L. Smith (1999) 'Evidence on the determinants of credit terms used in interfirm trade', *The Journal of Finance*, 54(3), 1109–29.

Cooley, P.L., R.L. Roenfeldt and I-K. Chew (1975) 'Capital budgeting procedures under inflation', *Financial Management*, 4(4), 18–27.

Copeland, T.E. and J.F. Weston (1989) *Financial Theory and Corporate Policy* (Addison-Wesley, 3rd edn 1992).

Crowder, W.J. and D.L. Hoffman (1996) 'The long-run relationship between nominal interest rates and inflation: the Fisher equation revisited', *Journal of Money, Credit and Banking*, 28(1), 102–18.

Fazzari, S.M. and B.C. Petersen (1993) 'Working capital and fixed investment: new evidence on financing constraints', *The RAND Journal of Economics*, 24(3), 328–42.

Francis, J., P. Olsson, and D.R. Oswald (2000) 'Comparing the accuracy and explainability of dividend, free cash flow, and abnormal earnings equity value estimates', *Journal of Accounting Research*, 38(1), 45–70.

Goedhart, M., T. Koller and D. Wessels (2010) 'When the balloon goes up…', *Financial Management (14719185)*, April, 14–16.
Hamada, R.S. (1979) 'Financial theory and taxation in an inflationary world: some public policy issues', *The Journal of Finance*, 34(2), 347– 69.
Horowitz, I. (2000) 'EOQ and inflation uncertainty', *Int. J. Production Economics*, 65(2), 217–24.
Huyghebaert, N. (2006) 'On the determinants and dynamics of trade credit use: empirical evidence from business start-ups', *Journal of Business Finance & Accounting*, 33(1&2), 305–28.
Jain, N. (2001) 'Monitoring costs and trade credit', *The Quarterly Review of Economics and Finance*, 41, 89–110.
Johnson, M.E. and E. Anderson (2000) 'Postponement strategies for channel derivatives', *The International Journal of Logistics Management*, 11(1), 19–35.
Kaplan, S.N. and R.S. Ruback (1995) 'The valuation of cash flow forecasts: an empirical analysis', *The Journal of Finance*, 50(4), 1059–93.
Kim, Y.H. (1979) 'Inflationary effects in the capital investment process: an empirical examination', *The Journal of Finance*, 34(4), 941–50.
Kim, Y.H. and J.C. Atkins (1978) 'Evaluating investments in accounts receivable: a wealth maximizing framework', *The Journal of Finance*, 33(2), 403–12.
Kroll, Y. (1985) 'On the difference between accrual accounting figures and cash flows: the case of working capital', *Financial Management*, 14(1), 75–83.
Lindblom, T., G. Sandahl and S. Sjögren (2011) 'Capital structure choices', *International Journal of Banking, Accounting and Finance*, 3(1), 4–30.
Mian, S.L. and C.W. Smith (1994) 'Extending trade credit and financing receivables', *Journal of Applied Corporate Finance*, 7(1), 75–84.
Miller, P. and T. O'Leary (1997) 'Capital budgeting practices and complementarity relations in the transition to modern manufacture: a field-based analysis', *Journal of Accounting Research*, 35(2), 257–71.
Mills, G.T. (1996) 'The impact of inflation on capital budgeting and working capital', *Journal of Financial and Strategic Decisions*, 9(1), 79–87.
Mishkin, F.S. (1992) 'Is the Fisher effect for real?' *Journal of Monetary Economics*, 30(2), 195–215.
Modigliani, F. and M.H. Miller (1958) 'The cost of capital, corporation finance and the theory of investment', *American Economic Review*, 48, 261–97.
Nilsen, J.H. (2002) 'Trade credit and the bank lending channel', *Journal of Money, Credit and Banking*, 34(1), 226–53.
Peterson, M.A. and R.G. Rajan (1997) 'Trade credit: theories and evidence', *The Review of Financial Studies*, 10(3), 661–91.
Rajan, R.G. and L. Zingales (1995) 'What do we know about capital structure? some evidence from international data', *Journal of Finance*, 50(5), 1421–60.
Schwartz, R.A. (1974) 'An economic model of trade credit', *Journal of Financial and Quantitative Analysis*, 9, 643–57.
Shinnar, R., O. Dressler, C.A. Feng, and A.I. Avidan (1989) 'Estimation of the economic rate of return for industrial companies', *The Journal of Business*, 62(3), 417–45.
Van Delft, C. and J.P. Vial (1996) 'Discounted costs, obsolescence and planned stockouts with the EOQ formula', *International Journal of Production Economics*, 44, 255–65.
Wilner, B.S. (2000) 'The exploitation of relationships in financial distress: the case of trade credit', *The Journal of Finance*, 55(1), 153–78.

7

Accounting for the Level of Success of Firms in Achieving Their Objectives for Using Derivatives

Frank Bezzina, Simon Grima and Joseph Falzon

1 Introduction

Derivatives can be viewed as a socially constructed and need-driven innovation in the financial economy, with their roots well ingrained in the events and circumstances of the real economy (Sharma, 2008). As the transition from a production-based economy to a financial economy was taking shape during the late 1960s and 1970s, the need to control highly increased volatility and fluctuations due to inflation problems, currency problems, debt defaults and many other factors increased in importance (Fischer, 1993). The increased need for controls such as regulation, risk management and audits is noted in literature as being the main reason for the increased global use of derivatives (Brenner, 2002). However, despite the fact that the trade of derivative products have mushroomed (Bank for International Settlements Quarterly Review, March 2010), derivative contracts have tended to make the headlines only when firms and financial institutions made spectacular financial losses (Hull, 2008).

Derivatives are used properly when they are neither misunderstood nor mishandled (Rutledge and Bertram, 1995; Tavakoli, 2001). According to Rutledge and Bartram (1995), financial derivatives can prove to be useful tools in pursuing an investment strategy when there is a full understanding of these instruments and responsible management of the risks. Recently, Bezzina and Grima (2012) identified five factors that affect the proper use of derivatives – namely

i) the use of risk management controls,
ii) expertise in handling derivatives,
iii) perception held on the usefulness of derivatives,
iv) awareness of the benefits that derivatives offer to firms when carefully handled, and
v) acknowledging that various factors such as personal greed or inappropriate standards encourage misuse, which in turn leads to losses.

This study extends the Bezzina and Grima (2012) study by investigating whether or not the five factors of proper derivatives use can account for the level of success of firms (both financial and non-financial) in reaching their goals for using derivatives. A discussion, together with suggestions for further research, will be presented in the light of the findings that emerge.

2 Literature review

In this section, we provide an overview of:

a) how derivatives have been described by theorists, critics and gurus in the world of finance;
b) two specific initiatives, namely the 'Derivatives: Practices and Principles' by the Group of Thirty (1993) and 'The Basel Accords' issued by the Basel Committee on Banking Supervision, that shaped today's best practice for risk management and risk control for derivatives usage, and
c) the constructs that make up the proper derivative use inventory (Bezzina and Grima, 2012).

2.1 Views and opinions on derivatives

Derivatives have been criticized for their supposedly destructive nature in the financial markets, with the effects of this spilling into the real economy (Sharma, 2008). The world of derivatives trading has been described as a world of beautiful lies (Das, 2006) and derivatives are widely perceived as financial instruments that have led to financial losses or failures of firms (Hull, 2008). Chancellor (1999) notes that during US Congress in 1994, American financier George Soros argued that some derivatives are so esoteric that the risks involved are not even understood by the most sophisticated of investors (including Soros himself). Soros claimed that the 'shaky' mathematics used in some derivative pricing models enabled institutional investors to gamble by taking more risks to increase profits, thus overreaching margin requirements which they would otherwise not be permitted to take (Chancellor, 1999). Some of the descriptions of derivatives, according to Jorion (1995, p. 4), include 'financial hydrogen bombs created by 26-year-olds with computers' by Wall Street wise man Felix Rohatyn; 'a monstrous global electronic Ponzi scheme' by Henry Gonzales, former House Banking Committee chairman; and 'highly exotic, little understood and virtually unregulated...and so unpredictable they could bring down the world banking system' by CBS TV Show *60 Minutes*. In the Berkshire Hathaway Inc. 2002 Annual Report, Buffett (2003) described derivatives as being 'financial weapons of mass destruction carrying dangers that, while now latent, are potentially lethal' (p. 15) and that 'the range of derivative contracts is limited only by the imagination of man (or sometimes, so it seems, madmen)' (p. 14).

This led Das (2006) to conclude that since this memorable description of derivatives was provided by Warren Buffett, there has been a thriller waiting to be written about them. More recently, Sammut (2012), a Swiss Management Center university professor, blamed collateralized debt obligations (CDOs) and credit default swaps (CDSs) for the financial crisis in 2007–2008. However, despite the role that derivatives played in the 2008 financial crisis, derivatives are not 'inherently bad' or a complete waste of time and money. In fact, during the Financial Crisis Inquiry in 2011, Buffett pulled back on his previous statement by claiming that derivatives 'are not evil *per se*', and that the real problem has to do with 'uninformed investors' and the 'exposure of banks' (Financial Crisis Inquiry Commission, 2011).

The reasons why the use of derivatives has led to losses and failures are varied. Some attributed this to the complexity of derivatives (Adams and Runkle, 2000), to the result of a 'can't lose mentality' which fails to see the downside of the investment (Muehring, 1995), and to misconceptions/myths that strongly affect investment and risk management (Siems, 1997). Davidson (2000) argued that derivatives don't 'kill' companies; traders and portfolio managers lose money because they do not know how derivative structures work and because companies do not have necessary internal controls in place to protect their assets in this highly risky area. She goes on to blame the media for making people believe that it is not so much people as the derivatives themselves that cause all the problems, somehow managing to slip into our investment portfolios to create losses without our knowledge. According to her, it is true that derivatives can be used as a weapon – but also that *not* investing in derivatives is like 'gambling on uncertainty' (p. 1). Dodd (2002), meanwhile, blamed derivatives users for their ineffective use of derivative instruments in increasing risk-to-capital ratios in the East Asian financial crisis. Economist David Hale of Zurich Kemper Investments blamed the global business culture for the negative attitude towards derivatives. As he put it: 'At fault may be a global business culture that lavishly rewards traders who take risks but not the people who are supposed to supervise them' (IBS Centre for Management Research, 2004, p. 1). This is because firms are generally ready to reach into their pockets to look at innovative ways of making profits and paying good salespeople, but are less willing to spend money and time to control the use of derivatives. In an environment where derivative traders are motivated with multimillion incentive packages, an inadequately funded oversight system is clearly not the appropriate tool to control and manage risk. This increases the gap between the incentive to take risks and the understanding and management of these risks. Baker-Said and Logutenkova (2008) noted that it is really the people within the organization that encourage misuse – not the market, the competition, the inadequacies in technology or the systems in place.

Although it has become fashionable for derivatives to make headlines when firms undergo spectacular collapses and billion-dollar losses, 'to blame derivatives is like blaming a car for causing a crash, rather than the driver who was drunk behind the wheel' (Bartram, 2009). Derivatives have proven to be immensely valuable to modern economies (Stulz, 2005) while Bodie and Merton (2005) argued that all financial intermediary developments (including derivatives) are a response to some or other existing market imperfection. The important benefits associated with derivatives usage include: hedging; speculation; the completing of markets and hence new investment opportunities; the enhancement of liquidity and hence the reduction of transaction costs; the improvement of market efficiency for the underlying asset; and price discovery (Acharya et al., 2009; CFA, 2009; Sill, 1997). According to Stulz (2005), a lack of awareness of such benefits could lead firms to miss out on the gains and protection that derivatives offer to those firms that use them properly.

2.2 Risk management control recommendations for derivative usage

Leslie Rahl, a principal in a financial consulting firm in New York, argued: 'It's not derivatives causing the problem, but a lack of management controls and process' (as cited in Bencivenga, 1994, p. 5). An important initiative that focuses on derivatives is the report entitled 'Derivatives: Practices and Principles' by the Group of Thirty (1993). This is a non-profit organization consisting of senior executives, regulators and academics, and the report provides a set of 20 recommendations related to: the role of boards and senior management; the implementation of independent risk management functions; and the various risks that derivatives transactions entail. The intention was to help users and end-dealers to manage their derivatives activities and continue to benefit from the use of derivatives. In this ground-breaking report, the Group of Thirty (1993) proposed a four-step management control system process for derivative use. This involves:

1) *Corporate Education*: In relation to derivatives and derivative exposure, top management must ensure a proper education for those responsible for anything related to the said financial tools.
2) *Setting of a corporate derivatives policy*: Once corporate education has been completed, the risk management policy should be instituted with the active participation of the board of directors and senior management. It should be clear and concise, should explain the purpose for the use of derivatives, and should include the extent to which derivatives can be used in pursuit of the overall business objectives. The risk management policy should also establish specific and consistent risk management expectations by setting limits to market and credit risk exposure. Guidelines are also needed to minimize legal and liquidity risk. Finally, these policies should be communicated unambiguously and distributed

in writing to those involved in any of the phases of the proposed management control system.

3) *Implementation of a sound investment strategy*: The third step is the implementation of a sound investment strategy, to aid the corporation in meeting the goals established in the derivatives policy. The general rule is that derivatives should be a means of shifting risk and not as a means of trading in risk. Specifically, the Group of Thirty (1993) recommended that: derivative use should correspond in quantity, complexity, and risk with the objectives of the corporation; unnecessary risk should be avoided in the areas of speculation and leverage; derivatives should be used almost exclusively for protection; hedging strategies should involve views on market direction; firms should adjust exposures to risk rather than use derivatives to increase expected short term profits; and leveraging should be avoided in most cases, because it magnifies the risk of a transaction. Other recommendations include: the avoidance of the use of derivatives that are extremely complex; the need for highly qualified personnel who are appropriately trained and informed of the firm's investment strategy and tolerance for loss; clear indication by the senior management of the lines of authority for decision making; and to have a timely derivative activities report given to senior management to keep them informed of the current derivatives investment status. In implementing these strategies, the active participation of the board of directors and senior management must be sought, and the implementation must be consistent with the board's authorization.
4) *Internal controls*: The final step is the establishment and maintenance of a key set of internal controls. In particular, all risk exposures should be quantified and monitored regularly by experts and that transactions are collated and disbursed through a system of checks and balances.

Other initiatives that shaped today's best practice for risk control and risk management are The Basel Accords, issued by the Basel Committee on Banking Supervision (BCBS) and which are available at the Bank for International Settlements website (http://www.bis.org). Pillar 1 of Basel II sets out the minimum capital requirement for credit risks, operational risks and market risks. Pillar 2 concerns the supervisory review process, and provides a framework for dealing with other risks such as systematic, liquidity, pension and legal risks. Pillar 3 focuses on market discipline, imposing greater disclosure standards on banks in order to increase transparency. It is recommended that the Basel III proposals will be completely in place by 2015, in an attempt to improve regulation, supervision and risk management in the banking sector.

2.3 The proper derivative use inventory

Derivatives are used properly when they are neither misunderstood nor mishandled (Rutledge and Bertram, 1995; Tavakoli, 2001). In a recent study,

Bezzina and Grima (2012) sought to identify a set of factors that affect the proper use of derivatives. After reviewing the literature and participating in various forums and sub-groups relating to controls and derivatives, they constructed a questionnaire related to 26 aspects that safeguard or hinder the proper use of derivatives. This questionnaire was presented to an online sample of 420 international users (consisting of managers, analysts, treasurers, brokers and investment bankers) and controllers (risk officers, auditors, compliance officers and regulators) of derivatives from financial and non-financial firms. The responses obtained from the survey were subjected to exploratory factor analysis, and five distinct dimensions of proper derivative use emerged:

1. *Risk management controls*: the importance of using risk management techniques and dedicating proper attention and resources to risk management;
2. *Expertise*: an awareness of the risks involved and having expert knowledge on how to handle derivatives, even in complex situations;
3. *Perception*: subscribing to the view that derivatives are valuable financial instruments in managing and shifting risk, since a negative perception (viewing derivatives as inherently 'bad' or as a complete waste of time and money) may lead firms to avoid dealing with them – and, as Adams and Runkle (2000) put it, avoiding them altogether may be irresponsible.
4. *Benefits*: an awareness of the gains and protection that derivatives offer to firms in managing and shifting risks;
5. *Misuse*: acknowledging that various factors such as personal greed, political interference, inappropriate standards and inadequate controls hinder the proper use of derivatives and encourage misuse (and misuse means losses).

Bezzina and Grima (2012) also found that that certain demographic characteristics of the respondents (experience with derivatives, level of education, position held within firm) produced a significant impact on the factor scores, and hence they recommended that 'any gaps that still need to be filled in order to ensure that derivatives are used properly may not necessarily relate to structures, regulations and process but also to the characteristics of personnel' (p. 430).

3 Research method

3.1 Research question

The main scope of this empirical quantitative study was to determine whether the five factors of 'proper derivative use' (use of risk management controls, expertise, perception, benefits and misuse), as proposed by Bezzina and Grima (2012), could account for the level of success of firms in achieving their objectives for using derivatives.

3.2 Measures

Proper Derivative Use: The 'proper derivative use' scales were adapted from the Proper Derivative Use Inventory (PDUI) by Bezzina and Grima (2012). The PDUI consists of the following five components:

1. Risk Management Controls, comprising nine items (Cronbach $\alpha = 0.94$) related to the importance of using risk management controls (for example, 'We evaluate both settlement and pre-settlement credit risk at the customer level across all products') and the importance of dedicating proper attention and resources towards risk management controls (for example, 'We have adequate support and operational capacity to accommodate the types of derivative activities in which our company engages').
2. Expertise, comprising five items (Cronbach $\alpha = 0.89$) concerning awareness of risks and competence in handling derivatives (for example, 'I am aware of any leverage in derivatives' positions, particularly in complex situations').
3. Perception, consisting of four items (Cronbach $\alpha = 0.77$) related to the view held as to whether derivatives are a necessity for firms in managing risks (for example, 'Managers and firms should encourage the use of derivatives') or whether they are a complete waste of time and money (for example, 'Derivatives are inherently "bad" financial instruments').
4. Benefits, with four items (Cronbach $\alpha = 0.78$) related to an awareness of the benefits that firms can gain from using derivatives properly (for example, 'Derivatives, when used properly, are potentially beneficial in managing and hedging unwanted risks').
5. Misuse, with four items (Cronbach $\alpha = 0.72$) related to an awareness that the catastrophic losses that can be incurred by firms when using derivatives are due not to the inherent nature of derivatives but to other factors which encourage misuse and hinder the proper use of derivatives (for example, 'Personal greed encourages misuse' or 'Inadequate controls encourage misuse').

The respondents were required to state their level of agreement with each of these 26 items on a standard five-point scale ranging from 'strongly disagree' (coded 1) to 'strongly agree' (coded 5). The factor scores were obtained by computing the mean score of the individual item scores pertaining to each factor.

Success of firms in achieving the objectives for using derivatives: The respondents were asked to respond to the following item: 'Our firm has been successful in achieving the objectives for using derivatives'. First, this item was presented with the 'proper derivative use' items, and the respondents were asked to rate their level of agreement with this statement on a standard five-point Likert scale ranging from 'strongly disagree' to 'strongly agree'. At a later stage of the questionnaire, the respondents were also asked to indicate whether this statement was true or false. This nominal variable allowed for dichotomous classification of the success of firms in reaching their objectives for using derivatives – successful versus unsuccessful group membership – and served as the independent variable in the statistical tests employed in this study which include multivariate analysis of variance (MANOVA) and the Mann–Whitney U test.

Demographic Information: The respondents were asked to indicate their gender (male/female), highest academic qualification achieved (diploma/undergraduate degree/post-graduate degree/doctoral degree) and experience with the firm (in years).

3.3 Sampling procedure and sample characteristics

Since the sampling frame of all international users and controllers of derivatives is not available, we resorted to critical-case purpose sampling (Saunders et al., 2012). So, all those subscribers on Linkedin, AuditNet, Global Derivatives and Wilmott who were responsible for derivatives, and who also occupied positions that enabled them to understand, determine and have full strategic information about their firm, were invited to participate in the survey.

The URL was set to limit surveys to one response per computer, but respondents were allowed to go back and edit their responses until the responses were submitted. We also collected the IP addresses and asked the respondents to provide us with their contact email address at their firm. These steps were taken to ensure as far as possible that we did not obtain multiple responses from the same organization. We assured the respondents about the privacy/confidentiality of their responses and that the responses were to be used only for research purposes.

The surveys were mainly carried out online via a weblink on kwiksurveys.com between March 2010 and August 2010, and 496 completed questionnaires were collected in all. The participants occupied the following positions within their firm: risk officers, analysts, compliance officers, managers, treasurers, internal auditors, regulators, brokers and investment bankers. Of the participating firms, 367 (or 74 per cent) were financial firms, and the remaining 129 (or 26 per cent) were non-financial. The majority of the respondents that responded on behalf of the firm were male (79.0 per cent), in possession of a post-graduate degree (73.2 per cent) and had, on average, more than 12 years of experience with their firm (M = 12.91; SD = 6.89).[1] The profile of the respondents, particularly with respect to their position occupied within the firm, experience and educational background, increased our confidence that overall the respondents were in a relatively good position to respond to the survey questions on behalf of their firm.

3.4 Analysis procedure

We started by estimating the factor scores, by computing the mean score of the individual items pertaining to each factor. We then computed summary statistics for the five factors overall and by group membership (the binary classification of the level of success of firms in reaching their objectives for using derivatives – successful versus unsuccessful). Multivariate analysis of variance (MANOVA) was then used to determine whether group membership had a statistically significant effect on the combined dependent variables (that is, the five proper derivative use factors). In the presence of a significant multivariate F statistic (for example, Wilks' λ),[2]between-subject effects were examined in order to interpret the respective effect. Here, the Type 1 error (generally denoted as α, and representing the probability of rejecting the null hypothesis when the null hypothesis is true) was corrected for the number of ANOVAs using a Bonferroni correction of α/m, where m is the number of ANOVAS conducted (Huberty and Smith, 1982). As such, we accepted statistical significance at $p \leq 0.01$.[3] For those factors that produced a univariate F-statistic, we also examined whether the level of success of firms in achieving their objectives for using derivatives produced a significant impact on the individual items scores pertaining to these factors. Since the individual items used the ordinal scale of measurement, the Mann–Whitney U test was used. This is a useful non-parametric alternative to the independent samples *t*-test or one-way ANOVA in cases where there are only two groups (Field, 2009). An alpha correction was made to account for multiple Mann–Whitney U tests run on items pertaining to the same construct (Miller, 1991). All statistical analyses were carried out in the IBM SPSS Version 20 software.

4 Results and discussion

4.1 Preliminary analysis

In this survey, we asked the respondents to rate their level of success in achieving their objectives for using derivatives on a dichotomous scale (successful versus unsuccessful) and on a standard five-point Likert scale ranging from 'strongly disagree' (coded 1) to 'strongly agree' (coded 5). Overall, 58.3 per cent of the respondents reported that their firms were successful in achieving the objectives for using derivatives ($M = 4.56$, $SD = 0.49$, $N = 289$),[4] while the other 41.7 per cent reported that they were unsuccessful ($M = 2.52$, $SD = 0.57$, $N = 207$). ANOVA revealed that these means were significantly different from each other ($F_{1,494} = 1784.19$, $p < 0.001$).

After calculating the factor scores by computing the mean score of the individual item scores pertaining to each factor, we generated descriptive statistics overall and by group membership. These are presented in Table 7.1.

Table 7.1 Descriptive statistics of factor scores overall and by group membership

Achieving objectives for using derivatives	Statistica	RMCb	Expertise	Perception	Benefits	Misuse
	N	289	289	289	289	289
Successful	M	4.22	4.41	4.02	4.43	3.84
	SD	0.62	0.50	0.56	0.50	0.68
	N	207	207	207	207	207
Unsuccessful	M	3.93	4.12	3.94	4.30	3.94
	SD	0.69	0.60	0.63	0.51	0.70
	N	496	496	496	496	496
	M	4.10	4.29	3.99	4.38	3.88
Overall	SD	0.47	0.56	0.59	0.51	0.69

Notes: [a] N = count, M = mean, SD = standard deviation ; [b] use of risk management controls.

To better understand how the factor scores were distributed for each group and to identify the presence of outliers and extreme values, box plots were obtained. These are portrayed in Figure 7.1. Both the means in Table 7.1 and medians in Figure 7.1 suggest that there may be sufficient differences between the groups to support statistical significance. The presence of outliers and extreme values are also evident in the box plots. The outliers (marked with a circle) are observations that range between 1 and 1.5 quartiles away from the box, while the extreme values (marked with a star) represent observations greater than 1.5 quartiles away from the end of the box. Following guidelines by Hair et al. (1998), these outliers and extreme values were retained, since after careful scrutiny we confirmed that they do not represent procedural errors – they in fact fall within the range of values of a standard five-point Likert scale and hence they represent valid observations in the population.

4.2 Multivariate analysis of variance

In MANOVA, the five factor scores were specified as dependent variables, while group membership (successful versus unsuccessful) was specified as the fixed factor (or independent variable). The first critical assumption in MANOVA is that that the dependent measures are significantly correlated (Hair et al., 1998). The Bartlett Test of Sphericity (statistic = 394.93, $df = 10$, $p < 0.001$)[5] confirmed that a significant amount of intercorrelation existed. The second critical assumption in MANOVA is that the within-group covariance matrices are equal. The Box M Test in our case had a significance level of 0.01. According to Hair et al. (1998), given the sensitivity of the test, this significance level is deemed acceptable since it is not significant at less than 0.001. Additionally, a violation of this assumption would have had minimal

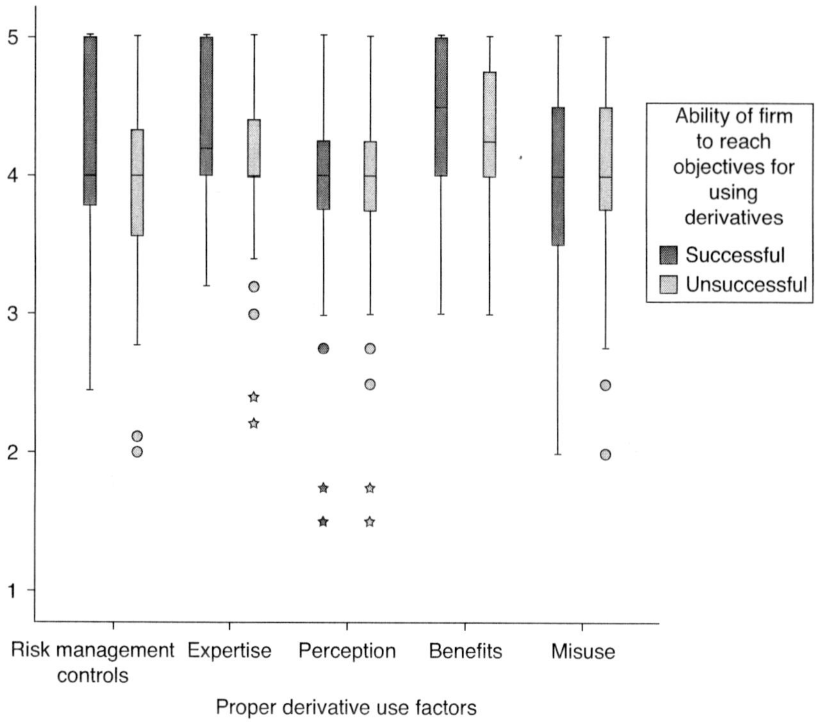

Figure 7.1 Box plots of factor score distributions by group membership

impact if the groups had been approximately equal in size. In our case, the largest group divided by the smallest group is 1.39, which is less than the critical value of 1.5 (Hair et al., 1998). So the MANOVA analysis proceeded.

The Wilks' lambda criterion (statistic = 0.92; $F_{5,490} = 8.57$, $p < 0.001$) had a significance level below the pre-specified level of 0.05, and this was also confirmed by Pillai's Trace criterion (statistic = 0.08, $F_{5,490} = 8.57$, $p < 0.001$). Additionally, the power for the multivariate test was 1.00, indicating that 'samples sizes and the effect sizes were sufficient to ensure that any significant differences would be detected if they existed beyond the differences due to sampling error' (Hair et al., 1998, p. 364). Hence, the level of success produced a statistically significant effect on the combined dependent variables.

In the presence of a significant multivariate F-statistic, we assessed the between-subjects effects. After applying a Bonferroni correction, statistical significance was set at $p \leq 0.01$. This analysis revealed that those firms which were successful in achieving their objectives for using derivatives reported:

a) a significantly greater use of risk management controls ($F_{1,494} = 20.35$, $p < 0.001$);
b) a significantly greater expertise in dealing with derivatives, particularly in complex scenarios ($F_{1,494} = 32.92$, $p < 0.001$); and
c) a significantly stronger awareness of an array of benefits that derivatives offer to firms ($F_{1,494} = 7.59$, $p < 0.01$).

However, the mean scores for perception ($F_{1,494} = 2.84$, $p = 0.092$) and misuse ($F_{1,494} = 2.70$, $p = 0.101$) did not vary as a function of group membership (the firms' level of success in achieving their objectives for using derivatives).

4.3 Examining group membership differences across the factor items

Given that the risk management controls, expertise and benefits factors produced statistically significant univariate F-effects, we investigated whether the scores of the items pertaining to each of these three factors varied significantly by group membership. Since the scales used for the items are ordinal, the Mann–Whitney U test was used. A summary of mean ranks and Mann–Whitney U test output is presented in Table 7.2.

With respect to risk management controls, the firms that were classified as being successful in achieving their objectives for using derivatives reported significantly higher mean ranks (with statistical significance set at $p \leq 0.005$, after applying Bonferroni correction) in all the nine items pertaining to this construct:

i) we evaluate both settlement and pre-settlement credit risk at the customer level for all products ($p < 0.001$),
ii) we assess potential exposure through simulation analysis or other sophisticated techniques ($p < 0.001$),
iii) in terms of market risk, we compare estimated market risk exposures with actual behavior ($p < 0.001$),
iv) we establish limits for market risk that relate to its risk measures and that are consistent with maximum exposures authorized by senior management and the board ($p = 0.005$),
v) in terms of market risk, we establish guidelines when establishing limits ($p = 0.001$),
vi) we assess the potential liquidity risks associated with the early termination of derivatives' contracts ($p < 0.001$),
vii) we allocate sufficient resources (financial and personnel) to support operations and systems development and maintenance ($p < 0.001$),
viii) we have adequate support and operational capacity to accommodate the types of derivative activities in which the company engages ($p < 0.001$), and
ix) we evaluate systems needs for derivative activities during the strategic planning process ($p < 0.001$).

Hence, the firms that were successful in achieving their objectives for using derivatives reported significantly greater use of risk management techniques, and dedicate more attention and resources towards risk management controls.

With respect to expertise, an analysis of the individual test items revealed that those firms that were successful in achieving their objectives for using derivatives reported significantly higher mean ranks (with statistical significance set at $p \leq 0.01$, after applying Bonferroni correction) that those that were unsuccessful in all the items pertaining to this construct. The items were the following:

i) We are aware of any leverage in derivatives' positions, particularly in complex situations ($p < 0.001$),
ii) We understand the risks associated with derivatives, particularly in complex scenarios ($p < 0.001$),
iii) We know our exit costs – What will it cost to unwind to a later position? ($p < 0.001$),
iv) We are prepared to face the challenges posed by derivatives ($p < 0.001$), and
v) We understand the purpose for using derivatives to hedge, speculate and reduce funding costs ($p < 0.001$).

These findings suggest that firms would benefit if they invest in personnel that are both knowledgeable and experienced, since this combination is more likely to contribute to better decision making due to the acquisition of analytical skills. A proper education helps to break down the barriers and makes the fearful known (Cowan, 1994), while past experience allows for a better understanding of the association between investment benefits and risks (Meir, 2005).

With respect to benefits, those firms who were classified as being successful when using derivatives reported significantly higher mean ranks (with statistical significance set at $p \leq 0.012$), after applying Bonferroni correction) than those who were unsuccessful in two specific items:

i) Derivatives, when used properly, offer inventory managers in the cash and commodity markets the opportunity to reduce their exposure to unexpected, unfavorable movements in the price of their product ($p = 0.002$), and
ii) Derivatives, when used properly, can reduce financing costs ($p = 0.003$).

The two items that did not produce a statistically significant difference across groups were the following:

i) Derivatives, when used properly, offer the possibility of large speculative gains (p = 0.271), and
ii) Derivatives, when used properly, are beneficial in managing and hedging unwanted risks (p = 0.357).

Thus, irrespective of the level of success in achieving the objectives for using derivatives, the firms strongly agree (on average) that derivatives are potentially beneficial in managing and hedging unwanted risk (M = 4.54, SD = 0.55, Median (Md) = 5, Range (R) = 3) and agree (on average) that derivatives offer the possibility of large speculative gains (M = 4.29, SD = 0.78, M_d = 4, R = 4). Hence derivatives are perceived to be valuable and beneficial by these firms, and this is in line with the general stand taken by most economists, that derivatives are a positive innovation of the last couple of decades (Cochran, 2007).

Table 7.2 Mean ranks and Mann–Whitney U test output

	Mean Rank		Mann–Whitney U Test	
	Achieved objectives for using derivatives?		U value (z score)	Asymp. Sig.
	No	*Yes*		
Statement	N = 207	N = 289		
Use of risk management controls			**Sig. set at p ≤ 0.005***	
We evaluate both settlement and pre-settlement credit risk at the customer level for all products	216.45	271.45	23278.0 (–4.67)	<0.001
We assess potential exposure through simulation analysis or other sophisticated techniques	218.86	269.73	23777.0 (–3.84)	<0.001
In terms of market risk, we compare estimated market risk exposures with actual behavior	221.61	267.76	24345 (–3.84)	<0.001
We establish limits for market risk that relate to its risk measures and that are consistent with maximum exposures authorized by senior management and the board	229.04	262.44	25883.0 (–2.82)	<0.001

Continued

Statement	Mean Rank: *Achieved objectives for using derivatives?* *No*	*Yes*	Mann–Whitney U Test: U value (z score)	Asymp. Sig.
	N = 207	N = 289		
Use of risk management controls			**Sig. set at p ≤ 0.005***	
In terms of market risk, we establish guidelines when establishing limits	225.53	264.95	25156.5 (–3.38)	0.001
We assess the potential liquidity risks associated the early termination of derivatives' contracts	224.39	265.77	24921.5 (–3.41)	0.001
We allocate sufficient resources (financial and personnel) to support operations and systems development and maintenance	221.17	268.08	24253.5 (–3.85)	<0.001
We have adequate support and operational capacity to accommodate the types of derivative activities in which the company engages	210.30	275.86	22005.0 (–5.43)	<0.001
We evaluate systems needs for derivative activities during the strategic planning process	214.54	272.83	22881.0 (–4.81)	<0.001
Expertise			**Sig. set at p ≤ 0.01***	
We are aware of any leverage in derivatives' positions, particularly in complex situations	216.93	271.11	22912.5 (–5.09)	<0.001
We understand the risks associated with derivatives, particularly in complex scenarios	213.66	273.45	23376.5 (–4.71)	<0.001
We know our exit costs – What will it cost to unwind to a later position?	212.36	274.39	22700.0 (–5.26)	<0.001

Continued

Statement	Mean Rank		Mann–Whitney U Test	
	Achieved objectives for using derivatives?		U value (z score)	Asymp. Sig.
	No	*Yes*		
	N = 207	N = 289		
We are prepared to face the challenges posed by derivatives	223.71	266.25	22429.5 (–5.26)	<0.001
We understand the purpose of using derivatives to hedge, speculate and reduce funding costs	282.31	224.28	24780.5 (–3.71)	<0.001
Benefits			**Sig. set at p ≤ 0.012***	
Derivatives, when used properly, offer the possibility of large speculative gains	240.89	253.95	28337.0	0.271
Derivatives, when used properly, offer inventory managers in the cash and commodity markets the opportunity to reduce their exposure to unexpected, unfavorable movements in the price of their product	227.8	263.33	25626.5 (–3.09)	0.002
Derivatives, when used properly, are beneficial in managing and hedging unwanted risks	242.44	252.84	28657.5 (–0.92)	0.357
Derivatives, when used properly, can reduce financing costs	227.79	263.33	25625.5 (–2.99)	0.003

Notes: *Statistical significance set after applying Bonferroni correction.

5 Conclusion

5.1 Contribution of the study

A significant contribution of this study is that it produced empirical evidence that accounts for the level of success of firms in reaching their objectives for using derivatives. The study shows that firms are more likely to be successful in reaching their objectives for using derivatives if they make greater use of risk management controls, if they have personnel with the right expertise to deal with derivatives even in complex situations, and if they are more aware of the array of benefits that derivatives provide to firms in managing and shifting risks. These are important findings, because they contradict the position taken by some theorists, critics and gurus in the world of finance that derivatives are inherently 'bad' and that their use leads to catastrophic losses (see Buffett (2003) and Jorion (1995) for such descriptions). The findings of our study lend weight to the claim that derivatives can be useful tools in pursuing an investment strategy, provided there is full understanding of these instruments and responsible management of the risks (Rutledge and Bertram, 1995).

5.2 Limitations of the study

There are some limitations to the findings, however, that must be noted. Firstly, the measures used in this study were obtained from self-reports, and hence it is possible that some respondents did not answer with objectivity and precision on a five-point scale. Secondly, this study made use of a judgmental sample, which is not a product of a randomized selection process, and so it may or may not represent the population accurately. Thirdly, this study has focused on five components of proper derivative use to try to account for the level of success of firms in achieving their objectives for reaching derivatives. These five factors are not exhaustive and there are undoubtedly various other aspects that could be investigated empirically and inductively in future studies. Fourthly, in determining whether the firms were successful in reaching their objectives for using derivatives, we did not define the objectives. Although this was done intentionally, in line with the objectives of the present study, it could be argued that we are not in a position to determine whether the objectives of firms in using derivatives have a speculative element.

5.3 Suggestions for further research

Despite widespread employment of derivatives with adequate risk management controls, not all firms are immune to derivative misuse, and this necessitates controls that constantly have to be kept up to date (Bank for International Settlements, December 2009). Risk management is a major concern that extends outside the risk management department if objectives for using derivatives are to be achieved successfully. However, with the growing volume and complexity of rules, standards, frameworks and regulations, it is now becoming ever more difficult to define the profession of risk management, let alone the controls that are required to be in place. There is a need for a more holistic, interdisciplinary and enterprise-wide approach to risk management, which combines all the lines of defense within a firm (accounting, economics, mathematics, operations, front offices and technology). The many framework standards, rules, guidelines and regulations are not always helpful in the development of robust rules that cover the whole categorization of risks.

Further research is also needed to determine whether the position of risk manager within a firm is held by the appropriate people, whether risk management education addresses the needs of the market appropriately, and whether the frameworks, standards, rules, guidelines and regulations addressing the needs of risk management are alive, or whether they are just rules set in stone. This should provide a better understanding of the gaps that need to be addressed to ensure that the objectives set for using derivatives are achieved successfully.

Notes

1. M = Mean, SD = Standard deviation.
2. Wilks' lambda, also known as the maximum likelihood criterion, is one of four principal statistics for testing the null hypothesis in MANOVA (Hair et al., 1998).
3. p = a conditional probability value – the probability of obtaining sample data that deviate as much or even more than the actual data observed, provided the null hypothesis is true. When $p \leq \alpha$, the null hypothesis is rejected and a statistical significant finding is reported.
4. N = number of participants.
5. *df* = degrees of freedom.

References

Acharya, V., M. Brenner, R. Engle, A. Lynch and M. Richardson (2009) 'Derivatives – the ultimate financial innovation', in V. Acharya and M. Richardson (eds), *Restoring Financial Stability: How to Repair a Failed System*. New York: Wiley, pp. 233–50.

Adams, E.S. and D.E. Runkle (2000) 'The easy case for derivatives use: advocating a corporate fiduciary duty to use derivatives', *William and Mary Law Review*, 41(2), 595.

Baker-Said, S. and E. Logutenkova (2008), 'UBS $100 Billion Wager Prompted $24 Billion Losses in Nine Months'. Available at: http://www.bloomberg.com/apps/news?pid=newsarchive&sid=a3sm9FOrsWcg&refer=home, Accessed on 12 January 2009.

Bank for International Settlements Quarterly Review (December 2009) 'International banking and financial market developments'. Available at: http://www.bis.org/publ/qtrpdf/r_qt0912.pdf. Accessed on 5 February 2010.

Bank for International Settlements Quarterly Review (March 2010) 'International banking and financial market developments'. Available at: http://www.bis.org/publ/qtrpdf/r_qt1003.pdf. Accessed on 18 May 2010.

Bartram, B. (2009) 'Derivatives Are Not Weapons of Mass Destruction'. Available at: http://www.standard.co.uk/business/derivatives-are-not-weapons-of-mass-destruction-6779663.html. Accessed on 12 January 2010.

Bencivenga, D. (1994) 'Derivatives litigation: parties argue over "degrees" of sophistication', *The New York Law Journal*, 1, 5.

Bezzina, F. and S. Grima (2012) 'Exploring factors affecting the proper use of derivatives: an empirical study with active users and controllers of derivatives', *Managerial Finance*, 38(4), 414–35.

Bodie, R.C. and Z. Merton (2005) 'Design of financial systems: towards a synthesis of function and structure', *Journal of Investment Management*, 3(1), 1–23.

Brenner, R. (2002) *The Boom and the Bubble: The US in the World Economy*. Verso: London.

Buffett, W.E. (2003) 'Berkshire Hathaway Inc. 2002 Annual Report'. Available at: http://www.berkshirehathaway.com/2002ar/2002ar.pdf. Accessed on 12 June 2009.

Chancellor, E. (1999) *Devil Take the Hindmost: A History of Financial Speculation*. Farrar, Straus and Giroux: New York.

Cochran, J. (2007) 'Carbon on Credit: Global Warming and the Derivatives Markets'. http://www.articlearchives.com/banking-finance/banking-lending-credit-services-consumer/347521-1.html. Accessed on 10 October 2008.

Cowan, D. (1994) 'Hedge your bets: OPEC', *The Middle East*, 238, 27.

CFA (2009) 'CFA Level 1 Purposes and Benefits of Derivatives'. Available at: http://www.investopedia.com/study-guide/cfa-exam/level-1/derivatives/cfa9.asp. Accessed on 18 May 2010.

Das, S. (2006) 'Traders Guns and Money: Knowns and Unknowns in the Dazzling World of Derivatives'. Available at: ftp://ftp.pearsoned-ema.com/HPE_Samples/PressReleases/0273704745-PR.pdf. Accessed 12 December 2008.

Davidson, B. (2000) *Auditing Derivative Strategies – The IIA Handbook Series*. Altamonte Springs, FL: Institute of Internal Auditors.

Dodd, R. (2002) 'The role of derivatives in the East Asian financial crisis', in J. Eatwell and L. Taylor (eds), *International Capital Markets: Systems in Transition*. Oxford: Oxford University Press, pp. 447–74.

Field, A. (2009) *Discover Statistics Using SPSS*, 3rd edn. London: Sage.

Financial Crisis Inquiry Commission (2011) *The Financial Crisis Inquiry Report: Final Report of the National Commission on the Causes of the Financial and Economic Crisis in the United States*. Financial Crisis Inquiry Commission: Washington, DC.

Fischer, S. (1993) 'The role of macroeconomic factors in growth', *Journal of Monetary Economics*, 32 (December), 485–512.

Group of Thirty (1993) *Derivatives: Practices and Principles*. Washington, DC: Group of Thirty.

Hair, J.F., R.E. Anderson, R.L. Tatham and W.C. Black (1998) *Multivariate Data Analysis*, 5th edn. Prentice-Hall, NJ: Upper Saddle River.

Huberty, C.J. and J.D. Smith (1982) 'The study of effects in MANOVA', *Multivariate Behavioral Research*, 17, 417–32.

Hull, J. (2008) *Options, Futures and Other Derivatives*, 7th edn. Prentice-Hall, NJ: Upper Saddle River.

IBS Centre for Management Research (2004) 'Sumitomo Corporation of Japan – The Commodity Derivatives Fiasco'. Available at: http://www.icmrindia.org/casestudies/catalogue/Finance/FINC029.htm. Accessed on 25 August 2010.

Jorion, P. (1995) *Big Bets Gone Bad: Derivatives and Bankruptcy in Orange County. The Largest Municipal Failure in US History*. San Diego, CA: Academic Press.

Meir, S. (2005) 'Normal investors, then and now', *Financial Analysts Journal*, 61(3), 31–7.

Miller, R.G. (1991) *Simultaneous Statistical Inference*. New York: Springer-Verlag.

Muehring, K. (1995) 'The year of the client', *Institutional Investor*, March, 31–2.

Rutledge, G.P. and R. Bertram (1995) 'A Brief Guide to Financial Derivatives'. Available at: http://www.psc.state.pa.us/corpfinance/derivatives.html. Accessed on 12 June 2009.

Sammut, J. (4 March 2012) 'Derivative Instruments and the Financial Crisis 2007–2008: Role and Responsibility'. Available at: SSRN: http://ssrn.com/abstract=2015786. Accessed on 12 July 2012.

Saunders, M., A. Thornhill and P. Lewis (2012) *Research Methods for Business Students*, 5th edn. Harlow, England: Pearson.

Sharma, S. (2008) 'Role of Financial Derivatives in Managing Risk in Financial Markets: Towards the Complex Exchange of Risk, Speculation, and Fundamental Value'. Available at: http://www.scribd.com/doc/15744801/Role-of-Financial-Derivatives-in-Managing-Risk-in-Financial-Markets-Towards-the-Complex-Exchange-of-Risk-Speculation-and-Fundamental-Value. Accessed on 12 June 2009.

Siems, T. (1997) 'Policy Analysis: 10 Myths about Financial Derivatives'. Available at: http://www.cato.org/pubs/pas/pa-283.html. Accessed on 25 February 2009.

Sill, K. (1997) 'The economic benefits and risks of derivative securities', *Business Review, Federal Reserve Bank of Philadelphia*, January, 15–26.

Stulz, R.M. (2005) 'Demystifying Financial Derivatives', *The Milken Institute Review*, Third Quarter 2005, 20–31.

Tavakoli, J. (2001) *Credit Derivatives and Synthetic Structures: A Guide to Instruments and Applications*, 2nd edn. New York: Wiley.

8
The Management of Foreign Exchange Exposures

Göran Bergendahl and Stefan Sjögren

1 Introduction

Since 1986, the international foreign exchange market has grown from US$208 billion in daily turnover (including spot, outright forward and foreign exchange swap transaction) to US$3.9 trillion in 2008 (Bank for International Settlement, 2010). The FDI[1] activity of mainly multinational companies (MNC) grew from around US$86.3 billion to around US$1.8 trillion in 2008 (UnctadStat, 2010). During the same period, international trade volumes grew from about US$2.4 million to about US$200 million (UnctadStat, 2010). These numbers demonstrate the globalization that has taken place during the last 25 years, and the increase in international activities by MNCs. This study investigates the foreign exchange exposure management of some Swedish and UK firms. The management of foreign exposure in global firms is considered today as a mature area with well established procedures and a choice of hedging techniques. This study aims at describing the development of these procedures and what factors that lie behind changes taking place. In contrast to other qualitative studies (for example, Aabo, 2006; Bartram, 2001; Brown, 2001; Dhanani, 2004 and Dhanani and Groves, 2001), we have had the opportunity of performing a longitudinal survey with repeated visits on three occasions during this period of extreme growth in the international financial markets, between 1986 and 2008. This study also contributes to the literature by focusing on how the decision maker's own perception on risk, market efficiency and shareholder influences their management of foreign exposure.

There is a controversy as to whether or not companies should hedge currency risks. Those who favor hedging support the principle that a company should not take financial risks but should leave those risks to financial institutions like banks. Those who do not recommend hedging support a view that all risks will even out in the long run. Furthermore, the combination of the risks of changes in the exchange rates (the currency risks) and the risks of sales that may grow smaller than expected (the sales risks) not only hit firms that export goods and services on the international markets – but will also influence many firms that solely work on the domestic markets (Allayannis and Ihrig, 2001; Dekle and Ryoo, 2007; Luehrman, 1991; Williamson, 2001). The reason is that such firms may suddenly realize that there is new competition from foreign companies making use of the advantages that can arise from changes in the exchange rates. Hedging against long-term real effects of currency changes, such as an increased demand for domestic labor (Gourinch, 1999) and changes in industrial structure (Williamson, 2001) is not possible using different financial instruments, and instead these exposures are part of the overall business risk, and are tightly interwoven with a firm's strategic decision making, whether or not the firm is operating on the global market.

A firm's hedging strategies are motivated by the existence of market imperfections, often referred to as transaction costs. The theoretical reasoning stretches back to Modigliani and Miller's *irrelevance proposition* (1958). In a Modigliani and Miller world, a firm should not hedge the kind of risk that diversified owners can in fact diversify by themselves. Subsequently, from a financial perspective it is the transaction costs that are the main motivation for hedging, and hedging activities can be viewed as redundant on an efficient market. The very extensive research on foreign exchange exposure management has in common an understanding and an explanation of how transaction costs, such as taxes, asymmetric information, the risk attitudes of owners and managers, imperfect currency and product markets, undiversified owners etc form the foundation for why, how and when firms choose to hedge currency risk.

This study differs from most other studies on foreign exchange exposure management (FEEM), as it also has a longitudinal aspect. In 1985 a first set of interviews were performed, referred to here as FEEM 85 (Bergendahl and Nyberg, 1986). These interviews were repeated in 1996, in a project which we have called FEEM 96 (see Bergendahl, 2001). Finally in 2008 we performed a third set of interviews, referred to as FEEM 08. In carrying out this study over the years, we have been able to observe changes in policies for individual companies of various sizes, from different business sectors, and from two countries facing different regulatory regimes, namely the UK and Sweden. This has also allowed us to study the differences in behavior between companies from Sweden, that operate with a small currency, and those from UK, a country with a currency that is traded in large volumes. This has been of special interest to us, as when we started this project in 1985, Swedish firms were controlled by currency regulation while UK firms were not. In addition, we will focus on behavioral aspects of treasury management such as risk attitudes and perception of market efficiency.

1.1 Main findings from the FEEM 85 and the FEEM 96 studies

In many companies today, the sales risks and the currency exchange risks are estimated regularly and simultaneously in terms of currency exposures. But in 1985, when the first set of interviews was carried out with 26 Swedish and UK firms, it was impossible to perform instantaneous and simultaneous measures of exposures. At that time we found (perhaps surprisingly), that the main objective for foreign exchange exposure management was to reduce payment costs and not the exchange rate risks; that was the concern for both the English and the Swedish multinationals, and perhaps more obviously so for smaller Swedish firms. The overwhelming part of the exposure management was concerned with the short-term trade; only two of the firms regularly managed their long-term economic exposures. For the 14 firms that actually measured and managed their exposure, forward contracts were the main instruments for hedging, and only a couple of firms issued debt in foreign currencies as a means of hedging. The exposure was either netted out month by month a year ahead (in four firms), once a month (in eight firms), or once a week (in a single firm). Only one firm performed netting on daily basis. For seven of these firms, the proportion to be hedged was 80 per cent or more out of their net exposure.

A project on international cash management ten years later (Bergendahl and Birts, 1998) revealed that a rapid change had taken place as to what was of concern in exposure management: first, the Swedish currency regulation had been eliminated; secondly, the financial markets had as of 1985 expanded beyond all imagination; and thirdly, interest rate risk management had become a central issue within companies. These changes motivated a new study to be performed on the same set of companies. It was observed (Bergendahl, 2001, pp. 253–266) in 1996, that a common approach in cash management was to invoice and to pay subsidiaries in their local currency in order to concentrate the management of currency risk at the headquarters. Net transfers were performed month by month in terms of a netting system. Furthermore, many firms measured and managed their interest rate exposures in terms of so-called Gap Management, and only a few firms used concepts like Duration, Volatility, and Value at Risk (VaR) for that purpose. It was also found that tender offers generated substantial economic exposures to the firms, and these exposures were seldom hedged by currency options. A few firms used currency clauses, but most firms relied on active management until a contract was signed. Since the first study, ten years beforehand, the firms investigated had increased their sophistication in the management of foreign exchange exposures.

1.2 Motivations for a third investigation, FEEM 08

Developments since 1996 motivated a third round of study. Risk as a concept has become much more refined, and risk management is nowadays (as at the time of writing, early 2013) treated as an extremely important topic, and is a well-developed, integrated and formalized part of treasury operations. The euro has taken a dominant role as a currency for trade and investments. We have seen a revolution in information technology (IT), which has completely changed the conditions for international payments and the control of international bank accounts, as well as enabling the use of instruments to hedge exposures to currency exchange risks and interest rate risks. Nevertheless, companies still face certain types of risk related to currency fluctuations and export/import activities, such as credit risk, antenatal risk, economic risk, market risk and price risk, and have to deal with them in different ways.

With this background, our aim for the FEEM 08 study is to investigate the principles and procedures used in MNCs management of foreign exchange, and to explain the driving factors behind foreign trade hedging strategies. This is achieved by examining the management of foreign exchange exposure in a set of Swedish and UK-based firms over the 25 years leading up to 2008. The focus is on describing the choice of currency; the exposure management processes; the organization of exposure management including how firms organize and create policies and set goals for their foreign exposure management; and how firms can manage their FEEM as a competitive advantage using currency denominations. The study also includes the respondents' own risk perception and aversion, and their individual experiences on how institutional changes have affected their hedging strategies.

2 Methodology and data

We use a qualitative research approach to investigate the foreign exchange exposure procedures. We consider this approach superior for the understanding of the motives behind these procedures, and the action taken by managers within their organizational setting (see for example Brown, 2001; Williamson, 2001; Dhanani and Groves, 2001; Dhanani, 2003, 2004). We use a *cross sectional approach* by interviewing representatives from a set of Swedish multinationals, and comparing them with a number of UK-based companies. We also use a *longitudinal approach*, by starting from the similar study (FEEM 85) carried out in 1985 (Bergendahl and Nyberg, 1986) followed up by a second study in 1996 (Bergendahl, 2001).

This chapter focuses on the results from a third set of interviews carried out in 2007/2008 among 15 Swedish and 3 UK firms. There is a particular interest on how the results from these interviews compare with earlier observations. We based the interviews on the questionnaire that was used in 1985 and 1996; the questionnaire covers the choice of currency of denomination, foreign exchange cash management, currency risk exposure, organization and stages of development. When the first study was done in 1985 (Bergendahl and Nyberg, 1986) the purposes were stated as follows:

- to analyze how foreign exchange exposures are measured and managed in a number of British and Swedish companies
- to find explanations for the different ways of managing the foreign exchange exposures
- to suggest alternative ways to measure, and to manage the foreign exchange exposures.

The companies included represented both a range of business sectors and a range of different firm sizes, based on large and medium-sized firms. The study in 1996 (see Bergendahl, 2001) was based on interviews with approximately the same Swedish and English firms as those of 1985. However, one firm had gone bankrupt since then, and others had changed their structures more or less completely. Consequently, out of the 26 firms of 1985, 18 Swedish and 5 English firms were interviewed once again in 1996.

The aim of FEEM 96 differed slightly from that of FEEM 85, as two more activities were added:

- to analyze the interaction between the management of foreign exchange exposures and interest rate exposures in these companies.
- to compare the principles of foreign exchange exposure management of 1985 and 1996.

The third set of interviews was performed with the general aim of following up earlier studies, and with the specific task of conducting the following research activities:

- to investigate the procedures for foreign exchange exposure management in a number of Swedish and British companies;
- to find explanations for the different ways of managing these exposures;
- to compare the principles of foreign exchange exposure management in 1985, in 1996 and in 2008;
- to explain how different perceptions on market efficiency and risk affect how firms organize and manage their exposures.

The fourth research activity required the inclusion of questions addressing the respondents' personal opinion on risk taking, and their perception of risk. We also added questions regarding issues we thought might have affected the companies' management during the period from 1996 to 2008.

It was not possible to cover the same companies consistently for over a quarter of a century; in that time companies have emerged, gone bankrupt, changed names and businesses, or have been acquired by other companies. This time, out of the 23 companies interviewed in 1996, we identified 18. We carried out telephone interviews with five companies that had been merged or acquired but still existed as subsidiaries within a group; the results from those interviews are not included in this survey. Of the 18 companies included in this last round, 11 companies are listed and seven privately owned. The majority are large multinational firms. The few medium-sized Swedish firms included have a large proportion of their sales in foreign currency. Companies interviewed in FEEM 08 and in FEEM 85 and FEEM 96 as well are:

Swedish: ABB, Atlas Copco, Atlet, Ekmans, Ericsson, Elof Hansson, Karner, Mölnlycke, SCA, Nimbus, SKF, Swedish Match, Transatlantic, Volvo.
English: BP, Rolls-Royce.

Companies not included in FEEM 08 but in FEEM 85 and in FEEM 96 are:

Swedish: ABV, ASG Celsius, Consafe, Esab, Wilson, Skandia.
English: BICC, Wimpey, Cadbury-Schweppes, and ICI.

In each company, we interviewed the head of the treasury department. Except for three company visits, we also met with one or two other employees from the treasury department. The duration of each interview was approximately 2–3 hours. The use of a semi-structured guide (see Appendix 8.1) allowed the respondent to articulate firm, specific details. During the interviews we often received written material, such as yearly reports, exposure data, and on one occasion the formal risk manual. This material, together with the structure of the interview guide made it possible to use a triangular method.

3 Risk perception and behavior: who favors hedging currencies?

In our survey, all firms but one hedge their currency exposures by use of instruments on the financial markets. Why firms choose to hedge is a controversial issue, and basically it depends on who will in the end carry the risk that originates from volatile exchange rates. From a shareholder perspective, the only risk a well diversified owner on an efficient market will get paid for is the systematic risk. A well diversified owner should therefore not be willing to pay to avoid this type of exposure, as it will only reduce the volatility of a single firm. In the presence of market imperfections, an investor may prefer to hedge on firm level if it is more efficient than to hedge via the stock market – that is, instead of holding a diversified portfolio, the investor chooses to allow managers to perform the hedging.

Exchange rate fluctuations are an important source of macroeconomic uncertainty (Levi, 1983; Oxelheim and Wihlborg, 1987, 2005), and the fact that the companies may face market inefficiencies such as convex tax shields or transaction costs of financial distress may make short-term hedging profitable (Smith and Stulz, 1985). Therefore, exchange rate exposures may have an effect on the value of a firm. Evidence on this effect seems to be more apparent among Europe-based multinationals (Muller and Verschoor, 2006a) compared to US-based ones (Bartov and Bodnar, 1994; Jorion, 1990). Meanwhile, Muller and Verschoor (2006b) and Hutson and Stevenson (2010) both argued that one reason for this difference may be that the US market is much more closed. The latter study shows both negative and positive exposure for European multinationals, indicating that on an aggregate firm level, hedging may be irrelevant to investor's portfolios. Allayannis and Weston (2001) showed that hedging increases firm value; they observed a positive relationship between the use of currency derivatives and Tobin's Q, and noted that hedging may increase firm value. However, Bali, Hume and Martell (2007) found that the use of derivatives is not related to firms' exposure or rate of return, and a negative relation between FX exposure and the use of financial derivatives is also reported (Hagelin and Pramborg, 2004). Bali et al. (2007) suggested other operational and economic factors as important. Géczy, Minton and Schrand (1997) found that the use of currency derivatives affects the cost of capital, and that hedging is supported by shareholders as being an efficient tool to reduce cash flow volatility and also to avoid precluding firms from exploring growth opportunities. They also found that firms that exhibit economies of scale from hedging costs may have a competitive advantage. Other evidence for the relevance of hedging is that that investors value cash flow volatility negatively (Rountree, Weston and Allayannis, 2008).

We asked the treasurers a range of questions on their perception of risk and goal congruence between their operations and their firm's objectives (Appendix 8.1, paragraph 6.) All but one of the respondents described their shareholders as undiversified, preferring hedging on a firm level. Respondents working in listed companies said that the shareholder view had influenced their decision making, and that there was an increased focus on cash flows. Two privately owned companies stated that they were handling the owners' money and were therefore obliged to reduce risk by hedging exposure. Some representative citations were: 'Yes they should, but we do it better,' 'It is our obligation to reduce short-term risk,' or 'We are transparent and clearly reveal our exposure strategies; shareholders have this information, and can price it accordingly.' This indicates that the managers in our sample do believe that hedging on firm level is more efficient than on the financial markets. It also seems as though managers have received some signals from their owners that they prefer hedging. The purpose of the hedging is reduced cash flow volatility, and the reported currency losses/gains play an important role in the analysis of the firm's performance. The fact that firms tend to hedge transaction exposures to a high degree and that economic exposures are seldomhedged lends support to the idea that investors are willing to let managers secure short-term exposures and leave costly long-term exposures unhedged; this is also supported by empirical research (see Allayannis and Weston, 2001; Bartov and Bodnar, 1994; Muller and Verschoor, 2006a; Hutson and Stevenson, 2010; Jorion, 1990 and Muller and Verschoor, 2006b)

Managers who believe that they are able to forecast a turn of the market are supposed to practise 'selective hedging' (Stulz, 1996). This type of hedging will also be affected by managers' attitudes towards risk and how their reward contracts are aligned with the various goals of the company. Kenyon (1981) makes a systematic classification of methods for the management of foreign exchange exposures. In his view, 'there are broadly three classes of implements: those which avoid risk, those which hedge it, and those which reduce the task of management' (Kenyon, 1981, p.49).

From an agency perspective, on the assumption that managers (agents) are risk averse, managers' behavior will be governed by their perception of risk and market efficiency, by their individual incentive structure and to what degree the owners are diversified. If managers are aligned with well diversified shareholders via incentive contracts, and forward rates are assumed to be unbiased predictors of future spot rates (market efficiency), hedging will not be undertaken. With the perception that markets are efficient and that managers' incentive contracts do not align them with well diversified shareholders, hedging will be undertaken in order to increase the managements' own utility. If managers base their decisions on the belief that markets are inefficient, either hedging or speculation will be the outcome, depending on the design of the incentive contracts and the owner's degree of diversification.

We asked the head of the treasury about his/her own perceptions of risk. The results did not provide unanimous answers; the most common was that they perceived themselves as being risk averse or risk neutral, and no respondent described herself or himself as a risk lover. Many described themselves as risk neutral, or risk averse leaning to risk neutral. We asked if they got a thrill out of taking on risk. A majority agreed, and some added that this thrill kept them alert and did not affect them in their daily operations. We also asked how they defined risk, if they were willing to accept risk, and if they were willing to take on risk in order to achieve higher returns. Even regarding these answers, no unanimous view could be found among the respondents. Some of them defined risk as the downside risk only, and others defined it (as if from a text book on finance) as 'a deviation from an expected value'. Some respondents were willing to take on higher risk for higher returns; others had been told to hedge all exposures (in this case transaction exposure).

When asking the respondents about their opinions on whether the market is efficient, many agreed that the currency markets were more stable than before, that is that there were fewer fluctuations in currency prices. Two of them said that markets had become more efficient and that nowadays (that is, at the time of our survey) it was not possible to beat the market in the long run. An experienced FE manager expressed this concept as 'there are no mispriced securities on the market'. Another respondent said that they regularly collected historical data to carry out their own tests on market efficiency, and that their findings confirmed market efficiency. Some respondents said that the markets were efficient in the long run, but in the short run they had to hedge their exposure. On the other hand, a few respondents, especially those that organized their treasury in profit centers (four companies), said that they regularly profited from taking positions.

The companies that organized their foreign exchange exposure management by the use of a profit centre (the treasury is a separate subsidiary, with a profit and loss account) had given their traders very strict mandates for action. Some firms operating with cost centers (treasuries being part of corporate finance) did allow their traders certain small mandates to take positions, arguing that such mandates would make them familiar and up to date with new instruments. Furthermore, firms with a profit centre, and even some of those with a cost centre had arranged bonus systems related to how well they performed relative to the market.

Our results contradict the findings of Brown et al. (2006) when investigating companies in the mining industry. They found that managers believed they had an information advantage, whereas in our study it seems that the respondents were more restrictive in taking positions. Brown et al. (2006) also found that managers rarely beat the market; this was also reported by some of our respondents, mainly those speculating (however implicitly questioned by a majority of respondents with a market efficiency view). Collier et al. (1990) investigated 51 firms in the US and the UK. They divided their sample into a highly risk-averse group and a risk-neutral group. The former was aiming to avoid currency risk, arguing that they are profitable in their operations and should not seek additional profit-taking currency positions. Here, the role of the treasurer is to hedge and to predict market development. In the other, risk-neutral, group the treasury aimed at managing currency flows by performing a selective hedging strategy, and they found a difference between UK and US firms; US firms were generally less willing to make selective hedging whereas UK firms more often hedged translation costs. But both US and UK firms perceived the market as inefficient. Our results rather point to the ideas of Bartram (2008) suggesting that managers take 'savvy' actions and reduce exposure to very low levels.

4 Measuring and hedging currency exposures

4.1 The principal use of hedging

There are different ways to hedge exposures: through the financial markets, using financial instruments such as futures and forwards; netting; using lead and leg; and to use operative hedging. It is also possible to pass through the risk related to exposure to customers. Bertram, Brown and Minton (2010), in a sample of 1150 manufacturing firms in the US, showed that pass-through to customers and operational hedging both decreased theoretical exposure by 10–15 per cent, and that financial hedging reduced it by about 40 per cent. Adler and Dumas (1984) and Kenyon (1990) made a distinction between foreign currency risk and foreign currency exposure. Risk was defined as the probability of a financial deviation from an expected outcome, and foreign currency exposure was related to what amount is at risk. Therefore, the notion of risk is market-related, and the exposure is how an individual firm will be affected in response to a certain event.

There are basically three different ways described in the literature on how to measure currency risks in a firm; *transaction exposure, economic exposure* and *translation exposure.*

The *transaction exposure* is described as the most apparent and easily identified form of exposure. In principle, a transaction exposure is usually related to the flows of funds that starts at the moment of pricing or, more precisely, at the moment an order is placed, and ends at the moment the payment is converted into the headquarters currency and placed on its current accounts.

The *economic exposure* is described as the long-term measure on how the value of a company will change relative to long-term changes in exchange rates. This measure extends the transaction exposure to cash flows that are not yet realized but may influence future sales volumes, prices and also input costs (Dhanani and Groves, 2001; Moffett and Karlsen, 1994). Economic exposure is a result of a misalignment between firms' future operative costs and future operative earnings. Consequently, other definitions are *operational exposure* or *business exposure*. Because of its long-term nature, and due to the fact that companies face competition from foreign companies, this exposure is argued to be best managed through natural hedges, and should be part of the overall strategy of the company (Chow et al., 1997; Pringle and Connolly, 1993).

A common definition of *translation exposure* is 'the net balance position of foreign currency translated at the currency exchange rate' (for example Oxelheim and Wihlborg, 2005, p. 62). It is not only a translation of financial (income) statements from affiliated firms into the parent firm, but also a translation of assets and liabilities denoted in foreign currencies into that of the parent. Theoretically, it is argued that this type of exposure is irrelevant to hedging, as it only relates to past performance and does not affect future cash flow. The hedging of translation exposure is rather explained by the fact that managers have their own perception on the importance of reported profit and loss statements, and that volatile earnings might be negatively pricedby investors (Rountree, Weston and Allayannis, 2008).

Volatile earnings also affect set targets on key ratios. This may create internal risk hedging behavior at different company levels, which would be more costly than smoothing accounting results at a headquarters level. Hedging can therefore facilitate internal control and budgets.

4.2 Choice of currency

The above theoretical description gives the background to the survey conducted on how firms manage their foreign exposure. In this section, we describe the factors for currency denomination (for questions see Appendix 8.1, paragraphs 1 and 2). Most problems of mismatching stem from the different conditions under which a firm purchases raw materials and components and sells its products. It could be, for example, that 35 per cent of the raw material is purchased from Germany according to price lists denoted in euros; at the same time, a large part of its final products is sold in US dollars and the pound sterling as a result of negotiations using short-term and long-term tenders. The degree of variation is large between the companies when it comes to the type of products that are sold and the choice of currency for these products. For example, one industrial company sells 75 per cent of its products in terms of projects, another 55 per cent, and a third 10 per cent. We find that some firms with customized products and long-term tenders did not include currency clauses; one firm said it was too expensive, and another said that they used currency clauses only for very unusual projects, when future uncertainty was high.

Both in 1985 and in 1996 the US dollar, the Deutsche mark and the pound sterling were the main currencies used for tenders. Since 2002, with no Deutsche mark, the euro has taken a leading role. Its introduction has resulted in change for most of the companies that are focused on trade. In 1985 and 1996, price lists were given in a large number of currencies for firms with export activities within the Eurozone, resulting in that many firms regularly devoting much effort to control currency risks. The introduction of the euro reduced the work related to foreign currencies. A larger share of the transactions are now netted, implying a reduction in currency exposure. Tender offers generate substantial economic exposures concerning projects with long-term transactions, as such transactions are not yet contracted. Certain firms carried out substantial trade in countries with small currencies; in such cases, the tender was always combined with a currency clause.

In most industrial sectors, products are sold in the currency of the purchaser. In 1985 and in 1996, about 50 per cent of the companies actively worked with price lists in foreign currencies, often set for half a year or a full year ahead. Nowadays, however, price lists are only provided for highly standardized products, as treasuries are aware that price lists of that type generate substantial currency risks. Consequently, the price lists that do still exist are continually revised in response to rapid changes in exchange rates or inflation.

Firms with a small domestic currency, like our Swedish companies, seem to be prepared to handle currency exposures; selling in the currency of the customer and buying in the currency of the supplier can be used as a competitive advantage. That implies a high degree of risk management. Respondents in some of the larger firms considered the cost of giving their suppliers and customers their transactions in their local currency worthwhile in terms of gaining a competitive edge. In most cases the foreign exchange risks were managed by the headquarters (more so in 2008 than in 1996); as a consequence the subsidiaries will have had to pay for their supplies in their own currency and to sell their products in their own currency. In 1985 the choice of currency was often open to negotiations, and one multinational firm found it easier to sell its products when the price was set in the customer's currency; that was the main reason why most firms in this study operated with a large number of currencies instead of pricing in the cost currency. When discussing this subject during the 1985 interviews, many of the respondents said that they tried to control which currencies to use, and sometimes a corporate finance department had discussions with the sales department about preferences for currencies. When using the foreign subsidiary's local currency the group could centralize their currency exposure in order to match payments and receipts. In a seller's market, however, the use of the Swedish krona as a sales currency dominated in order to avoid currency exposure.

In the case of actions in affiliated organizations, transactions, assets and liabilities may be managed with a much higher degree of flexibility than when selling to separate customers. A common procedure is to concentrate foreign exchange management at the head office, and to invoice and to pay subsidiaries in their local currency. Furthermore, any lending and borrowing between subsidiaries and the head office should be performed in the local currency, providing a platform for central management of costs and risks related to currency exchange. An exception was made by one manufacturing firm. That firm decided that each production unit must invoice in the currency of the purchasing unit, and at the same time, the unit had to hedge each such invoice and cover the cost of hedging.

In certain sectors a dominant currency is used, like the US dollar for petroleum products, paper and pulp, and the pound sterling for copper (in 1996). The choice of currencies of denomination is often dependent on the sector in which the firm operates. For example, the US dollar is the dominant currency for a company that sells minerals and mineral products, whereas the pound sterling is a currency often used by another company that exports machinery. One treasurer said: 'We want to increase our assets in US dollars, because everything is oriented towards dollars.'

To summarize, we notice that the reasons for mismatch and the choice of currency were more or less the same in 2008 as in both 1996 and 1985. We witnessed an increased centralization (discussed later in this text) but companies still utilize currency denominations for competition. Tender offers and long-term projects create exposures, which are more difficult to hedge than are standardized products with price lists. In 2008, currency clauses became much more common.

4.3 The hedging procedures

In 1985 we found that the companies which hedged their transaction exposures followed the following principles:

1. Estimate future transaction exposures for a relevant set of time periods.
2. Plan to net out as much as possible of these exposures.
3. Then, the residual (net) exposure can either be hedged by forward contracts, local borrowing etc., or be left open, to be exchanged in the spot market.
4. Hedge a certain percentage (say 50–75 per cent) of these exposures month by month, one year ahead.

Obviously, both transaction ('contracted') exposures as well as a potential part of their economic ('estimated') exposures were hedged. One treasurer expressed it as follows: 'We forecast transaction exposures a year in advance based upon a multi-lateral netting system. Then we cover about 50 per cent of these amounts in order to allow for changes in the sales volumes.' Another treasurer stated: 'We don't have any cash management system. Every morning, we cover 80 per cent of our new sales. On average we aim at 70 per cent cover, but in certain currencies we cover 100 per cent.'

In 2008, and also in 1996, the majority of the investigated firms stated that they used a 'staircase policy'. For example, they might hedge 25 per cent of the expected net inflow 12 months ahead, an additional 25 per cent nine months ahead, another 25 per cent six months ahead, and the remaining 25 per cent three months ahead. The argument for this policy is that the closer you get to the dates of delivery the more certain the exposures become. Another example of this staircase policy comes from firms that stated that they hedged their transaction exposures to 100 per cent four months ahead. Beyond those four months they made a proportional hedging of 40–60 per cent in several cases. Motivations for using a staircase policy were mainly to maintain flexibility. Two interviewees said 'We only hedge 50–70 per cent of the exposed values, just to preserve flexibility in case any estimated sales are not realized,' and, 'We would like to be flexible. That means that we hedge 30–60 per cent of the annual flow of foreign currencies.'

Several firms still did not create any separation between an economic exposure and a transaction exposure. They often included estimated but non-contracted transactions in their transaction exposures. On the other hand, those firms seldom hedged 100 per cent of such an exposure merely because it was not completely contracted. Most firms measured their transaction exposures once a month, and at least three months ahead. Two firms indicated that their estimations went up to six months and two others aimed at a nine-month planning horizon. In those cases, the transaction exposure was actually converted into one of economic exposure, as most transactions were estimated but not confirmed. Longer economic exposures were sometimes covered by using interest rate swaps.

Economic exposure arises from several actions by a firm; however, the major source seems to be price lists and tender offers. A company producing services in foreign countries issues tenders in local currency, and production capacity might be chartered from a subcontractor at the same time (and in local currency). If the tender is not accepted, there is a risk that the services from the subcontractor cannot be efficiently utilized, even if the production costs (in a reporting currency) are avoided. One 2008 firm made the following comment: 'The tender period is a difficult one; you don't know where the raw material will come from.'

Transaction exposures arise from two broad categories of a company's business (Donaldson, 1987); one is long-term contract business where individual contracts have to be bid for and, when won, are executed over a period, possibly several years; and the other is regular sales or service business, where single or unconnected multiple transactions take place at irregular intervals. The first category covers companies producing customized products. The second covers companies with price lists for a large number of standardized products or services.

The companies investigated differed in the degree of standardized and customized products, which affected their choice of exposure measure. In our sample there were eight companies with very standardized products. Four companies had more or less customized products only, and five companies had a mix of customized and standard products. For standard products, often accompanied by a price list, the transaction exposures are easier to predict than are those for customized products. When selling customized products, payment takes place during production, and in discrete and larger sums, all affecting the accuracy of exposure measurement.

Another source of long-term economic exposure is foreign direct investments. We found that these exposures were mainly hedged by currency loans in both the 1996 and the 2008 survey. One construction firm declared: 'The customer has to cover the currency risk. We cannot possibly use long-term currency clauses, and currency options are too expensive'. Another construction firm stated: 'It's too expensive to hedge everything. If we do so, we take away the opportunity of earning money.'

The use of interest currency swaps was not very common in the companies in question, in any of the three surveys. However, one firm active in the large-scale construction industry presented a case with an economic exposure of as long as ten years or more; to manage the corresponding risk, they used both currency loans and interest rate swaps. For most of the firms in

2008, forward contracts were the most common instrument for hedging; about 8–10 firms in the 2008 survey confirmed a simultaneous use of options for that purpose.

Just a few companies were concerned about translation exposures, except for the time when closing the accounts. Some treasurers measured the exposures regularly in order to reduce balance sheet risks. One of them expressed it as follows: 'We measure the translation exposure every quarter of the year. We may then use it when we choose the currency of the loans that we take in order to buy a foreign company.' Another firm said: 'We must cover the equity in our foreign subsidiaries by loans in the same currency. For that purpose we take short-term credits, which we renew regularly.' One firm even performed a regular hedging on the translation exposure 'in order to preserve the net capital intact'. But no other firms in our 2008 survey hedged this kind of exposure.

In sum, our results do not differ from those of other currency management studies. Most firms measure transaction exposure currency by currency on the contracted net inflow of funds per time period (usually measured month by month on a predetermined date) and use derivatives such as forwards and options (see, for example, Brown, 2001; Collier et al., 1990 and Dhanani, 2003), netting and occasionally leading and lagging payments (for example, Dhanani, 2004). In so doing, the transaction exposure is often used to estimate the immediate effect of unexpected changes in the exchange rates. A longitudinal observation is that in 1985 and 1996 many firms did in fact hedge a substantial part of their non-contracted economic exposures. But in 2008 most firms seemed to be more cautious and concentrated their hedging onto their contracted transaction exposures. As most of the trade in 2008 took place in a period of 3–6 months from contract to payment, with a staircase policy, the hedging took place over the corresponding period of months; that is a substantial change from 1985 and 1996, when most firms in our survey hedged a large part of their non-contracted economic exposures, which could run for one year or more.

4.4 The use of netting

In 1985, we observed that only some of the companies used bilateral netting; at that time it was unusual to include external transactions in a netting system. In 1996, one group used netting with its subsidiaries in the country of the parent company only, and seven of the companies operated a multilateral netting system. In most cases, netting was carried out once a month. However, one firm did so twice a month, another firm every fourth week and a third firm once a week.

In 1985, netting was not that common. In 1996, several firms included both affiliated and non-affiliated companies in their netting systems. Often the non-affiliated companies were large customers with a stable demand for which it was fairly easy to forecast the transaction volumes. Taxation systems, laws, and regulations created a framework for the accumulation of liquidity in different countries, but in 2008 this was not so common; in fact, only one firm offered foreign exchange exposure services to some of its major customers.

In 1996, a treasurer made the following comment: 'The netting procedure takes us 10 days per month. Consequently, we cannot do it more frequently than once a month.' Nowadays, the electronic revolution has resulted in netting being easily carried out more often than once a month; in 2008, one firm stated that 'we net as often as needed', and many firms carried out their netting daily. Otherwise, the same procedures used in 1996 were also used in 2008.

4.5 The use of lead and lag

In 1985, we observed a number of firms that were using lead and lag in order to reduce the currency risk exposures both from internal and external transactions. At that time, many of the companies used lead and lag regularly for internal group payments. A couple of firms actively controlled lead and lag from their headquarters; for them, it was an easy way of handling short-term liquidity problems within the group, even if it did not have any effect on the total exposure. By 2008, this was a natural part of the cash management system, and we found no firm making active use of lead and lag for the purpose of exposure management.

4.6 The use of natural hedging

A natural hedge is available when, for example, payment inflows from sales in a foreign currency are balanced by the equivalent outflow of payments for purchasing and production in the same foreign currency. The netting of cash flows is a measure of the extent to which a firm has a natural hedge. Increasing the natural hedge can be done by strategic decisions on, for example, changing suppliers into other currency areas, by FDI in production or sale capacity, the location of new R&D activities, or to pay salaries in different currencies. Research has found that FDI reduces the economic exposure (Miller and Reuer, 1998). However, it seems that an increased network of activities through location of subsidiaries does not reduce the exchange rate exposure; geographically dispersed firms tend to use financial hedging to a larger extent, and operational hedging seems to be effective only in combination with financial derivatives (Allayannis et al., 2001; Kim et al., 2006).

In our study, all the companies had more or less widespread export activities. However, we met with a near-unanimous response that export strategy, the location of R&D and other FDIs was not directly influenced by the currency exposure (see questions under Appendix 8.1, paragraph 3). Three respondents said that the decision on where to invest in R&D facilities mostly depended on where to find centers of excellence. The choice of markets is often described as finding opportunities from logistical and other cost minimization or revenue-seeking rationales; however, although all the respondents acknowledged the positive effects of creating a natural hedge, only one said that this actually had affected any strategic decisions. Dhanani (2003) found that the firm in question actually made use of operational hedging, and that this hedging was a complement to financial hedging. Dhanani and Grooves (2001) reported that MNCs were seeking to minimize their strategic exchange risks by operative hedging and that financial hedging was often short-term. This was not, however, the case in our study. We found firms that used financial instruments for hedging over one year, and even used interest swaps and currency loans to hedge contracts of up to ten years.

4.7 The use of bank services

In 1996, most firms performed a regular rating of existing and potential banks in order to assure that they got the best possible services for their money. Most firms laid a stronger emphasis on service quality than on low prices. It was common practice to use one bank (say the Citibank) for international transactions and another (say SEB)[2] for their local services. Many of the firms used the same international bank as their preferred one for international payment services, but a few firms made use of different banks. Finally, there were firms that switched regularly between banks.

Since 1996, we have observed an increase in the activity of evaluating bank services and in the number of banks used. It seems as if most firms have established an evaluation system which includes price and quality comparisons. Firms are approaching several banks for different currency regions and countries, in order to obtain more competitive services (see questions under Appendix 8.1, paragraph 2). When the 'best' banks have been chosen, detailed contracts are often set up for a period of two to three years. The following comments illustrate this situation:

- 'We have had 50 per cent of our Swedish services with Bank A, and 50 per cent with Bank B. But last year we changed that to 70 per cent with Bank A and 30 per cent with Bank B. The main reason was that Bank A offered much better services abroad.'
- 'We make use of five banks for the main part of our transactions – Den Danske Bank, Handelsbanken, Nordea, SEB and Swedbank.'
- 'We operate with about 30 banks, out of which one Swedish bank is a coordinator, 10 banks are the main foreign banks, 10 other banks are supplementary banks and the remainder are used only sporadically.'

It seems as though banks have become more specialized. For example, one Swedish firm selling capital goods reported that it used one bank for payments inside Sweden, another for its payments in US dollars, a third for payments in Denmark, a fourth for payments in France, and a final one for its liquidity needs. This seemed to be the case for the UK-based firms as well; one firm reported that one third of its foreign sales were in US dollars, one third in euros and one third in pounds sterling, and that they used different banks for different currencies.

5 Organization and policy

A vast amount of literature confirms that netting and strategic hedging are important tools for the firms (Bergendahl, 2001; Dhanani, 2003 and 2004; Donaldson, 1987; George, 1983; Earl, 1985; Kenyon, 1981 and 1990; Pramborg, 2002). When interviewing 12 large MNCs, Dhanani and Groves (2001) found that companies made operational adjustments and actively managed their strategic exposure, and that these actions were often planned and executed by the financial department. It was obvious that the organization of the foreign exchange management affected the ability to effectively manage the currency exposure, even if that factor had not been directly investigated in depth in earlier research. There is a need for some centralization in order to deal with these issues in an efficient manner.

5.1 The formation of the treasury

In small and medium-sized firms, the foreign exposure management activities often take place inside the accountancy unit, and are often administrated by a single individual. In the large firms, the currency management is performed in a special unit, either inside a certain treasury department or financial department or as a separate department. The tasks for such a Corporate Treasury unit/department are often specified as shown in Table 8.1.

We categorized the companies as either centralized (eight companies) or very centralized (ten companies). In the very centralized group, the treasury set out the policy, often acted as an internal bank, collected information on all currency flows, and conducted netting and hedging; these tasks were performed by the treasury unit either as a cost or as a profit centre. In firms belonging to the centralized group, the CFO at the subsidiary was responsible both for the currency risk and for the policy being adhered to; it was very rare (in only one company) that subsidiaries were allowed to perform currency or interest hedging on the market by themselves. This is in line with other observations such as those made by Collier and Davies (1985) and Dhanani (2003), who argued that central coordination can help negotiate superior financial contracts better than can subsidiaries. It also allows companies to take full advantage of internal netting. However, a disadvantage of such a principle is that there will be little stimulation locally to utilize local conditions. The manager of one subsidiary expressed these fears as 'We have had enough of centralization. It takes away the competence. And

Table 8.1 Task and topics for the corporate treasury

Tasks for the corporate treasury	Topics
• Formation of the capital structure • International cash management • Liquidity management • Currency exposure management • Interest rate risk management • Bank relations	• Value and finance of debt, short and long term lending • Control and transactions of international payments, currency exchange and losses in float • Control and placement of cash surplus on collection accounts and currency accounts. • Forward and future contracts, currency options and swaps, etc • Borrowing and lending to fixed or floating rates, interest rate swaps, etc • Different banks for different currencies and different tasks such as payments, lending, finance of long term investments.

people will lose interest in being efficient managers.' In another company it was up to the subsidiaries to find out if the local bank could provide it with better conditions than the treasury function. If so, they were allowed to use that local service. Back in 1996, the treasury in many firms was more decentralized than was in 2008; there has been a trend towards centralizing these activities.

In 2008 only three companies operated their treasury as a profit centre. That was a substantial change since 1996, and the reasons given by companies were that excessive speculation had led to substantial losses, and that a new risk avoidance policy would be better suited to a cost centre. In two firms, the profit centers were separate companies which could sell their services to other companies within the group or, in one case, even outside the group.

From 1996 to 2008, it seems that more and more firms carried out the hedging of their transaction exposures centrally, in their headquarters. In the present study, we found only one firm that instructed each subsidiary and division on how to hedge its own net exposure. Such a hedge may be done either with a local bank or in terms of internal forward contracts with the treasury. Another consequence of the increased centralization is the way in which firms deal with the transaction exposure with the aim of effective cash management. A majority of all foreign transactions are organized as bank payments without reimbursements or similar instruments. A procedure employed is to direct these payments into currency accounts of the head office or into collection accounts for the subsidiaries and then report to the head office.

Dhanani et al. (2003) concluded that industry would shape the management processes. We could not find clear evidence of this when looking at our cross-section case either with companies operating in different industries or between UK-based and Swedish-based companies. However, it seemed that firms with standardized products were more centralized than firms with customized products. Furthermore, in 1985 and especially in 1996 we did find a size effect, in that larger firms tended to be more decentralized than smaller ones. In 2008, this difference was not particularly obvious, as larger firms tended to be more centralized than before.

5.2 Policy documents

The control of the treasury function may be formalized in terms of a 'financial policy document'. Such a document will then include a set of rules specially designed for currency issues and for interest rate policies.

Back in 1996, the interviews demonstrated significant differences between British and Swedish companies in how to form a policy for, and how to control the management of, the foreign exchange exposure. In some firms, the policy was made operational in terms of frames and limits for the daily exposures/positions. In others, the corporate finance department operated with a finance committee which made the decisions on a day-to-day basis. That is a dramatic change from 1985, as in those days only a very few companies had formulated a written policy. In 2008, all of our larger firms had a written policy, and in only two of the small companies did a written policy not exist. Among those with such a policy, it is signed by the managing director or by the treasurer, and approved by the special committee or the head of corporate finance, and the board. In most cases the respondents said that the policy document was often expressed in general terms. Some companies were forming their policy in terms of maximum and minimum limits for the amount that had to be hedged or as expressions in general terms about the exposure balance, whereas other companies let their treasury department form the group policy and implement it within the rest of the group. The latter policy is more oriented towards a control of financial tasks at other organizational levels than at the treasury level. Below is an example of the points in the financial policy of one particular firm:

- currencies the company is dealing with,
- ways of measuring currency exposures,
- types of currency risks,
- the time period for currency management,
- the financial impact of the policy,
- restrictions because of currency exchange controls,
- acceptable deviations from the policy,

- the responsibility for each organizational level within the finance function.
- a general policy on how to handle currency risks.

The policy is also used for educational purposes, introducing both new employees at the treasury department as well as responsible managers at subsidiaries about the operations and routines. One respondent declared that the policy was distributed to many junior managers and salespeople in order to make them aware of the risk related to foreign exposures.

In some of the companies we investigated in 2008, the policy documents had not been changed for a long time. The most common answer to our enquiry was that the policy had often been up for discussion (at least every year) and that since 1996 the policy had changed due to different factors such as new netting and administrative systems, new hedging techniques and new guidelines regarding risk mandates. The last factor was seen as very important as it related to the overall objectives of the treasury department.

We asked the respondents if these objectives were formalized and if they were related to the overall objectives of the firm. In 7 out of 18 firms the respondents did not declare any formal objective. One respondent stated that: 'We have no formal goal, but we cover all risk except business risk. This is in line with the overall goal of the company.' Not all respondents with a formal objective agreed that it was related to the overall goal of the firm; one respondent said: 'Our goal is very specific, but we cannot say if this goal is related to the overall goal of the firm. We shall reduce risk'. The objectives differed in the level of specification. Some corporate treasury departments even used quantitative measures like 'the impact on overall goal profit should be less than XXX dollars', while others had more qualitative measures like 'stability, and to measure and hedge all transaction risk', or 'our goal is to take no exchange rate risk'. Other objectives discussed but not clearly formalized were: to maximize the return on financial management; to minimize the risks caused by variations in currency exchange rates and interest rates; to minimize the costs of payments, domestically and internationally; to coordinate all inflow and outflow of liquidity; to provide the departments and subsidiaries with financial services that are competitive; to treat issues of taxes and regulations in an efficient way.

6. Respondents' views on important factors influencing their foreign exchange management

So far we have discussed the respondents' answers on questions common to the interviews in 1985, 1996 and 2008. In this section, we report the respondents' answers on specific changes that were explicitly expressed in that last interview round. It is difficult to pinpoint each change that has taken place and may have had an effect on currency hedging strategies as well as on the organization of currency management; both macro factors (such as changing interest rates or inflation, oil price volatility and turmoil following geopolitical events), and micro factors (such as new administrative systems and new hedging derivatives adopted by organizations) may all have different impacts depending on each company's unique business setting. For this reason we asked our 2008 respondents the following explicit questions (Appendix 8.1, paragraph 6):

> What major trends on the international markets have had most influence on decisions made during the last years concerning foreign exchange exposures and interest rate exposures?

1. New techniques for hedging and administration.
2. The introduction of the Eurozone.
3. The weakening of the dollar.
4. The increased focus on shareholder value.
5. The new legislation.

The development of new techniques refers to both new administrative systems and new, more advanced, hedging strategies. None of the respondents said that they were employing new hedging derivatives to any large extent, even if such new instruments were being promoted by their banks. Most respondents found them very expensive, and one respondent described them as 'nothing more than the emperor's new clothes'. Instead, many respondents said that they were using simple hedging techniques, such as forward contracts or loans in the actual foreign currency. One treasurer accentuated that: 'We want simple products, which are easy to manage. We do not even use currency options – they are too complicated.' However, some of the companies allowed their staff to explore new derivatives under certain mandates; the purpose was to keep the staff updated on developments, and maximize knowledge within the company. The adoption of new treasury management systems (TMSs), often interlinked with administrative enterprise systems such as SAP,[3] was adopted and refined by almost all companies.

Over the 23 years observed, we noted the importance of the rapid development of information systems. Whereas in the 70s and 80s it was a hard task for an MNC to manage netting and hedging even once a month, by 2008 the information systems allowed many MNCs to carry out netting once a day.

In some companies new TMSs have also influenced the organizational structure, and changed the methods of measuring the exposure. In one company the new system was introduced after the acquisition of a company using a more advanced system. Other firms have bought special TMSs, and almost every firm in our sample could instantly measure the exposure and take immediate action. The few companies that still lacked top of the range systems were in the process of introducing them. The introduction of new systems was also accompanied by an increased centralization of the decision making relating to hedging.

The introduction of the euro to replace a set of national currencies made the management of the foreign exchange less cumbersome. The formation of the Eurozone seemed to have had a very limited impact on the companies in our sample. In response to a direct question, the answers ranged from no impact at all to a small degree of relief in not having to measure the same amount of currencies. Two companies in our sample actually found it slightly negative, as the reduced number of currencies decreased their comparative advantage in exposure management.

Some respondents stressed that the choice of dollar as the trading currency had declined in favor of the euro. This picture was not, however, shared by others. One respondent said that their customers switched to US dollars after the introduction of the euro. Another respondent claimed that the US dollar would remain as the major trading currency, and its importance might even increase with increased globalization.

A fourth factor that we expected should have influenced the management of foreign exposure was the increased general focus on the shareholder perspective. Seven of the companies (three English and four Swedish multinationals, listed on stock market) said that the increased focus on shareholder value had resulted in increased attention being paid to the effects of foreign exchange exposure. Policy changes had been preceded by a discussion on what type of currency risk should be hedged. In one company it had been decided not to perform financial hedging on any currency exposure; the company representatives had argued that the risk was diversifiable by their owners, and that they were operating in a market where long-term negative currency changes could be passed through to their customers. Another respondent said that the increased focus on shareholder value had led to increased centralization.

Ronner and Blok (2001) investigated the consequences of the introduction of FAS 133[4] on hedging for foreign currency exposure; they found that FAS 133 might have led to strategic choices that would not increase shareholder wealth. Firms implementing FAS 133 at lower entity level would increase their systems, labor and bid-offer spread costs. It also seems that that accounting standard for derivative instruments had the effect of increasing prudence by firms in their risk management (Zhang, 2009). The implementation of IFRS in our investigated companies led to increased centralization; the new reporting standards, stipulating how to report the value of different hedging positions, more or less required a centralized unit to collect information and accounting knowledge. The respondents argued that using decentralized decision making was not possible, as knowledge on how to report these issues was too expensive to gain at different sub-units. For firms already centralized, IFRS had no effect on the organization. The new accounting standard was generally, however, considered as yet another administrative burden.

To summarize the results on how different factors influenced the management of foreign exchange, it is possible to argue that the introduction of the Eurozone, new administrative systems and the new IFRS system, together with an increased focus on shareholders have had a centralizing effect on the organization of foreign exchange management within the investigated companies.

7 Conclusion

Over the period from 1985 to 2008, the financial markets have expanded dramatically. At the same time most firms have become more cautious in the control of their international payments and foreign exchange exposures. It seems that advanced cash management and foreign exchange management systems have encouraged more centralized organization. This centralization has also been a result of an increased focus on shareholder maximization, and legislation in the form of new accounting standards. The introduction of the Eurozone seems to have had a minor effect on the firms we investigated. Many globalized Swedish firms have tried to take advantage of trading with a small currency, offering their suppliers and customers the option of trading in their chosen currency.

Some firms in our 2008 survey pointed out that earlier mistakes in taking positions had made them more risk averse. The respondents mostly agreed on being risk averse in any case, and the majority thought that the foreign exchange market was efficient enough for them to avoid taking positions. However, some firms still did take positions and allowed their traders to have a mandated amount for speculation. This selective strategy was profitable, according to these firms.

Firms with concentrated ownerships and firms with family owners seemed to be more risk averse and centralized in their FEEM. Almost all respondents had shareholder maximization as the objective for their operations. However, they did not discuss risk in terms of systematic and non-systematic, and they strove to smooth revenues and avoid liquidity crises. The task was merely to minimize the risk for their owners, and some said that they did this better than the owners themselves. It was our perception that it was the management perspective rather than a shareholder perspective that prevailed within many firms. Agency costs, financial distress costs, and bonuses seemed to affect risk taking, and were factors that explained the firms' FEEM procedures. We consider this an important topic for further research.

The reasons for a mismatch of currency flow have not changed since 1985. In 2008, tender offers were still a major source for exposure, and dealing with this risk has become an important task. Within some markets, for example oil, copper and other minerals, there is a tradition to use a specific currency for all international trading. Affiliated organizations are not included in the netting procedures which some firms used to carry out earlier.

The use of financial hedging techniques has not changed dramatically. Forwards and options are still the most common hedging techniques, and new derivatives are not so popular. It seems as though the time horizons for hedging have decreased; in 1985 and in 1996 many firms hedged a substantial part of their non-contracted economic exposures, for up to 12 months, whereas in 2008 the most common time horizon was between 3 and 6 months, and these related to contracted transaction exposures. Netting is easily performed now and is done daily if necessary within firms with advanced systems. Contrary to 1985, when very few firms performed multilateral hedging, almost all firms have done this in 2008 on onward. In 1985 many firms estimated their expected flows in terms of economic exposures. In 2008, however, most firms concentrated on short-term transaction exposures. Those companies observed that if they hedged economic exposures they would actually take the risk of contracting future exchange operations for transactions that are uncertain.

Reducing operational exposure by taking advantage of a natural hedge is not a primary goal in the companies' strategic decision making. Location of R&D, new production facilities and new markets are all guided by other factors. The use of lead and lag is an interlinked procedure within the cash management system.

The operation of FX exposure within profit centers had declined in 2008 compared to 1996. One reason for this change was the excessive speculation during some earlier periods, which led to substantial losses. New policies are better suited to a cost centre. It also seems like many multinationals operate today with a more stable customer base than 20 years ago.

Finally, the controversy on pro hedging and con hedging has not yet been resolved. Many of our 2008 treasurers stated that they had taken a position not to speculate. On the other hand, they might well hedge expected exposures, even if such actions increased the currency risks. So even if they support the arguments in favor of hedging, the controversy is whether or not to hedge economic exposures. This issue is still open at the time of writing in early 2013, has not yet led to a satisfactory solution and requires further research.

Appendix 8.1

Interview (compressed)
Personal Interviews – Guide

1. **Choice of currency of Denomination**
   Which currencies are used for tenders?
   Which currencies are used for international transactions?
   Which currencies are used for internal loans?

2. **Foreign exchange cash management**
   Which formal procedures do you have for your cash management?
   How are the cash management systems operated?
   Do you use several banks? Why? Are the bank services efficient? Do the prices correspond to the costs?
   Which are the gross and the net amounts of transaction?
   How often do you perform netting and payments for transactions?
   Do you include both affiliated and non-affiliated companies?
   Where and how do you accumulate liquidity?
   Do you have separate systems and procedures for internal and external payments?
   Which is the use of lead and lag?
   Can you give a short overview of the currency stream?

3. **Currency risk exposure**
   Which are the measures of currency exposure?
   Which are the elements of these exposure measurements?
   Are tenders included in these exposures?
   How can you use these exposures to reduce risk?
   How frequently do you measure these exposures?
   From where do you get data for these exposures?
   From where do get data for these measures and which data do you use?
   Do you use alternative strategies to reduce currency exposures? Why?
   What do you use the currency exposure for?
   Follow up?
   Short-term operation activities?
   To determine the extent of forward cover?
   Do you cover 50 per cent, 75 per cent, or 100 per cent of the exposure?

4. **Interest rate risk exposure**
   Which measures do you use? Do you manage short term or long term?
   Which policy do you have?
   How does this policy interact with the foreign exchange risk management?

Which are the proposals for future changes of the management of FEE and IRE?

5. **Organization**
   Is the organization of FEE and IRE centralized or decentralized?
   Which influence does the organization structure have on the currency risk management?
   In which way does your financial department participate in the management of different exposures?
   Which emphasis does the management put on the management of FEE and IRE?
   When and why have there been changes in policies?

6. **Goal congruence**
   Have your organization declared a formal goal for your FEE and IRE?
   To which extent is this goal related to the overall goal of the organization?
   Not at all *To a high extent*
   Which of the below statements will describe in the best way your definition of risk.

   a) The probability that the outcome will be different from expected outcome
   b) The probability that the outcome will be worse than expected
   c) The length of the exposure
   d) The amount of exposure in relation to firm size (sales)
   e) Other

To which extent are you willing to take on risk in order to obtain a better return?
Not at all *To a high extent*
Would you consider your export activities as very diversified or do you focus on special geographic areas?
Diversified *Specialized*
Would you consider your R&D activities diversified or focused on specific geographical areas?
Diversified *Focused*
The following statements concerns your/your company's view on FEE decision making

1. Your FEE-strategy decisions are made solely on the value they create for the shareholders

2. A successful company has high profitability, while it is exposed to, relatively speaking, less FE-risk.
3. By eliminating risk managers increase the possibility of earning high returns

In your opinion a successful manager of FEE is good at:

a) Choosing the optimal level of exchange exposure.
b) Taking advantage of short term mispriced currencies

In your opinion your decisions concerning hedging of currencies can be considered as:

Highly *risk averse risk neutralrisk loving*
A FEE manager's risk aversion varies over time
Agree *Disagree*
The risk aversion will change as the decision-maker becomes more professional/skilled.
Agree *Disagree*
There is a level of attractiveness/thrill in the exposure to risk
Agree *Disagree*
From a shareholder perspective it is better to diversify by spreading equity among currency regions rather than allowing manager to hedge exposure
Agree *Disagree*
The consequences of taking much risk are primarily seen in an economic recession?
Agree *Disagree*

Which of the following statements describes best your willingness to accept or avoid risk in FEE or IRE decisions?

a) we never accept risk
b) we accept risk in order to receive profit
c) we are trying to match our risk with that of competitors
d) We are more aggressive in taking on risk compared to competitors
e) We are less aggressive in taking on risk compared to competitor

Which of the following statements do you think best describe the markets that you operate in?

a) Fierce competition with many competitors
b) Fierce competition but with few large competitors
c) Fierce competition with many foreign competitors

d) Fierce competition with few foreign competitors
e) Ease competition
f) Monopoly situation

Which of the following statements describe in the best way the macro factor relations presented below?

a) The purchasing power parity holds in the long run/short run (the law of one price) (the difference in inflation are perfectly matched by differences in forward and spot rates)
b) The fisher parity holds in the long run/short run (the capital market equilibrium) (the differences interest rates are perfectly matched by differences in inflation rates)
c) The expectation hypothesis holds in the long run/short run (forward rate = future spot rate)
d) Interest rate parity holds in the long run/short run (today's interest differences are perfectly matched by differences in forward and spot rates.

Do you think your company are doing a good job in hedging FEE and IRE compared to competitors?
Better *average worse*
Do you think your company takes on more/less risk than competitors?
More risk average less risk
What major trends on the international markets have had most influence on decisions made during the last years concerning FEE and IRE?

a) The development of new techniques for hedging purposes.
b) The change in fluctuation in interest and currency rates.
c) The introduction of the Euro zone.
d) The increased focus on shareholder value
e) Other

How has the introduction of a single currency, and the fact the Sweden/GB did not join, affected your company's profitability?
How has the above affected your work with FEE and IRE?

Notes

1. FDI = foreign direct investment.
2. SAP is a brandname of SAP AG. A major producer of enterprise software.
3. FAS 133 = *Accounting for Derivative Instruments and Hedging Activities*, a standard issued by the Financial Accounting Standards Board.

References

Aabo, T. (2006) 'The importance of corporate foreign debt in managing exchange rate exposure in non-financial companies', *European Financial Management,* 12(4), 633–49.

Adler, M., and B. Dumas (1984) 'Exposure to currency risk: definition and measurement', *Financial Management,* Summer.

Allayannis, G. and J. Ihrig (2001) 'Exposure and markups', *The Review of Financial Studies,* 14(3), 805–35.

Allayannis, G., J. Ihrig and J.P. Weston (2001) 'Exchange-rate hedging: financial versus operational strategies', *AEA Papers and Proceedings,* May.

Allayannis, G., and J.P Weston (2001) 'The use of foreign currency derivatives and firm market value', *Review of Financial Studies,* Spring, 14(1), 243–76.

Bali, T.G., S.R. Hume and T.F. Martell (2007) 'A new look at hedging with derivatives: will firms reduce market risk exposure?' *The Journal of Futures Markets,* 27(11), 1053–83.

Bank for International Settlement (2010) Triennial Central Bank Survey. Foreign Exchange and Derivatives Market Activity in April 2010. ISBN 92–9131–840-X.

Bartov, E. and G.M. Bodnar (1994) 'Firm valuation, earnings expectations, and the use of foreign currency derivatives', *Journal of Finance,* 49, 1755–85.

Bartram, S.K. (2008) 'What lies beneath: foreign exchange rate exposure, hedging and cash flows', *Journal of Banking and Finance,* 31, 1508–21.

Bergendahl, G. (2001) 'The management of foreign exchange exposures and interest rate exposures in a number of UK and Swedish firms between 1985 and 1996', in E.P.M. Gardener and P.C. Versluijs (eds), *Bank Strategies and Challenges in the New Europe.* Palgrave: Hampshire, UK.

Bergendahl, G. and A. Birts (1998) 'The management of international cash transactions and associated foreign exchange transactions: a comparative study of practices in the UK, Sweden, Scandinavia and Europe', in D.F. Birks (ed.), *Global Cash Management in Europe.* Palgrave Macmillan.

Bergendahl, G. and M. Nyberg (1986) *Foreign Exchange Exposure Management. An Analysis of the Practice in 26 British and Swedish Firms,* FE-Report 265–1986, Department of Business Administration, University of Gothenburg.

Brown, G.W. (2001) 'Managing foreign exchange risk with derivatives', *Journal of Financial Economics,* 60, 401–48.

Brown, G.W., P.R. Crabb and D. Haushalter (2006) 'Are firms successful at selective hedging? *Journal of Business,* 79(6).

Chow, E.H., W.Y. Lee and M.E. Solt (1997) 'The economic exposure of US multinational firms', *The Journal of Financial Research,* 20, 191–210.

Collier, P. and E.W. Davis (1985) 'Currency risk management in UK MNCs', *Accounting and Business Research,* Autumn, 327–35.

Collier P., E.W. Davis, J.B. Coates and S.G. Longden (1990) 'The management of currency risk: case studies of US and UK multinationals', *Accounting and Business Research,* 20(79), 206–10.

Dekle, R. and H.H. Ryoo (2007) 'Exchange rate fluctuations, financing constraints, hedging, and exports: evidence from firm level data', *International Financial Markets, Institutions and Money,* 17, 437–51.

Dhanani, A. (2003) 'Foreign exchange risk management: a case in the mining industry', *The British Accounting Review,* 35, 35–63.

Dhanani, A. (2004) 'The management of exchange-rate risk: a case from the manufacturing industry', *Thunderbird International Business Review*, 46(3), 317–38.

Dhanani, A., and R. Groves (2001) 'The management of strategic exchange risk: evidence from corporate practices', *Accounting and Business Research*, 31(4), 275–90.

Donaldson, J.A. (1987) *Corporate Currency Risk. A Reappraisal*, Financial Times Business Information, London.

Earl, M. (1985) A Stage Model of Measuring and Managing Foreign Exchange Exposure, The Treasurer, March.

George, A.M. (1983) 'Currency exposure management', in A.M. George and I.M. Giddy (eds), *International Finance Handbook*, Vol. 2, Wiley-Interscience.

Géczy, C., B.A. Minton, and C. Schrand (1997) 'Why firms use currency derivatives', *The Journal of Finance*, LII(4).

Hagelin, N. and B. Pramborg (2004) 'Hedging foreign exchange exposure: risk reduction from transaction and translation hedging', *Journal of International Financial Management and Accounting*, 15(1), 1–20.

Hutson, E., and S. Stevenson (2010) 'Openness, hedging incentives and foreign exchange exposure: a firm-level multi-country study', *Journal of International Business Studies*, 41, 105–22.

Jorion, P. (1990) 'The exchange rate exposure of US multinationals', *Journal of Business*, 63, 331–45.

Kenyon, A. (1990) *Currency Risk and Business Management*. Basil Blackwell: Oxford.

Kim, Y.S., I. Mathur and J. Nam (2006) 'Is operational hedging a substitute for or a complement to financial hedging', *Journal of Corporate Finance*, 12, 834–5.

Luehrman, T.A. (1991) 'Exchange rate changes and the distribution of industry value', *Journal of International Business Studies*, 22(4), 619–49.

Miller, K.D. and J.J. Reuer (1998) 'Firm strategy and economic exposure to foreign exchange rate movements', *Journal of International Business Studies*, 29(3), 493–513.

Modigliani, F. and M.H. Miller (1958) 'The cost of capital, corporate finance and the theory of investment', *American Economic Review*, 32, 261–97.

Moffett, M.H. and J.K. Karlsen (1994) 'Managing foreign exchange rate economic exposure', *Journal of International Financial Management and Accounting*, 5(2).

Muller, A. and W.F.C. Verschoor (2006a) 'Foreign exchange risk exposure: survey and suggestions, journal of multinational financial', *European Financial Management*, 12(2), 195–220.

Muller, A. and W.F.C. Verschoor (2006b) 'European foreign exchange risk exposure', *European Financial Management*, 12(2), 195–220.

Oxelheim, L. and C. Wihlborg (1987) *Macroeconomic Uncertainty*. Wiley.

Oxelheim, L. and C. Wihlborg (2005) *Corporate Performance and the Exposure to Macroeconomic Fluctuations*. Nordstedts: Stockholm.

Pringle, J.J. and R.A. Connolly (1993) 'The nature and causes of foreign currency exposure', *Journal of Applied Corporate Finance*, 6(3), 61–72.

Ronner, A. and M. Blok (2001) 'Hedging foreign currency exposure: consequences of FAS 133', *Journal of Applied Finance*, 11, 23–34.

Rountree, B., J.P. Weston and G. Allayannis (2008) 'Do investors value smooth performance', *Journal of Financial Economics*, 90, 237–51.

Smith, C., and R. Stulz (1985) 'The determinants of firms' hedging policies', *Journal of Financial Quantitative Analysis*, 20, 391–405.

Stulz, R. (1996) 'Rethinking risk management', *Journal of Applied Corporate Finance*, 9, 8–24.

Williamson, R. (2001) 'Exchange rate exposure and competition: evidence from the automotive industry', *Journal of Financial Economics*, 59, 441–75.
Zhang, H. (2009) 'Effect of derivative accounting rules on corporate risk-management behavior', *Journal of Accounting and Economics*, 47, 244–64.

9

Risk Governance in Pension Funds: Management Control in Dutch Pension Funds

Leo A. van Eerden

1 Introduction: risk as a management problem in Dutch pension funds

In the decade leading up to the time of writing, early 2013, the performance of Dutch pension funds dropped seriously after a period of gloomy investment results in the nineties. This was partly due to the spread of the international financial crisis, born of the American subprime debt crisis and extending to inter-bank and sovereign debt crises. This turbulence has had a great impact on the development of stock market and investment returns for pension funds in the Netherlands. Markets, and the use of different popular financial instruments, showed severe losses in investment returns. Even after five years of financial crises and (public) efforts to deal with resolution plans, we can suppose that recovery in investment performance is not to be expected in the short and medium term. Over-liquidity in the international financial system, stimulated by a flood of liquidity creation by the European Central Bank and the American Federal Reserve, can rescue banks from defaulting but it negatively affects pension fund investments.

One of the main dangers of the present time is that traditional financial intermediation is threatened by a mismatch between aggregate savings and borrowing needs. Furthermore there seems to be a great distrust in financial institutions. Pension funds, as financial institutions, are in this case no exception. In the Global Consumer Survey (Wyman, 2012), 63 per cent of the respondents trust only themselves to manage their retirement savings.

In the world of banking, trust is the lifeblood of the business. For pension fund investments, trust in its management and long-run perspectives is critical.

However pension fund management has some other major challenges to deal with; these include the problem of an ageing society and diminishing amounts of new entrants to help replenish pension funds.

This results in a particular problem for the financing of defined benefit (DB) schemes, but more and more also for defined contribution (DC) schemes. For both type of contracts, dependence on money and capital markets is growing. Forces operating in these markets are to a large extent out of control of the majority of national policy institutions.

Nowadays, ex post, it became painfully clear that many pension funds have invested in financial products of bad quality and unacceptable risk. The marketing of these products was the result of the trading activities of banks and shadow banks; overoptimistic promises relating to high and extra returns created a smokescreen concealing the risks taken on behalf of the customers.

However it was not only on the micro level that unacceptable risks were created and accepted. At the beginning of this century, supervisors, too – in most cases central banks – recognized the riskiness of this business, but did not apparently have the power to correct this – embarrassingly so for national financial system agencies whose self-declared main task is 'to safeguard financial stability'.

Financial markets have grown tremendously in complexity over the last 20 years. Without doubt, the situation is the same with risk management. The pension fund board governs, in most cases, from a distance. Basic tasks are outsourced. Strategic objectives are translated into tactical policies by asset managers and service providers. There is, in the Dutch case, a practice of controlling outsourced activities through the use of commitment papers, protocols and effort obligations with SAS[1] declarations on its quality. In the Netherlands, Frijns et al. (2010) analyzed the investment and risk management policies of a representative part of the Dutch pension fund industry. One of the conclusions from this research is that pension funds structurally pay too little attention to risk management and the execution of investment policy; this criticism was also brought up by the supervisor De Nederlandsche Bank (DNB) (2011). Research from DNB on investment policy and practice of Dutch pension funds made clear that in an overwhelming number of the cases studied, pension fund boards were not sufficiently in control of the investment risk taken.

The attention paid to investments and risk management has been largely influenced by the insights of mainstream financial economics. With the Efficient Markets Hypothesis and CAPM[2] approach, the sight on the development of financial bubbles and crisis events was outside the scope of (neoclassical) analyses. Even the popular Value at Risk approach seems to have major deficiencies in completely explaining the financial risks to investment. This is not the place to analyze these deficiencies in more depth.

In general, there is a need for a better understanding of financial risks and risk management, by introducing and linking the human factor into the analysis. With this human factor, we can understand the way people are working together to deal with risk in the organization. It is about the development of the organizational processes and the way investment risks are assessed; as Cools (2010) states: 'risk management is first of all looking after conduct and then after systems'.

There are good grounds for a paradigm change combining quantitative models with a qualitative and multidisciplinary approach regarding risk processing.

The DNB, supervising pensions funds, demands the boards of these funds to be, and to remain, 'in control' of investment practices and risk management.

As shown in this chapter, risk management as such needs to be expanded from mere quantitative analyses, to true risk governance encompassing the human management factor in the working of pension fund boards.

2 Pension fund management in the Netherlands

2.1 The Dutch pension fund system: some key elements

The first Dutch pension fund, the Dutch Railroads (Hollandse IJzeren Spoorwegmaatschappij) dates from 1845, then in 1846 the Dutch Civil Servants' Fund (ABP) was founded. Over time these pension funds have been developed as important players in the Dutch pension fund landscape. Nevertheless changes in the structure of the economy and labor relations have created a base for the present Dutch pension system. This system can be

Table 9.1 Pillar system

Pillar	Character	Who exercises Control?	What is it?	Funding
1st	Public	Regulated by law	Basic state pension: AOW	Pay-as-you-go (PAYG): today's contributors pay for today's retirees
2nd	Private	Regulated by law	Supplementary pension (collective schemes)	Pension contributions paid in the past and accumulated by investment results
3rd	Private	Individual action	Supplementary pension (individual): annuities, endowment	Pension contributions paid in the past and accumulated by investment results

Source: Ministry of Social Affairs and Employment.

Table 9.2 Types of pension schemes (2000–2008) (expressed as a percentage of active members)

	2000	2001	2002	2003	2004	2005	2006	2007	2008
Defined benefit									
Final pay scheme	59	56	54	49	12	11	10	3	1
Career-average scheme	31	32	32	35	73	74	77	85	87
Other	8	8	8	10	10	9	9	1	0,5
Defined contribution	1	3	3	3	3	4	4	5	5
Other	2	1	3	3	3	2	0,5	3	2

Source: DNB Statistics Bulletin, December 2008, *op. cit.* Dutch Ministry of Social Affairs and Employment.

characterized as a three-pillar system (Table 9.1) with different stakeholders involved in the management of the pension funds. These three pillars together determine the amount of money that its pensioners will receive in their retirement.

The *first pillar* of the Dutch pension system is based on a state pension (AOW) with a statutory insurance system. The system provides state pensions for people aged 65+ years. It also provides incomefor people with a deceased partner and with children younger than 16 years.[3] It is a pay-as-you-go system funded by people under the age of 65.[4] In 2007, about 2.7 million people received a state pension with a total amount of more than € 25 billion.

The cost of the Dutch state pensions is paid by the workforce in the form of contributions; additional funding stems from government public funds. This means that everybody, with or without paid work, contributes directly or indirectly.

The *second pillar* is an occupational pension scheme. It is the largest pillar in the Dutch pension fund system, and is based on contributions of employers and employees. Usually the employers pay more than 50 per cent of the pension contributions. This is a part of and a result of the wage determination process between employers and employees. The associated pension schemes are administrated by a pension fund or by an insurance company. The pension funds are legally and financially independent of companies. The greatest part of Dutch pension money is under management by pension funds.

This pillar is financed by capital funding; in other words, it is financed by the contributions of members in the pension scheme and from the return on investment on previous contributions.

The *third pillar* consists of individual pension products. These products are mostly used by self-employed people and employees in sectors without any collective pension scheme.

Basically there are three forms of pension funds: industry-wide, corporate pension funds and pension funds for independent professionals.

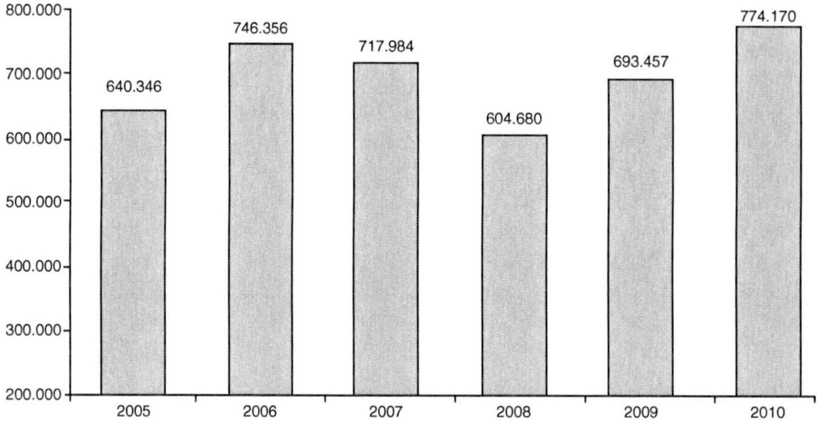

Figure 9.1 Balance sheet total pension funds (in € millions)
Source: DNB.

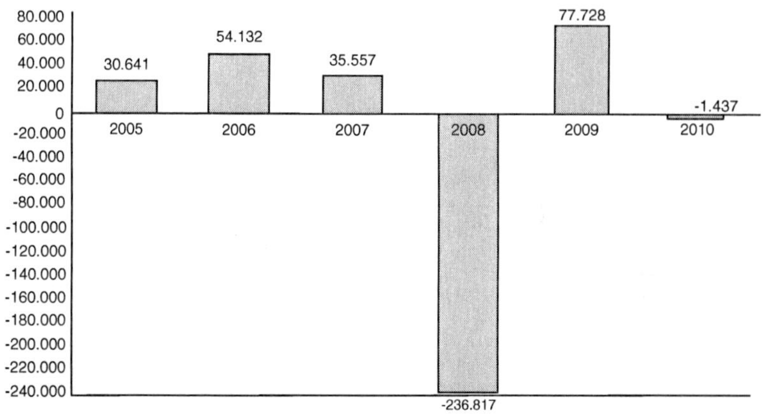

Figure 9.2 Results pension funds (in € millions)
Source: DNB.

In the Netherlands there is no obligation by law to become member or participant in a pension fund. But if social partners decide to provide a pension scheme for their employees, the government can make their pension scheme mandatory (VB OPF, 2010).

There are three types of pension schemes (Table 9.2) in the form of a Defined Benefit (DB), Defined Contribution (DC) and a Collective Defined Contribution (CDC) scheme.

The majority of Dutch DB schemes are not pure DB schemes but more hybrid. (VB OPF, 2010). In cases of financial difficulties, all participants: employers, employees and pensioners have to contribute to the fund's recovery. Basically there are three routes to fo llow: increasing pension contributions, limiting indexation and reducing pension rights.

As we can see from Figure 9.1, in 2010 the balance sheet total from Dutch pension funds was back at the 2006 level. These figures are on an aggregate level and do not differentiate between funds with liabilities under pressure or funds with a profile skewed to higher ages.

The international financial crisis of 2007 had an great impact on the results of the pension funds. As we can see in Figure 9.2, the swing in results is large. Major parts of the investment portfolio are in stocks and in fixed interest rate investments; the latter, with extremely low interest rates, are responsible for a fall in investment returns.

The performance of Dutch pension funds is under severe pressure. Failing investment returns have a had a great impact on the coverage ratio of pension funds. Many of them have been forced by the supervisor, DNB, to accept recovery plans. Several funds, not meeting the required recovery, had to adapt a reduction of their payment obligations to pensioners. Besides losses in investments, Dutch pension funds are confronted with an ageing population and an ever-diminishing will in contributors to make a larger contribution to pension funds.

Hit as by a bolt from the blue by the financial crisis of 2007/2008 and beyond, the pension fund management have had much discussion about their role in managing investment and risk.[5] The pension law passed since that crisis has addressed issues of pension fund management and ageing.

The risk of the outbreak of financial and banking crises is a feature central to the history of capitalism (cf. Reinhart and Rogoff, 2009). Even if financial crises occur at various times, the intensity, depth and effects of these crises may differ. What also differs is the involvement of public supervisors and regulators. The 2007–2010 financial crisis was not just a terrible accident happening outside the reach of policymakers and financial market forces. Debt and over-indebtedness were the main issues, and these, combined with failures in supervision and regulation, were the ingredients of this systemic crisis (cf. Barth et al., 2012). New to that crisis was that outside the mainstream operating of the banks, shadow banks became of great importance (Adrian and Shin, 2009). The emergence of shadow banking, encompassing hedge funds, private equity and institutional investors, changed the traditional dominance of banks in financial intermediation. The outbreak of the international financial crisis in 2007–2008 highlights the structural changes which have taken place in financial intermediation and investments over the last 25 years. This means also that the position of pension funds as institutional investors was changing more to so-called 'shadow-intermediation' and hence became more vulnerable in the killing fields generated by the new financial instruments and products.

2.2 Supervision and regulation

The Dutch government and parliament are responsible for the development and implementation of pension law. The check on the execution is delegated to two supervisory agencies: the Dutch Central Bank (DNB) and the Authority Financial Markets (AFM).

The DNB is the supervisor that examines the short- and long-term financial position of pension funds. The DNB is also responsible for substantive regulation in terms of monitoring and organizing of pension funds according to the standards set.

As part of the Pension Act there is a Financial Assessment Framework (FTK) which sets out the requirements for pension funds. Central to the assessment of a fund's performance is the coverage ratio, the relation between assets and the pensions to be paid in the future. This minimum coverage ratio is fixed at 105 per cent (that is, capital must amount to 105 per cent of the liabilities). (VB OPF, 2010)

In addition to this coverage ratio, pension funds need to have buffers to safeguard against financial setbacks; so added to the coverage ratio there must be 125 per cent capital. There is a charge for taking more investment risk and the average age of the pension fund members. It is important that the capital of the fund and the liabilities are valued at market prices.

If the coverage ratio falls below 105 per cent, the fund has to submit a recovery plan to the DNB with the obligation to be back at the 105 per cent level within three years. Rebuilding the required buffers may take 15 years. In exceptional circumstances the DNB can extend the recovery time; for example, due to the effect of the credit crisis the three-year recovery time has been extended to a five-year period.

The AFM is the monitoring institution for behavior of pension funds. The focus is especially on the provision of information to pension fund members.

3 Investment policies and risk management

For several years, a discussion has been initiated about the future of the Dutch pension system.[6] In this discussion, the report by Frijns et al. (2010) has an important place. It presents an analysis of investment policy and risk management in a representative number of Dutch pension funds. In addition to other conclusions, this report emphasizes the complex character and heterogeneity of the pension fund sector. Ageing population and low birth rates contribute to the increasing vulnerability of pension funds. The report also stresses the inadequate translation of the specific character of pension funds in investment policy. There is also a focus on the necessity of improving the governance. From this research, encompassing a representative part of the Dutch pension fund industry, it has become clear that almost all pension funds have undervalued the importance of risk management and the implementation of investment policy.

A selection of recommendations of the commission (2010, p. 5/6):

Risk management

1. Boards must only accept pension contracts that are not only explicit and well-balanced in terms of the pension commitments and the agreements on contributions, but also in terms of the allocation of risks.
2. Boards must establish a strategic risk framework laying down an appropriate balance for the fund and the members between return and risk. The appetite for risk and the risk acceptance level among the members of the fund must be defined and should form the starting point for the investment policy to be pursued. A situation whereby the investment policy is in fact mainly return driven should be avoided.
3. The board of the fund should ascertain what the attitude of the members of the fund and the contributing employers is with regard to sustainability. This should then form the starting point for the risk and investment policy. Each year the board renders account with regard to the sustainability performance of the investments.
4. A real aim must serve as a guide. The pension fund must develop an assessment framework in which both short-term funding ratio risks and long-term indexation risks are taken into account. This must be detailed and given concrete form in an ALM context, with the liability structure acting as reference point.
5. The board must ensure that even under extreme market conditions, the fund does not drop below the critical nominal or real funding ratio. The board must determine the lower limit for the nominal and the real funding ratio based on the specific characteristics of that fund and the risk acceptance level and risk appetite of the fund members.
6. The board must render account to the members with regard to the strategic investment framework and the exchange of return against risk that has been opted for within that framework and with regard to the shape and details of the accompanying risk management. As a mandatory element of this accountability, the fund should inform the members via the website and at least yearly via an annual report about the presumed risk appetite of the members, the current risk profile, the effective nominal and real funding ratio as well as the critical lower limit for the nominal and real funding ratio set by the board.

Investment policy

7. The investment policy must be aimed at achieving a correct balance between the real objective (ambition) and the interim nominal and real funding ratio risk. The investment policy forms an integral whole with the risk and sustainability policy. The strategic risk framework and the investment policy are determined in combination with one another.
8. The board must base the investment policy on current and realistic return and risk expectations. In particular, the board must satisfy itself that critical funding ratio limits are not exceeded, even under extreme circumstances.
9. The board must make explicit choices regarding the structuring of the investment policy in all its aspects and must render account in this regard. The board must take a critical stance with regard to the assumed benefits of alternative investments and forms of active investment policy and must analyze and identify the burdens and risks of that policy in addition to the expected benefits.
10. The board should adopt a monitoring framework in order to be able continuously to assess the result of the investment policy relative to its real aim.

Implementation of risk management and investment policy

11. The board must be effectively in control with respect to risk management at all stages of the investment process. This applies to the implementation of the strategic, tactical and operational investment policy. The board should set this out in a control statement.
12. The results of the investment policy must be put against the aims, the risk profile and the risk acceptance level as they have been determined based on the pension contract.
13. The information processes must be structured in such a way that the risks of asymmetrical information are reduced to a manageable level. This requires that management monitoring processes be organized in such a way that this yields actual insight into and transparency of risk management and the entire investment process. Additionally, it requires the selection of executors who fit the selected investment policy.
14. The board must be able to form an effective countervailing power to the professional executors and (commercial) providers of investment products. This also applies in the event that implementation takes place in house.

These recommendations play an important role in the pension law passed in 2012 and the managerial renewal in the Dutch pension funds. In general there is a plea for a better management and board involvement in risk management and investment control. But there is also a plea for more expertise in the management of risk in the board of pension funds.

In a study by Hinz (2011, p. 29), the Dutch Pension System is marked as very consistent with the World Bank Multi/Pillar Framework. For the World Bank, a greater reliance on individual accounts to achieve optimal incentives and sustainability on the road to an optimal system, would be better.

This addresses the issue of measuring the performance of pension systems. Hinz et al. (2010) presented a study about the performance of pension funds. The performance of a pension system is to a large extent determined by the fundamental issues of system design and the operational efficiency (Ambachtsheer, 2010). To label a system as 'good' there are, according to Ambachtsheer, four criteria which need a high score:

1. population/workforce coverage,
2. income replacement adequacy,
3. intra- and intergenerational fairness, and
4. system efficiency.

In the World Bank study most contributions focus on the latter only. Then, measuring the overall system efficiency this is driven by four factors (Ambachtsheer, 2010, p. 244):

1. the long-term risk-free real interest rate,
2. the gross risk premium on risky investments, less the costs of passive implementation,
3. the gross value-added from active management less the cost of active implementation, and
4. the cost of benefit administration.

Nevertheless there should also be integration with the three other criteria mentioned. In addition, an assessment of pension fund design and institutional implementation needs to be considered before concluding whether systems are 'good' or 'bad'.

3.1 From FIRM to FOCUS!

Since 2005 the Dutch supervisor has used the FIRM[7] model as a framework and point of reference for assessing the risk and financial performance of pension funds.[8]

Beside the long list of risk items (Annex 9.1) and well known as such from the economic literature, FIRM adds some new dimensions to the assessment

Table 9.3 Control categories and control items

Control item	Description
Management quality and structure	The manner in which the institution's leadership function is effectively performed. Cases in point are: • the competence of the (board of) management as a whole to manage the institution; • the extent to which the (board of) management is adequately balanced in terms of expertise and background; • the extent to which the management structure and composition match the size and complexity of the operations; • the extent to which responsibilities have been assigned in an adequate matter to individual members of the (board of) management, and the extent to which an adequate span of control have been realized; • the extent to which (the board of) management sets an example for the institution's staff (for instance, by propagating ethical norms and standards); • the (board of) management's leadership style and the extent to which the (board of) management is respected within the institution.
Strategy	This concerns: • the manner in which the strategy is formulated within the institution; • the extent to which this process takes place on an institution-wide basis; • the transparency of the process; • the substance and consistency of the strategy; • the degree of specificity of the strategy, and • the extent to which the institution's strategy is clearly and consistently communicated.

Continued

Table 9.3 Continued

Control item	Description
Risk/control attitude	This concerns: • the extent to which the (board of) management is aware of and interested in, and has an insight into, the risks to which the institution is exposed; • the preparedness of the (board of) management to use adequate controls (both in-house and underlain by statutory rules), and to make sufficient funds available for that purpose; • the extent to which the (board of) management is prepared to take risk and, when doing so, to perform an adequate risks-benefit analysis; • the extent to which the (board of) management complies with the existing internal controls.
Management and decision making	The extent to which the (board of) management is sufficiently actively and substantively involved in operational management and results. This is reflected in such aspects as the frequency, degree of substantiveness, intensity and action-oriented nature of management consultations. This also concerns the effectiveness of the delegation of powers to (decision-making) bodies (such as risk committees).

Source: DNB, FIRM Manual, November 2005.

of risk management. More attention is paid in this model to the participation and involvement of pension fund board and management.

The model is also the starting point for risk-based supervision.[9]

These control items are to be added to the risk items presented in Annex 9.1. Although the different forms of risk are well known, an extension with more managerial elements is necessary. However as presented in Table 9.3 it is not very clear how these management and board activities can be measured and assessed.

With the follow-up of FIRM in FOCUS!, the risk methodology has been improved. The pension funds have been divided into five supervision classes, each with a different risk analysis. The idea behind this classification is that the bigger the impact of the problems of the pension funds, the more intensive the risk analysis. In addition to the micro-focused elements from FRIM there is now also a linkage to macro-developments. There is, further, an explicit assessment of the business model, strategy, conduct and culture.

The DNB uses now a top–down way of working:

1) Macro- and sectorial risk
2) Business model and strategy
3) Conduct, culture and governance
4) Infrastructure and IT
5) Risk management
6) Risk position
7) Capital / liquidity.

From several studies of investment performance and risk management in Dutch pension funds (DNB, 2010) there arises a picture of lack of grip and control on the investments and the risks taken. In many cases, pension fund management is driven by representatives of 'social partners', employers and employees with a predominantly general focus; investments and asset management, and sometimes risk management as well, are outsourced to external business partners. These partners are specialists in their professional areas; nevertheless these specialists can take their fund principals by surprise with unexpected and unwanted results of the outsourcing. Our experience over the years with different management assessments in pension funds, is that pension fund managers need to be more in control of their investments. Management needs to develop and to be responsible for 'investment with a vision' (Cf. Koedijk and Slager, 2011). As Ambachtsheer (2008) makes clear, better investments are realized in cases of pension funds with an explicit and clear investment vision and with a better and explicit governance of investment by the management.

As Van Eerden (2013) posits, management of 'risk with a vision' is also required. In this vision it is preferable that the pension fund management be actively involved in the risk management of the fund; they need to be aware of the risk, to understand the grade of acceptance of risk, and to monitor risk processes and communicate this to all stakeholders. As stated by Koedijk and Slager (2011), financial economics is not an exact science, regardless of the numbers of figures and formulas used in investment modeling. In almost all investment practices these models and associated concepts lack the human factor in decision making and decision taking.

The same topic has a role in risk management. For many years, risk management has been dominated by the mathematics of the Value at Risk formulas. Quite apart from certain technical deficiencies in these common approaches, they give a false impression of a risk-free or managed live. But for effective risk management we also need to integrate the human factor and to expect the unexpected.

In the case of pension fund management, we need to move from the traditional concept of risk management to a form of risk governance that includes risk management processes and control.

4 Towards risk governance

The present financial crisis developed out of a period of structural change in financial intermediation. The broad use of new financial products in and outside traditional banking and the growing importance of non-bank financial intermediaries and deregulation transformed the financial order. This new order was processed by so-called 'financialization'.[10] Economic growth has become more and more finance-led (van Eerden and Graafsma, 1998). This finance-led dynamics means that the developments in the money market and capital market have had a strong impact on investment and economic growth. As a consequence, the relevance of taking macroeconomic developments into account, linked to micro-institutional risk performance, is of great importance. In the Netherlands, DNB is setting out now to judge how best to be in control of the risk management of the investment portfolio of pension funds, using this macro-analysis as starter.

4.1 Risk Governance[11]

The concept of risk governance[12] is a broad concept encompassing risk management, risk analysis and risk-related decision-making. The latter in particular is an important extension, because it also highlights a range of involved actors. It requires co-ordination and a profusion of roles, perspectives, goals and activities. Risk governance means taking account of factors like historical and legal backgrounds, guiding principles, value systems, perceptions and organizational imperatives. As Renn remarks, the risk governance framework offers two major innovations by the inclusion of the social context and the new category of 'risk-related knowledge'.

Risk governance uses concepts that link risk assessment with risk perception and the social processing of risk. It is also a concept linking physical risk analysis with financial, economic and social risk. In addition, the concept links risk theory with organizational capacity building and management competency.

Behind the risk governance framework are three value-based premises and assumptions (Renn, 2006, p. 12):

- First, the framework is inspired by the conviction that both the 'factual' and 'socio-cultural' dimension of risk need to be considered if risk governance is to produce adequate decisions and results.

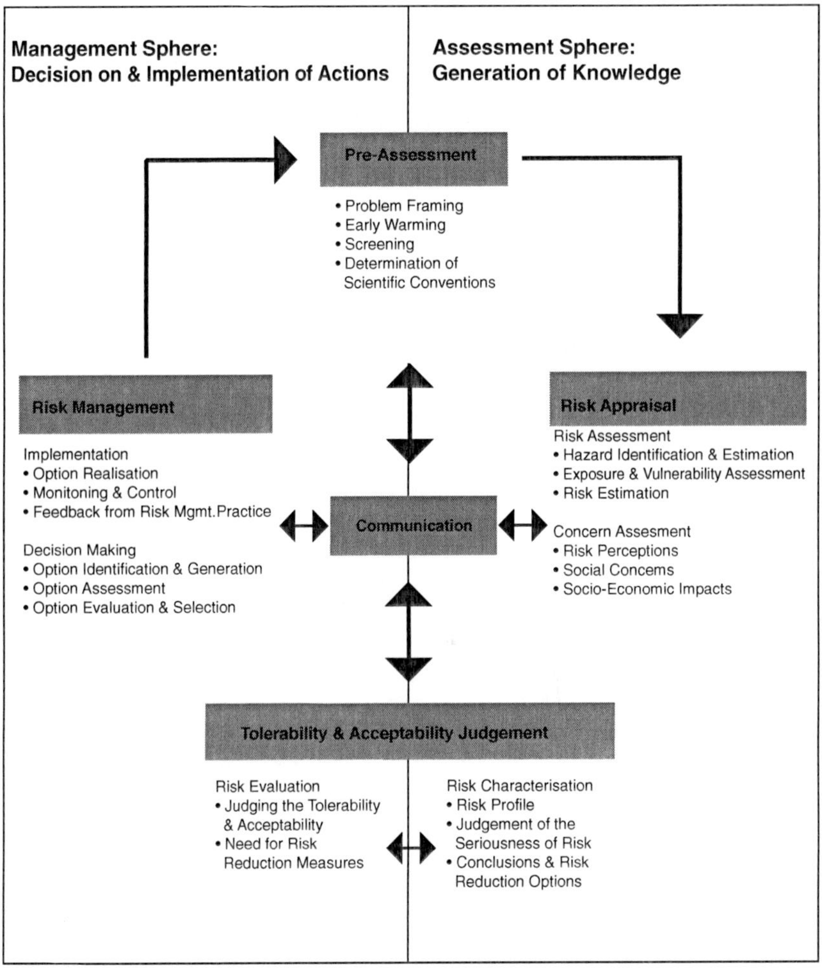

Figure 9.3 Risk governance framework
Source: Renn (2006, p. 13).

- The second major premise concerns the inclusiveness of the governance process, which is seen as a necessary, although not sufficient, prerequisite for tackling risks in both sustainable and acceptable manner and consequently, imposes an obligation to ensure the early and meaningful involvement of all stakeholders and, in particular, civil society.
- A third premise involving values is reflected in the framework's implementation of principles of 'good' governance: beyond the crucial commitment to participation these principles include transparency, effectiveness and efficiency, accountability, strategic focus, sustainability, equity and fairness, respect for rule of law and the need for the chosen solution to be politically and legally realizable as well as ethically and publicly acceptable.

A risk governance framework can be built up from different basic blocks: a) Pre-assessment, b) Risk Appraisal, c) Risk Management, and Tolerability and Acceptability Judgment. These blocks are analytically connected, but address the Management Sphere with Decision and Implementation of Actions, and an Assessment Sphere with the Generation of Knowledge. This framework is presented in Figure 9.3.

Important elements of the risk governance frame are (Renn, 2006):

- Acknowledgement of different frames
- Distinguished strategies to deal with uncertainties and ambiguities
- Importance of both risks and concerns
- Need for explicit risk and benefit evaluation including the consideration of equity impacts
- Need for global governance mechanisms (monitoring, control, supervision)
- Importance of effective risk and benefit communication programs
- Need for inclusive governance integration government, industry, civil society and science
- Need for gaining public trust and support.

Lessons learned from the present financial crisis and the risk management practices in the nineties are that risk management has problems in handling risk (see the summing up above). In line with Renn, four risk management regimes should be used to deal with the new risk challenges:

- simple risk management: standard risk assessment,
- risk-informed management: expanded risk assessments; seeking expert consensus and epistemological clarification,
- precaution-/resilience-based management: negotiated safety level under uncertainty; seeking stakeholder consensus and relying on containment and resilience,

- discourse-based management: value-based orientation; seeking more public input and stakeholder involvement for interpretative variability and normative controversy.

The Dutch Central Bank has introduced a stronger focus on the human factor in pension fund management with explicit attention to conduct, culture, management quality and governance.[13]

5 Conclusions

We highlight here the fact that risk management in the financial service industry has become a major focus of attention. However, in many cases risk management practices involve the management processes and responsibilities too little. Especially in pension funds, with a rich tradition of outsourcing, a widening of the scope of risk management to risk governance can be important to deal with risk in the organization.

With the use of the risk management framework and risk management regimes, boards and management of pension funds can take better control.

Annex 9.1

Risk categories	Risk items
Matching/interest rate risks	Interest rate
	Currency
	Liquidity
	Inflation
Market risks	Price volatility
	Market liquidity
	Concentration and correlation
Credit risks	Default probability
Insurance technical risks	Concentration and correlation
	Loss given default
	Exposure at default
	Mortality
	Disability
Environmental risks	Loss
	Concentration and correlation
	Competition
	Dependence
Operational risks	Reputation
	Business climate
	(Pre)acceptance/transaction
	Processing

Continued

Annex 9.1 Continued

Risk categories	Risk items
Outsourcing risks	Payment/clearing/settlement
	Information
	Product development
	Cost
	Staff
	Sensitivity to fraud.
	Business continuity
	Integrity
IT risks	Quality of services
	Strategy and policies
Integrity risks	Security
	Controllability
	Continuity
	Prejudice to third parties
	Insider trading
Legal risks	Money laundering
	Financing of terrorism
	Improper conduct
	Legislation and regulation
	Compliance
	Liability
	Enforceability of contracts

Source: DNB: FIRM Manual, 2005.

Notes

1. SAS = Statement on Auditing Standards; an auditing standard produced by the American Institute of Certified Public Accountants.
2. CAPM = Capital Asset Pricing Model; describes the risk–return relationship, and is used to help price risky securities.
3. According to the Dutch Surviving Dependents Act, ANW.
4. In a law passed in 2012, the Dutch parliament changed the 65-year norm to add, over a longer period, a month's extra labor time before attaining pension age of 67 year.
5. Frijns et al. (2010) not only highlight the necessity of improving the investment policies and risk management of pension funds, but they also formulate real, not just nominal, payment goals to pensioners.
6. Van Ewijk (2009); Goudzwaard et al. (2010).
7. FIRM = Financial Institutions' Risk analysis Method. It is a method for risk analyses and an application for reporting.
8. FIRM replaces the RAST of DNB and MARS from the Pension and Insurance Board.
9. For the risk-based supervision approach, see Brunner et al. (2008); IOPS (2008); Stewart (2010).

10. 'Financialization is a process whereby financial markets, financial institutions and financial elites gain greater influence over economic policy and economic outcomes. Financialization transforms the functioning of economic systems at both the macro and micro levels' (Palley, 2007).
11. The notion of Risk Governance was developed by Otwin Renn (2006). This subsection is closely linked to his work; we use his concepts here, and extend them with the element of financial risk, an element not addressed by Renn.
12. Governance refers to the actions, processes, laws, traditions and institutions by which authority is exercised and decisions are taken and implemented. Risk Governance refers to the actions, processes, law, traditions and institutions by which decisions about risk handling are prepared, taken and implemented.
13. More data will become available relating to these supervisory activities.

References

Adrian, T. and H.S. Shin (2009) 'The shadow banking system: implications for financial regulation', Federal Reserve Bank of New York, *Staff Report,* no. 382.

Ambachtsheer, K. (2008) 'The Canada Supplementary Pension Plan (CSPP). Towards an Adequate affordable pension for all Canadians', *The Pension Papers,* 265.

Ambachtsheer, K. (2010) 'Future directions in measuring the financial performance of pension funds: a roundtable discussion', in R. Hinz, H. Rudolph, P. Antolin and J. Yermo (eds), *Evaluating the Financial Performance of Pension Funds.* Washington D.C., World Bank, 244–51.

Barth, J.R., G. Caprio Jr and R. Levine (2012) *Guardians of Finance. Making Regulators Work for Us.* Cambridge: MIT Press.

Brunner, G., R. Hinz, R. Rocha (2008) 'Risk-based supervision of pension funds: a review of international experience and preliminary assessment of first outcome', *Policy Research Working Paper,* 4491. Washington DC: The World Bank.

Cools, K. (2010) 'Risk management out of control', *Financial Management,* 23–08–2010.

De Nederlandsche Bank (2011) *Resultaten Beleggingsonderzoeken 2010* [Results Investment Research 2010], Amsterdam.

Eerden, L.A. van (2013) Risk with a Vision, forthcoming.

Eerden, L.A. van and C. Graafsma (1998) 'Een zoektocht naar nieuwe financiële verhoudingen', in B. van Riel et al. (eds), *Het kapitalisme sinds de jaren zeventig* [The search after new financial relations]. Tilburg University Press, 157–79.

Ewijk, C. van (2009) 'Credit crisis and Dutch pension funds: who bears the shock', *De Economist,* September.

Frijns, J., J. Nijssen and L. Scholtens (2010) *Pension: 'Uncertain Security'.* Investment Policy and Risk Management Committee. Eindhoven.

Goudzwaard, K., R. Beetsma, Th. Nijman and P. Schnabel (2010) 'Een sterke tweede pijler'. *Commissie Toekomstbestendigheid Aanvullende Pensioenregelingen,* The Hague.

Hinz, R. (2011) 'The world bank's pension policy framework and the Dutch pension system. A paradigm for the multi-pillar design? Netspar Discussion Papers, 2011–043, Tilburg: Tilburg University.

Hinz, R., H. Rudolph, P. Antolin and J. Yermo (2010) *Evaluating the Financial Performance of Pension Funds.* Washington D.C., World Bank.

IOPS (2008) 'Supervisory oversights of pension fund governance', Working Paper 8.

Koedijk, K. and A. Slager (2010) *Investment Beliefs. A Positive Approach to Institutional Investing.* Houndsmill: Palgrave Macmillan.

of liquidity. The author found that the exploitation of network externalities led to an increase in the demand for trading services and a rise in profits for both stock exchanges and intermediaries.

The above-mentioned works are relevant in that they underlie the role of liquidity as a value driver in the exchange industry. That role has been widely recognized in literature, and has been augmented following the intensification of consolidation efforts during the first decade of the 21st century. The liquidity-based literature focuses more precisely on the relations between trading values and revenues. Thus, exchanges strive for attracting more investors and issuers in order to increase both trading values and IPOs.[1] Growing trading values and listed companies, in turn, would prompt positive liquidity effects permitting exchanges (and their shareholders) to take benefit of revenues increases (Pagano et al., 2001). The most recent literature in this field explores the rationale of consolidation in the industry in light of the improving effects on liquidity and revenues (see for example, Pownall et al., 2012, with reference to the case of Euronext).

At the same time, the ongoing consolidation process stimulates a field of research which assesses the conditions of economic efficiency (Schmiedel, 2001; Schmiedel and Schönenberger, 2005) and the technical efficiency of stock exchanges (Serifsoy, 2007) alongside a body of literature dealing with value creation. Some of the literature on the value of exchanges focuses on share performances, while some builds on operative performances and, in particular, on accounting measures of operative performances (RoE, RoA[2] operating margins). The prevailing contributions in this field (Mendiola and O'Hara, 2004; Otchere, 2006; Otchere and Oldford, 2011) are mainly empirical, and deal with comparisons of the pre-privatization operating performances of listed exchanges with the post-privatization performances. Other studies try to answer the question of whether the consolidation of stock exchanges creates value for shareholders. Song et al. (2010) address the issue by comparing short-run stock price response to the announcement of mergers and alliances.

What is missing is a conceptual framework for understanding value creation for stock exchanges. In this chapter we try to bridge the gap; our aim is to provide a basic model which captures value drivers for exchanges. Drawing on the liquidity-based literature, we assume trading values and the number of IPOs as measures of market liquidity, and model their relations with costs, revenues and performances. In particular, we develop an accounting measure of operative performance based on the *return on capital employed* (Roce). A paper which is somewhat related to our work is that by Otchere (2006) although the aim is different; in particular, it assesses the effects of self-listing on the economics of exchanges comparing post-listing profitability, leverage and operating efficiency measures (cost to income ratio and operating expense ratio) with those of a control group of non-listed exchanges. Despite its different aims, Otchere's study is of interest, as it links market activity measures (trading volumes and market liquidity) with financial variables, an approach on which we build in our work. Similarly, Otchere and Oldford (2011) compare operating performances across a sample of mutually-owned, demutualized and privately-owned exchanges focusing on measures of performances such as RoA and RoE.

We have, then, complemented the analysis by modeling a *risk-based metric* for stock exchange performance aimed at capturing the implications of risk exposure on value. Here we have built on the capital-based performance literature. Capital-based metrics are of course a key tool for business management in financial institutions, and to that end they may serve a variety of purposes (James, 1996), including the management of the corporate leverage and risk–return assessments. This approach allows for treating an exchange as a portfolio of businesses in which the contribution of each business unit to the overall portfolio risk can be estimated, and the corresponding capital at corporate level can be defined and then allocated to the different units (Zaik et al., 1996). Capital assignment here is part of a system of computing a risk-adjusted rate of return for different businesses with the aim of measuring their contribution to value creation.

Our analysis may have several implications along a variety of dimensions related to the management of stock exchanges. First of all, it could usefully support the valuation of exchanges in M&As and the definition of the terms of the deal. On the other hand, assuming an industrial organization perspective, it would be useful in supporting strategic decision making with reference to those choices related to geographical diversification or to the addition of new product lines (developed internally or acquired on the market). Finally, our approach will have obvious implications for the corporate governance of the exchange. In fact, deriving RAP measures would help the top management in setting performance targets to each business unit according to the risks entailed, and monitoring deviation from those targets.

This chapter is mainly conceptual, in that it provides a theoretical ground for value creation and measurement in the exchange industry. Notwithstanding that, it will provide some evidence as well. The chapter is organized as follows. In Section 2 we discuss some relevant issues related to the economics of exchanges; in Section 3 we define the cost and revenue functions of exchanges and discuss the value drivers in the exchange industry; this section sets out the building blocks that we will use for defining our model. Section 4 provides the basic model for analyzing the performances and risks relating to exchanges; here we start by developing an accounting measure of operative performance based on the Roce. In Section 5 we provide some evidence on the relations between revenues and market activity of the main listed exchanges. Section 6 concludes.

2 Value creation for exchanges: the traditional tale and what is missing

Almost all securities exchanges around the world are managed as organizations that are privately owned for profit; many of them are listed companies engaged in value creation for shareholders. This objective function has been widely used to explain recent developments in the securities industry; for many years the competitive policies of exchanges have been targeted to reinforce consolidation in the securities industry. So the basic arguments accompanying the strategic choices of exchanges focus on cost and revenue functions.

The rationale of mergers in the exchange industry lies in the features of cost functions. More precisely, the problem could be stated as follows.

> *Proposition 1 – As stock exchanges operate largely with fixed-cost functions, mergers would be a compelling need in order to achieve cost efficiencies.*

Building on the dataset of the Federation of European Securities Exchanges (FESE), we aim to give some degree of concrete character to this proposition. In particular, we consider revenues and costs for 25 securities exchanges, including exchanges belonging to transatlantic groups. For the latter, we consider the data related to European operations, over a time span of nine years, from 2002 to 2010.[3]

From a methodological point of view, we define a linear relation between costs and revenues, and regress the former on the latter in order to provide an estimate of the fixed and variable components of costs. The function is $C = \alpha + \beta \cdot Rev$ where C is the costs and *Rev* denotes the revenues. Table 10.1 summarizes the main results, showing the parameters α and β, the *r-square* and the relative standard deviation for costs and revenues.

Evidences are quite mixed across exchanges. The data show a well defined linear relation between costs and revenues, as implied by the high values for *r-square*. The β parameter expressing the incidence of variable costs varies across exchanges, but is generally low with an average value which equals 0.3386 and a median value of 0.325. We then observe that the *relative standard deviations* for costs are generally lower than those for revenues. These patterns confirm the prevalent feature of a fixed cost business for managing securities exchanges.

Nowadays the main competitive advantage for exchanges derives from the efficiency of the trading platforms that claim large investments in technology while their marginal costs from increasing trading volumes are negligible. Cost efficiencies are of course strongly recommended in order to help counteract the ever more aggressive competition from the alternative trading systems operating with lower costs than traditional exchanges.

Value creation is, then, the function of risks. The main source of risk entailed in exchange business, which we may define as *operational risk*, is related to the volatility of revenues. Since revenues are function of trading volumes, which are typically dependent on the cycle, stock exchanges are forced to diversify their business model. This is consistent with securities exchanges, at least those listed, organizing themselves into large conglomerate groups.

Table 10.1 The relation between costs and revenues

Exchange	R^2	α	β	*Rsd Rev.*	Rsd Costs
Athens Exchange	0.7881	19.685	0.1465	0.4	0.2
Bolsas Y Mercados Españoles (BME)	0.6239	76.401	0.0731	0.3	0.1
Bratislava Stock Exchange	0.7334	0.5689	0.5642	0.2	0.1
Bucharest Stock Exchange	0.814	1.1123	0.3092	0.7	0.5
Budapest Stock Exchange	0.9221	1.5791	0.4138	0.3	0.3
Bulgarian Stock Exchange	0.507	0.6395	0.3415	0.7	0.5
Cyprus Stock Exchange	0.0085	5.8724	0.0372	0.4	0.2
Deutsche Börse Group	0.7996	744.03	0.2025	0.2	0.1
ICE Futures Europe	0.7164	23.429	0.1174	0.6	0.2
Irish Stock Exchange	0.8563	1.8276	0.5954	0.3	0.3
Ljubljana Stock Exchange	0.5577	1.8552	0.2415	0.3	0.1
London Metal Exchange	0.817	12.418	0.4393	0.3	0.2
Luxembourg Stock Exchange	0.9532	5.183	0.5159	0.2	0.1
Malta Stock Exchange	0.856	0.7545	0.4593	0.1	0.1
Nasdaq Omx Group	0.5486	143.89	1.0868	0.2	0.4
Prague Stock Exchange	0.3823	4.6618	0.3945	0.1	0.2
Swiss Exchange	0.2569	254.85	–0.3158[4]	0.1	0.1
Warsaw Exchange	0.4182	13.678	0.242	0.1	0.2
Wiener Börse	0.8739	13.415	0.2572	0.2	0.1
Nyse Euronext	0.557	0.8539	0.65	0.3	0.7

Proposition 2 – Business diversification results in exchanges stabilizing their revenues. In particular, derivatives trading is seen as a countercyclical business. Moreover, business diversification would be beneficial for exchange performances.

As the evidence suggests, the main exchanges could be seen as portfolios of different value-generating activities. Cash markets sometimes take a relatively lesser role, as complementary activities (such as post-trading and data sales) become increasingly important. However there is no clear understanding on how these activities affect the economics of the trading industry. In other words, in multi-business exchanges pricing a service not only depends on the elasticity of demand for that service but also is conditional on the demand for complementary services. The most obvious case is the relation between listing and trading services, the typical activities for a stock exchange, which can be analyzed within the *two-sided markets* framework (Rochet and Tirole, 2006).

Proposition 3 – Listing and trading activities entail cross-networks effects, as exchanges need to attract issuers in order to attract order flow on those stocks.

At the same time, capturing order flow, giving rise to liquid securities markets, is crucial for attracting listings.

It should be expected that the maximization problem for securities exchanges is affected by these cross-effects. Competing on the listing side could result in pressures on trading revenues, and this may explain why derivatives markets generally present greater margins (Cantillon and Yin, 2011). Similarly, in two-sided markets there is also an interdependence of risks. Even though in several exchanges listing revenues present a low incidence in total revenues, changes in issuers' preferences may negatively affect trading revenues. So the cost of capital should be different across different business models.

In terms of strategic management, the above-mentioned features of exchange business carry relevant implications with them. We start by defining the production function of a securities exchange focused on traditional business (that is, listing services and trading services). At first, the exchange defines the technology, which comprises listing standards, the trading platform and the trading rules. Then the exchange admits issuers to listing; at that point, information is the fundamental input of the production process, whereas the output is reflected in the number of companies listed. Then trading begins; at that point, the inputs are the orders delivered by market participants which, through the technology employed (platform and trading rules), give rise to the output (namely, the trades which could be measured in terms of trading volume).

The problem for the exchange management is to make a strategic choice of both the technology and the price schedule for its services. It is generally acknowledged that competition takes place on the technology side; strict admission standards, in particular, would raise the reputation of the exchange and succeed in attracting issuers. This view is well established in the theoretical literature. On the other hand, the effects of increasing competition, from alternative trading systems in particular, are to claim high-quality trading platforms. In our view, the most compelling challenge for exchanges is to attract a strong issuer base; this would enable the exchange to set trading fees and sustain the investments needed in order to develop efficient trading platforms.

For the sake of completeness, it should be noted that in many exchanges business units such as derivatives trading and post-trading have greater margins than cash trading. Moreover, the market has been seemingly benign in valuing the consolidation process in the industry, as implicitly suggested by some high multiples in previous mergers.

However, there is no evidence of overall greater efficiency for conglomerate exchanges. What is missing is an in-depth analysis of either the cost or revenue functions of stock exchanges; in particular, there is no clear understanding of the factors impacting on revenue dynamics. On cost structure, a deeper understanding of the magnitude of both fixed and variable costs is required.

Assuming a managerial perspective would have relevant implications for strategic planning. In fact, while it permits diversification of revenues, business diversification may induce increasing complexity at corporate level. Moreover, business expansion requires the allocation of capital to each business unit. Indeed, principles of capital management do not constitute a well established field of research in studies related to the exchange industry, as they do in the banking sector. However, applying certain well known methodologies in bank capital management would be supportive of efficient decision making in terms of risk management and pricing of risk.

To that end, the main developments in economics of exchanges would be the setting out of principles for efficient capital budgeting, based on the following steps: the measurement of capital absorbed at business unit level, the allocation of capital; and the definition of a target rate of return coherent with the risks involved by each business unit. This approach requires two problems to be overcome: the first being the provision of a *capital at risk measure,* and the second the definition of an appropriate methodology for estimating the cost of capital.

3 The value drivers for exchanges

The description of the economics of exchanges required us to specify the sources of value in the exchange industry. To accomplish this task we identified the industry-specific sources of value. Methodologically, we followed a top–down approach by defining a framework in which exchange outputs are dependent on macroeconomic developments; building on that framework we then modeled the revenue and cost functions of exchanges.

As noted in the previous section, exchanges have the features of two-sided platforms, as they accommodate two types of customer: listed companies and traders. Their output may be measured in terms of the number of companies listed and the value of trading on the two respective sides. On a theoretical basis, Otchere's study (2006) stressed the relevance of volumes of market activity on the basis of the relation between value creation and governance arrangements. In particular, he pointed out that exchanges with slow-growing profits but with strong dynamics in market activity are likely to go public. Others streams of literature which assume the same perspective stress the relevance of market activity for value creation.

As in the extant literature, our main variables were the value of share trading and the number of companies listed as value drivers for securities exchanges. Incidentally, this approach, which is shared by investors, financial analysts and rating agencies,[5] is of interest, in that it permitted us to explore the relations between market activity and the dynamics of the economic cycle, thus creating endogenous macroeconomic conditions in the process of creating value. By adopting a top–down approach we first explored such relations; then we modeled the relations between liquidity measures and revenues. We are aware that in today's exchange industry the business of running securities exchanges goes well beyond the mere supply of listing services and management of cash markets; service revenues, for example, are becoming even more important. However, in our stylized model we chose to focus on a simple business model consisting in listing and cash trading. Our purpose, in fact, was to set down the conceptual framework of a risk-based approach for measuring performance.

The exchange business is regarded as a cyclical business. Economic growth, in fact, affects the decisions of both issuers and investors. The former seek equity or debt financing when they have viable investment projects to support. Traders' market activity, on the other hand, is mainly driven by their risk attitude; during periods of high market volatility and uncertainty trading volumes flatten. GDP and corporate earnings expectations should, therefore, play a relevant role in driving the behavior of issuers and traders. Obviously, the economic cycle is not the only driver of market activity; at a microeconomic level, the ability to attract either issuers and traders depends on a variety of features, such as the reputation of the exchange, its competitive positioning, the efficiency of its trading platforms and the design of its price schedule.

The macroeconomic environment is, then, related to the dynamics in interest rates and, in particular, the yield curve. We expect the yield curve to affect the valuation of an exchange through the standard impact on discounted cash flows and its relation with economic cycle; for example, an inverted yield curve is generally associated with expectations of an economic downturn which, in turn, would of course have a negative impact on the turnover of the exchange, and therefore on expected revenues.

According to the previous observations, we may define the exchange output as a linear function of the GDP, the corporate earnings and the yield curve. Equation (10.1) expresses the relation.

$$TV, L = \alpha + \beta_{Gdp} \cdot GDP + \beta_E . E + \beta_y \cdot Y \tag{10.1}$$

where *TV* is the trading values and *L* is the number of companies listed,[6] *E* identifies the corporate earnings and *Yield* expresses the yield curve.

Since exchanges typically operate as multi-business companies, we should investigate the relations between different business units. This is an approach we adopted widely throughout the chapter in defining our risk-based model for measuring performances.

In particular we modeled a simplified business model focusing on listings and trading on cash markets in which revenues are function of the outputs of the exchange business and prices. The outputs are the number of listed companies, which we denote with *L*, and the trading volumes, which we denote with *TV*, and could more properly be interpreted as the value of share trading.

To express the interrelations between business units we accordingly modeled trading values as a function of the number of companies listed. We define the following linear function:

$$TV = \alpha_1 + \beta_1 L \tag{10.2}$$

According to Equation (10.2), the value of equity trading is dependent on the parameter $\beta 1$, which we can see as the marginal increase in trading value as L increases. We can think of this variable as dependent on the production technology which we may identify with the cross-externalities that the exchange may develop across business units, and on its reputation. Another factor which may impact on the coefficient is related to the type of companies listed, in terms of size and liquidity. In light of the theory of network economies, we may expect highly liquid companies to attract higher volumes of share trading.

We may now continue by introducing the revenue function for securities exchanges. Given our previous analysis, we may express revenues as dependent on the dynamics in listed companies and value of trading – which, in turn, are a function of the macroeconomic environment and the prevailing conditions on financial markets. Accordingly, we may define total revenues as the sum of listing revenues and trading revenues:

$$\mathrm{Re}\,v_{Tot} = L_{\mathrm{Re}\,v}(Gdp, E, Yield) + CT_{\mathrm{Re}\,v}(Gdp, E, Yield) \tag{10.3}$$

The next step was to characterize in more detail both the listing and trading revenues and the relations between them. More precisely, we modeled the cross externalities between business units. We express listing services revenues as a linear relation with the number of companies listed:

$$L_{\mathrm{Re}\,v}(GDP, E, Yield) = \vartheta + \nu L \tag{10.4}$$

We also assumed a linear function between cash trading revenues (CT_{Rev}) and trading volumes. Therefore, the function could be expressed as follows:

$$CT_{\mathrm{Re}\,v}(GDP, E, Yield) = \alpha_{TV} + \beta_{TV} TV \tag{10.5}$$

Consistent with our approach in modeling the relations between different business units we draw on Equation (10.2) in order to express cash trading revenues as a function of the number of companies listed. Accordingly, we define the following linear relation between trading revenues and primary market activity:

$$CT_{\mathrm{Re}\,v} = \alpha_L + \beta_L L \tag{10.6}$$

A comment is needed on the variables θ, α_{TV} and α_L and β_L in the above equations. These items could be seen as expressive of fixed revenues. In particular, θ could be seen as annual fees paid to the exchange by listed firms, whereas α_{TV} could reflect the fees paid by intermediaries for the right to use exchange platforms. But in fact, the exchange pricing schedules often set these fees up in different ways; for example, security exchanges may adopt either a flat trading fee based on volumes or a regressive pricing structure. But whatever the specific pricing schedule, such fees are variable. As for the other coefficients, α_L could be seen, like θ, as a membership fee, and we may in fact assume the two coefficients to be equal. On the other hand, β_L expresses the marginal increases in trading revenues as the number of listed companies increases. In that aspect, it has the same conceptual meaning as β_1 in Equation (10.2), and its value is dependent on the production technology and the reputation of the exchange.

However, the magnitude of the two coefficients may be quite different from one another. The increase in trading revenues as the number of listed companies increases may slow down when the exchange faces high levels of competition. Actually, it is reasonable to assume that β_1 and β_L vary with volumes according to the levels of competition and the competitive policies of the exchange. For example, as competitive pressures rise, the exchange may be forced to cut fees in order to expand trading volumes. As a result the relation between trading values and revenues may substantially weaken. We will return later, when discussing the cost function, to the business risk of losing revenues and its impact on the operative leverage.

For the moment, though, we need to clarify how cross-network effects may drive across business units. According to the previous discussion, network externalities between trading services and listing services may be defined in the following terms. A high sensitivity of TV on L may imply that competition on listing services is effective. If this were to be the case, lower marginal cash trading revenues for an increase in TV could reflect a strategic choice by the exchange to compete on listings. Moving the reasoning forward, we now define a model for measuring cross-effects. Let us suppose that the exchange only provides cash trading services; revenues would then be defined according to Equation (10.5). As the exchange adds listing services to its business model we may express cash trading revenues by combining Equations (10.2) and (10.5) into the following:

$$CT_{rev}(L) = \alpha_{TV} + \beta_{TV}(\alpha_1 + \beta_1 L) \tag{10.7}$$

We can say that the cross-effects (on the cash trading side) are produced if marginal revenues are greater when combining listing and trading services, compared with a mono-business exchange. Therefore the following condition has to hold:

$$\frac{dCT_{Rev}(TV)}{dTV} < \frac{dCT_{Rev}(L)}{dl}$$

which means that $\beta_{TV} < \beta_1\beta_{TV}$. We may perceive the right-hand term of that expression as a measure of market power; it is clear that the greater the β_1, the greater the stream of liquidity (measured by the value of equity trading) gained by the exchange. Arguably, the exchange may become a price setter as regards the pricing schedule for trades taking place on its platforms. This means that it may have the power to set β_{TV}.

Obviously, it would be possible to measure cross-effects on the listing side. It means investigating the return effect of increases in trading volumes on the issuers' choices, and also the ability of the exchange to extract rents on listings as more issuers choose to be listed on that exchange. In the context of the present study we do not, however, address that issue; since listing revenues tend to become an ever lower portion of total revenues, in large conglomerate exchanges at least, we assume that we may reasonably neglect it. Rather, we assume as more appropriate a setting in which exchanges compete in listings (through primary standards and raising their reputational capital) in order to gain power on trading side.

The characterization of the revenue function in multi-business exchanges is more complex. In order to accomplish this task, we need to identify and measure the typical output for each business line and find a relation with the revenues relating to that business. For the sake of simplicity, here we are considering only listing and (cash) trading services. As we have noted in the previous section, listing revenues are sensitive to the number of companies listed according to a consistent linear relation.

Finally, we have to derive a cost function. As stated in the previous section, the evidence suggests a defined linear relation between revenues and costs. Therefore, we express the cost function as: $c = \alpha + \beta \, Rev$, where the intercept α represents fixed costs and the coefficient β captures variable costs. Recalling the formulation of revenues, as in Equations (10.4) and (10.5), costs become a function of the number of companies listed and the trading values: $c = \alpha + \beta(\theta + \vartheta L + \alpha_{Ty} + \beta_{Ty} Tn) = \alpha + \beta[\theta + \vartheta L + \alpha_{Ty} + \beta_{Ty}(\alpha_1 + \beta_1 L)]$. Costs, therefore, depend on the productive factors and the production technology employed by the platform operator.

The relative magnitude of both fixed and variable costs assumes particular relevance, since it has implications for the operative leverage. The development and setup of trading platforms, together with the organizational arrangements for performing the monitoring functions that are entrusted to exchanges, imply relevant costs which are substantially fixed. Notwithstanding that, securities exchanges often reward liquidity traders with rebates. Such cost items are dependent on trading volumes and, therefore, are variable at most.

In fact, liquidity rebates are a relevant tool for pricing the competition alongside trading fees, at least for certain exchanges. The combination of trading fees and rebates may have different impacts on the economics of exchanges. Where cuts in trading fees may turn out to weaken the relation between trading volumes and revenues, putting pressures on margins, high liquidity rebates may alter the relative magnitude of both fixed and variable costs, at least to some extent. In turn, changes in the operative leverage alter the impact on margins for a given variation in revenues.

Starting from cost and revenues functions, we define the main risks that exchanges are exposed to. In particular, we refer to the *business risk* and the *financial risk*. We encompass those kinds of risk within the concept of leverage, which may, in turn, be broken down into *operative leverage* and *financial leverage*.

We recall that operative leverage is: $Ol = \frac{(\mathrm{Re}\,v - \beta \mathrm{Re}\,v}{(1-\beta)\mathrm{Re}\,v -}$ or $Ol = \frac{(1-\beta)\mathrm{Re}\,v}{(1-\beta)\mathrm{Re}\,v - \alpha}$.

Given the formulation of our revenue function, the operative leverage is a function of market volumes on both primary and secondary markets, $Ol = f(L, Tv)$, and decreases with increases in the number of companies listed and trading volumes. Everything else being equal, we expect exchanges to reduce their operative leverage during the upward phases of the cycle and, in contrast, to expand it during downturns. Therefore, volatility in margins would also be reduced in good times and increased in bad. However, the magnitude of the operative leverage varies with other factors as well, such as the measure of both fixed and variable costs and also the coefficients expressing fixed and variable revenues that are implicit in the above-mentioned expressions of the operative leverage. Given the role of both fixed and variable costs, we draw your attention to the incidence of the factors impacting on the revenues; should the competitive landscape force the exchanges to cut their fees (in particular trading fees), breaking the link between revenues and market outputs (in particular reducing the coefficients β_{Tv} and β_1) as defined above, we expect the leverage to decline as a result of a reduced responsiveness of the revenues to the outputs.

The financial leverage, on the other hand, apparently poses particular problems for those exchanges moving forward with sizeable acquisitions, as shown by the recent consolidation process.

On grounds of the risks expressed above, in the next section we will develop an accounting measure of operative performance. In particular, we derive measures of profitability in terms of return on capital employed (Roce) and return on equity (RoE).

Business and financial risks have not been widely investigated so far. However they are of major concern for securities exchanges, in particular for their value implications. In such a context, we aim to develop a model for measuring risk adjusted performances and their relations with value creation in the securities industry..

4 The model

In this section, we have provided the basic model for analyzing the performance of exchanges. First we build on the relations we have sketched in the previous section, in order to derive a comprehensive revenue function. Then we model a performance measure to unravel the main levers that create value for shareholders.

If we take into account the cross-effects between listing services and trading services, we may express total revenues as function of either L or TV. If we assume an exchange exploiting the cross-effects on trading services, we may define revenues as a function of the number issuer listed:

$$\mathrm{Re}\,v_{tot} = \theta + \vartheta L + \alpha_{TV} + \beta_{TV} TV = \theta + \vartheta L + \alpha_{TV} + \beta_{TV}(\alpha_1 + \beta_1 L) \tag{10.8}$$

and, rearranging, we obtain $Rev_{Tot} = \theta + \alpha_{Tv} + \beta_{Tv}\alpha_1 + (\vartheta + \beta_{TV}\beta_1)L$ or simply $Rev_{Tot} = \tau + \omega L$, where τ is the sum of fixed factors, and $v = \vartheta + \beta_{T_v} + \beta_1$ is the sum of the variable factors. We therefore assume a model in which exchanges compete on listings in order to increase overall revenues.

Defining total revenues in terms of number of companies listed is then useful in that this permits us to make explicit the impact of the number of companies listed on cash trading revenues. In order to measure this impact, we derive the cash trading revenues per unit of listing revenues, dividing Equation (10.7) by Equation (10.4). This expresses the amount of trading revenues yielded by one unit of listing revenues, and may be seen as a proxy of potential synergies between listing services and trading services. We thus obtain:

$$Rev_{CTu} = \frac{\alpha_{T_v} + \beta_{T_v}(\alpha_1 + \beta_1 L)}{\theta + \vartheta L} \tag{10.9}$$

where $\mathrm{Re}\,\omega_{CTu}$ is the cash trading revenues per unit of listing revenues.

We are now ready to define performances in terms of *return on capital employed* (*Roce*), thus:

$$Roce = \frac{Ebit}{Ce} \tag{10.10}$$

where *Ce* denotes the *capital employed*. Making reference to this indicator, we can express the performance as a function of the intensity of capital, business risk and financial structure. Expressing costs as (linear) function of revenues, $C = \alpha - \beta \mathrm{Re}v$, we may define Ebit as $Ebit = (1-\beta)\mathrm{Re}v - \alpha$, and Equation (10.10) then yields:

$$Roce = \frac{(1-\beta)\mathrm{Re}\omega - \alpha}{Ce} \tag{10.11}$$

Recalling the formulation of revenues we obtain: $Roce = \dfrac{(1-\beta)[\tau + \varphi L] - \alpha}{Ce}$

or, rearranging, $Roce - \dfrac{(\tau - \alpha) + \varphi L(1-\beta) - \beta\tau}{Ce}$. Focusing on the numerator, Roce is a function of three terms: the first, $(\tau - \alpha)$, is the difference between fixed revenues and fixed costs; the second expresses variable revenues net of variable costs; and the third is a residual item. Given τ and α, and neglecting β (which for several exchanges assumes low values), Roce is an increasing function of L and ω which, as noted, can be assumed as a measure of market power for the exchange.

Rearranging the terms on the right-hand side, we may obtain a modified version of Equation (10.11) which will be useful in capturing the effects on performances deriving from risks involved in the management of exchanges. In order to capture the overall exposure of exchanges to the business risk, we rewrite the numerator in Equation (10.10) in terms of *operative leverage*. Expressing revenues as function of L, we obtain: $Ol = \dfrac{(1-\beta)(\tau + \varphi L)}{(1-\beta)(\tau + \varphi L) - \alpha}$.

Then by rearranging the terms in Equation (10.11) we obtain:

$$Roce = \frac{(\mathrm{Re}\,v - \beta)}{Ce} \cdot \frac{1}{ol}$$

We may, then, obtain the return on equity based on the previous measure of Roce and the financial leverage:

$$Roe = Roce + [Roce - K_d] \cdot Fl \tag{10.12}$$

where K_d is the cost of debt (net of taxes) and Fl is the financial leverage that we may express as $\dfrac{Ebit}{NetIncome}$. Equation (10.12) could then be expressed as follows:

$$Roe = \frac{\mathrm{Re}\,v - \beta}{Ce} \cdot \frac{1}{Ol} + \frac{\mathrm{Re}\,v - \beta}{Ce} \cdot \frac{Fl}{Ol} - kd.Fl$$

The equation above expresses the profitability of exchanges in terms of the three main strategic areas, namely: business structure, financial structure and capital management. More precisely, business structure is dependent on costs and revenues functions, and defines the operative leverage; at this level, the main risks are related to the effects stemming from declining market activity and to losses in the number of companies listed which, in turn, puts pressures on revenues. Moreover, changes in the industry structure may play an important part. Such changes may have an impact on the marginal revenues through changes in those variables (θ, β_L, β_{TV}) that convert a marginal increase in L or TV in revenues. For example, the success of alternative systems in stealing large flows of liquidity from established exchanges may force widespread price cuts. All other things being equal (in particular, the cost structure of the exchange), the operative leverage would increase.

The financial risk refers to the risks inherent in the financial structure of the exchange. In particular, we expect the financial risk to be particularly compelling for those exchanges moving forward with sizeable acquisitions supported by an increased recourse to debt financing. Moving forward, we define a capital management framework for exchanges. We think of this metric as an useful decision tool for managing risks and measuring performance in different strategic business units (SBUs). Similarly, it would be useful to drive capital allocation to each business unit. We do this by modeling a *risk-adjusted performance (RAP)* metric for stock exchange performance. This is a quite new approach in stock exchange management, although some exchanges are already adopting certain metrics for measuring risk. Considering the exchange as a portfolio of different business units, we first derive a *Rap* metric at business-unit level.

An useful starting point is to define a risk-adjusted measure for the earnings. For a multi-business exchange, the determination of such a measure at a SBU level would help the management gain better insight into the economics of each business unit, driving the relevant strategic choices. We express earnings adjusted for risk as $Ebit - n\sigma(Ebit_i)$, where i denotes the *i-th* business unit and $n\sigma Ebit$ is the *earnings at risk (Ear)*. Assuming a normal distribution for the Ebit and n=3, this means covering potential losses up to 99.7 per cent of cases. Further, we may derive the exchange's *capital at risk* just by calculating the present value of such a rent at an appropriate *risk-free* rate. Formally: $Car = \dfrac{n\sigma(Ebit)}{i}$.

For multi-business exchanges, it becomes imperative to measure the capital absorbed at corporate level. When thus deriving the cost of capital we must obviously take the effect of correlations between single business units into consideration. According to the traditional tale, business diversification would reduce overall risk by assuming a reduced correlation between cash trading and other businesses (mainly derivatives trading). We may formally express the earnings at risk at a corporate level as follows:

$$Ear_c = \sum_{i=1}^{n} Ear_i + \sigma(Ear)_{i,j} \tag{10.13}$$

where $\sigma(Ear)_{i,j}$ is the covariance between the *Ears* of the *i-th* and *j-th* business unit. From Equation (10.13) we obtain the capital at risk at a corporate level:

$$Car_c \frac{Ear_c}{i} = \frac{\sum_{i=1}^{n} n\sigma(Ebit)_i + \sigma(Ebit)_{i,j}}{i}$$

Knowing the capital at risk, at either a business-unit or a corporate level, will help the management in its strategic decision making process, allowing it to monitor the risks entailed by the business and the capital absorbed, and to set targets in terms of risk-adjusted return. However, we may think of capital management in two possible ways: the first is to measure the capital absorbed by the business and the return on that capital; the second is to assign an explicit limit to the capital absorbed by each unit.

We are now able to derive a risk-adjusted performance measure that we can define in terms of *risk-adjusted performance on risk-adjusted capital*. Engaging in exchange business absorbs resources which should be rewarded by adequate remuneration. (Resources comprise human capital, intangibles and the capital allocated against business risk.) Therefore, the price schedule should be defined in order to remunerate both the production inputs and the cost of the economic capital. More precisely, we express these metric for the *i-th* business unit in terms of expected return and capital at risk. Formally:

$$\overline{Raroc_i} = \frac{E(R_i)}{Car_i} \tag{10.14}$$

where $E(R_i)$ is the expected return for the *i-th* business unit and Car_i is the capital at risk of that SBU. In more detail, we may express the minimum expected return in terms of the cost of capital Ke_i for the *i-th* business unit: $\overline{Raroc_i} = \frac{Ke_i car}{Car_i}$. Therefore, the $\overline{Raroc}$ expresses the minimum target risk-adjusted return in order to create value for shareholders.

Posing the problem in these terms, a business unit becomes profitable when it yields a return which at least equals the opportunity cost of the capital allocated to that unit. In particular, we may think of the cost of capital as a function of a combination of different economic and market variables (for example, earnings per share, number of listed companies, value of share trading and the operative leverage).

An obvious extension of the model is to apply the portfolio theory to the strategic management of exchanges. Treating the exchange as a portfolio of different strategic business units implies consideration of the contribution of each business unit to both the yield and the risk of the portfolio. Formally, we may define a *Rap* measure at a corporate level as a linear function of the performance of each business unit and the cross-selling opportunities. Formally:

$$Rarorac_c = \sum_{i=1}^{n} x_i \cdot Rarorac_i + \beta\gamma_{i,j} \tag{10.15}$$

where $Rarorac_C$ is the corporate's Rarorac,[7] $Rarorac_i$ is the risk-adjusted return for the *i-th* business unit, x_i is the weight of the *i-th* business unit which, may be intended as the capital invested on that unit, and finally $\gamma_{i,j}$ is a term expressing the return from cross-selling opportunities between the two business units *i* and *j*. This return could be seen as the ratio between cross-selling opportunities and the capital at risk. Indeed, this term would reflect the synergies stemming from combining different business units.

Moving on, along with the reasoning, the model we propose represents a different way of assessing the consolidation process in the securities industry, resulting, in almost all cases, in large conglomerate groups with a diversified business model and diversified geographical extension.

So far, the prevailing theoretical contributions have addressed the problem of assessing efficiency for diversified exchanges adopting either a concept of *technical efficiency* or *economic efficiency* based on a simple Ebit measure. We will now, however, express the economics of exchanges in a slightly different way. In particular, we define the performance of the exchange (or of each business unit) in terms of *value added* (VA), which could be expressed as follows:

$$VA = (\overline{Rarorac} - K_a) \cdot Ca \tag{10.6}$$

When *Rarorac* equals the cost of capital, the *value added* clearly becomes null. If we reason at a SBU level, this therefore represents a cut-off value for the acceptability of an investment project (such as adding a new business unit). However, the management may define a certain minimum threshold for the *value added* attributable to a particular unit. In this case, expanding the business model by adding a new SBU turns out to be a rational choice as far as the value added exceeds this threshold. If we imagine a value added target at a corporate level, this has implications relevant to the behavior of the exchange. Let suppose that the management sets a minimum target, $\overline{VA}$, for the value added. Therefore, the exchange has to obtain a Rarorac that satisfies the following: $\overline{VA} = (Rarorac - Ke)Car$. So the following has to hold:

$$Raroc > \frac{\overline{VA}}{car} + Ke \tag{10.17}$$

Since Rarorac is the expected return divided by Car, if we multiply each member by Car, then Equation (10.17) yields $E(R) > \overline{VA} + KeCar$, where E(R) is the minimum level of the expected return coherent with the VA target.

Defining the problem of value creation in terms of a *Rarorac* measure as above, requires a focus on two related issues: the first is the definition of an appropriate measure for the cost of capital; the second relates to the pricing policies of exchanges. To measure the cost of capital we should take into consideration the entire business structure of the exchange. Our hypothesis is that the cost of capital is dependent on certain variables capturing economic performance (for example, total revenues, Ebit, earning per share), risks and some market variables.

In particular, we model the cost of capital as function of the Ebit, trading volumes, operative and financial leverage and yield curve. Formally, the relation is as follows: $K_e = \alpha + \gamma_1 Ebit + \gamma_2 TV + \gamma_3 Ol + \gamma_4 Fl + \gamma_5 yield$. We expect both the Ebit and the trading volumes to have an inverse impact on the cost of capital, at least as long as increases in volumes reinforce the competitive positioning of exchanges and lead revenues to rise. Alternatively, we might have used a measure of economic activity such as the GDP instead of the trading volumes, since in our model the outputs from the exchanges are dependent on the cycle. Increasing competition, however, may lead (as is happening in today's exchange industry, as at the time of writing, in early 2013) to aggressive pricing policies which may turn out to exert pressures on margins. Operative and financial leverage captures the business and financial risks that exchanges are exposed to; we expect them to have a direct impact on the cost of capital. The yield curve captures the risk of cyclical downturns which would adversely impact outputs and revenues.

Our model requires an in-depth analysis of the pricing behavior by the exchanges. Broadly speaking, the price (for both listing services and trading services) should cover fixed costs, marginal costs and the cost of economic capital. As we have seen, marginal costs for an additional unit of output are expected to be negligible once the exchange has set all the infrastructures (rules, standards and trading platforms) required to run the business. Therefore, we can express revenues as follows:

$$\tau + \beta_{TV}(\alpha_1 + \beta_1 L) = \alpha + \beta[\tau + \beta_{TV}(\alpha_1 + \beta_1 L)] + Kecar \qquad (10.18)$$

Positing $E(R) = \mathrm{Re}v - Costs = Kecar$, in order to satisfy Equation (10.17) the following have to hold: $(\mathrm{Re}v - Costs) > \overline{VA} + Kecar$. Building on Equation (10.18), this means:

$$\tau + \beta_{TV}(\alpha_1 + \beta_1 L) - \alpha - \beta[\tau + \beta_{TV}(\alpha_1 + \beta_1 L)] > \overline{VA} + Kecar \qquad (10.19)$$

Equation (10.18) is useful insofar as it permits us to define the revenues and costs function of the number of companies listed. In turn, we may derive the pricing policies of the exchange in order to satisfy Equation (10.19). To that end, we assume the cost structure of the exchange as given – and, therefore, the weight of both fixed and variable costs. As for revenues, we may also assume as given the items expressing fixed revenues, such as the fees paid by intermediaries for the right to use trading platforms and the annual fees paid by issuers. Finally, we assume β_1 as a variable not directly under the control of the exchange. We can think of that variable as dependent on the production technology of the exchange and, to a considerable extent, on the reputation of the exchange. Therefore, the exchange chooses β_{Tv} which reflects the pricing schedule for the trades taking place on its platforms. We derive the value of such a variable in order to satisfy Equation (10.19):

$$\beta^{*}_{Tv} > \frac{\overline{VA} + KeCar + (\alpha - \tau)}{(\alpha_1 + \beta_1 L)(1 - \beta)} \tag{10.20}$$

Assuming a broader perspective, a risk-adjusted performance metric might be used for other purposes – specifically within the internal control function and when managing business combinations between exchanges.

To that end, the metrics we have presented may be useful for defining the *fair value* of the exchange on the occasion of an eventual business combination. More precisely, we may derive from a *Rap* measure the value that a bidder would be willing to pay to acquire a portfolio of activities, given the yield and risks of that portfolio. This is a different way of assessing the value of exchanges. So far, the issue of the value of exchanges in mergers has been addressed by observing the implied multiples in merger agreements and comparing those multiples with market multiples. Building on Equation (10.15) we derive the Rarorac for the exchange target as it was combined with the exchange bidder; in other words, it represents the risk-adjusted performance that the target company would yield to the bidder, taking into account the synergies between the two parts.

$$Rarorac_{Tc} = Rarorac_{T} + \gamma_{T,B} \tag{10.21}$$

Whereas $Rarorac_{Tc}$ is the risk-adjusted performance of the exchange target assuming a combination with the bidder, $Rarorac_{T}$ is the performance of the exchange target considered as *stand alone*, and $\gamma_{T,B}$ are the synergies potentially stemming from the combination. We may, then, derive the cost of capital for the exchange target under the combination agreement. More precisely, this would reflect the risks of the exchange for the bidder, and it is a function of the correlation with the other value-generating activities of the enlarged group. Formally:

$$Ke_{Tc} = Rarorac_{Tc} \cdot Car_{Tc} \tag{10.22}$$

where Ke_{Tc} is the cost of capital for the exchange target assuming the perspective of the bidder and Car_{Tc} is the capital absorbed by the exchange under the combination agreement; it is a function of the contribution of the exchange target to the overall risk of the overall group. Defining the cost of capital for the exchange target under the bidder's point of view, we may derive the value that the bidder would be willing to pay by discounting expected earnings (comprising the effect of synergies) at that cost of capital.

5 Some evidence

The purpose of this section is to provide some evidence across the main listed exchanges as to the relations between market activity measures (listed companies and trading values) and exchange revenues. From a methodological point of view, we performed a quarterly analysis of the exchanges considered for the period 2007–2011. Following our top–down approach, we started by providing evidence on the relations between trading volumes, macroeconomic dynamics (expressed by the GDP), evolutions in corporate

Table 10.2 Trading volumes, GDP, yield curve and price-to-earnings ratio

Nasdaq	**TV**	**GDP**	**10y2y**	**P/E**	**Nyse Euronext (US markets)**	**TV**	**GDP**	**10y2y**	**P/E**
TV	1				TV	1			
GDP	0.7113	1			GDP	0.7211	1		
10y2y	–0.0507	–0.0248	1		10y2y	–0.4771	–0.0248	1	
P/E	–0.0939	0.0206	0.3914	1	P/E	–0.2331	0.0206	0.3914	1
Tmx	TV	GDP	10y2y	P/E	LSEG	TV	GDP	10y2y	P/E
TV	1				TV	1			
GDP	0.9692	1			GDP	0.754	1		
10y2y	–0.3343	–0.3426	1		10y2y	–0.5072	0.0815	1	
P/E	–0.1453	–0.1693	0.1796	1	P/E	–0.4796	–0.7946	–0.1418	1
Deutsche Börse	TV	GDP	10y2y	P/E	Nyse Euronext (European markets)	TV	GDP	10y2y	P/E
TV	1				TV	1			
GDP	0.9212	1			GDP	0.9448	1		
10y2y	–0.1238	–0.0979	1		10y2y	–0.1427	–0.0754	1	
P/E	0.1848	0.1484	0.3676	1	P/E	–0.181	0.2038	0.272	1
BME	TV	GDP	10y2y	P/E					
TV	1								
GDP	0.9712	1							
10y2y	–0.1026	–0.1138	1						
P/E	–0.4843	–0.4744	–0.5457	1					

Source: Our elaborations on Datastream data (GDP, yield curve and price-to-earnings ratio) and Wfe statistics (trading volumes).

earnings (expressed by the average *price-to-earnings* ratio of the index constituents) and the conditions of the financial markets (captured by the difference between the ten-year and two-year government bond yields). Table 10.2 summarizes the results.

Market activity is tightly related to the dynamics of GDP. The degree of correlation between both the value of share trading and the domestic economic growth rate is quite high across all market centers. In contrast, market volumes and GDP show a generally negative correlation with the differential between the ten-year and two-year government bond rates, which we assumed as a proxy of the yield curve. Indeed, during downturns short-term yields are generally bound at low levels while higher rates on the long-term spectrum of the curve could be regarded as expressive of expectations of recovery in the economic cycle. Finally, the results in Table 10.2 report a negative correlation (with the exception of Deutsche Börse) between the value of share trading and the price-to-earnings ratio. It is unsurprising that the volumes traded tend to decrease with low earnings relative to share prices, and this reinforces the positive relation between exchange outputs and the overall macroeconomic environment. When examining the correlations between different business units (Table 10.3), the evidence is rather mixed.

Listing services and cash trading show, as expected, a certain degree of correlation. As for the derivatives business, we observe great differences across exchanges. In some cases (for example, Deutsche Börse), we observe a positive correlation between the number of derivative contracts traded and the volume of equity trading in cash market, whereas in other cases (especially relating to the BME exchange),[8] derivatives markets and cash markets show a negative correlation. Instead, we always observe a positive correlation between the number of companies listed and number of derivative contracts traded. When trying to explain exchange revenues as a function of GDP and the yield curve, our model is apparently quite significant (the left-hand side of Table 10.4). The GDP is particularly significant in explaining the evolution in revenues; in contrast, the significance of the yield curve is more or less negligible (except for the London Stock Exchange Group). The exception that proves the rule is the Nyse Euronext exchange, for which neither the

Table 10.3 Correlations among business units

	Deutsche Börse	LSEG	Nyse Euronext	Nasdaq Omx	BME	Tmx
Corr_L_CT	50.5%	88.7%	–70.4%	77.3%	33.2%	65.45
Corr_L_DT	63.6%	–30.3%	20.5%	–86.7%	45.3%	–36.7%
Corr_CT_DT	33.9%	–27.6%	–30.8%	–81.9%	–50%	–28%

Note: L denotes listed companies, CT denotes trading values and DT denotes the number of derivatives contracts traded.

Table 10.4 The revenue (left side) and cost function (right side)

	GDP	Yield curv.	R-sq		Intercept	Rev	R-sq
Deutsche Börse	1.7138 (***)	–1277.22 ('')	0.4266	Deutsche B	744.3	0.2025 ('')	0.1
BME	0.0006 (***)	–3.6564 ('')	0.5358	BME	22142	0.06 (**)	0.27
LSEG	0.00352 (***)	23.2573(***)	0.6835	LSEG	–31.579	0.90 (***)	0.5
Nasdaq Omx	0.222 (***)	64.79 ('.')	0.7966	Nasdaq Omx	143.89	1.08 (***)	0.98
Nyse Euronext	–0.0533 ('')	54.34 ('.')	0.2118	Nyse Euronext	–1636	2.34 ('.')	0.18
Tmx	0.0006 (***)	–3.6564 ('')	0.5358	Tmx	–1.99	0.47 (***)	0.93

Note: Significance codes: 0 '***', 0.001 '**', 0.01 '*', 0.05 '.', 0.1 ' '.
Source: Our elaborations on exchanges' financial data.

Table 10.5 A pooled model

	Intercept	Estimates θ	β_{TV}	p-value (DB test)	r-sq.	D-Watson
L_{rev}	3.378	0.006 (**)	0.010 (***)	0	0.65	0.73819
CT_{rev}	50.771	–0.002 (' ')	0.077 (***)	0	0.73	0.3934

Note: Significance codes: 0 '***', 0.001 '**', 0.01 '*', 0.05 '.', 0.1 ' '.
Source: Our elaborations on exchanges' financial data.

GDP nor the yield curve are significant in explaining revenues; the *r-square* is fairly low as well.

When examining the relation between costs and revenues (right-hand side of Table 10.4) the evidence is quite mixed. Revenues are significant in explaining costs in four cases (the Spanish exchange, the London Stock Exchange, the Nasdaq Omx Exchange and the Canadian Exchange); however, the magnitude of variable revenues (expressed by the β in the relation we presented in Section 3) is quite different across these exchanges. Lseg and Nasdaq seem to have the highest levels of variable costs among those four exchanges; in the others, the significance of revenues in explaining costs is quite negligible.

For the next step, we want to investigate the relations between exchange outputs and revenues. The aim is to gain better understanding of the extent to which revenues are sensitive to variations in output. Apart from being of particular interest when studying the securities industry structure, it would have implications for the exchange pricing policies. We focus on listing and trading revenues. As for the methodology employed, we test a linear relation in which both listing and trading revenues depend on number of companies listed and value of trading.

We have collected six groups of data representing the exchanges selected. For each exchange we have quarterly data for revenues and outputs. We apply a pooled model. The Table 10.5 summarizes the results.

Trading volumes are apparently the most significant variable in explaining both listing and trading revenues, while listings appear to have a certain significance only with respect to listing revenues. As for trading revenues, the impact of listings is apparently contradictory, as it would suggest a negative relation. When performing the Durbin-Watson test, this reveals autocorrelation; we address that problem by using a lag model (Table 10.6).

Looking in more detail at the single exchanges, the evidence is mixed. Table 10.7 shows the relation of listing revenues to number of companies listed and trading values. We find that the number of companies listed

Table 10.6 A lag model

		Estimates			p-value (DB test)	r-sq.
	Intercept	Θ	Lag	β_{TV}		
L_{rev}	1.3863	0.002 (' ')	0.6518(***)	0.0038 (***)	0	0.80733
CT_{rev}	3.047	–0.001 (' ')	0.8027 (***)	0.020 (***)	0	0.96

Note: Significance codes: 0 '***', 0.001 '**', 0.01 '*', 0.05 '.', 0.1 ' '.
Source: Our elaborations on the financial data of the exchanges.

Table 10.7 Regression of listing revenues on listed companies and trading value (turnover)

	Deutsche B.	BME	LSEG	NasdaqO.	Nyse E.	Tmx
Intercept	109.96 (***)	–11.484 (' ')	47.011(' ')	295.41(' ')	112.58 (**)	170.72 (' ')
Lcompanies	–0.114 (**)	0.0052 (*)	–0.0103 (' ')	–0.0607 (' ')	0.00106 (' ')	–0.0394 (' ')
Turnover	–0.0058 (' ')	0.00614 (**)	0.0110 (***)	0.0024(' ')	–0.0021 (*)	0.0587 (' ')
P>F	0.0008	0.0006	0.0000	0.5061	0.0093	0.5696
r-sq	0.5652	0.5833	0.7627	0.077	0.4234	0.0641
D-Watson	0.6474	1.240232	3.067925	2.614901	0.701795	0.362995

Note: Significance codes: 0 '***', 0.001 '**', 0.01 '*', 0.05 '.', 0.1 ' '.
Source: Our elaborations on exchanges' financial data.

does not explain the variation in listing revenues to any great extent; for some exchanges, there is a negative relation between listings and listing revenues. These results seem to be coherent with the decreasing weight of listing services on total exchange revenues, and may reveal a strategic choice by exchanges to compete on listings in order to exploit network effects. In contrast, trading values seem to be significant (at least for some exchanges) in explaining listing revenues. However, in some exchanges there remains a high degree of autocorrelation.

Table **10.8** presents the relation of trading revenues with number of companies listed and trading values.

The number of companies listed and the value of equity trading does not appear to explain a great portion of variations in cash trading revenues, except for Deutsche Börse, Lseg and the Spanish exchange, for which *r square* is high. For these three exchanges trading volumes are significant in explaining revenues, but for the other exchanges Nasdaq and Nyse Euronext especially, the significance of volumes traded is negligible. In Nyse Euronext the sign is negative. Arguably, these results should be put in relation with increasing competitive pressures. Perhaps unsurprisingly, Nyse Euronext, which is among the exchanges suffering more from competition, is particularly exposed to pressures on revenues.

Finally, we try to explain the cost of capital in light of the explanatory variables that we have presented in the previous section. In particular, building on quarterly data, we express the cost of capital as a linear relation of the trading values (*Turnover*), the *Ebit*, the *Operative* and *Financial leverage* and the *yield curve*, approximated by the differential between the ten-year and two-year government bond yield.

We calculated the cost of capital, applying the Capm model, taking the quarterly ten-year treasury rates for the euro area, the US and Canada as the

Table 10.8 Regression of trading revenues on listed companies and trading value (turnover)

	Deutsche B.	BME	LSEG	NasdaqO	Nyse E.	Tmx
Intercept	–8.7476 (‘ ’)	32.4666 (‘ ’)	34.598 (‘ ’)	254.35 (‘ ’)	1076.14 (‘ ’)	14.014 (‘ ’)
Lcompanies	0.00389 (‘ ’)	–0.00146 (‘ ’)	0.0062 (‘ ’)	0.0606 (‘ ’)	–0.115 (‘ ’)	–0.0018 (‘ ’)
Turnover	0.18777 (***)	0.06244 (***)	0.0234 (***)	0.01308 (‘ ’)	–0.0237 (‘ ’)	0.0612 (*)
P>F	0.0000	0.0000	0.0000	0.3469	0.5283	0.0091
r-sq	0.8747	0.7657	0.8478	0.1171	0.0723	0.4247
D-Watson	0.8349166	2.82529	1.279517	0.6476235	0.9843092	1.359313

Notes: Significance codes: 0 ‘***’, 0.001 ‘**’, 0.01 ‘*’, 0.05 ‘.’, 0.1 ‘ ’.
Source: Our elaborations on exchanges' financial data.

Table 10.9 Regression of cost of capital on market turnover, E_{bit}, operative and financial leverage, and yield curve

	Nasdaq Omx	Nyse Euronext	Tmx	Lseg	Deutsche Börse	BME
Intercept	0.092	0.302	0.089	0.89	0.103	0.069
Turnover	0.000	0.0004	0.0001	0.0001	0.000	0.000
	(***)	(**)	(‘ ’)	(‘ ’)	(‘ ’)	(‘ ’)
Ebit	0.000	–0.002	–0.00004	–0.0001	–0.0001	–0.00001
	(‘ ’)	(***)	(‘ ’)	(‘ ’)	(‘ ’)	(‘ ’)
Op. Lev	–0.0003	–0.079	–0.005	0.401	0.004	0.0004
	(‘ ’)	(***)	(‘ ’)	(‘ ’)	(‘ ’)	(‘ ’)
Fin. Lev	–0.0002	0.0066	–0.003	–0.008	0.0008	0.0031
	(‘ ’)	(‘ ’)	(‘ ’)	(‘ ’)	(‘ ’)	(‘ ’)
Yield	–0.001	–0.285	0.0009	0.002	0.001	0.11
	(‘ ’)	(‘ ’)	(‘ ’)	(‘ ’)	(‘ ’)	(**)
r-sq	0.23	0.82	0.07	0.16	0.57	0.49

Notes: Significance codes: 0 ‘***’, 0.001 ‘**’, 0.01 ‘*’, 0.05 ‘.’, 0.1 ‘ ’.
Source: Our elaborations on exchanges’ financial data.

risk-free rates and deriving the betas from the Datastream database. Table 10.9 gives the results. In particular, the volatility in trading volumes is one of the main risk factors as it may impact on exchanges’ revenues and profitability. Obviously, this is particularly challenging for exchanges moving forward with sizeable acquisitions and, therefore, reporting high goodwill.

The evidences are quite mixed. Only in one case (namely, Nyse Euronext) is the model apparently satisfactory in explaining the cost of capital (the r-square is 0.82). For Deutsche Börse and the Spanish exchange there is no clear evidence of the predictable properties of the model, while for the other exchanges (Nasdaq Omx, Tmx and London Stock Exchange Group) this seems not to explain the cost of capital so well.

As for the explanatory variables, the turnover seems to be significant in explaining the cost of capital for Nasdaq Omx and Nyse Euronext. For the latter, the Ebit and the operative leverage are significant as well. The other variables appear not to be significant in explaining the cost of capital. What is a surprise, however, are the signs of the relations; the direct relation of the turnover, in particular, with the cost of capital seems to be quite counterintuitive. In some cases also the signs of the two leverage variables are not as expected (and especially the inverse relation with the cost of capital observed for some exchanges).

6 Conclusions

Value creation for securities exchanges is far from being a well established field of research. Theoretical literature focuses on the main features of the economics of exchanges and, in particular, the presence of relevant network externalities. Other contributions deal with efficiency matters in relation to conglomerate exchanges. But there is a lack of knowledge about the main drivers of value for exchanges, and this chapter has tried to bridge the gap. First we provided a picture of the main features of exchange business; we found that exchanges operate with a prevalently fixed-cost function, and this lends support to the hypothesis that consolidation in the industry will be beneficial for exchanges.

However, the most recent developments in the industry (recall the Intercontinental Exchange bid for the Nyse Euronext, and the convergence between western exchanges and Asian exchanges, mirrored by the Hong Kong Stock Exchange bid for the London Metal Exchange) raise the relevant issue of who is going to lead the consolidation process in the near future. Value creation is particularly challenging in this regard. This is why it is important to shed light on the value drivers in the exchange industry, finding the main relations between the macroeconomic environment and the competitive levers of exchanges. Arguably, those exchanges, located in fast growing economies, will enjoy a competitive advantage in the consolidation process.

In addition, the viability of the business in terms of sustainability of growth in revenues is another source of competitive advantage. Derivatives are traditionally seen as a countercyclical business compared with the cycle-dependent cash markets. Although derivative exchanges are exposed to increasing competitive pressures as well, they are seemingly more resilient to downturns than are cash markets. Specialization in certain product lines which are particularly relevant in today's economic environment (such as certain commodities, metals or energy products) may be another lever for competitive advantage. While the ongoing competitive pressures and the efforts to cope with them may disclose relevant opportunities for global exchanges, notwithstanding they underlie relevant risks for the viability of exchange business.

The competitive forces that are reshaping the industry exert pressures for a well established and properly designed framework for managing risks, especially strategic risk. Such a framework should be based on a widespread use of metrics, targeted to support the strategic decision making process by measuring the contribution of each business unit or line to the overall corporate risk. In such a context, value creation is function of the capital absorbed by each business line to cover risks and the cost of capital. On the one hand, value added lies on the generation of risk-adjusted returns in excess of the cost of capital. On the other, such an approach provides the basis for defining the exchange pricing schedule.

Notes

1. IPO = Initial Public Offering.
2. RoE = Return on Equity; RoA = Return on Assets.
3. The FESE collects and publishes data annually on the operating costs and revenues of the member exchanges. Revenues are broken down in order to show the contribution of each business area to total revenues. Here we consider the relation between operating costs and total revenues.
4. Although the negative value for the beta may turn out to be somewhat counterintuitive, it may depend on a variety of reasons related to the pricing policies of the exchange or cuts in costs. Specifically, the Six Group, which manages the Swiss Exchange, cut costs by 26 per cent during the timeframe we considered.
5. See, for example, Standard & Poor's rating methodology for exchanges and clearing houses, which assesses the viability of the business on the basis of supply and demand of listed products.
6. Alternatively, the output on primary markets could be expressed in terms of capital raised.
7. Rarorac = risk-adjusted return on risk-adjusted capital.
8. BME = the Spanish exchange, entitled Bolsas y Mercados Españoles Sociedad Holding de Mercados y Sistemas Financieros SA.

References

Andersén, A. (2005) 'Pricing of stock exchange trading. The role of network externalities', Helsinki School of Economics, Working Paper.

Cantillon, E. and P.L. Yin (2011) 'Competition between exchanges: a research agenda', *International Journal of Industrial Organization*, 29(3), 329–36.

Di Noia, C. (1999) 'Competition and integration among stock exchanges in Europe: network effects, implicit mergers and remote access', Wharton, Working Paper, no. 3.

Economides, N. (1993) 'Network economics with application to finance', *Financial Markets, Institutions and Instruments*, 2(5), 89–97.

Economides, N. and Flyer F., 1997, *Compatibility and market structure for network goods*, Discussion Paper EC-98-02, Stern School of Business.

James, C. (1996) 'RAROC based capital budgeting and performance evaluation: A case study of bank capital allocation', Wharton Financial Institutions Center, Working Paper, no. 40.

Mendiola, A. and M. O'Hara (2004) 'Taking stock in the stock markets: the changing governance of exchanges', SSRN Working Paper.

Otchere, I. (2006) 'Stock exchange self-listing and value effects', *Journal of Corporate Finance*, 12, 926–53.

Otchere, I. and E. Oldford (2011) 'Can commercialization improve the performance of stock exchanges even without corporatization?' *The Financial Review*, 46(1), 67–87.

Pagano, M., O. Randl, A. Röell and J. Zechner (2001) 'What makes stock exchanges succeed? Evidence from cross-listing decisions', *European Economic Review*, 45, 770–82.

Pownall, G., M. Vulcheva and X. Wang (2012) 'Increasing liquidity on global stock exchanges: the structure of Euronext', SSRN Working Paper.

Rochet, J.C. and J. Tirole (2006) 'Two-sided markets: a progress report', *Rand Journal of Economics*, 37(3), 645–67.

Schmiedel, H. (2001) 'Technological development and concentration of stock exchanges in Europe', Bank of Finland, Working Paper no. 21.

Schmiedel, H. and A. Schönenberger (2005) 'Integration of securities market infrastructures in the euro area', European Central Bank, Occasional Paper no. 33.

Serifsoy, B. (2007) 'Stock exchange business models and their operative performance', *Journal of Banking and Finance*, 31(10), 2978–3012.

Shy, O. and J. Tarkka (2001) 'Stock exchange alliances, access fees and competition', Research Discussion Papers, Bank of Finland, no. 22.

Song, L., H. Schmiedel and I. Hasan (2010) 'Growth strategies and value creation. What works best for stock exchanges?' European Central Bank, Working Papers, no. 1201.

Zaik, E., J. Walter, G. Kelling and C. James (1996) 'RAROC at Bank of America: from theory to practice', *Journal of Applied Corporate Finance*, 9(2), 83–93.

11

Does Private Equity Investment Positively Impact on Firm Profitability and on the Growth of the Target Company?

Giusy Chesini and Elisa Giaretta

1 Introduction

Private Equity (PE), with around 45.5 billion invested in target companies in Europe in 2011, is a core tool that allows the funding of businesses with high potential. The amount of the funds invested in the PE industry grew during that year, as investments slightly increased, that is by 6 per cent, over 2010 (EVCA Yearbook 2012).

PE is a short-to-medium-term investment that provides equity capital to enterprises not quoted on a stock market.

PE investment is typically carried out through a limited partnership structure in which the PE firm serves as the general partner (GP). The limited partners (LPs) mostly consist of institutional and other investors, who provide the capital for deals. We refer to each individual limited partnership as a fund. The LPs commit to providing a certain amount of capital to the fund. The GP has an agreed time period – usually five years – in which to invest the committed capital; the GP also has an agreed time period in which to return capital to the LPs – usually of the order of 10–12 years.[1]

As GPs during the limited partnership select investments, structure deals, monitor investments and design the appropriate exit strategies on behalf of the LPs, we refer to GPs as PE investors (Burgel, 2000).

The aim of PE investors is to create value by helping company growth and making firms more efficient (Achleitner and Klöckner, 2005); in exchange, they receive a management fee and a share of the overall returns of the fund. In general, when a GP identifies an investment opportunity, it 'calls' money from its LPs and channels it to the target company (Phalippou and Gottschalg, 2009). PE investors provide the target company with advice, incentives, networking and knowledge through a range of specific investment structures.

One particularly controversial issue is the ways in which PE investors affect the economic performance and size growth of the target companies. In fact, there are conflicting opinions and heated debate on the effects of PE investments on target companies. GPs are active investors, with seats on the board of directors, and they benefit from detailed pre-purchase due diligence and full, timely information on the operations of the businesses in which they invest. PE investors' expertise in monitoring may enable firms to improve performance through exploiting opportunities for both cost efficiencies and growth. For this reason, PE investments may lead to improvements in performance in a variety of measures, including revenue and employment growth, profitability, operating performance and cash-flow, productivity and innovations. Moreover, PE investors can improve the performance of companies in failure situations. However, active investors need time to successfully restructure and improve a company's performance.

Firms can raise capital either by raising debt or by issuing equity, but in the former case, lenders have the legal right to interest payments and repayment of the debt, irrespective of the success or failure of the firm. In contrast, equity is provided in exchange for the redemption of ownership rights. Equity providers thus become co-owners of the firms, and share risk and returns to the extent to which they participate in the firm, so their returns depend directly on the growth and profitability of the firm. Equity providers realize their returns through selling their stake in an investee company at a higher price than they paid for it (Burgel, 2000).

Recent studies have criticized the PE instruments, and they argue for the failure of the PE industry (see for example Davidoff, 2009; Cheffins and Armour, 2007). It has been strongly stated that this type of deal leads to short-term performance horizons, reductions in employment, and increased insolvency risk, particularly in an economic downturn. For instance, the Service Employees International Union (2007), a prominent critic of PE, offers the following assessment: 'It's easier to decrease costs quickly by cutting heads, which is why buyouts have typically been accompanied by layoffs.' Overall, evidence suggests that PE investors implement rationalization policies, making PE-backed companies more focused. These operations result in job losses in the company areas where are inefficiencies, and at the same time there are expansions and job creations in core strength areas. Cost reduction and strategic refocusing are used to mitigate the downside problems of mature firms and to create value following the transfer of ownership (Bruining et al., 2005). As argued by Davis et al. (2011), employment growth in the target company, like size growth in general, is not the specific goal of profit-oriented PE companies, given their overriding interest in firm value. On the other hand, a key advantage of company growth is evident: it allows early diagnosis of firm development while investment is being made. Further, high growth is directly connected with an increase in firm value in most cases, and hence represents an appropriate early diagnosis indicator.

In the traditional PE literature (see Jensen, 1993; Wright et al., 2000) it tends to be argued that cost reduction predominates, as managers introduce efficiencies and reduce post-deal costs. PE investments may therefore actually reduce employment (Kaplan, 1989).

Since economists have a longstanding interest in how changes in ownership affect profitability and size growth, this chapter aims to analyze and measure the effect of PE investments on target companies. The key question has to do with the way in which PE investments have an impact on PE-backed companies in terms of certain profitability and growth indicators.

The structure of the chapter is as follows. In Section 2 we discuss the specific literature about the phenomena and develop our hypotheses. Section 3 describes the research method and sample characteristics. The empirical results are presented and discussed in Section 4, while Section 5 concludes.

2 Literature review

There are many studies related to both profitability and size growth in PE-backed companies. Most of studies analyze the impact of only one subtype of PE, such as buyouts, leverage buyouts (LBOs), reverse LBOs or venture capital investments.[2]

A very important study for our analyses is that by Wilson et al. (2012). They assessed the recent economic and financial performance of UK buyouts. The results reveal that buyout firms achieved superior economic and financial performance in the period before and during the recent global recession, relative to comparable non-buyout firms. The authors' regression results imply positive differentials of 5–15 per cent in productivity and approximately 3–5 per cent in profitability for buyout firms relative to non-buyout firms. Another key finding was that revenue and employment growth for PE-backed firms were positive during the sample period.

Kaplan (1989) considered 76 public-to-private LBOs during the 1980s. He found that the median firm lost 12 per cent of employment on an industry-adjusted basis from the end of the fiscal year prior to the PE transaction to the end of the fiscal year after the transaction. Kaplan's findings also suggest a significant increase in operating returns. He claimed that LBOs[3] generally bring positive improvements to the firm's operations and increase its value.

Smith (1990) found that between 1977 and 1986 the operating returns of 58 public firms significantly increased from the year before completion of buyout to the year after. He also found no effects on employment.

Muscarella and Vetsuypens (1990) studied 72 reverse LBOs. The 92 per cent of random samples underwent a median percentage change in employment larger than that of the reverse LBOs over a similar time period. The low employment growth seen in reverse LBO firms was, however, attributed to divestiture activities after the LBO. Owing to accounting write-ups at the LBO, measures of profitability were likely to be biased against finding evidence of increased efficiency. An analysis of conventional accounting measures of performance revealed that reverse LBOs experienced significant improvements in profitability when compared with random samples of publicly traded firms over similar time periods; these improvements in profitability resulted mainly from the ability of the sample firms to reduce costs rather than to generate more revenues or to improve asset turnover.

In the early years post buyout, Wright et al. (1996) identified no significant differences in the return on assets ratio (RoA).

Buttignon et al. (2009) studied a sample of 21 buyouts carried out in Italy during the 1990s. Some of the variables identified – such as turnover and EBITDA[4] – were not statistically significant. In an attempt to identify some patterns of behavior, the authors clustered firms on the basis of turnover and EBITDA margin trends, and found that PE intervention generally caused a discontinuity in the life of a firm, generating a shift in performance trends from bad to good and vice versa. Almost a third of firms that had been analyzed achieved very good performances, measured as Turnover and EBITDA, after the PE investment, while another third displayed some signs of failure. A number of mixed situations emerged in the remaining firms, where growth was achieved at the expense of profitability or where profitability increased as growth diminished.

Badunenko and Baum (2010) analyzed 159,425 firm-years of observations, including firms with annual operating revenues in excess of €5,000. They found that short-term PE investments had, on average, a detrimental effect on firm performance. The performance of PE-backed firms was lower than that of non-PE backed firms in the first year of PE investment. That effect, however, disappeared if PE investments continued for an uninterrupted six-year term. In the short run, the presence of PE investors in the firm's shareholders had, on average, a negative impact on the firm's performance, measured in terms of RoA. However, if the PE investment time horizon was long enough, its effect on company performance was significantly positive.

Davis et al. (2011) constructed and analyzed a dataset of 3200 target firms and their 150,000 establishments, covering PE transactions in the US from 1980 to 2005. The authors compared the outcomes to controls that were similar in terms of industry, size, age, and prior growth. Their establishment-level analysis yielded three main findings: first, employment shrank more rapidly, on average, at target establishments than at controls after PE transactions; the average cumulative difference in favor of controls was about 3 per cent of initial employment over two years, and 6 per cent over five years. Second, the greater decline in post-transaction employment at target establishments wholly reflected the higher rates of job destruction at shrinking and exiting establishments; in fact, the post-transaction creation of new jobs at expanding establishments was greater for targets than controls. Third, mean employment growth rates were similar for target and control establishments in the two years before buyout, and targets grew more rapidly in the transaction year.

A synoptic table summarizing the literature can be found in Appendix (Table 11.A). The vast number of results from the literature invites further investigation of the phenomenon. The key question we investigated is whether investments in PE result in profitability improvements and size growth in comparison with the pre-investment situation. More specifically, we examined the following research question: *Do PE-backed companies outperform non-PE-backed companies after acquisition by the institutional investor in terms of growth and profitability?*

Despite the heightened interest in PE and the potential importance of PE investments for the economy as a whole, we have only a limited understanding of the dynamics of performance and the growth of target companies. One of the main obstacles is the lack of available data, as PE firms are largely exempt from the disclosure requirements that public firms are subject to. Studies on the effect of PE have serious limitations:[5]

- most studies rely on surveys with incomplete and selective responses;
- the data offers little scope for control in comparable firms. When a firm backed by PE sheds 5 per cent of some of the variables analyzed, the interpretation depends greatly on whether comparable firms grow by 3 per cent or shrink by 10 per cent. For example, Achleitner and Klöckner (2005) compared percentage employment growth of European PE-backed firms with total employment growth in Europe. But this comparison was not appropriate, since it compared companies differing in terms of size and industry sector. In contrast to that method, measurement of the growth of PE-backed companies must be based on a comparison of similar businesses;
- there are many studies that discuss the economic effects of PE transactions based largely on case study evidence (see for example Shleifer and Summers, 1988; Rasmussen, 2008); most studies analyzed only those companies that went public after the deal (see for example, Bruton et al., 2010). However, an IPO[6] often represents the first liquidity event in the life cycle of a target company when its founders and initial investors begin the process of realizing the value of their ownership stake in the company (Bruton et al., 2010).

The aim of our study was to overcome these weaknesses, so we constructed and analyzed a dataset that achieved this goal.

Our work differs from the existing literature by using a more appropriate dataset for the control sample. The novelty of our work also lies in the area analyzed. Specifically, we decided to limit our work to a small area where there were many PE investments in the first decade of the 21st century, in order to compare companies operating in the same territory, with the same environmental characteristics, accounting principles and legal framework that could contribute to the performance of the investment.

3 Data and methodology

Data on the performance of PE investments can be gathered either at company level, or at fund level. While fund-level data have the advantage of being net of fund fees and carried interest, aggregation at fund level also implies loss of leveraged recapitalization. In contrast, company-level data allows researchers to more explicitly control for the selection bias arising from lack of observation on the final outcomes of unsuccessful investments.

Our data sources and sample selection scheme are detailed in this section. We provide descriptive statistics for both PE sample and non-PE sample and document via a Probit model showing how the two samples differ in terms of fund characteristics. We also describe how performance is typically computed in the literature.

3.1 Data sources

Data on PE investments is obtained from the PEM Private Equity Monitor Report database constructed by the PEM Observatory at the Carlo Cattaneo University – LIUC, which focuses on investments in Italian private companies, and aims to map out the main industry trends and to identify future developments. Certain selection criteria were applied. Only initial rounds of investments undertaken by non-state-related PE investors were considered. Moreover, we only considered investments in companies post the start-up phase. Hence, our study excludes the following types of deals:

- Deals undertaken by government institutions and regional government agencies;
- Seed and start-up deals;
- Second-round financing deals.

To analyze investments we constructed a sub-sample of PE-backed companies (PE sample) in the period 2002–2008.

The initial dataset consisted of 106 PE-backed companies, from which we eliminated 38 firms with insufficient pre- or post-deal data. The final sample consisted of 68 firms, as follows:

Table 11.1 Distribution of deals during the years

Year (T)	No. of deals	%
2002	5	7
2003	13	19
2004	7	10
2005	8	12
2006	15	22
2007	9	13
2008	11	16
Total	*68*	*100*

The impact of PE on target firm performance was directly analyzed by comparing firms with and without PE shareholders through a paired sample design approach. We created a control sample of 204 non-PE-backed companies (NPE sample) to compare with the PE sample. For each company in the PE sample, we generated three draws of firms with the following characteristics from the Bureau Van Dijk database:

- Same industrial classification code (two-digit NACE code);
- Similar (+/– 20%) number of employees in the year of the deal;
- Registered office in the same area.

Each randomly selected firm was matched to its corresponding PE-backed firm in the sense that we measured the variables over the same calendar period as the PE-backed company. We used the term 'before the deal' for companies in the NPE sample to indicate the years prior to the investment for the corresponding company in the PE sample. In the same way we used the terms 'during the deal' and 'after the deal for the companies in the control sample, by indicating the periods during and after the deal for the matched PE-backed company.

We chose to study only PE-backed companies located in an Italian area where PE investments are numerous and growing – which includes Veneto, Friuli Venezia Giulia and Trentino Alto Adige – because we wanted to compare companies operating in the same territory, with the same environmental characteristics, accounting principles and legal frameworks.

3.2 Methodology

In this sub-section, we report descriptive statistics on the performance of the 68 PE-backed companies and the 204 non-PE-backed companies; in addition, we describe the methodology applied and we debate the variables chosen in order to analyze the companies.

We decided to use financial statement analysis to explain the key characteristics of PE investments. This is due to our willingness to adopt the data available for all companies and not to investigate the investments by means of surveys.

The relationship between company characteristics and the probability of being PE-backed can be seen via a Probit model (see for example Phalippou and Gottschalg, 2009, for other studies on PE performance via a Probit model). The dependent variable is a dummy variable that takes the value 1 if the company is in the PE sample and 0 otherwise. The explanatory variables should reflect the differences between PE-backed companies and the companies covered in the control dataset.

We expected that PE-backed companies would show better profitability and size growth than non-PE-backed companies.

In order to test for the performance of PE-backed companies we needed to define the variables to analyze.

The financial variables employed in this study were selected in order to reflect the traditional dimensions of performance evaluation within the constraints of data availability. The precise constructs are detailed in the Appendix (Table 11.B).

As regards the economic performance of target companies, profitability was measured by four variables, namely: profit, sales, RoE and EBITDA:

Profit is the company's remaining revenues after all expenses and taxes have been paid. Profit is the financial benefit that is realized when the amount of revenue gained from a business activity exceeds the expenses, costs and taxes required to sustain the activity. This measure is important, as any profit that is made goes to the company's owners, who may or may not decide to spend it on the business.

The total amount of sales refers to the amount of money a business has brought in during the time period covered by the income statement. Sales are calculated by multiplying the price at which goods or services are sold by the number of units or the amount sold. Sales are important because a business must bring in money to make a profit, and for companies that have not yet made a profit the sales can serve as a gauge of potential profitability in the future.

RoE is profit after tax less exceptional items deflated by shareholders' equity. RoE represents the situation after tax and interest payments, and indicates the profit available to shareholders. It is therefore more important to PE providers than other measures such as RoCE, that can be affected by asset valuation.

EBITDA is widely used as a measure of profitability by PE investors, who need to analyze the financial statements of target enterprises considered to be in need of financial restructuring. As target companies are often distressed enterprises that are not making a profit, PE investors need a variable to measure the potential ability of the target company. EBITDA gives some idea of the availability of cash to deal with the repayment terms of debt, ignoring the current financing structure of the target enterprise. EBITDA gives an opportunity for the comparison of companies with different financing structures, by looking at the profit before interest and concentrating on the cash generated in the company. EBITDA is not distorted by expenses outside a company's business (interest and taxes) and non-cash charges due to allocation of historical cost of an asset (depreciation and amortization). The result given by EBITDA, although not the same as a cash flow forecast, give an indication of the value of the target company and its suitability as a target for a PE investor.[7]

With regard to company growth, one problem that must be faced is the definition of firm size. If all companies produced the same good, then we could use a physical measure of output. But as we are studying companies that produce different goods there is no common physical measure of output. An obvious solution to the problem is to use the value of the output: the sales. However the value of the sales is a better indicator of company profitability than its size growth. A general alternative to measuring the size of output is to measure input – but again, since companies produce different goods, they use different inputs. However, virtually all companies have employees. As a result, some economists have used the number of employees as a measure of firm size (see for example Evans, 1987; Amaral et al., 1997). Another value of inputs is the book value of the equity, as it is the input from the shareholders of the firm. We must remind you, however, that equity is not directly affected by PE investments, which mostly increase debt in the target company, as investors usually operate using high leverage. Moreover, equity is not directly affected by buyout investments, as it is only subjected to a change in the property.

In order to estimate how target firms were affected by the PE activity, we analyzed the following variables: EBITDA, profit, sales, RoE, equity and employees (see Appendix, Table 11.B). We aimed to answer the main research question by measuring the positive effect of PE investment, in terms of both size growth and profitability. The first four variables – EBITDA, profit, sales and RoE – were designed to measure company profitability, while the last two variables – equity and number of employees – were used to measure company growth.

Table 11.2 summarizes the descriptive statistics of the two samples by indicating the mean and median values for each variable analyzed in three different periods – two years before the deal, during the deal year and two years after the deal. We chose to study the situation before the deal by analyzing the variables just two years before the deal, as data was not always available for any earlier periods. We also analyzed the situation after the investment by studying the two years afterwards, because if we had used a longer time period we should have had to omit the later deals; when we carried out the analysis, data for three years after the deal was not yet available for acquisitions made any later than 2008.

As you can see, the characteristics of the two samples two years before the deal were similar. However, in general companies in the PE sample showed higher EBITDA – as it is considered an important indicator for investors (Manigart et al., 2000).

We decided to use a Probit model[8] in order to explain the relationship between the probability of a company being subject to PE investment and the variables analyzed. The model comprises the values of the profitability and growth variables two years after the deal. We decided to include the year of the deal in our model as well, as a control variable.

Table 11.2 Descriptive statistics in different periods

	PE sample	NPE sample		Pooled sample
Panel A: before the deal				
Profit	948,639	839,967		867,135
	(536,468)	(223,544)		(271,394)
Sales	78,201,324	75,678,870		76,309,483
	(30,208,268)	(25,160,046)		(26,128,631)
EBITDA	9,076,669	5,006,036	*	6,023,694
	(3,534,606)	(2,060,430)		(2,383,055)
ROE	-0.00305	-0.21866		-0.16456
	(0.115622)	(0.062869)		(0.070201)
Equity	20,730,579	13,231,923	*	15,106,587
	(7,318,031)	(4,012,609)		(4,523,771)
Employees	328	205		236
	(140)	(121)		(123)
Panel B: during the year of the deal				
Profit	2,195,828	1,291,051		1,517,245
	(387,467)	(195,650)		(276,658)
Sales	81,235,940	91,928,358		89,255,253
	(32,643,354)	(30,891,251)		(32,264,083)
EBITDA	10,346,595	6,129,536	*	7,183,801
	(2,759,908)	(2,365,971)		(2,506,182)
ROE	-0.19198	0.113311	*	0.036988
	(0.04451)	(0.062307)		(0.054998)
Equity	32,295,252	15,446,967	**	19,659,038
	(11,538,717)	(5,826,680)		(6,422,423)
Employees	369	242		274
	(149)	(126)		(134)
Panel C: after the deal				
Profit	-4,485,843	1,351,044	*	-113,562
	(-46,991)	(132,285)		(112,551)
Sales	75,770,741	97,666,479		92,172,345
	(29,894,298)	(29,628,506)		(29,850,004)
EBITDA	8,857,074	5,626,291		6,436,967
	(2,710,295)	(1,976,404)		(2,188,729)
RoE	-0.2512	0.026173		-0.0419
	(-0.0050)	(0.039451)		(0.0325)
Equity	32,967,801	17,664,369	*	21,504,345
	(11,590,594)	(6,251,642)		(7,213,749)
Employees	283	247		255
	(131)	(123)		(126)

Notes: Sample includes 68 PE-backed firms and 204 non-PE-backed firms in 2002–2008. Variable definitions and data sources are listed in the appendix. Financial data are in euros. Statistical tests are t-tests for equality in means. Median values are in brackets. *, **, *** Significant difference between PE and non-PE values at 10%, 5% and 1% levels.

We analyzed the following Probit model:

$$PROB\_PE = \beta 1 + \beta 2\ PROFIT\_T + 2 + \beta_3\ SALES\_T + 2 + \beta_4\ EBITDA\_T + 2 + \beta_5\ ROE\_T + 2 + \beta_6\ EQUITY\_T + 2\ \beta_7\ EMPLOYEES\_T + 2 + \beta_8\ YEAR + u$$

Table 11.3 Probit model

	Expected sign	*Coefficient*		
Profitability variables				
PROFIT_T+2	–	–6,3496e–09	(0,00033)	***
SALES_T+2	+/–	–5,7774e–01	(0,00124)	***
EBITDA_T+2	+	7,5909e–09	(0,00978)	***
ROE_T+2	–	–2,9336e–07	(0,97960)	
Growth variables				
EQUITY_T+2	+	1,8354e–09	(0,01718)	**
EMPLOY_T+2	+	2,3924e–08	(0,08486)	*
Control variable				
YEAR		0,0063826	(0,62855)	
Const		–12,5982	(0,63398)	
Number of observations			272	

Notes: The sample consists of 68 PE-backed Italian companies and 204 non-PE-backed Italian companies. The dependent variable is a dummy variable for PE backing. The independent variables include EBITDA, profit, sales, RoE, equity and number of employees in T+2 and year, as defined in Appendix. P-values are in brackets. * Significant at 10% confidence level; ** Significant at 5% confidence level; *** Significant at 1% confidence level.

where:

PROB_PE is a dummy variable which explains the membership of the PE sample (1 for PE-backed companies, 0 otherwise)

PROFIT_T+2 explains the value of profit in year T+2

SALES_T+2 explains the value of sales in year T+2

EBITDA_T+2 explains the value of EBITDA in year T+2

ROE_T+2 explains the value of Return on Equity in year T+2

EQUITY_T+2 explains the value of total equity in year T+2

EMPLOYEE_T+2 explains the number of employees in year T+2

YEAR explains the deal year (T)

Statistical results are summarized in Table 11.3.

We tested for collinearity for the variables used, and we did not find any collinearity problems, as reported in Table 11.4. We reported the correlation matrix for the variables analyzed in Table 11.5.

Table 11.4 Variance inflation factors

Profitability variables	
PROFIT_T+2	1.04
SALES_T+2	2.06
EBITDA_T+2	2.53
ROE_T+2	3.10
Growth variables	
EQUITY_T+2	1.67
EMPLOY_T+2	3.10
Control variable	
Year	1.03

Notes: Minimum possible value is equal to 1.00. Values larger than 10.00 may indicate a collinearity problem.

Table 11.5 Correlation coefficients

	YEAR	PROB_PE	ROE_T+2	PROFIT_ T+2	EQUITY_ T+2	EMPLOY_ T+2	SALES_ T+2	EBITDA_ T+2
YEAR	1.0000	0.0000	0.0254	–0.0482	–0.1532	0.0319	–0.1379	–0.1576
PROB _PE		1.0000	0.1155	–0.1750	0.1588	0.1528	–0.0474	0.1041
ROE _T+2			1.0000	0.0851	–0.0344	0.8228	–0.0291	–0.0320
PROFIT_T+2				1.0000	0.0876	0.0682	0.1188	0.1882
EQUITY_T+2					1.0000	–0.0440	0.5176	0.6231
EMPLOY_T+2						1.0000	–0.0380	–0.0411
SALES_T+2							1.0000	0.7118
EBITDA_T+2								1.0000

Note: 5% critical value (two-tailed) = 0.1190 for n = 272.

A possible weak point of our analysis at an aggregate level is that there are companies in different situations – some exhibiting good performance before the deal and some in failure situations – thus throwing the entire picture out of focus. As a consequence, a better understanding could be obtained through the identification of more homogeneous groups of companies, since completely different patterns of behavior seem to coexist. We therefore clustered companies according to the trend in the observed variables in the pre-deal period, and we subsequently divided the companies in sub-groups according to the trend in the post-deal period. We analyze performance changes before and after the deal year also to emphasize the discontinuity impact of the PE investments.

Operationally, for both the PE sample and the control sample we calculated the value of each performance variable two years before the investment

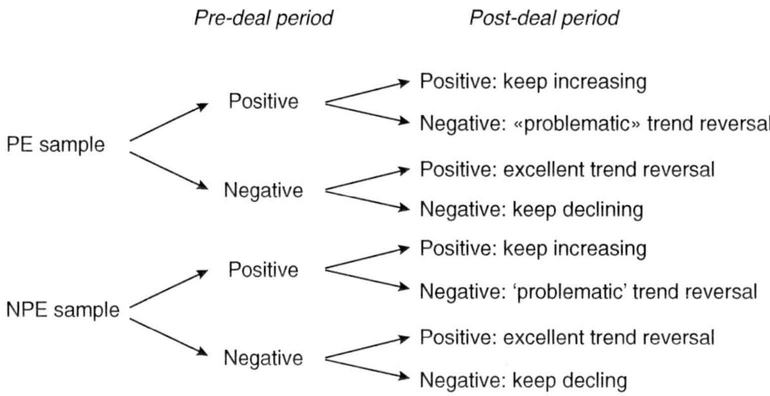

Figure 11.1 Analysis of performance variation

Note: This figure illustrates how we divided the two samples in the pre-deal period and in the post-deal period.

Table 11.6 **Comparison of PE and control (NPE) samples**

	Δ < 0 pre-deal		Δ > 0 pre-deal	
	Δ > 0 post-deal	**Δ < 0 post-deal**	**Δ < 0 post-deal**	**Δ > 0 post-deal**
PE sample				
Profitability variables				
Profit	51%	49%	66%	34%
Sales	54%	46%	38%	63%
EBITDA	58%	42%	59%	41%
ROE	49%	51%	68%	32%
Growth variables				
Equity	60%	40%	43%	57%
Employee	35%	61%	60%	37%
NPE sample				
Profitability variables				
Profit	64%	36%	61%	38%
Sales	44%	56%	48%	51%
EBITDA	53%	46%	65%	35%
ROE	57%	43%	73%	27%
Growth variables				
Equity	61%	37%	34%	66%
Employee	34%	64%	52%	48%

Notes: We analyzed the changes in performance by comparing the two samples. In the second and third columns we calculated the percentage of companies showing a negative change in performance from T-2 to T that showed a positive (column 2) or a negative (column 3) change in performance from T to T+2. In the fourth and fifth columns we calculated the percentage of companies showing a positive change in performance from T-2 to T that showed a negative (column 4) or a positive (column 5) change in performance from T to T+2.

year (T-2), in the year of the investment (T) and two years later (T+2). We calculated the performance change in the pre-deal period (from T-2 to T) and in the post-deal period (from T to T+2). We analyzed the changes in performance by comparing the two samples. Our aim was to check in the two samples whether a positive change in performance from T-2 to T corresponded to a positive change in the performance from T to T+2 (the performance was continually increasing) or if it corresponded to a negative change (the company was showing a 'problematic' trend reversal). Then we checked whether a negative change in performance from T-2 to T corresponded to a positive change in the performance from T to T+2 (the company was showing an excellent trend reversal) or to a negative change (the performance was continually declining) as explained in Figure 11.1. Table 11.6 shows data for the PE sample and for the control sample.

4 Results

From Probit model (1) it can be seen that five variables had a statistically significant impact. These variables were profit, sales, EBITDA, equity and employees.

The effect of PE investment on EBITDA, equity and number of employees was positive. A positive relation between EBITDA and PE investments means that if a company is acquired by an institutional investor, that company should record an increase in its EBITDA two years after the deal. In the same way, PE investments should lead to an increase in equity and in the number of employees.

The relationship between the probability of having a PE investment and profit was negative – PE investments brought about a decrease in profit two years after the deal. In fact, the profits of PE-backed companies should decline as the result of M&A operations conducted by institutional investors. PE investments are usually made through the creation of a new company which merges with the company subject to the investment. PE-backed companies would be expected to show some minor performance, related to higher post-merger annual depreciation or goodwill amortization and impairment tests, with effects on profit – but not on EBITDA.

Also the relationship between PE investments and sales was negative. This might be because investors usually implement rationalization policies that decrease revenues in order to achieve greater cost savings.

The relation between PE investment and RoE was not statistically significant. This is because there are many aspects that can affect the post-deal ROE ratio – in a positive or negative way. Similarly, the relation between PE investment and the year of the investment was not statistically significant.

As can be seen in Table 11.6, PE-backed companies that had a negative change in performance in the first period showed, in more than 50 per cent of cases, a positive change in performance in the second period – with the exception of employees. In particular, for sales and EBITDA, the excellent performance reversal – from negative to positive – in the PE sample was reported by a higher number of companies. For equity and employees the reversal trends in the two samples were similar. It follows that as early as two years after the deal, PE investments can bring about improvements in business performance and company growth in firms with an initial deficit situation – improvements that would not be achieved without PE backing. Consequently, for companies that are initially declining, PE investments can lead to improvements in business performance after two years.

In the PE sample there is a lower number of companies showing a reversal trend from positive to negative compared to the control sample in the following variables: sales, EBITDA and ROE. Nevertheless, for profit, equity and employees, the performance reversal – from positive to negative – in the PE sample was reported by more companies.

5 Conclusions

To analyze the effects of PE investments, we first constituted a sample of 68 PE-backed companies in the period 2002–2008. The impact of PE investments on firm profitability and company growth was directly analyzed by comparing firms with and without PE shareholders. We set up a control sample of three companies for each PE-backed company with a similar number of employees in the year of the deal, with territorial proximity and working in the same industry.

We started with a Probit model to explain the relationship between the probability of a firm receiving a PE investment and six variables already adopted in recent literature analyzed in year T+2 (profit, sales, EBITDA, RoE, the number of employees and equity). Then we calculated performance changes in the pre-deal period (from T-2 to T) and the post-deal period (from T to T+2).

From the results of the model, five variables emerged as statistically significant: profit, sales, EBITDA, equity and employees.

The relationship between the probability of having a PE investment and profit and sales was negative, and the impact on EBITDA, equity and number of employees of PE investment was positive. This means that PE-backed companies should record an increase in EBITDA, equity and employees and a decrease in profit and sales after two years.

The findings of our further analysis on EBITDA confirmed the regression results. In general, PE investments led to growth in EBITDA two years after the deal. Also the negative effects on profit were confirmed by the later analyses. The effects on sales were confusing, however: the negative results from the regression were not confirmed by the subsequent analyses. Also the effects on the ROE were ambiguous – in some cases we found a negative effect from the PE investments, while in other cases we found a positive effect. The positive effects on equity and employees were partially confirmed by the second round of calculations.

Our study partially confirmed the previous results from the literature.

The results from the Probit model on the number of employees confirmed the study of Wilson et al. (2012) which found an increase in the number of employees of the target companies after the PE investment. In contrast, our analysis gave different results from those obtained by Kaplan (1989) and Davis et al. (2011), according to which the PE investments should have negative effects on the number of employees in the target company.

The positive value of equity does not find confirmation in other previous studies.

Our analyses showed positive effects of PE investments on EBITDA. This result is similar to the finding of Kaplan (1989) and Smith (1990), which obtained the positive effects of PE investments on the profitability of target firms measured as operating revenue – with variable construction very similar to the one we used – and the various measures of profitability used by Wilson et al. (2012). On the other hand, in Badunenko and Baum (2010) the effects on operating revenue in the short term are negative.

As with Wright et al. (1996), who did not find statistical significance for RoA, we did not find statistical significance for RoE.

Our analysis suggests that PE investments have, on average, a positive effect on firm profitability and company growth. In the second year after the deal, the performance of a PE-backed company is higher in more cases than that of a firm without PE investments.

This work has some limitations that can be overcome with further research. An appropriate next step of our work would be to consider the impact of PE investments in subsequent years. We would also like to consider other measures of profitability and company growth. Another step could be to analyze the impact of PE investments in other areas with a high number of PE deals.

Appendix

Table 11.A Outcomes from the literature review

Author(s)	Sample	Topic	Outcomes
Kaplan, 1989	76 public-to-private buyouts	Profitability and size growth	Significant increase in operating returns. The median firm lost 12% of employment.
Smith, 1990	58 public-to-private buyouts	Profitability and size growth	Significant increase in operating returns. No employment effects.
Muscarella and Vetsuypens, 1990	72 reverse leverage buyouts	Profitability and size growth	Significant increase in profitability. Median percentage change in employment smaller in 8% of cases.
Wilson et al., 2011	32,474 observations on buyouts	Profitability and size growth	Positive differentials in productivity (5–15%) and in profitability (3–5%). Positive revenue and employment growth.
Wright et al., 1996	Sample A 158 buyouts Sample B 251 buyouts	Profitability	No significant differences in ROA in the early years post buyout.
Buttignon et al., 2009	21 family buyouts	Profitability	No significant differences in turnover and EBITDA.
Badunenko and Baum, 2010	159,425 observations	Profitability	Lower RoA in the first year of PE investment, higher RoA in a six-year term.
Davis et al., 2011	3,200 target firms	Size growth	Positive differentials in employment (3% over two years, 6% over five years).
Achleitner and Klöckner, 2005	66 target firms	Size growth	Employment grew by an average rate of 5.4%

Table 11.B Variable definitions and data sources

Variable	Definition	Data Sources
Profitability variables		
Profit	Net income for the year before deduction of minority interests, if any (Profit after taxation + Extraordinary and other profit).	Bureau Van Dijk – Registro delle imprese
Sales	Revenues from sales and services	Bureau Van Dijk – Registro delle imprese
EBITDA	EBITDA (Earnings Before Interest, Taxes, Depreciation and Amortization) calculated as Operating profit (E_{bit}) + Depreciation (Total depreciation, amortization and write-downs)	Bureau Van Dijk – Registro delle imprese
RoE	(Net income / Shareholder funds) * 100	Bureau Van Dijk – Registro delle imprese
Growth variables		
Equity	Shareholders' Funds Total equity (Capital + Other shareholders funds)	Bureau Van Dijk – Registro delle imprese
Employees	Total number of employees included in the company's payroll	Bureau Van Dijk – Registro delle imprese
Control variable		
Year	For companies in the PE sample: year of the deal For companies in the NPE sample: year of the deal of the corresponding company in the PE sample	Private Equity Monitor

Notes

1. For a more detailed discussion of private equity funds, see Gompers and Lerner (2000), and Kaplan and Schoar (2005).
2. A buyout is a PE investment that leads to the purchase of a controlling interest in a single target company. The transaction is financed by a mix of debt and equity. LBO is a buyout in which the target company's capital structure incorporates a particularly high level of debt, much of which is normally secured against the company's assets. Reverse LBOs are PE investments in companies which had been private in the past, either in a full LBO or in a divisional buyout, and that have gone public again.

Venture capital is an investment in a new business that is perceived to have excellent growth prospects but does not have access to capital markets. Venture capital finances companies in the early stages (seed and start-up) or expansion venture. See EVCA glossary for a more detailed description of type of PE investments.
3. LBO = leveraged buyout.
4. EBITDA = earnings before interest, tax, depreciation and amortization.
5. See for example Davis et al. (2011) and Kaplan and Schoar (2005) for more detailed discussions about limitation in PE studies.
6. IPO = Initial Public Offering.
7. These variables have already been employed in the analyses of PE investments. See for example Badertscher et al. (2011) and Weir et al. (2007).
8. A Probit model is a popular specification for an ordinal or a binary response model that employs a probit link function. For a detailed discussion on the Probit model, see for example Ai and Norton (2003).

References

Achleitner Ann-Kristin and Klöckner Oliver (2005) 'Employment contribution of private equity and venture capital in Europe', Research for EVCA.

Ai Chunrong and Edward C. Norton (2003) 'Interaction terms in logit and probit models', *Economics Letters*, 80, 123–9.

Amaral Luis A. Nunes, Buldyrev Sergey V., Havlin Shlomo, Leschhorn Heiko, Maass Philipp, Salinger Michael A., Stanley Eugene H. and Stanley Michael H. R. (1997) 'Scaling behavior in economics: I. Empirical results for company growth', *Journal de Physique*, 7(4), 621–33.

Badertscher Brad, Katz Sharon P. and Rego Sonja O. (2011) 'The impact of private equity ownership on portfolio firms' corporate tax avoidance', Working Paper, University of Notre Dame, Columbia University and Indiana University.

Badunenko Oleg and Baum Christopher F. (2010) 'Does the tenure of private equity investment improve the performance of European Firms?' *Financial Systems, Efficiency and Stimulation of Sustainable Growth*, 1–21.

Bruining Hans, Boselie Paul, Wright Mike and Bacon Nicolas (2005) 'The impact of business ownership change on employee relations: buy-outs in the UK and the Netherlands', *The International Journal of Human Resource Management*, 16(3), 345–65.

Bruton Garry D., Filatotchev Igor, Chahine Salim and Wright Mike (2010) 'Governance, ownership structure, and performance of IPO firms: the impact of different types of private equity investors and institutional environments', *Strategic Management Journal*, 31(5), 491–509.

Burgel Oliver (2000) 'UK venture capital and private equity as an asset class for institutional investors', BVCA Research Report.

Buttignon Fabio, Vedovato Marco and Bortoluzzi Paolo (2009) 'Family business investor buyouts: the Italian case', *Economy & Management*, 2, 1–39.

Cheffins Brian and Armour John (2007) 'The eclipse of private equity', Working Papers from ESRC Centre for Business Research, 2007.

Davidoff Steven M. (2009) 'The failure of private equity', *Southern California Law Review*, 82, 481.

Davis Steven J., Haltiwanger John C., Jarmin Ron S., Lerner Josh and Miranda Javier (2011) 'Private equity and employment', NBER working paper series.

Evans David S. (1987) 'Tests of alternative theories of firm growth', *Journal of Political Economics*, 95, 657.

EVCA Yearbook 2012, European Venture Capital and Private Equity Association.

Gompers Paul and Lerner Josh (2000) 'Money chasing deals? The impact of fund inflows on private equity valuation', *Journal of Financial Economics*, 55, 281–325.

Jensen Michael C. (1993) 'The modern industrial revolution: exit, and the failure of internal control systems', *Journal of Finance*, 48, 831–80.

Kaplan Steven N. (1989) 'The effects of management buyouts on operating performance and value', *Journal of Financial Economics*, 24, 217–54.

Kaplan Steven N. and Schoar Antoinette (2005) 'Private equity performance: returns, persistence, and capital flows', *The Journal of Finance*, 60(4), 1791–823.

Manigart Sophie, De Waele Koen, Wright Mike, Robbie Ken, Desbrières Philippe, Sapienza Harry and Beekman Amy (2000) 'Venture capitalists, investment appraisal and accounting information', *European Financial Management*, 6(3), 389–403.

Muscarella Chris J. and Vetsuypens Michael R. (1990) 'Efficiency and organizational structure: a study of reverse LBOs', *The Journal of Finance*, 45(5).

PEM Private Equity Monitor Report, PEM Observatory at the Carlo Cattaneo University – LIUC.

Phalippou Ludovic and Gottschalg Oliver (2009) 'The performance of private equity funds', *The Review of Financial Studies*, 2(4), 1747–76.

Rasmussen Poul N. (2008) 'Taming the private equity fund "Locusts"', *Europe Today*, 8 (Spring), 130–3.

Service Employees International Union (SEIU) (2007) *Behind the Buyouts: Inside the World of Private Equity*. Washington, SEIU.

Shleifer Andrei and Summers Lawrence H. (1988) 'Breach of trust in hostile takeovers', in A.J. Auerbach (ed.), *Corporate Takeovers: Causes and Consequences*. Chicago: University of Chicago Press.

Smith Abbie J. (1990) 'Corporate ownership structure and performance: the case of management buyouts', *Journal of Financial Economics*, 1(27), 143–64.

Weir Charlie, Jones Peter and Wright Mike (2007) 'Public to private transactions, private equity and performance in the UK: an empirical analysis of the impact of going private', Working Paper, Nottingham University.

Wilson Nick, Wright Mike, Siegel Donald S. and Scholes Louise (2012) 'Private equity portfolio company performance during the global recession', *Journal of Corporate Finance*, 18(1), 193–205.

Wright Mike, Hoskisson Robert E., Busenitz Lowell W. and Dial Jay (2000) 'Entrepreneurial growth through privatization: the upside of management buyouts', *Academy of Management Review*, 25, 591–601.

Wright Mike, Wilson Nick and Robbie Ken (1996) 'The longer-term effects of management-led buy-outs', *Journal of Entrepreneurial & Small Business Finance*, 5(3), 213–22.

Index

Printed and bound by CPI Group (UK) Ltd, Croydon, CR0 4YY